GREAT
GENERALS OF
THE ANCIENT
WORLD

For Hallie Gabriele Marcaccio
a la famiglia!

and

My beloved, beautiful, and kind Susan

GREAT GENERALS OF THE ANCIENT WORLD

The Personality, Intellectual and Leadership Traits That Made Them Great

By Richard A. Gabriel

Pen & Sword
MILITARY

First published in Great Britain in 2017 by
PEN & SWORD MILITARY
an imprint of
Pen & Sword Books Ltd
47 Church Street
Barnsley
South Yorkshire
S70 2AS

ISBN 978-1-47385-908-1

A CIP catalogue record for this book is available from the British Library.

Printed and bound in England By
CPI Group (UK) Ltd, Croydon, CR0 4YY.

Pen & Sword Books Ltd incorporates the Imprints of Pen & Sword Aviation, Pen & Sword Family History, Pen & Sword Maritime, Pen & Sword Military, Pen & Sword Discovery, Pen & Sword Politics, Pen & Sword Atlas, Pen & Sword Archaeology, Wharncliffe Local History, Wharncliffe True Crime, Wharncliffe Transport, Pen & Sword Select, Pen & Sword Military Classics, Leo Cooper, The Praetorian Press, Claymore Press, Remember When, Seaforth Publishing and Frontline Publishing.

For a complete list of Pen & Sword titles please contact
PEN & SWORD BOOKS LIMITED
47 Church Street, Barnsley, South Yorkshire, S70 2AS, England
E-mail: enquiries@pen-and-sword.co.uk
Website: www.pen-and-sword.co.uk

CONTENTS

CHAPTER ONE

WHAT MAKES GREAT GENERALS GREAT?

Great generals cannot be judged to be so apart from the military context in which they fought, the nature of the armies they commanded and the political and social conditions that marked the societies in which they lived. Too often, generals are thought of as great field commanders even when their conduct of war was so restricted by these factors as to make their contribution to victory or defeat nearly irrelevant. Claims about a commander's genius for war must take into account the level of sophistication of warfare at the time in which he fought. In this regard, the scope, complexity, range, size and lethality of the armies of the late Bronze and Iron ages (2500 BC–AD 600), the period in which the great commanders examined herein fought, was not exceeded in the West until at least the Napoleonic era and, in many respects, not even until the First World War.

What makes a military leader great? Of the thousands of officers who served in history's armies, why is it that only a few are remembered as remarkable leaders of men in battle? What confluence of personal and circumstantial influences conspire to produce great military leaders? This book examines the role of human will and intellect as evident in the lives of ten selected military commanders of the ancient world whose achievements crucially shaped their respective societies, and in doing so set in motion ideas, beliefs and practices that shaped the larger direction of these societies and, sometimes, even civilization itself. Underlying this effort is the conviction that by understanding the role of the vital human qualities of intellect and will that made these captains great, we can draw lessons that aid us in rediscovering the central place of these human qualities in the management of our own civilization and even, perhaps, our own lives. For it is surely true that the human drama is never really about things, no matter how wondrous or even magical they may appear at the moment. It is, instead, always about ourselves.

But why study the great commanders of antiquity? Because the world of antiquity is not as distant from us as we might believe. Those who lived then were like us in most things that matter to human experience. Moreover, ancient societies often confronted technological challenges equal in difficulty to those we face today. The introduction and management of new technologies in the ancient world was just as difficult and disruptive as in modern times. Thutmose III of Egypt, for example, reformed an Egyptian military system that had remained unchanged for 2,000 years, and then used it to force a country that had been largely sealed from the outside world for those two millennia to embark upon the road to empire. The new Egyptian military order he created lasted for more than half a millennium. The challenges faced by the great commanders of antiquity were often no less daunting than those faced by military leaders today. It is worthwhile to enquire into the personalities, traits and habits of these commanders to see what made them great, and to ask what we might learn from them.

Two sets of factors seem relevant to the success of great commanders. The first are traits of personality and character that permit the development of an intellect that comprehends its environment and can cope with it without paralyzing apprehension. The great commander understands his world even as he sees beyond it, bringing to it a vision of change and objectives toward which he wishes to advance. The second set of factors are the historical circumstances that form the political and social environment in which the commander must act. Great commanders can only emerge when challenging times provide opportunities for their abilities to manifest themselves. Grave social and military crises create opportunities for commanders to rise who, in normal times, would probably have lived quite ordinary lives. The circumstances of history create the stage upon which the commander possessed of the right personality and character is allowed to perform.

With three exceptions, the great commanders examined here all experienced war at an early age. Thutmose III was the commander of the Egyptian army at 16, and a year later led his first military expedition into Nubia. Two years later, he commanded an expeditionary force to recapture Gaza. He was not yet 22 when he fought his famous Battle of Megiddo. Cornelius Scipio was a cavalry troop commander at the Battle of the Ticinus River at age 17. A year later, he fought at the Trebia River, and a year after that at Cannae. He assumed command of the Roman armies in Spain at 26. Hannibal accompanied his father to Spain at the age of 9, and was raised in a military camp while his father conquered Spain. He was 26 when he assumed command of the Carthaginian armies in Spain. Philip of Macedonia took part in the cavalry battles that characterized the Macedonian tribal wars when he was 16, and was a military governor at 18. Marcus Agrippa enlisted in Caesar's mercenary army at 14, and fought in many of Caesar's battles, including Munda. As part of Sargon the Great's military training as a young warrior, he was placed in a walled courtyard armed with a bow and spear. A lion was let loose and Sargon had to kill it or be killed! Alexander led his first expedition against the tribes in Thrace at 16. Only Moses, Julius Caesar and Muhammad never experienced war until they assumed command of their respective armies.

The great commanders of the ancient world were all educated people, formally trained by the educational establishments of their respective times. Sargon II was perhaps the best educated, the modern equivalent of a classics scholar; fluent in ancient languages, a military historian and trained in the school of pragmatic politics at a special college whose purpose was to educate and prepare the leaders of the Assyrian state. Thutmose III was educated as a priest of Amun, and Scipio and Caesar received classical educations at the hands of private Greek tutors. Hannibal was educated in the manner of any Hellenic noble of the day, and spoke Punic, Latin and Greek. Philip II of Macedon was formally educated while a hostage at Thebes, and could speak several languages; he surrounded himself with artists and philosophers. It was Philip who recruited Aristotle, his boyhood friend, to instruct his son, Alexander, for three years at the academy at Missa. Moses may well have been educated, if not at the court of Pharaoh as the Bible tells us, then certainly at one of the many Egyptian scriptoria. We know nothing of Muhammad's formal education, but his experience as a caravaneer and businessman suggest at least literacy and some level of formal education. He seems to have been particularly well-informed about the theological and social history of Arabia.

Rigorous intellectual training provides the commander with the confidence to trust his intellect to explain the world in which he lives by demonstrating that the mind can make reasonable sense of one's environment and even, to some lesser extent, the future. Educated people think in terms of cause and effect, of one thing leading to another, of chains of action, where one might bring about ends with some degree of certainty by setting in motion events yet far removed from those ends. Soldiers educated in this manner are far less likely to accept the world as it is, and far less likely to permit cultural and theological explanations to guide their actions. Formally educated leaders are far more likely to see themselves as controlling their own fate, as being able to change the course of events rather than having to acquiesce in them. Without this perspective, it is difficult to see how one could become a great commander.

All the great commanders possessed a remarkable confidence in their own ability and will, traits only partly, if at all, acquired through formal education. Educated leaders possess the *potential* for greatness precisely because they can understand their environment and discern how to control it, a habit of mind developed through study and thought. Uneducated leaders often fail because they are prisoners of their environment insofar as important aspects of it escape their purview. While such leaders might master their world for a while, eventually they will be overwhelmed by it. Hitler, Stalin, Lenin and Mao, to mention some of the great disrupters of the past century, fell victim to precisely this shortcoming. If the great commanders of the past excelled at anything, it was their ability *not* to become victims of unanticipated change.

To adjust to changing circumstances requires a mind receptive to new ideas and open to new possibilities. Thutmose III's adoption of new military technologies, Philip's development and use of new tactical cavalry doctrines, Scipio's redesign and tactical employment of the infantry cohort and Sargon's new doctrine of pre-emptive war are all examples of leaders willing to entertain and apply new possibilities, as are Agrippa's design of new ships and naval tactics, Moses' creation of the new Israelite army at Sinai and Muhammad's invention and execution of the theory and practice of insurgency. The purpose of new ideas is to control events so as to bring about desired outcomes. This often requires that new ideas be placed in service of already extant goals, although new ideas can themselves become vehicles for determining new goals. Thus, Thutmose III's adoption of the chariot and composite bow for the Egyptian army made sense only because he had already set the objective of driving the Asiatics from the Palestine land bridge. Moses' redesign of the Israelite army made sense only in relation to his strategic objective of conquering Canaan.

An open and receptive intellect permits a commander to challenge existing assumptions about his world and generate new paradigms that structure novel thinking as a means of adjusting one's intellectual processes to a new environment. This is an intellectual achievement of the first order, and characterizes the thinking of history's great commanders. Caesar was able to see a new future for Rome only after he had conceived of the Roman world in a completely new way; that is, as the creator of a new, peaceful, just and prosperous empire based on the integration of conquered peoples into a new social order. Hannibal, too, saw his military campaign against Rome as the vehicle for creating a new world order in which states of relatively equal military and economic power coexisted in peace and harmony. Scipio reached for the same vision after Carthage's defeat, yet his failure set Rome on the road to empire. Philip's ability to dream of a unified Greece under the benign tutelage of Macedonia sought to create a world that no Greek had ever before conceived of as possible.

Thutmose brought about a fundamental shift in the paradigm of Egyptian thinking when he forced Egypt to turn away from 2,000 years of isolation and brave the new world beyond the Nile. Sargon of Assyria changed the impetus of 200 years of previous wars of conquest, redirecting Assyria's energies to consolidating the empire and focusing on its domestic requirements. Moses and Muhammad radically changed the world with their new ideas. In the sense that the great commanders changed the fundamental paradigms of their age, they created new futures for their civilizations. Some of these futures, like those of Rome and Egypt, lasted for hundreds of years after the men who had brought them into being had turned to dust. Others, like Judaism and Islam, are still very much with us.

All of the great captains possessed imagination as a regular habit of mind. Imagination resides in the consciousness between sensory experience and intellect. It is not primarily the ability to conceive of the fantastic. More pragmatically, imagination is the ability to envision alternative sets of circumstances that *might* realistically be brought into being by human will and action. Imagination, thus, is the ability to foresee what may be foreseen under the reasonable conditions of knowledge that one possesses. It is closely connected to extrapolation, and is a highly pragmatic intellectual skill.

All the great commanders were highly imaginative in this pragmatic sense. Philip of Macedon, for example, completely reinvented the Macedonian army in order to deal with a set of circumstances – the conquest of Greece and eventually of Persia – that did not yet exist, but which Philip could imagine to exist. In the process, he gave Greece a completely new type of army, one that the Greeks themselves could never have conceived without him. Thutmose fashioned new military and diplomatic instruments to deal with the new world confronting Egypt because he could imagine how that new world would be and connect that vision to the means necessary to control it. The great commanders often succeeded because they possessed the ability to imagine the world not as it was, but as it would be if circumstances permitted.

These traits – (1) conceptual thinking from cause to effect, (2) receptivity to new ideas, (3) thinking beyond existing paradigms and (4) practical imagination – are all intellectual achievements that transcend technology, formulaic reasoning and cultural influence. Together, they constitute what might be called *imaginative reasoning*, where all relevant aspects of problem-solving, human and techno-logical, come together to make mental sense of the world outside the mind. The human individual, not formulas, culture or technologies, remains at the centre of the process, for only humans can conceive of *possible* worlds. To substitute formulas or technologies for imaginative thought as guides to action, especially on the battlefield or in the world of power politics, is to court disaster. Thus, the Roman armies that fought Hannibal, for example, were defeated repeatedly because their commanders employed them again and again precisely as they were designed to be used. The trouble was that Hannibal fought in a manner completely different from what the Roman armies had been designed for. Roman commanders continued to employ the same military system in defeat after defeat, precisely because they could not sufficiently integrate all the new elements in their drasti-cally changed environment to formulate a successful response to the changes. The Egyptian army, too, met its death in the wars against the Hyksos for the same reasons, by employing an existing successful military system in radically changed circumstances. This same lack of integrated thinking characterized the American military effort in Vietnam. Unable to grasp the changed circumstances under which the old tactical and strategic formulas had to operate, American com-manders continued to do what was most familiar to them, with disas-trous results.

While certain traits of intellect are important to understanding the success of history's great commanders, *intellect, per se, is not sufficient for greatness.* Whatever else the great captains of antiquity were, they were first men of action and will. It is one thing to conceive of great things, quite another to attempt them. And to attempt great things requires personality traits more related to character and will than to intellect. All the great commanders were leaders possessed of strong self-confidence and will. The ability to trust one's thoughts, experi-ences and judgment is central to the strength of personality required to give sound thinking the force of action.

Tradition and religion determined a great deal of human behaviour in ancient civilizations. The 'drag' of cultural inertia made innovation difficult. New ideas and actions required not only clear thinking, but a great deal of self-confidence and will to make them happen. The roots of a commander's self-confidence, then, do not lie in formal education but, more likely, in the strength of personality shaped by experience and practice. It is an old soldier's maxim that one can train a frightened soldier to be less frightened, but one cannot make him brave.

The roots of a leader's self-confidence are difficult to determine. With the exception of Moses, Muhammad and Caesar, none of whom seem to lack the self-confidence so necessary to success, all the great commanders received military training and experienced war at an early age, an experience that may have taught them self-reliance, the ability to endure difficult circumstances and how to cope with uncertainty. The major goal of military training, at least at the basic level, is not so much to inculcate military skills, most of which are easily learned. Rather its point is to shape the psychology of the soldier so that he comes to trust his own abilities in an uncertain environment. Myra McPherson's study of Americans during the Vietnam war, *Long Time Passing: Vietnam and the Haunted Generation*, suggests that Vietnam veterans manifested higher levels of self-confidence in their lives than non-veterans. Self-confidence is a necessary requisite for the strength of will and intellect needed to make a commander great.

All the great captains were risk-takers. It is the riskiness of the professional gambler, not the enthusiastic amateur, which the great commander must possess, for he knows that the mere knowledge of circumstances is insufficient to master them. The battlefield is among the most uncertain places in human experience, a world that can never be completely known or turned completely to one's will. There is always uncertainty, always the unknown, to be confronted. The great commander confronts uncertainty with the willingness to take risks, to reduce the threat of the unknown by plunging into it and making it known. Hannibal and Scipio were experts at taking risks. Hannibal's movement over the Alps marked his propensity to take risks on a grand scale. At Trasimene, he relied upon the fog to hide his troops when a sudden wind would have revealed them to the Roman enemy. At Cannae, Hannibal exposed his centre to draw the Romans into a trap. Had his cavalry not returned in time, he would have faced disaster. Scipio's swift march against New Carthage depended entirely upon guessing correctly that the enemy could not react in time to meet him. Scipio's campaign in Africa, undertaken below strength and without adequate supplies, remains a classic study in military risk-taking, as does Thutmose III's willingness to risk his army by moving down a narrow mountain trail to achieve tactical surprise at Megiddo. Without the ability, as Rudyard Kipling put it, 'to make a heap of one's winnings and risk it all on one turn of pitch and toss', the great captain cannot master the uncertainties of the battlefield or those of his larger world that threaten to frustrate his will. There is always danger in taking risks. But for the great commander, the greater danger lies in doing nothing.

Beyond their intellectual and character traits, all the great leaders possessed some element of physical presence that made others love, respect or fear them. Scipio manifested an air of quiet calm and dignity that gave his soldiers confidence. Hannibal's physique and demeanour was that of the combat-hardened soldier, fearless and competent in the face of danger. Philip of Macedon, his large head atop a body crippled and scarred from battle wounds, seemed every bit the rough warrior chief, even as he was among the most sophisticated military thinkers of his time. Thutmose was tall and robustly built, with a large hawk-beaked nose and thought by his troops to be a god. Muhammad, too, was said to be physically imposing, as were Agrippa and Caesar. Moses enhanced his mysterious sense of command presence by always wearing the mask of a Midianite priest. Only Alexander, 5ft 2in tall, of blonde hair and fair skin, and cursed with a high voice, seems to have lacked a manly warrior-like presence.

The physical presence of these commanders was further enhanced by their willingness to suffer the hardships and dangers of battle. Sargon died leading an attack in battle, Caesar personally led the attack at Alesia – distinguishing himself by his red cloak – Thutmose personally led the attack at Megiddo, Hannibal always fought in the middle of the line, and Philip was wounded five times, Alexander seven and Muhammad twice. There is a mysticism in the attraction of ordinary people for brave men that is not completely explainable in rational terms. Whatever personal charisma was required to convince troops to follow them into the crucible of combat, to persuade them to risk their lives, and to risk the horror of blindness, paralysis and loss of limb from wounds, the great commanders possessed it. It remains a maxim of military life that a combat leader cannot manage soldiers to their deaths. Soldiers must be led. They follow their commanders for the most basic of reasons, because they love, trust and admire him for who he is and what he does.

Great captains can arise only when there are great challenges to be dealt with, or when social turmoil and revolution loosen the constraints that restrain the exercise of social power in normal times. Without great challenges, leadership is confined to a narrower scope of events and concerns. Then, mere competence passes for leadership. In these circumstances, great commanders remain only potentially so, carrying out their duties, their abilities permitted by circumstance to rise only to the level of competence permitted by the environment, but never to greatness. It was, of course, always so. The analysis of great commanders ought not to obscure the fact that in the ancient world great captains were rare.

The secular, democratic, technologically advanced, free economy, post-industrial societies that characterize the modern West necessarily restrict opportunities for military greatness because of the inherent structural limitations placed on power of all types. There are strong institutional barriers to the emergence of great commanders. The fundamental premise of democracy requires the limited exercise of *all* power. Unlike antiquity, modern generals rarely become political leaders, and political leaders never take the field as military commanders. One of the fundamental characteristics of the great commanders of the past, the fusion of military and political power, is institutionally absent in the modern Western world.

The advent of high-tech warfare has further reduced the degree of greatness associated with military achievement. Wars are now thought of as being fought by rival 'technological systems' in which military commanders are interchangeable. Wars are fought and won through planning combat 'scenarios' executed with almost complete predictability, so that there is far less room for brilliance, innovation and daring than in the past.

There is, too, the degree of political control over military operations required by modern states seeking to execute military policy within the constraints of fragile public support and the transparency of events made possible by instantaneous communications. This condition under which military men have had to labour is not new, however. Hannibal was completely hamstrung by Carthage's failure to supply him with adequate resources for his campaigns, and Scipio's invasion of Africa was done at the margin because the Roman Senate refused to provide him with money or authorize the troops he requested. Caesar, too, had to reckon with a hostile Senate, and even Alexander was strongly dependent on Antipater and Greece for troops for his Asian adventures. It is, everyone knows, the political leader who will fall if things fail militarily. Since political leaders are prevented from being field generals, the next best thing is to make certain that one's field generals remain sensitive to the requirements of the political leadership's survival at the polls. The congruence of military and political power so necessary to greatness in the ancient world is almost prohibited in the modern one.

Still, there is no doubt that great captains will emerge from time to time in the future, as they have in the past. The lesson learned from studying the great commanders of antiquity is that human nature will ensure that the great commanders yet to come will be just as remarkable and every bit as human as those who have already come and gone. There is, then, perhaps much that present and future generals might learn from studying what it was that made the great generals of antiquity as great as they were.

I suppose any list of the greatest generals in the ancient world will be subject to objections. But having spent forty-two years studying and writing about military subjects in antiquity, I think it probable that my list might be as well-regarded as any other. I have more than a passing interest in my subjects. I have written military biographies of seven of the ten generals examined herein (Thutmose III, Moses, Philip of Macedonia, Hannibal, Scipio, Muhammad and Alexander), and authored extensive chapters and articles on the remaining three (Julius Caesar, Sargon the Great and Marcus Agrippa). In addition, it seemed only logical to include those generals that the ancient historians themselves regarded as the greatest. Thus, Caesar, Scipio, Alexander, Hannibal and Sargon were obvious choices.

But military historians of the ancient world would immediately recognize this list as incomplete. It would, for example, omit perhaps the greatest general of them all, Thutmose III of Egypt. It would also omit Marcus Agrippa, the forgotten genius behind Augustus and the soldier responsible for most of the important victories and achievements commonly attributed to Augustus. The list would also leave unexamined two of the world's most influential generals, Moses and Muhammad, whose world-changing achievements rested squarely upon their previous military achievements. Without these achievements, two of the world's greatest religions may well have never emerged. Finally, the list would omit one of the period's greatest military commanders, Philip II of Macedonia, surely one of the great strategists and military innovators of the period, and the man who made Alexander's conquests possible.

In choosing what generals to include, I have given great thought to the historical period in which each general fought, especially the nature, complexity, innovation and weapons lethality that characterized war in each period. Thutmose III and Moses lived and fought in the Bronze Age, a period of often unappreciated innovation in warfare. The Bronze Age witnessed the emergence of all the weapons that were employed in war for the next two millennia. The period introduced the helmet, body armour, sickle sword, penetrating axe, socketed axe, composite bow and chariot, all of which wrought great changes on the way armies were formed and warfare conducted. The rarity of tin and cost of manufacture of bronze weapons limited the size of large armies to the major nations of the period. The introduction of plentiful iron and cheap manufacture of weapons in the Iron Age made possible warfare of greater size armies whose scope, range and lethality increased enormously. Sargon II's campaigns offer an excellent example of the conduct of Iron Age warfare at its height.

Philip and Alexander are representatives of the conduct of war in the late Greek classical period during which many changes in weapons and tactics occurred. Hannibal's army, tactics and strategic thinking offer a good example of warfare in the late Hellenistic period in which infantry and combined arms manoeuvres once more made an appearance. Scipio portrays the Roman practice of war during the Roman Republic during a period of transition, and Caesar and Marcus Agrippa are examples of the combined tactics and changed equipment that followed in the Roman Imperial period. It might be objected that Muhammad lived and fought in the period of *late* antiquity, when the eastern empire of Rome was on its last legs. Nonetheless, the Roman practice of war during that time was very much akin to the way the imperial troops had fought for centuries. Even at this late date, the military orders, titles and field commands were given in Latin, not Greek, and the soldiers and their officers thought of themselves as Romans.

Though the nature of warfare was different in each period in which they fought, it comes as little surprise that the psychological, intellectual and leadership traits of the great generals were more or less the same over time. Perhaps this is because warfare is first and foremost a human endeavour carried out by human beings, and the nature of the human animal has remained unchanged over time in its psychological and social fundamentals. The fears and hopes of the soldiers who fought and died at Megiddo, Marathon, Chaeronea and on scores of other battlefields in antiquity, were no different than those who fought at Verdun, Bastogne, the Ia Drang valley or Fallujah. Little wonder, then, that the skills necessary to successfully command men in war have not changed much either.

I will leave it to the readers to judge if my selection of great generals meets muster. It is my hope that this book will be read by military professionals as well as general readers. For it is those who fight wars and command men in battle who may have most to gain for their efforts.

Richard A. Gabriel

CHAPTER TWO

THUTMOSE III (1504–1450 BC)

The Archaeological Museum in Cairo is the final resting place of Thutmose III, the greatest warrior pharaoh of the ancient world. His shrunken corpse rests in a casket-like glass case, half-covered with a cloth of royal purple, its skin parchmentized brown. He is swathed completely in linen wrappings, except for those pulled back to reveal his face. The face is oval with full lips, smooth cheekbones and a prominent brow stretched tight against the age-darkened skin. One can easily recognize the set of the jaw and the nose that bears a strong resemblance to his father and grandfather.

When the mummy of the great king was discovered in 1881, Egyptologists were horrified to learn that grave robbers had almost destroyed the corpse. All four limbs were torn from the body, the feet were missing, most of the nose was gone and the head had been severed at the neck. The sight of this great man desecrated in this manner so disturbed the Egyptian government that it declared a five-year moratorium on future examinations of royal mummies.[1]

The autopsy of Thutmose's corpse was performed by the famed Egyptologist and physician, G. Elliot Smith. Smith measured the body and declared Thutmose to have been 5ft 3in tall. The combination of Thutmose's well-known military prowess and his short stature led Egyptologists to call Thutmose III 'the Napoleon of Egypt', a description that may have originated with James Henry Breasted, the famous American Egyptologist.[2] It seems, however, that Smith did not account for the corpse's missing feet when taking his measurements. Another examination revealed the king's height to be 1.71 metres, or approximately 5ft 6½in, taller than the average Egyptian of his day and taller than all of the pharaohs of the Eighteenth Dynasty except Amenhotep I.[3]

He was quite a remarkable fellow, this warrior prince of Thebes, and the greatest of all generals in Egyptian history. Unlike many generals before him and since, he did not permit his military training and experience in war to narrow his intellect. He was no military mechanic, no mere technician of war, but an integral man who retained his interest in things botanical, biological, religious, literary, aesthetic and architectural to the end of his life. His broad understanding of his world sharpened a mind already literate, well-read and prepared by his early education and training to think clearly. And he was a brilliant strategic thinker. To him, Egypt owes the conception and implementation of a new strategic vision that permitted this once defeated and insular society to become a great nation of imperial dimensions for more than five centuries.

Thutmose III was one of the great captains of the ancient world. His record of military activity is remarkable. He fought more battles over a longer period and won more victories than any general in the ancient world. In the sixty years prior to Thutmose's reign, the great warrior kings of Egypt – from Ahmose to Thutmose II – fought one foreign campaign every 4.6 years. In the seventy years following Thutmose, from Amenhotep II to Amenhotep III, there was one foreign campaign every 10.5 years. In the nineteen years between regnal years twenty-three and forty-two of Thutmose's thirty-two-year reign, he fought seventeen campaigns in Canaan and Syria, or an average of one military campaign every 1.2 years.[4] In the six years between assuming command of the army and ascending the throne in his own right, Thutmose fought a major campaign in Nubia and, perhaps, another for which there is only tentative evidence, and led the army that liberated Gaza from rebels.[5] By the time Thutmose ruled Egypt in his own right, sometime in his twenty-second year, he was already an experienced combat commander. In his first major campaign against the combined Canaanite-Syrian armies at Megiddo in his twenty-third year, Thutmose revealed himself to be a first-rate strategist, tactician and logistician, qualities gained by extensive experience in the field prior to ascending the throne. Thutmose transformed Egypt into a military state. With Egypt's great resources at his command, he set events in motion that shaped Egypt and the Levant for the next 500 years.[6]

Paradoxically, Thutmoses' magnificent military record remained unknown for most of history. The Greek and Roman occupation of Egypt produced no histories of the great man, and the Arab invasion and occupation of Egypt from the sixth century to the present completely obliterated any knowledge of Egyptian history in the West. It was not until Napoleon's occupation of the country and the discovery of the Rosetta Stone that historians were able to read the surviving ancient hieroglyphic records revealing Thutmose's achievement. Even these were not fully recorded and published until the early twentieth century. For much of history, then, military historians were simply unaware of Egypt's greatest warrior king.

Thutmose is often portrayed as a devout and respectful servant of the gods. As a young man, he was trained as a priest of Amun before being sent to the army as a teenager. The humility of the man is reflected in his tomb; it is small and sparsely decorated. Compared to other tombs in the Valley of the Kings, Thutmose is buried in the funereal equivalent of the simple military coffin. There are no descriptions of his great military victories inside his burial chamber. Still, no other general in antiquity can claim as remarkable a record of military success as Thutmose III of Egypt. Despite his ferocity on the battlefield, the great general seems to have been a compassionate man. In all his campaigns, there are no reports of massacres or atrocities, and he often showed mercy to the inhabitants of captured towns. He shared the spoils of war generously with his officers and soldiers, and seems to have taken great delight in rewarding his men with decorations for valour in battle. Along with the traditional gold of honour, he introduced a number of other military decorations for his troops.[7]

Thutmose possessed an enquiring mind, and his intellectual interests ranged beyond military matters and affairs of state to include history, religion, architecture, pottery and even jewellery design. His reign witnessed a period of prodigious art production of all forms, and he was one of history's greatest patrons of the arts.[8] He had an abiding interest in botany and took special scribes with him on campaign whose task was to find and record any strange flowers and plants they might encounter. Animals, too, interested him, and he seems to have been enchanted by the story of his father having encountered a white rhinoceros in Nubia. Returning from one of his campaigns, Thutmose spent several days in the vicinity of the marshes of Niy in Syria studying and hunting elephants.

Thutmose was one of Egypt's great builders and constructed more temples, shrines, votive buildings, pylons and fortresses than any of his predecessors and all of his successors, with the possible exception of Ramses II, who enjoyed the longest reign (sixty-seven years) in Egyptian history.[9] The Hyksos invaders had destroyed much of the monumental architecture in Middle Egypt, and it was probably not until Thutmose's time that events and resources made possible an attempt at large-scale rebuilding of the destroyed buildings. Thutmose also had to administer an empire that required the construction of new military garrisons and fortifications in Canaan and Nubia.[10] It was Thutmose who introduced the basilica as an architectural form to Egypt.[11]

Thutmose's administrative responsibilities were different and considerably more difficult than those of his predecessors. The wars against the Hyksos and the need to re-establish control over Nubia had led to a gradual centralization of administrative authority in the hands of the pharaoh, but much remained decentralized until the reign of Thutmose III. The need to conscript, train and equip a large army and a new naval arm, and keep both in the field, required centralized planning and control over all national resources. While the trend toward centralization was already evident under earlier kings, Thutmose's large-scale and almost constant wars accelerated and increased the trend toward centralization, turning Egypt administratively into a military state. Although Nubia had come under Egyptian administration by the reign of Thutmose I, it still had to be governed, goods extracted, garrisons staffed and repaired and occasional revolts suppressed. The great expansion of the Amun priesthood and the remarkable building programme, with all that entailed with regard to the extraction of resources and the conscription of labour, required constant attention. There was also the need to administer the Egyptian military and economic presence in Canaan, while at the same time being attendant to the threats from Syria and the Mitanni. Unlike any of his predecessors, Thutmose had to govern an imperial realm, and he proved an excellent administrator equal to the task.

Thutmose III was probably born in 1504 BC, the son of Pharaoh Thutmose II by a concubine named Isis. Pharaoh's great wife and half-sister, Hatshepsut, produced only a daughter, Neferure.[12] While still very young, it is probable that Thutmose was married to his half-sister, Neferure. Marriage to sisters and half-sisters was common among the royalty of Egypt, since the bloodline of succession followed the female line. Marriage to these royal blue blood females was sometimes a means of legitimizing the rule of a non-royal who had been appointed to succeed a pharaoh who died without a male heir. Thutmose I became pharaoh in exactly this way by marrying the sister of his predecessor, Amenophis I, who had left no surviving male heir. So, too, did Thutmose II, born of a non-royal mother, who married Hatshepsut, the daughter of Thutmose I and his royal wife, Ahmose. Thutmose II died while his son was still an infant, and although his son was recognized as pharaoh from this early time, real power passed to Queen Hatshepsut, Thutmose III's stepmother/aunt, who governed as regent.

We are lacking the details of his early adolescence, but it seems that the boy-king was sent to one of the temples, the Houses of Life, perhaps the *scriptorum* of the temple at Karnak, where he was taught to read and write, first in the common hieratic script and then in the more complex system of hieroglyphics.[13] The 'instruction houses' of the temples taught much more than basic literacy, however, and Thutmose would have been exposed to the books of the temple library, including the historical accounts of the accomplishments of his predecessors.[14] It was probably around this age that Thutmose was apprenticed to the priesthood at the temple of Amun at Karnak. For a few years, Thutmose served as a priest of Amun at Karnak. The experience made him deeply devout for the rest of his life.

We do not know exactly when Thutmose completed his temple education and went to the army for military training. It may have been a year or so before he reached his age of majority of sixteen years, when Queen Hatshepsut appointed him commander of the army.[15] The training of an Egyptian officer was rigorous, physically demanding and required familiarization with all combat arms of the fighting force – infantry, archers and chariotry. He endured poor food (march rations of sour milk, fish with salt, hard bread and a canteen of water), forced marches and rowing of boats. The Egyptian army held regular field exercises in which young officers participated, and there were jousts, mock combats and weapons competitions where they might demonstrate their skills to their superiors.

Thutmose was very young, perhaps only a 'nursling' when his father died. Although he was recognized as the legitimate king and dated his regnal years from his time as an infant, the effective day-to-day governance of Egypt was left in the hands of the dead king's great wife, Hatshepsut, who assumed the role of regent for the young Thutmose. But Hatshepsut did something no other female regent had ever done. When Thutmose was 7 years old, Hatshepsut declared herself king, assumed the entire titulary of a pharaoh and even began to dress in male attire, complete with the false beard of Egyptian royalty.[16] The two kings, one male and one female, ruled side-by-side for some fifteen years, but with Hatshepsut wielding the real authority of office until Thutmose removed her from the throne when he was 22.[17]

We do not know the circumstances under which Thutmose assumed his rightful position as sole king of Egypt sometime in 1482/1481 BC, or what happened to Hatshepsut, now a woman of more than 50 years of age. It is not unimaginable that by year twenty-two of her reign, Thutmose, commander of the army and the rightful male king, now found it appropriate to press his claim to the throne with the support of the army and court elites and removed his aunt.[18] Whatever the circumstances, within six months of Thutmose coming to the throne, Canaan exploded in revolt, and Egypt was threatened with another foreign invasion.

Thutmose III's great achievements on the battlefield inevitably lead one to think of him mostly in military terms, as a great general who excelled in the art of war. It is certainly true that there are few generals of the ancient world who can claim a record of battlefield achievement equal to that of the great pharaoh. Still, there is more to military greatness than winning battles. It is often an appreciation for the *political* dimension of war and the *personal* dimension of leadership that give victories on the battlefield any meaning beyond the body count. Thutmose knew and appreciated these strategic dimensions of military performance and demonstrated them often.

Perhaps the most important and far-reaching of Thutmose's achievements was to change the psychology of Egyptian national character, to set forth a new paradigm altering the way Egyptians thought about themselves and their world. For more than two millennia, Egypt had been an isolated society, almost hermetically sealed by her vast desert borderlands from the great cultural changes that were occurring in the rest of the Levant. For as long as there was recorded history, Egyptians lived as if there were no other lands at all. In all this time, one is hard pressed to find any significant examples of cultural or technological change within Egypt that came about as a consequence of contact with lands beyond its borders.

The Hyksos invasion of Egypt (circa 1650 BC) and 108 years of occupation provided a shocking awakening to this peaceful view of things. But even then, the goal of Egyptian leaders was only to rid *Kemit*, the Black Land, of the invaders and return to the old ways. Thutmose was the first to realize that there was no going back. To return to the past would achieve nothing but to place Egypt at risk once more. It was Thutmose who led a closed Egyptian society into a new era of awareness and interaction with other cultures. How traumatic it must have been for the Egyptians to abandon their *two millennia* of history and face the world anew. Thutmose gave Egypt a new vision of itself and its place in the world, and that vision remained unchanged in its essentials for the next 500 years.

The new security strategy was partially dictated by a change in the nature of the threat. The 'sand dwellers' of the Canaan land bridge, whom the Egyptians continued to view as the descendants of the hated Hyksos, had matured to the point where they now constructed sophisticated and powerful military establishments and fortifications. These circumstances meant that the armies of the small states of the area, especially in coalition with the larger and more powerful Hittite and Mitanni states, were dangerous instruments that had to be dealt with if Egypt was to be secure.

At the same time, new and more powerful kingdoms were emerging. The most proximate threats were the Mitanni, who occupied the land beyond the great bend of the Euphrates in northeast Syria, and whose client states extended south and west to the Litani River into southern Syria (modern Lebanon). To the northwest, the powerful and dangerous Hittites were beginning to appear as major players on the international scene. Both states eventually became competitors with Egypt for hegemony in Syria. The key to the dominance of Canaan, and thus to protecting the Nile, was the ability of Egypt to control events in Syria. The larger city-states of the area, particularly Kadesh, Qatna and Tunip on the Orontes River, could affect Egyptian influence considerably. It is testimony to the sophistication of Egyptian strategic thinking that they realized that the defence of the Nile began far away in the mountains of Syria.

Egypt required a new national security strategy to guide its policy in the new and hostile environment in which it was now forced to live. Thutmose's strategic vision of Egyptian security guided Egyptian diplomatic, commercial and military policy for a half-millennium. In this view, Egypt had no safe borders. The security of the nation lay in Egypt's ability to control political and military developments in the Canaan-Lebanon-Syrian theatre of operations. The goal of Egyptian defence policy was to prevent any major power or coalition of Asiatic city-states from assembling an alliance powerful enough to threaten Egypt. This required for the first time the full involvement of Egypt in the politics, economics and military affairs of the states on the Palestinian land bridge.

Under Thutmose, Egyptian defence policy became dynamic and pro-active, requiring preventive military interventions in support of political objectives, as well as economic policies that guaranteed Egypt access to important strategic materials such as hard wood for ships, buildings and chariots, and tin for making bronze weapons. After his first foray into Canaan, where he destroyed a coalition of Canaanite and Mitanni princes planning to invade Egypt at Megiddo, Thutmose intervened with military force in the area no fewer than sixteen times.[19] His son, Amenophis II, was kept busy with one campaign after another in similar fashion, as were most of the pharaohs who followed for the next 500 years.

New empires and great powers rose and fell during this time, and most challenged Egyptian hegemony on the Canaanite land bridge at one time or another. Two centuries after Thutmose had defeated the Mitanni, Ramses II fought the Hittites to a draw at Kadesh. A century and a half later, Ramses III defeated the Sea Peoples in a great land and sea battle at the mouth of the Nile, saving Egypt from the devastation that overwhelmed and destroyed every major city from Syria to Canaan. And so it went, on and on, Egyptian policy guided by the same national security goals and strategic vision that Thutmose had forged for Egypt so many centuries before. It was 'a sustained military and administrative effort unequaled in Egyptian history'.[20]

By the reign of Thutmose II and immediately thereafter with Hatshepsut, the process of Egyptian military modernization was still incomplete and unsupported by a new strategic doctrine to under-pin its implementation. That new strategic vision was provided by Thutmose III. As long as Egypt remained a strategically defensive power, the existing military establishment, relatively small, equipped with bronze weapons but not having large chariot squadrons, would suffice. It was Thutmose III who shifted the Egyptian strategic paradigm from defence to offence.

In this new strategic perspective, the defence of Egypt required the military and political subordination of the city-states of Canaan and Syria. Given the nature of the enemy forces equipped with bronze weap-ons and armour, its fortified cities and the open terrain that required rapid movement and manoeuvring to dominate, a newly structured Egyptian force was required. The new army would have to be larger, better-equipped and better logistically organized to carry out expedi-tionary campaigns for months on end. Garrisons had to be constructed and manned, the professional cadre expanded to organize and train large numbers of conscripts, and new administrative positions created and staffed. Transport of Egyptian forces by sea required the expansion and modernization of the navy, which required new shipyards and a large ship-building programme. Sources of important strategic materi-als also had to be secured, and thousands of new workshops established and manned with skilled craftsmen to produce the new weapons and war machines in substantial numbers. While the restructuring of the new army probably began under Hatshepsut and incorporated previ-ous improvements in supplying new weapons, most of the credit is due to 'the military genius of Thutmose III'.[21]

The new Egyptian national army was raised by conscription, with the levy being one man in ten instead of the traditional one man in 100.[22] It was centrally trained by professional officers and non-commissioned offi-cers, and Pharaoh himself stood as commander-in-chief and personally led his troops in battle. The Vizier served as Minister of War, and there was an Army Council that served as a general staff. The field army was organized into divisions, each of which was a complete combined-arms corps, including infantry, archers and chariots. These divisions contained approximately 6,000 men each, including logistics and support person-nel, and each was named after one of the principal gods of Egypt. Later,

Ramses II organized Egypt and the empire into thirty-four military districts to facilitate conscription, training and the supply of the army.[23] The army's administrative structure was also improved, and there were professional schools to train and test officers and scribes in the military arts.

The two major combat arms of the Egyptian army were chariotry and infantry. The chariot corps was organized into squadrons of twenty-five machines, each commanded by a 'charioteer of the residence', equal to a modern company commander. Larger units of fifty and 150 vehicles could be rapidly assembled and employed in concert with other forces.[24] It was common practice to assemble units whose size depended upon the nature of the mission and terrain, an example of the modern practice of tailoring a unit to a specific function. The chariot corps was supported logistically by staffs who procured and trained horses, and by craftsmen to maintain and repair the machines. Egyptian divisions also had mobile chariot repair units to ensure the operability of the vehicles when the army was in the field. The fact that Pharaoh was often portrayed as leading a chariot charge suggests that the chariot forces were the status elite of the field force, if not its primary combat striking arm. Figure 1 portrays a typical Egyptian mixed arms combat division of 5,500 men and 1,000 horses. A full field army usually comprised four such divisions.

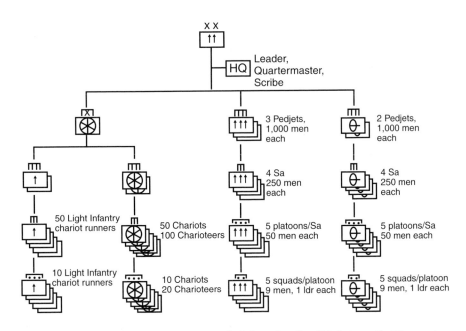

Organization of an Egyptian Division in the Eighteenth Dynasty

Thutmose III's strategic vision brought into being another important development, the Egyptian imperial navy. Egypt could not bring Canaan and Syria under its control if it had to move its army overland each time that control was threatened by revolt. The overland march was 350 miles long, took a high toll on the army's men and machines, was difficult and expensive to support logistically, conceded the tactical initiative to the enemy and took too much time, sacrificing any possibility of surprise. In addition, the transit time through Canaan reduced the effective campaign season to such a degree that the Egyptian army would be incapable of conducting sustained operations against the Mitanni across the Euphrates. Maintaining permanent troop garrisons of sufficient strength in Syria was expensive and probably not possible in terms of manpower. To achieve Egypt's strategic goals in Canaan and Syria, Thutmose had to find a way to move his army quickly into the zone of operations and to do so at low cost.

Thutmose's solution was to transport his army by ship along the Canaan-Lebanon coast, landing it in secure harbours logistically prepared in advance, and then strike inland against the adversary. Instead of invasions, Thutmose planned to conduct rapid expeditionary operations. The Egyptians had been sailors and ship-builders from time immemorial, but only on the Nile and never on the open sea. The navy had been an integral part of the army until Thutmose I, and had considerable experience in transporting troops and equipment over long distances up and down the Nile. The wars against the Hyksos and the conquest of Nubia had been successfully achieved by naval operations transporting troops to the battle areas, sometimes over distances of more than 1,000 miles. To fulfill Thutmose's mission, however, the navy would have to construct more and larger ships, learn how to transport and unload horses, and, most important, learn how to sail upon the open Mediterranean Sea.

Early in his reign, Thutmose ordered the expansion of the army and naval presence at the new town of Perunefer (literally, 'good sailing' or 'bon voyage') located on the western edge of the old Hyksos capital of Avaris on the Pelusiac branch of the Nile leading to the open sea.[25] A large army, logistics and naval base was constructed there that became the main operational base from which troops and equipment were transported to carry out military operations in Asia.[26] A large dockyard for building new ships was established, where the Egyptians began to construct new and larger vessels.

They built sea-going horse and troop transports.[27] Six years after Thutmose's attack on Megiddo, he transported his army by sea, landed on the Lebanon coast and attacked Kadesh, conducting the 'first great amphibious operation in history'.[28] Over the next three years, Thutmose gained control of a number of the Lebanese port cities, converting them into safe harbours and logistics bases for future expeditionary operations. From this time forward, Egypt had no rival for control of the coastal Mediterranean.[29]

Thutmose's success on the battlefield offers a case study in those personality traits that make a general great. First and foremost is a penchant for clear thinking unclouded by ideological or religious precepts. Thutmose was a deeply religious man. Yet, when it came to war, he appears to have assessed situations with a cold eye. He fought no wars for ideological purposes. He rarely destroyed the temples of other people's gods, and then only to make a political point. Thutmose was a commander always open to new ideas, and his inquisitive mind permitted him to find them everywhere. Whether it was adopting new weapons, using the four-wheeled wagon for the first time in Egypt's history, dragging boats over mountains, recognizing the value of naval power to ground warfare or incorporating the Syrian chicken into the army's food rations, Thutmose was an innovative commander in things large and small. The willingness to accept innovation is the mark of a stable, self-confident personality, one who trusts his own experiences and intellect to make sense of his world.

The strength of Thutmose's personality is revealed, too, in his willingness to challenge the unknown. He moved armies 800 miles from Egypt into territory about which Egyptians knew little. Time and again, he forged ahead into unknown land, trusting in his ability to learn and adapt to its very strangeness. Today, with so much of the world known and mapped, it is difficult for us to appreciate the apprehension such journeys could generate in the Egyptian mind, with its millennia-long history of isolation. To challenge the unknown requires a personality of strong will and confidence, and Thutmose's strength of will was prodigious. It was revealed when he overruled the objections of his senior officers to his plan of advance at Megiddo, and imposed his own tactical vision upon the plan of battle. One can only imagine how many more times the young and adventurous pharaoh overruled his more conservative military advisors. The risks and scale of the Euphrates campaign against the Mitanni must have shocked his generals. It is a maxim of military leadership that an army is an instrument of a commander's will. If so, then it is a good idea to begin with a commander who possesses a will of iron, as Thutmose did.

Brilliance, clear-headedness, a sense of risk and a strong will are the qualities of a good general, but they are qualities that must be augmented by others if soldiers are to be willing to follow a commander into battle at the risk of their own deaths. No soldier dies for grand strategy or for the glory of his king or country. Thutmose possessed the qualities of a good combat commander, including the all-important willingness to share the risks of his soldiers. Thutmose did this at Megiddo when he personally led the army down the dangerous, narrow track he had selected over the objections of his senior officers. The lesson was clear: if he made a mistake and the enemy ambushed the column, he would have been the first into the fight ... and the first to die. During the battle itself, Thutmose led the chariot attack in the centre of the line, a place of great danger but also of high visibility. As every combat officer knows, officers must be seen by their men when it comes time to fight and die. In every one of his campaigns for which we have records, Thutmose is portrayed as always participating fully in the battle.

There is, too, the need for a combat commander to care for his men, and Thutmose seems to have taken great care to be close to his troops, to see to it that they were well-fed and well-trained. He rewarded bravery in battle often, and there are many stories where he bestowed gold and other awards upon brave men. He seems to have taken a special pleasure in presenting common soldiers with the Fly of Valour, a gold housefly on a chain, the highest Egyptian decoration for bravery in battle, which Thutmose himself introduced. He was one of those great captains of antiquity who shaped his world in ways that most men of his time could not have imagined.

Thutmose III set in motion a series of events that shaped and influenced the Levant and Egypt for the next 400 years and his reign can be regarded as a watershed in the military and imperial history of the entire eastern Mediterranean. Thutmose inherited only a rudimentary military establishment that was gravely inadequate to the task of fostering his imperial ambitions. It was Thutmose who forged the new model army of the New Kingdom, introducing major reforms in logistics, conscription, weapons, chariotry and a new naval arm capable of supporting ground operations far from Egypt itself. The army that Thutmose brought into being lasted almost four centuries without major changes, remaining a reliable instrument of force projection in the hands of his immediate successors, the rest of the Eighteenth Dynasty, and most of the Nineteenth. Had he not done so, Egypt's conquest and administration of the eastern Levant would have been impossible.

Megiddo

Thutmose's military and political genius is clearly revealed in three of his major campaigns to establish his new strategic vision in Canaan and Syria. The first, and most famous, is his campaign against the city of Megiddo, where thirty-four Canaanite and Mitanni princes were gathering with their armies as a prelude to attacking Egypt.[30] In April 1481 BC, an Egyptian army comprised of two combined arms corps – each having 5,000 infantry and a chariot brigade of 500 vehicles – marched out of Egypt along the coastal road toward Gaza.[31] The army's advance to Megiddo was divided into four operational phases, each influenced by time, terrain and enemy reaction. First, Thutmose had to move his army from Egypt to Gaza. The army covered the 125 miles from Sile to Gaza in ten days, a rate of march of about 12 miles a day.[32] Thutmose remained in Gaza only overnight, ordering the army back on the march the next day.

The second phase required traversing the terrain from Gaza to Yehem (modern Yemma), a distance of 80 miles, much of it across the open Sharon plain, perfect for an Asiatic chariot attack. Yehem was a key road junction controlling the entrance to the Aruna road that led over the Carmel mountains to Megiddo and the Esdraelon Plain, the Classical Greek name for the Jezreel Valley. The danger in the movement from Gaza to Yehem lay in the possibility of discovery by Asiatic reconnaissance units or even a collision with the advance units of the Asiatic main force making its way across the Sharon plain en route to attack Egypt. Under these circumstances, security of the Egyptian force was paramount, and Thutmose covered the 80 miles in nine days. When the Egyptian army arrived at Yehem, it had been on the march for nineteen days.[33]

Phase three required the army to move over the Carmel mountains and gain the open plain next to the ridge upon which Megiddo sat without being attacked, worn down by enemy harassment along the way or ambushed as it exited the mountains on to the plain. Only after Thutmose's army forced the exits and gained the Esdraelon plain could it bring the enemy to battle in phase four.

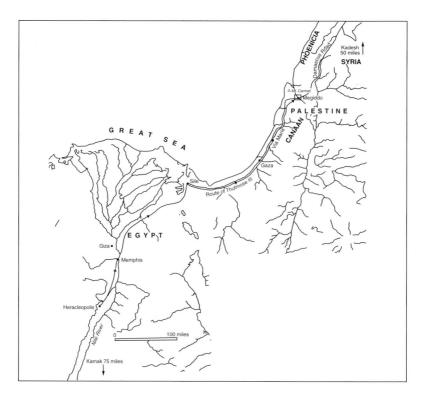

Thutmose's Route To Megiddo

Thutmose spent three days at Yehem, during which time his reconnaissance units explored the routes leading to Megiddo and discovered the disposition of the enemy force on the Esdraelon plain. Three roads led from Yehem to the valley. One led to Ta'anach at the southern end of the valley and was heavily guarded by an enemy chariot force. The second led through Aruna, and debouched less than a mile in front of Megiddo itself. It, too, was heavily guarded. A third road led to Djefty, some 5 miles from the city. On 18 May, the Egyptian army left Yehem, entered the Wadi Ara through the Carmel Mountains connecting to the Aruna road, marched 13 miles to the village of Aruna and then encamped. Below in the valley, some 300 enemy chariots blocked the exit at Aruna and another 600 guarded the exit from Ta'anach. The two forces were only 4 miles apart and could easily reinforce one another.[34] It was only when the Egyptian army arrived at Aruna that the enemy finally learned of its presence. Thutmose had successfully achieved strategic surprise.

But the tactical problem of how to get his army from Aruna on to the Esdraelon plain without being attacked when it exited the ridge remained. Egyptian reconnaissance units had discovered a narrow path running left off the Aruna road that debouched on the plain near the Kina brook, about a mile from Megiddo itself. The path was narrow, steep and ran 6 miles from Aruna to its exit on the valley floor. Thutmose proposed to his officers that his army take the path, and arrive outside the city and behind both enemy forces blocking the other exits. To a man, his senior generals opposed the plan as too dangerous. The 22-year-old Thutmose, now commanding his first major field operation, overruled them and ordered his army down the path on the morning of 19 May. With himself in the lead, the van of the army reached the plain in 3 hours, around noon, and began to deploy for battle on the plain using the Kina brook as a defensive obstacle to enemy attack. Outmanoeuvred and surprised, the enemy chariot detachments at the Aruna and Ta'anach exits deployed rearward to defend the city.[35]

The battle of Megiddo took place the next day. Greatly outnumbered and forced into a narrow tactical box by Thutmose's deployment of his infantry on the wings, the enemy chariots clashed with the Egyptians in the centre while the Egyptian infantry pressed inward from the flanks. Squeezed between the two combat elements, the enemy broke and fled, some taking refuge inside the city, others fleeing behind the city on the road to Hazor, 20 miles distant. Thutmose placed Megiddo under siege, and on 27 June, sixty-six days after the Egyptians had left Egypt, the city surrendered.[36] The capture of Megiddo placed control of the key communication routes from Egypt to Canaan, Syria and Mesopotamia firmly in Egyptian hands. Thutmose now turned his attention to getting control of the Lebanon coastal ports as he began the second phase of his grand strategy.

Canaan and the Lebanon Coast

It required three years of successive demonstrations of military power, threats, dismantling of fortifications, taking of hostages, heavy tribute and enforced loyalty oaths for Thutmose to bring all of Canaan and parts of southern Lebanon under effective Egyptian control following the victory at Megiddo. Over the next two years, the new system of Egyptian hegemony was reinforced by regular military visits, albeit by smaller contingents led by generals and not Pharaoh, and the imposition of small military and commercial garrisons who oversaw the operation of the imposed tax system. The effort to pacify Canaan took the Egyptians over five years.

In regnal year 29, (1472 BC), Thutmose embarked upon a major military expedition deep into Lebanon, the first Egyptian advance beyond the northern limits of the first campaign begun at Megiddo. The years of effort to win over the cities and towns of Canaan now paid dividends in enabling Thutmose to move north without too much concern about revolts occurring across his line of communications. Moreover, the newly established supply depots in Canaan made it possible to support the army logistically on its long march from Egypt to southern Lebanon, a distance of more than 300 miles. The Egyptian army numbered around 10,000 troops. It took the Egyptian army thirty-eight days to complete the march to Byblos.[37]

The expedition took Egyptian forces deep into Lebanon and engaged Kadesh and Tunip, allies of the Mitanni, who were of particular concern since both maintained substantial forces and were close to Thutmose's zone of operations. Thutmose's immediate objective was to bring the port of Byblos back into the Egyptian orbit after it was threatened by troops from the city of Tunip. Thutmose's army overwhelmed two Tunip garrisons that had blocked the mouth of the Eleutheros Valley that connected the Syrian interior to the military routes along the Orontes River to the Lebanon coast.[38] The Egyptians now controlled the invasion route to the interior. Of equal importance, Thutmose gained access to the Arka plain. Full of fertile fields, small towns, livestock and situated close to the coastal ports, the Arka plain could provide all the logistics support that an Egyptian army required to conduct sustained operations in the Syrian interior and, more importantly, north against the Euphrates and the Mitanni homeland.

The following year (1473 BC), Thutmose invaded Lebanon by sea with the goal of transforming the area west of the Lebanon mountains into a strategic platform for conducting further military operations. The Egyptian amphibious force comprised 12,000 troops, 500 chariots, 1,250 horses and 2,000 pack animals transported in eighty ships. The force covered the distance of 340 miles to Byblos in seven days at sea.[39] Thutmose quickly captured many of the coastal towns, transforming them into logistics depots, and then gained control of the exit to the Eleutheros Valley and the Arka plain by defeating the city state of Kadesh. He then conducted a demonstration tour of

Egyptian military power, capturing Avad, the last remaining major port outside Egyptian control.

The Egyptian campaign was a success. Thutmose had demonstrated his ability to conduct a large-scale amphibious invasion of the Lebanon coast, giving Egypt a new military advantage that greatly increased its ability to project power throughout the Levant. The Egyptians could now respond more rapidly to any rebellion or crisis, deploying large numbers of troops in ready fighting condition hundreds of miles from Egypt's shores, a military capability heretofore unknown in antiquity until Thutmose showed the world how to do it. He further built upon the new amphibious capability by demonstrating his ability to move inland and operate far from his coastal base, thus overcoming the strategic barrier of distance, behind which the powerful city states of Tunip, Kadesh and Qatna had relied for their protection against Egyptian retaliation for their mischief in Lebanon and Canaan. With their Syrian cat's paws now vulnerable to Egyptian attack, it was only a matter of time before Egyptian power would be directed at the Mitanni.

The Euphrates Campaign

In nine years, Thutmose had mounted seven military expeditions in Canaan and Lebanon, the last three coming in quick and effective succession. The decade of military operations was a prelude to the larger goal of confronting and defeating the Mitanni, the great power that Egypt saw as the major strategic threat and the source of its troubles in Syria. In 1471 BC, only eighteen months after his last campaign, Thutmose once more invaded the Lebanon coast.

The campaign plan called for the Egyptian army to deploy 600 miles from its base in Egypt, and maintain itself in the field for more than five months. During that time, it would have to fight its way across the Syrian interior, cross the Euphrates River, engage and defeat the Mitanni army in its homeland and return by overland march, passing again within striking distance of the military forces of the city-states with which it had to deal on its way out.

Thutmose's army included three infantry divisions, each of 5,000 infantry. Two brigades of 500 chariots each gave the army a combat capability of 1,000 vehicles. Two chariot brigades required 2,000 horses, and another 500 in reserve to compensate for losses to disease, lameness and combat actions. Two thousand drivers and charioteers comprised the personnel complement of the chariot brigades.

Another 1,000 groomsmen were taken along to care for the horses. Four thousand mules and donkeys were needed to provide the army's ground transport, and 600 smiths and carpenters to keep the army's equipment in ready repair. Another 1,000 or so human porters and other hangers-on that usually accompanied the armies of antiquity brought the number of personnel in Thutmose's army to almost 20,000 and the number of animals to almost 7,000. It was the largest army that Egypt had ever put in the field.[40]

It is an axiom of sound military thinking that political realities determine a commander's strategic vision, that strategy determines the campaign plan, and the campaign plan determines the operational plan to be carried out by the field force. The political configuration of the Mitanni system of alliances imposed significant limits on the way any Egyptian campaign could be waged against it. The powerful city of Aleppo to the north was under strong Mitanni influence, as were the mid-Syrian city-states of Qatna, Tunip and Kadesh that controlled the Orontes River valley.[41] Each of these states occupied an important location, control of which could seriously hinder the Egyptian advance.

But even in antiquity, military force was the handmaiden of politics. Thutmose used the time during which he was preparing his army to attempt to reduce the threats posed by some of the Syrian city-states by diplomacy. Thutmose achieved by diplomacy what would have required great effort to achieve by force, and gained unhindered access to the Orontes crossing as well as an unimpeded axis of advance to the north along the east bank of the river. In mid-April, the Egyptian army sailed from the new port city and dockyard at Perunefer bound for the Lebanon coast. Approximately 170 ships were needed to transport the army for the eight-day journey.

Once ashore on the Lebanon coast, Thutmose ordered the construction of landing craft. It was operational planning at its best. The Euphrates is a formidable barrier, in some places almost 2 miles wide where it touches northeastern Syria. Without boats to cross this mighty barrier, the campaign against the Mitanni would not have been possible. The landing craft were rafts fashioned from cedar logs, disassembled and loaded upon four-wheeled wagons pulled by oxen, to be reassembled when the army reached the Euphrates. Thutmose's use of four-wheeled wagons during his campaign is the first use of this technology in Egyptian military history.[42] At 9 miles a day, Thutmose's army and its wagons would take thirty-five days to reach the Euphrates.

The most direct axis of advance from the debarkation ports on the Lebanon coast to the Orontes River valley of northeast Syria was through

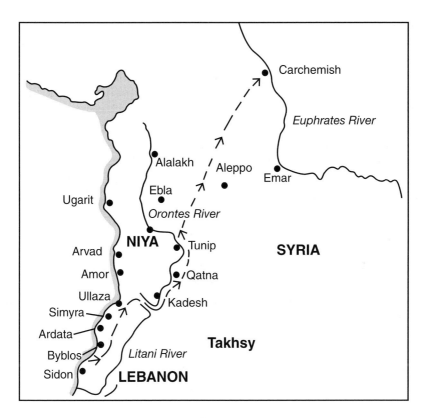

Thutmose's Route of March to the Euphrates

the Eleutheros valley. Thutmose was already in control of the valley's entrance, the Arka plain and some of the inland agricultural towns in the valley itself. But the exit from the valley was guarded by the powerful city-state of Kadesh. When the van of the Egyptian army approached the plain around Kadesh, its body stretched back for 12 miles.[43] The Egyptian force was larger by several orders of magnitude than anything Kadesh could put in the field, and the prince of Kadesh thought discretion the better part of valour and kept his main force inside the city walls. The grand army of Egypt passed through the plain of Kadesh and into the Orontes valley without incident.

Thutmose's route of march took him through the fertile agricultural belt of the Orontes valley, under the walls of the city-states of Qatna, Tunip and Niy, and on toward Aleppo. By a shrewd combination of diplomacy and intimidation, Thutmose had moved his army from the Lebanon coast to the outskirts of Aleppo without having to fight a single battle. Along the way, his army had been well-supplied with food and water, and except for the 'wastage' of men and animals that inevitably took its toll on any army on the march, the Egyptian force was in good fighting condition as it prepared for its first battle of the campaign outside Aleppo.[44] Beyond Aleppo, it was 70 miles to Carchemish and the Euphrates.

Geography, politics and logistics made some sort of skirmish around Aleppo inevitable. Aleppo was a key ally of the Mitanni, and the last allied state between the Egyptians and the Mitanni homeland, the last military obstacle to Thutmose's advance. Aleppo was also on the edge of the last agricultural region before the barren steppe that separated the city from the Euphrates. The Egyptian army had been on the march for eight days since leaving Tunip, and most of their field rations were already gone. Thutmose ordered his army to march west of Aleppo, plundering the countryside for the supplies he needed to cross the steppe and march on Carchemish.

Thutmose made no attempt to attack Carchemish itself, and the rulers of the city closed their gates and waited for the Egyptians to pass. Thutmose had no interest in attempting to overcome Aleppo, at least not yet. Seizing its food supply was sufficient. The area around Carchemish was a rich agricultural region stretching in a 4-mile wide strip 3 miles north and 6 miles south of the city itself on the Euphrates' west bank. A larger fertile area almost 8 miles wide and running south for 13 miles occupied the east bank.[45] The army rested and replenished itself from the stores confiscated from the farms on the west bank of the river. The crossing of the steppe between Aleppo and Carchemish occurred without incident. The area was sparsely settled by pastoral nomads, and there were few settlements from which opposition might have been mounted.

At Carchemish, the Euphrates narrows into two streams separated by a number of large islands. The distance from the west bank to the large island is only 75 metres. The island itself is about 300 metres wide. The second stream on the far side of the island is 100 metres wide. Using the islands as a mid-point, Thutmose's army crossed the Euphrates in three days.[46] The terrain between the Euphrates and the cities of the Mitanni was sparse, and afforded few opportunities for an invader to live off the land, making it unlikely that Thutmose thought it possible to drive inland and attack the Mitanni capital, Washshuganni, some 145 miles away. Thutmose's crossing of the river was designed to draw the enemy army to him, forcing it to fight on the borders of its territory and distant from its supply bases.

The Gebel Barkal stela tells of a great battle between the Egyptians and the Mitanni that took place on the east bank of the Euphrates in which 'the numerous army of the Mitanni was cast down in one hour. They have disappeared completely as those who never were, like an end of the Devourer, by act of the arms of the great good god, strong in battle, who causes slaughter among everyone.'[47] The stela implies that the battle was with the Mitanni king. But the list of booty taken from the defeated army belies the claim that a great battle was fought. At best, the Egyptians seem to have defeated only a local garrison of Mitanni troops, and certainly not the main army of the king. There must, however, have been some sort of engagement, for the texts tell of Thutmose conducting a pursuit of an enemy force that fled before him. In all likelihood, Thutmose ravaged the fertile areas on the eastern bank of the Euphrates and probably engaged and destroyed some local militia units. The Mitanni king, meanwhile, had refused to march to the river to fight the Egyptians and remained outside his capital waiting for them to come to him. They never did.

Years before, Thutmose's grandfather, Thutmose I, had led a military expedition to the banks of the Euphrates, where he had erected a victory stele on the east bank of the river. Now his grandson did the same thing. According to the *Annals*, 'He set up a tablet east of this water [Euphrates River]; he set up another beside the tablet of his father, the king of Upper and Lower Egypt, Okheperkere (Thutmose I).'[48] Placing a victory stela on the heights of Carchemish had great symbolic and political importance to the Egyptians. To them, the stela marked the new boundary of Egyptian influence and power. Its erection on Mitanni territory signified that the Mitanni were now a client state of Egypt, subject to Pharaoh's rule.[49] In reality, of course, no such thing was true.

Thutmose's raid had not changed the balance of power between the antagonists at all, and the Mitanni remained a great power for another fifty years. But in Egyptian eyes, Thutmose had defeated the great power to the east. Equally important, all the territory from the Lebanese coast to the banks of the Euphrates was now considered under Egyptian hegemony, including the city-states Thutmose had bypassed on his march to the river.

Thutmose and his army lingered only long enough to replenish their supplies to sustain them on their return march. Upon his return to Aleppo, Thutmose destroyed the settlements in the region that were allied with Aleppo and the Mitanni that he had presumably left unmolested on his outward march. It was a warning that Egyptian power could fall upon the city at a later date. After a march of more than 100 miles from the banks of the Euphrates, the Egyptian army arrived at Niya, between Tunip and Aleppo, where it rested to regain its strength. One of the objectives of the Euphrates campaign was to place under Egyptian control the area south and west of Aleppo and the Orontes valley as far south as the headwaters of the river at modern Baalbek. Egyptian diplomacy had neutralized the power of Tunip and Qatna, if only temporarily, and the march to the Euphrates had isolated Aleppo, whose agricultural regions the Egyptians had demonstrated could now be ravaged at will, even though the city itself had not been captured. This left Kadesh the only remaining obstacle to Egyptian success.

It must have been early August when Thutmose moved against Kadesh. The march from Kadesh to Egypt would take some thirty-seven days, bringing Thutmose back to Egypt around late September or early October. Consequently, Thutmose did not have sufficient time to over-come Kadesh by siege, which, given the Egyptian lack of siege technol-ogy, meant starving out the defenders. The harvest was already in, and the city's stores were sufficient to last the winter. If Kadesh was to be captured, Thutmose would have to entice its defenders into a battle on open ground or take the city by storm.

The terrain around the city was ideal chariot country, and it seems that some sort of chariot battle or at least a skirmish may have taken place there. Kadesh's army was a chariot-heavy force of *maryannu* war-riors, and it would have been logical for them to try to engage the Egyptian chariots on familiar ground. Whatever skirmish or battle was fought on the plain of Kadesh must have been inconclusive, with the *maryannu* retiring behind the safety of the city's walls. Thutmose then mounted an attack on the city by storm. There may have been repeated attempts to storm the city, but in the end Kadesh's defences held and the city did not fall.[50] The *Annals* are silent regarding the out-come of Thutmose's attack against Kadesh. The repeated Egyptian attacks undoubtedly produced high casualties, and after several failed attempts Thutmose may have thought better of it and simply withdrawn.

The Euphrates campaign was a great success. It represented a brilliant example of strategic deception by the psychological con-ditioning of Mitanni thinking regarding Egyptian intentions. Thutmose's previous military expeditions had convinced the Mitanni that he harboured no strategic interests beyond southern

Syria. This permitted him to move his army to within ten days' march of the Euphrates without arousing Mitanni suspicions. By then, however, it was too late for the Mitanni to react. Thutmose's use of the sea, the construction of river rafts and their transport overland with four-wheeled wagons, a military technology heretofore unknown to the Egyptians, all combined to inflict strategic surprise upon the enemy, and represents an excellent operational example of the projection of force in which all elements of the campaign plan were conceptually integrated and executed perfectly. The military expertise required to move an Egyptian force of 20,000 men and more than 7,000 animals first by sea for more than 300 miles, and then overland for another 270 to reach the objective, and to do so without being detected, surely stands as one of the most outstanding military feats of the Bronze Age.

Thutmose was 42 years old and in the third decade of his reign when he mounted his last campaign in Syria-Lebanon to put down another revolt by Kadesh. After this, he spent his last years building temples and indulging his intellectual interests. And then one day the greatest of the warrior pharaohs was gone, dead from natural causes.

'Lo, the king completed his lifetime of many years, splendid in valour, in might, and in triumph; from year 1 to year 54, third month of the second season, the last day of the month under the majesty of King Menkheperre, triumphant. He mounted to heaven, he joined the sun; the divine limbs mingling with him who begat him.'

He had lived fifty-three years, ten months and twenty-six days, and in his time had changed Egypt and the world forever.

Notes

1. Dennis Forbes, 'Menkheperre Djehutymes: Thutmose III, a Pharaoh's Pharaoh', *KMT* 9, no. 4 (Winter 1998–99), p.63.
2. Ibid. p.62.
3. R.B. Partridge, *Faces of Pharaohs: Royal Mummies and Coffins from Ancient Thebes* (London, Rubicon Press, 1994), pp.77–80.
4. David O'Connor, 'Thutmose III: An Enigmatic Pharaoh', in Eric Cline and David O'Connor (eds), *Thutmose III: A New Biography* (Ann Arbor, University of Michigan Press, 2008), pp.5–6.
5. Ibid.
6. Donald B. Redford, 'The Northern Wars of Thutmose III', in Cline and O'Connor, *Thutmose III: A New Biography*, p.325.

7. Richard A. Gabriel, *Thutmose III: The Military Biography of Egypt's Greatest Warrior Pharaoh* (Dulles, VA, Potomac Books, 2009), p.6.
8. Arielle P. Kozloff, 'The Artistic Production of the Reign of Thutmose III', in Cline and O'Connor, *Thutmose III: A New Biography*, p.317.
9. Forbes, 'Menkheperre Djehutymes', p.183.
10. Ibid.
11. Piotr Laskowski, 'Monumental Architecture and the Royal Building Program of Thutmose III', in Cline and O'Connor, *Thutmose III: A New Biography*, p.229.
12. Gabriel, *Thutmose III: Military Biography*, p.9.
13. See the classic work by Adolf Erman, *Life in Ancient* Egypt, trans. H.M. Girard (New York, Dover Books Reprint, 1971), especially chapter 14, 'Learning', pp.328–68.
14. Some idea as to how extensive the temple's libraries were can be gained from the example of Manetho, the high priest of Ptah at Memphis. When Ptolemy I assumed control of Egypt in the wake of Alexander's death, he asked Manetho to produce a history of Egypt. In a few short months, he was able to produce a comprehensive account of Egyptian history, reaching back to the third millennium BC, by drawing on the historical records in the temple library.
15. William Petty, 'Hatshepsut and Thutmose III Reconsidered', *KMT* 8, no. 1 (Spring, 1997), p.47.
16. Peter F. Dorman, 'The Early Reign of Thutmose III: An Unorthodox Mantle of Coregency', in Cline and O'Connor, *Thutmose III: A New Biography*, pp.39–68.
17. O'Connor, 'Thutmose III: An Enigmatic Pharaoh', p.5.
18. Petty, 'Hatshepsut and Thutmose III Reconsidered', p.48.
19. Gabriel, *Thutmose III: Military Biography*, p.19.
20. Redford, 'The Northern Wars of Thutmose III', p.325.
21. R.O. Faulkner, 'Egyptian Military Organization', *Journal of Egyptian Archaeology* 39 (1953), p.42.
22. Raymond W. Baker, *Encyclopedia Britannica*, 15th ed., s.v. 'History of Egyptian Civililization'.
23. Alan R. Schlman, *Military Rank, Title, and Organization in the Egyptian New Kingdom* (Berlin, Bruno Hassling Verlag, 1964), p.54.
24. Ibid.
25. Manfred Bietak, 'The Thutmosid Stronghold of Perunefer', *Egyptian Archaeology* 26 (Spring, 2005), pp.13–14.
26. Torgny Save-Soderbergh, *The Navy of the Eighteenth Egyptian Dynasty* (Uppsala, Sweden, Uppsala University Press, 1946), p.39.
27. Ibid. p.34.

28. Ibid. p.42.
29. Ibid. p.34
30. The Battle of Megiddo is the first battle in history for which we have a name and a sufficient account of events from which to reconstruct a portrait of the strategy and tactics employed by the antagonists. In this sense, it can be said that the Battle of Megiddo is the starting point for the study of military history.
31. Gabriel, *Thutmose III: Military Biography*, p.84.
32. R.O. Faulkner, 'The Battle of Megiddo', *Journal of Egyptian Archaeology* 28 (1942), p.2.
33. Gabriel, *Thutmose III: Military Biography*, p.87.
34. Ibid. p.96.
35. Ibid. pp.99–104.
36. Ibid. pp.106–12.
37. Ibid. p.127.
38. The name of the Eleutheros Valley is taken from *Strabo*, Histories, xvi, 2, 12, and was used throughout classical times. The name appears in the *Bible* (Maccabees 11:7 and 12:30), but we do not know by what name it was known to the Egyptians.
39. William F. Edgerton, 'Ancient Egyptian Steering Gear', *American Journal of Semitic Languages and Literature* 43, no. 4 (July, 1927), pp.255–65; see also by the same author, 'Ancient Egyptian Ships and Shipping', *American Journal of Semitic Languages and Literature* 39, no. 2 (January, 1923), pp.116–17.
40. Gabriel, *Thutmose III: Military Biography*, p.161.
41. Donald B. Redford, *The Wars in Syria and Palestine of Thutmose III* (Boston, Brill, 2003), p.232.
42. Mordchai Gichon, 'Military Camps on Egyptian and Syrian Reliefs', *Assaph: Studies in Honor of Asher Ovadiah* (Tel Aviv, Department of Art History, Tel Aviv University, 2005–6), p.571.
43. An army of 20,000 troops marching four abreast forms a column 7 miles long. Add to this number the 6,500 animals and wagons, and an estimate of 10–12 miles for the length of Thutmose's column seems reasonable.
44. British staff officers in the First World War invented the term *wastage* to describe the number of soldiers who became unfit for duty for a variety of reasons each day.
45. For a description of the agricultural region around Carchemish and the west bank of the Euphrates in antiquity, see Irene J. Winter, 'Carchemish', *Anatolian Studies* 33 (1983), pp.177–97.
46. Gabriel, *Thutmose III: Military Biography*, 171.

47. The inscription appears on the Rebel Baikal stela, 3, in Sethe, *Urkunden der 18 Dynastie.*
48. James Henry Breasted, *Ancient Records of Egypt, vol. 2, The Eighteenth Dynasty* (Urbana, University of Illinois, 2001), p.202.
49. It is for this reason – the conquered country became part of Pharaoh's realm – that the texts frequently portray the military expeditions of the Egyptian king as 'extending the boundaries of Egypt'.
50. Redford, *The Wars in Syria and Palestine of Thutmose III*, p.240.

CHAPTER THREE

MOSES (1200 BC?)

While the *Bible* is primarily a religious text, it can also be read as an after-action report detailing the military history of the early Israelites. Whoever recorded the saga of Moses in the book of *Exodus* was well acquainted with the strategies, tactics and military techniques of the day. Examined as military history, *Exodus* tells the tale of a great general who sacked an Egyptian supply depot, outmanoeuvred the Egyptians in a desert campaign, fought the Amelekites to a draw, created and trained the first Israelite national army, won a great victory on the plain of Jahaz, destroyed fortified cities in the Jordan Valley and bequeathed his successor a large, well-equipped, combat-hardened and professionally led military force with which to attack Canaan. This great Israelite general's name was Moses.

Contrary to popular belief, the Israelites in Egypt were neither slaves nor a rag-tag band of wandering Bedouins, but a tribal coalition of *habiru*. *Habiru* is not a designation for an ethnic or racial group, but a class of wandering peoples in Palestine and Syria who came into contact with the Egyptians during the New Kingdom. The *habiru* comprised much larger groups than Bedouin, and their social structure was more complex. They were a people without a country, with no national identity, united now and again in common journeys for pasture and plunder.[1] And they were armed to the teeth!

The *habiru* sometimes remained in an area for very long periods and became clients of the host kingdom, where their military arm performed military service as mercenaries. They 'operated as armed groups, semi-independent in the feudal structure, available for hire, as auxiliary troops or resourceful in carrying out free booting, either on their own or at the instigation of one city-state against another'.[2] The military arm of the *habiru* typically comprised military professionals sufficiently experienced in war whose task was to protect the community. *Habiru* units were formidable military assets, proficient in combat in rough terrain and experts at hit-and-run raids, ambush and surprise attack. The size of their units varied. When David fought for the Philistines before becoming king of Israel, his command numbered 600 men. Other *habiru* forces were larger, one comprising 1,436 infantry,

80 charioteers and 1,000 archers.[3] The settlement of the Israelites in Goshen in exchange for military service, as told in the Bible, is a typical pattern of *habiru* military employment found elsewhere.

The tale of the Exodus in the original Hebrew is explicitly told in military terms. *Exodus* 13:19 says that the Israelites were armed when they left Egypt: 'Now the Israelites went up armed out of Egypt.' The term *hamushim* is used to denote their possession of weapons.[4] *Exodus* 12:37 describes the Israelites as having 'six thousand footmen – the males besides the dependants'. The term employed for 'footmen' is *ragli,* literally 'he of the leg', meaning infantry.[5] *Exodus* 12:41 describes these infantry units as being formed into brigades: 'All Yahweh's brigades went out from the land of Egypt.' The biblical account tells us that the Israelites departed Egypt with their weapons in hand and their military units formed up in march formations. Against this background, the adventures of Moses and the Israelites described in *Exodus* take on new meaning as military history.

Moses' Personality

Next to Yahweh, Moses is the most intriguing character of the Old Testament. Held in awe as the founder of one of the world's great religions, respected as a national patriot who led his people out of slavery and the subject of endless writings and speculations, Moses has become a figure of history. And yet there is scant evidence beyond the Bible itself that the man ever existed. The Bible tell us that Moses was born in Egypt to Israelite parents. We have no knowledge of where within Egypt or when he was born. It is likely, however, that he was an Israelite leader of some standing, for only a leader would have returned from exile to lead his people and expected them to follow him. We know nothing, however, about what position he may have held.

But the Bible does reveal elements of Moses' behaviour that shed considerable light upon his personality, and one of the more interesting elements is the man's bloodthirsty and violent nature. I am not referring here to the murder and mayhem committed by Moses at the command of Yahweh, itself terrible enough, but rather to the violence and killing that Moses committed at his own initiative in the absence of Yahweh's directives.

We first encounter Moses as an adult when he murders an Egyptian overseer. This was no act of rage. It was, instead, premeditated murder. The Bible says, 'he looked this way and that, and seeing there was no one about, he struck the Egyptian down.'[6] Moses showed no sign of panic, and coolly dragged the dead man away and 'hid his body in the sand'. Moses then calmly went about his business for a few days before returning to the scene of the crime, where he learned that witnesses had reported the killing to the authorities. Fearing apprehension, Moses fled.[7] Moses was clearly not a man easily upset by violence, and the murder of the overseer was a portent of his willingness to use violence whenever it suited his purpose.

In another violent incident, Moses returned from Mount Sinai to discover the Israelites worshipping a golden calf. He convinced Yahweh not to exterminate the Israelites for their sin, and Moses took it upon himself to punish them. Moses called upon his Levite praetorian guard and ordered, 'Put ye every man his sword upon his thigh, and go to and from gate to gate throughout the camp, and slay every man his brother, and every man his companion, and every man his neighbour.'[8] The Levites were Moses' clansmen, and comprised the police force that Moses used time and again to keep his people in line. Three thousand Israelites were put to death that day, and then only after Moses had crushed the idol into powder, mixed it with water and forced the apostates to drink it before being killed.

The next murderous outburst came when the Israelites were camped on the border of Moab and Canaan. Some Israelite men took up with the 'daughters of Moab', taking them as concubines and fornicating with them. Moses ordered the death of every Israelite male who 'committed harlotry with the daughters of Moab'.[9] Some Midianite women had apparently joined the Moabites in seducing the Israelites. Yahweh ordered Moses to exterminate the Midianites, a particularly cruel command since Moses' wife, Zipporah, and father-in-law, Jethro, were Midianites. Moses was being asked to kill his blood clansmen, and he complied without pity. He gave command of the expedition to the religious zealot, Phinehas, son of the high priest. Moses ordered Phinehas to exterminate the Midianites. No one was to be left alive.

Phinehas attacked the Midianites with a cruel vengeance, slaughtering every adult man and woman. But even this cold *apparatchik* could not bring himself to slaughter the children. When Moses saw that Phinehas had spared the helpless, he flew into a rage. 'Have ye saved all the women alive!' Moses then ordered everyone but the virgins to be killed. 'Now therefore kill every male among the little ones, and kill every woman that hath known man by lying with him.'[10] The young virgins were turned over to Moses' troops to do with as they wished. The slaughter and rape were so hideous that the officers of the army turned their share of booty over to Moses 'to make atonement for our souls before the Lord'.[11]

It is important to note that while the Moabites were slain because of their sexual proclivities, Moses slaughtered the Midianites because they seduced the Israelites into worshipping idols; that is, they were killed for religious reasons. Moses' killing of the Midianties is the first religious genocide in recorded history.[12]

Moses had a well-developed flair for the dramatic, for the mysterious gesture that confounds the comprehension of his clansman at almost every turn. The Bible suggests Moses' encounter with Yahweh on Mount Sinai may have left him with some sort of disfigurement. *Exodus* says that 'the children of Israel saw the face of Moses, that the skin of Moses' face sent forth beams.'[13] A more likely explanation of Moses' condition is that he may have been afflicted by one of the six plagues that the Bible says the Israelites suffered on the desert trek, plagues that the text tells us killed nearly 40,000 people in all. Whatever disfigured Moses must have left a serious facial injury that encouraged him to cover it up.

From the moment he returned from Mount Sinai, Moses always wore a mask, removing it only when he spoke with Yahweh in the 'tent of meeting'. The effect of walking around the Israelite camp with a mask covering his face no doubt marked Moses as a mysterious man somehow chosen by God. The Bible uses the word *masweh* to denote the mask that Moses wore. The word denotes the kind of mask commonly worn by pagan priests when addressing their gods.[14] To further mystify his actions, Moses ordered the 'tent of meeting' moved to the centre of the camp, and mounted an armed Levite guard around it. If anyone came near the sacred tent, 'the common man who draweth nigh shall be put to death'.[15] Moses had arranged the circumstances of his leadership so that he remained the only connection between the people and their god.

Ritual as a mechanism of personal power is nothing new, and Moses may have found himself in a difficult spot when it came to keeping the Israelites in line. He may have had desperate need for recognizable ritual to rally his followers. Some of these he may have recalled from the old Israelite rituals, as when he fashioned the magic-soaked ritual of Passover with its sacrifice of the lamb and smearing of blood on the door posts of the Israelites so that Yahweh would know his own people as he went about exterminating the Egyptians.[16] Others he may have adopted from Egyptian rituals, as when 'Moses made a serpent of brass, and set it upon the pole, and it came to pass that if a serpent had bitten any man, when he looked unto the serpent of brass, he lived'.[17] Showmanship is the stock in trade of any successful leader, secular or religious, and Moses knew how to mix magic, mystery and mastery with the best of them to convince the crowd.

Moses the General

Exodus has been presented to the world mostly by theologians and religious historians, not military historians, with the result that its account has been largely overlooked as a significant source of military history. Yet even a cursory examination of *Exodus* reveals more than a few examples of the military art practised with an expertise sufficient to hold the attention of any serious student of strategy and tactics. Seen from a military perspective, the Exodus is the saga of a people equipped and familiar with weapons, led by experienced and tactically proficient commanders, who were not Egyptian slaves, and whose military proficiency and operational capability improved greatly during the desert trek until, with remarkable clarity of strategic aim, they were able to achieve their ultimate objective of conquering the land of Canaan. First and foremost is the evidence of military competence and greatness revealed in the strategies and tactics employed by Moses, the Israelite commander, in leading his people out of Egypt and fighting his way to Canaan.

What follows is an examination of Moses' actions as the field commander of the Exodus from this new perspective that analyzes a number of events described therein from the viewpoint of a military historian trying to make sense of the Moses tale in military terms. To help the reader see the story with a soldier's eye, it is useful if the reader could set aside any reliance upon divine explanations for these events, and see them instead from the perspective of a combat field commander. Where I thought it helpful, I have attributed the military commands of Yahweh and Moses as reported in the Hebrew text to Moses alone. Hopefully, this literary device will help the reader see that these commands often make surprisingly good military sense.

With Moses in command, the Israelites prepared to leave Egypt. Evidence of a first-rate military mind is seen quickly in the choice of which routes to take. *Exodus* 13:17–18 tells us: 'Now when Pharaoh let the people go, Moses did not lead them by way of the land of the Philistines, although it was nearer; for Moses said, "The people may have a change of heart when they see war, and return to Egypt." So Moses led the people roundabout, by way of the wilderness at the Sea of Reeds.' Moses decided to avoid the coastal road, the most direct route to Canaan, because it was well-guarded by Egyptian forts and troop garrisons. The Canaanite towns along the coastal road were also protected by their own military forces, some including other *habiru* serving as mercenaries to their Canaanite kings. Moses feared his people might be attacked and 'have a change of heart when they see war, and return to Egypt'. His decision to avoid the coastal road made sound military sense.

But having received permission to leave Egypt, why would Moses be concerned about the Egyptians? *Exodus* 14:5–6 tells us only that Pharaoh changed his mind, but not why. A clue may lie in *Exodus* 14:8, which says that the Israelites were 'departing defiantly, boldly'. It is important to recall that the *habiru* were not only mercenaries, but brigands and freebooters who could quickly turn from allies to brigands if circumstances required. *Exodus* 12:39 tells us that 'because they had been expelled from Egypt and could not tarry … they had made no provisions for themselves'.

Moses must have known that to take the Israelites into the desert without sufficient provisions was to face almost certain death, especially since the Israelites in Goshen were surrounded by the very provisions they required. Goshen was filled with 'store cities', logistics depots for the Egyptian army in the Delta, and royal estates and farms. Everything the Israelites needed to support themselves on the trek to Canaan was there for the taking. It is a reasonable guess that the Israelites sacked one of the towns on the way out of the country to provision themselves for the desert trek. *Exodus* 12:35–36 tells the outrageous tale of how Moses proposed to solve the provision problem by simply asking the Egyptians for them! Thus, 'The Israelites had done Moses' bidding and borrowed from the Egyptians objects of silver and gold, and clothing. And Moses had disposed the Egyptians favourably toward the people, and they let them have their request; thus they stripped the Egyptians.' But the text clearly implies otherwise. The Hebrew word used to describe what happened to the Egyptians is *nitzeyl*, usually used to mean 'despoiled', so that the Israelites 'despoiled Egypt'. It is not plausible that the Egyptians provided food, clothing, gold and silver merely for the asking. Far more likely is that Israelite brigands took them at the point of the sword. If the news of the Israelite sack of an Egyptian town reached Pharaoh's ears, it may have provoked him to punish the Israelites. Perhaps this is why Moses avoided the coastal road.

The Pillar of Fire and Smoke

The Israelites began their march along the well-travelled road leading from Raamses to the edge of the desert. The first day's march, about 10 miles, brought them to Succoth. The end of the next day found them in Etham, 8 miles from Succoth. All along the way, the Israelites were accompanied by a strange phenomenon, a pillar of cloud and a pillar of fire. *Exodus* 13:20–22 describes it this way: 'They set out from Succoth, and encamped at Etham, at the edge of the wilderness. The Lord went before them in a pillar of cloud by day, to guide them along the way, and in a pillar of fire by night, to give them light, that they might travel day and night. The pillar of cloud by day and the pillar of fire by night did not depart from before the people.' Again and again throughout the journey, the pillars appear.

Miraculous explanations aside, the pillars appear to have two functions. One, to guide the Israelites as they move over unfamiliar terrain; two, to signal the Israelites when to camp and when to break camp. And so *Exodus* 40: 36–37 tells us: 'When the cloud lifted from the tabernacle, the Israelites would set out on their various journeys; but if the cloud did not lift, they would not set out until such times as it did lift.' *Numbers* 9:17–18 is even more explicit: 'And whenever the cloud lifted from the tent, the Israelites set out accordingly; and at the spot where the cloud settled, there the Israelites would make camp. At the command of Moses the Israelites broke camp, and at the command of Moses they made camp.' What the pillar of cloud and fire appears to be is not so much a divine totem but a practical device to improve Moses' command and control over his followers, yet another indication of Moses' knowledge of Egyptian military practices.

This same signalling device is found in the writings of Quintus Curtius, a Roman historian. In his *History of Alexander,* Curtius describes how after conquering Egypt and returning to Babylon, Alexander prepared his army for movement further east. These preparations included a number of changes in his regular methods of command and control. As Curtius tells it, 'Also in the military discipline handed down by his predecessors Alexander made many changes of the greatest advantage.'[18] Curtius goes on to describe one of these changes: 'When he [Alexander] wished to move his camp, he used to give the signal with the trumpet, the sound of which was often not readily enough heard amid the noise made by the bustling soldiers; therefore he set up a pole [*perticam*] on top of the general's tent, which could be clearly seen from all sides, and from this lofty signal, visible to all alike, was watched for, [*ignis noctu fumus interdieu*] fire by night, smoke by day.'[19]

Until very modern times, Arab caravans, including those making their way to the *hajj*, were commonly preceded by a signal brazier of some sort.[20]

Was the pillar of fire and smoke an Egyptian military signalling device, as Alexander's use of it implies? Just such a device is portrayed in the reliefs in the Luxor Temple depicting Ramses II's military camp at the Battle of Kadesh. Standing behind Ramses as he sits upon his throne are two figures, each holding a long straight pole. Atop one of the poles appears to be a portrayal of a brazier in full flame. The other figure is holding a second pole, atop which sits the bottom half of a partially covered brazier. A brazier covered in this manner would dampen the flame and produce smoke. If the Ramses relief is indeed portraying a covered brazier and one in full flame, then it might be an Egyptian portrayal of the pillar of smoke and fire described in *Exodus*.

There is one more clue as to the device's Egyptian origins. When Pharaoh's chariots approached the Israelite camp near the Reed Sea, they saw the pillar of smoke change into a pillar of fire and shift position. But these 'miraculous' events produced no reaction at all on the part of the Egyptian commanders and soldiers, and the Egyptians calmly went into their night encampment and waited for dawn. This suggests that the Egyptians were observing something which they had often seen before, a commander's signal for his troops to encamp for the night. That Moses was familiar with Egyptian military practices is not surprising in light of the fact that the Israelite *habiru* military arm served in the Egyptian army as mercenaries.

The Crossing of the Reed Sea

Perhaps no event in *Exodus* has captured the imagination more than the crossing of the Reed Sea. When examined from the perspective of military technique, however, it is clear that what happened at the Red Sea was only a tactical manoeuvre, the night crossing of a water obstacle, and not a miraculous occurrence. Moses and the Israelites had lived in Goshen for a long time, perhaps as long as four generations, and were thoroughly familiar with the area, including the marshy tract (the Reed Sea) where the fertile land met the desert. For years they had taken their herds down the same road they were travelling now to pasture them in the Sinai steppe during the rainy season.[21] The main road led directly from the edge of Goshen to a junction where it joined the road to Beersheba and then on to Canaan. As mercenaries serving in Goshen, Israelite commanders were also aware of the locations and strength of Egyptian troop garrisons in the area.

It is pointless to attempt to locate the exact place where the Israelites crossed the Reed Sea. Suffice it to say that the terrain where Goshen met the desert was marshy and wet, deep in places and shallow in others, neither sea nor lake for the most part, yet subject to strong tidal flows, all elements attested to by other writers in antiquity.[22] The tidal flows of the general area are attested to in antiquity. Strabo seems to be describing them when he notes that, 'During my stay in Egypt the sea rose so high near Pelusium and Mount Cassius as to overflow the land and to convert the mountain into an island.'[23] That the marshy terrain was dangerous to ground troops is clear from the description offered by Diodorus Siculus, a first-century CE Greek historian, who records that during Xerxes' invasion of Egypt in 340 BC, a troop unit of his army drowned in the place.[24] It is not difficult to imagine a company of Persian troops walking across a shallow muddy flat only to be trapped and drowned when the tide suddenly came in. As Moses marched the Israelites down the road to the desert, he had the advantage of knowing the enemy troop dispositions and how to navigate the marshy terrain.

Moses must have been aware that the Israelite column would have to pass directly beneath the Egyptian fortress that guarded the road junction. As one of the four major fortresses of the area, the Egyptian garrison would have been large and well-armed. Moses depended upon a peaceful passage. If he had to fight his way through, the results would be a catastrophe, for his people were no match for the Egyptian professionals. Perhaps this was when a message reached Moses that Pharaoh's troops had already left Raamses, and were fast closing in on the road behind him, trapping him between them and the Egyptian fortress to his front. If he remained where he was, Moses would find himself caught between the classic 'hammer and anvil'. With the Egyptian garrison to his front and Pharaoh's chariots closing from behind, the situation was already desperate. In a few hours it would be hopeless.

Moses assembled his commanders. 'Tell the Israelites to turn back and encamp before Pi-hahiroth, between Migdol and the sea, before Baal-Zephon; you shall encamp facing it, by the sea.' (*Exodus* 14:2–2) The order must have struck some of the Israelite troop commanders as insane, for Moses had just instructed the Israelite column to leave the road and head directly into the desert! Unwilling to risk forcing his way through the Egyptian fort to his front, Moses manoeuvred to neutralize its tactical significance by moving his people south and west, away from the Egyptian garrison. But why did Moses move further into the desert? *Exodus* 14:3 tells us what was in his mind when it explains: 'Pharaoh will say of the Israelites, "They are astray in the land; the wilderness has closed in on them."' It is an axiom of war to deceive the enemy as to your intentions, to mislead him into thinking one thing while you prepare to do another. Here, *Exodus* provides us with an example of tactical deception at its best. Moses intends to convince the Egyptians that the Israelites are lost when, in fact, having lived in Goshen for many years, Moses knows exactly where he is.

The Israelites marched into the desert. When they reached a place where the firm ground to their front met the watery marsh to their rear, they encamped and waited for the Egyptian chariots to arrive. Now Moses manoeuvred to deceive the Egyptians further. *Exodus* 14:19 tells us: 'The angel of God who had been going ahead of the Israelite army, now moved and followed behind them; and the pillar of cloud shifted from in front of them and took up a place behind them, and it came between the army of the Egyptians and the army of Israel.' Moses moved his command tent and its characteristic signal, the pillar of smoke atop a pole, around behind the column to strengthen the impression that the Israelites were facing in a direction of march leading further into the desert. The goal was to convince the Egyptians that the Israelites were indeed 'astray in the land'.

It must have been near dusk when the Egyptian chariot units arrived, for they went immediately into camp. From the Egyptian camp, it looked like the Israelites were facing in a direction of march that would take them deeper into the desert. Behind the Israelites lay the tidal salt marsh. As dusk gave way to darkness, the pillar of smoke atop the Israelite signal standard burst into flame and 'the pillar lit up the night, so that the one camp could not come near the other all through the night'. (*Exodus*, 14:20)

The bright flame atop the pillar drew the attention of the Egyptian sentries, completely blocking their ability to see behind it. Today's soldiers are taught when training in night discipline that any bright object at night affects the eye, making it incapable of seeing in the dark behind the light. Moses could now safely manoeuvre his troops behind the light, as long as the direction of movement was to the rear of the Israelite encampment. For all practical purposes the Egyptians were blind.

Now the *ruah qadim*, or forward wind, began to blow. It was spring-time, the time of the sirocco winds that blew out of the eastern desert with terrific force and great noise. Because the Israelites oriented themselves for religious reasons toward the sunrise, the translation of *ruah qadim* as east wind, the forward direction, is correct.[25] As the wind grew stronger, the noise increased. Now the Egyptians were deaf as well. The shallow water covering the sandbar just below the surface began to move as the tide flowed out to sea. With the desert wind pushing from the southeast and the tide pulling it northward, the water was gone in a short time and the ground dry enough to hold the weight of men and animals. Moses called his troop commanders together and ordered them to withdraw across the marsh and gain the desert on the other side.

Exodus 14:24 tells us that the Egyptian pursuit began 'at the morning watch', or shortly after daybreak. The Egyptians attempted to follow the Israelites, but the wheels of their chariots became 'locked' so that 'they moved forward with difficulty'. (*Exodus* 14:21–23) This seems to be nothing more mysterious than chariot wheels stuck in the mud. While struggling to free their machines, 'the waters turned back and covered the chariots and the horsemen'. The tide came in and perhaps some of the Egyptian troops and horses drowned. The incoming tide filled the

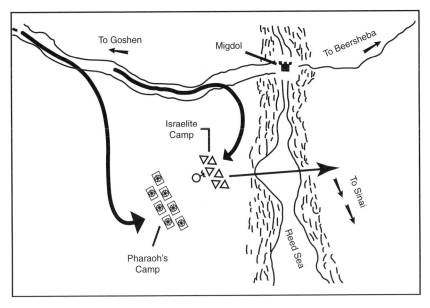

Night Crossing Of The Reed Sea

marsh, preventing any further pursuit for at least 8 hours until the tide receded again.[26]

The Israelites had crossed the marsh and gained the desert. But Moses knew that they were still in danger. The plan had been to return to the land of Canaan. To return to their original route, however, would have required them to turn north to reach the Beersheba road and taken them close to the Egyptian fort at the junction of the Beersheba–Goshen road. Egyptian reconnaissance chariots regularly patrolled the road and might easily discover the Israelites and bring them under attack. Once more, Moses did the unexpected. He turned not toward the land of Canaan, but away from it. *Exodus* 15:22 says: 'Then Moses caused Israel to set out from the Sea of Reeds. They went into the wilderness of Shur.' And so began the great desert trek of the Israelites in their attempt to return to Canaan.

The Battle with the Amalekites

Moses' decision took advantage of his knowledge of the terrain over which the Israelites would have to travel. The Israelites did not simply 'wander' guided only by fortune (or divine design) to stumble upon Sinai and then Kadesh-Barnea. The texts tell us that Moses had spent many years among his Midianite relatives tending flocks in the Sinai desert, an occupation that would surely have equipped him with a knowledge of the area and the locations of the wells. The Israelites were also helped by Midianite guides 'who serve as eyes for Israel'. These hardy desert Bedouins also instructed the Israelites how to 'encamp in the wilderness', that is, how to live off the land.[27]

Little more than a month after crossing the Reed Sea, and somewhere in the Sinai near Rephidim, the Israelites were attacked by the Amalekites and forced to fight their first battle. The centre of the Amalekite territory was north of Kadesh-barnea in the Negev desert in the southern part of Canaan, with their tributary camps radiating out into the Sinai Peninsula and northern Arabia. It was probably Amalekites from one of these tributary camps that the Israelites encountered. The biblical text suggests an engagement that occurred in two phases. The first was an ambush in which the Amalekites caught the Israelites in column of march and attacked their rear. *Deuteronomy* 25:17–19 describes the ambush: 'Remember what the Amalek did to you on your journey, after you left Egypt – how, undeterred by fear of god, he surprised you on the march, when you were famished and weary, and cut down all the stragglers in your rear.' The Amalekites engaged again in the morning. Moses placed command of the Israelite fighting men in the hands of a young troop commander named Joshua, and then 'stationed myself on the top of the hill, with the rod of God in my hand'. It is an old military maxim that commanders must be seen by their soldiers to be effective in battle. The text tells us that for the entire day Moses stood in plain view on the hill overlooking the battle 'until the sun set', while on the battlefield below 'Joshua overwhelmed the Amalek with the edge of the sword'. (*Exodus,* 17:9–13)

What is the historian to make of the account? First, there can be no doubt now that the Israelites are armed, and they are armed with the sword. This sword is the sickle-sword, the basic second weapon of the Egyptian spear infantryman, called the *khopesh* or 'foreleg' of an animal. The weapon was so completely identified with the Egyptian army, although Canaanites used it as well, that the *khopesh* replaced the mace as the symbol of pharaonic authority.[28] Where, then, did the Israelites acquire such weapons in sufficient numbers if they did not, as *Exodus* tells us, already possess them *before* they left Egypt? Given the expense and difficulty of bronze manufacture, especially so for a people on the move, we may rule out the Israelites having manufactured the weapons after they left Egypt.[29] If the Israelites at Rephidim were armed with standard-issue Egyptian weapons, this could only be because they possessed them during their mercenary service in Egypt. Thus it was, as *Exodus* says, that the Israelites 'went up out of Egypt armed'.

The Amalekites were tribal nomads whose military capability was confined to camel-riding infantry armed with the simple bow. Camel infantry was well suited to ambush and hit-and-run raids of the type described as having occurred at Rephidim. In uneven or narrow terrain, however, it was at a severe disadvantage, and could not effect a tactical decision without having its riders dismount and fight as infantry. It was precisely this combined capability that made the later Arab armies under Muhammad so successful. But dismounted bowmen are not as effective as dismounted spear infantry, a fact that forced the Amalekites to fight mounted, often with two men upon a single camel.[30]

Joshua's main tactical problem was to neutralize the enemy camel infantry. Joshua took up positions at the rear of the Israelite column, while its main body took refuge behind his soldiers in a narrow defile protected by hills on either side. The moderately steep hills prevented any flanking attack or envelopment by the Amalekite camels, in much the same manner as the Greek army at Marathon neutralized the Persian cavalry by deploying in a narrow gap between the hills to make it impossible for the Persian cavalry to flank or envelope the Greek position. Arranged in phalanx, Joshua's spear and shield infantry would have offered an impenetrable wall of spear points. Behind the spear infantry were Joshua's archers, armed with the Egyptian composite bow, of greater range than the simple bow of the Amalekites. Scattered upon both sides of the hills were slingers capable of throwing stone shot the size of a tennis ball 100 yards. The Amalekites could rush the wall of spears again and again, only to have their camels pull up short as long as the Israelite infantry held fast. Each Amalekite attack would be subject to long-range slinger fire before it reached the wall of spears and shields. Once the Amalekites closed with the Israelite infantry, Joshua's archers could pick off individual targets. *Exodus* 17:12–13 tells us that the battle lasted until sunset, and that when it was over 'Joshua overwhelmed the people of Amalek with the edge of the sword'.

It is clear that from a defensive position, Joshua could have done no such thing, since at any time the Amalekites could have broken off the attack and given up the fight. Joshua's infantry could not have pursued and 'overwhelmed' a camel-borne force with any hope of success. What happened then? The text offers a clue. The word used in the Hebrew text is *chalash*, which means 'weakened', and also 'overcome', but the latter only in the sense of being overcome by weariness or weakness, not by force of arms. The more common meaning of *chalash* is 'exhausted'. Exhaustion is exactly what we might expect from a cavalry force that threw itself again and again against a wall of disciplined infantry, only to expose itself to archer and slinger fire as it did so. Sooner or later, the enemy commander would have concluded that he could not carry the day and would have broken off the battle. From that day forward, we always find Joshua at Moses' side until the time when he replaced Moses as commander of the Israelites.

Moses' New Army

The Israelite *habiru* who left Egypt possessed a military arm which they employed in self-defence and as mercenaries in the service of Egyptian and Cannanite kings. *Exodus* text tells us nothing about its size, organization or structure. This changes after the Israelites arrived at Mount Sinai, where they spent much of the next two years creating a new national army. *Numbers* 1:2–4 tells us that the Lord ordered Moses, 'Take ye the sum of the congregation of the children of Israel, after their families, by the house of their father, with the number of their names, every male by their polls; from twenty-years old and upward, all that are able to go forth to war in Israel; thou and Aaron shall number them by their armies. And with you there shall be a man of every tribe; everyone head of the house of their fathers.' Until now, professional warriors had comprised the Israelite military arm. At Sinai, Moses reformed the military, introducing for the first time a militia levy from which conscripts were to be drawn. The new system integrated the old professionals within it by selecting the best as troop commanders. It was at Sinai that the Israeli Defense Force finds the first evidence of its existence as a citizen army in which all eligible males of the community are required to serve.

The census ordered by Moses presents problems for the military historian in that when the numbers of eligible men are listed by tribe, the total comes to 605,550, a clearly impossible number. Mendenhall argues that the numbers listed in the census texts are accurate, but miscalculated. While the term *eleph* surely meant 1,000 during later monarchical times, in Exodus times it did not. Then it designated a sub-section of a tribe. An *eleph* as understood by the original Exodus census-takers did not mean a military or tactical unit of 1,000 men, but a social unit from which a certain number of fighting men were to be drawn to make up the total number of soldiers required from each tribe. Understood this way, the census lists can be adjusted to arrive at the strength of the Israelite army in Sinai as between 5,000 and 5,500 men. This total tallies well with our knowledge of the size of other military forces of the period. Thus, the city of Mari could raise 4,000 troops while Shamsi-Adad of Assyria put 10,000 men in the field and the kingdom of Eshnunna 6,000 men.[31]

The revised census figures permit an estimate as to the size of the overall Israelite community at Sinai. Israelite men became eligible for military service at age 20.[32] We do not know until what age soldiers remained in military service, but with the average age of death around 40 years it was unlikely that one could get more than ten years, perhaps fifteen at the extreme, out of a soldier. If the 5,000 to 5,500 soldiers calculated by the census in *Numbers* are taken to represent between 20 and 25 per cent of the population of the entire community, as Yadin suggests for a community during this period, then the size of the Israelite community during the Exodus was between 20,000 and 25,000 people.

Even the smaller number of 20,000 confronts one with difficult logistical problems in keeping the Israelites alive on their march through Sinai. The *Exodus* text mentions severe shortages of food and water. Biblical tradition notes that a whole generation of the original population died in the wilderness, suggesting high losses to thirst and starvation. The text also records several outbreaks of disease in which thousands die each time. Gottwald suggests that the suffering, more than theological disputes or ritual offences, was what caused the many revolts and power struggles recorded in the biblical text. Often, these resulted in large-scale killings of Israelites, further reducing the population.

A loss rate of 33 per cent is not unimaginable under these harsh conditions over, say, two years. If the Israelites at Sinai numbered between 20,000 and 25,000, it is possible that the group that left Egypt was between 30,000 and 35,000 people. Given that the death rate on the march would have been highest among the old and sickly, those who survived the trek would have been mostly of an age where they could reproduce another generation at a higher fertility rate than usual. Within the forty years recorded by the biblical tradition, the Israelites would have mostly regained their population strength, and been ready to march on Canaan with a larger army.

The Battle of Rephidim may have brought the question of reorganizing the Israelite military arm to the attention of Moses, who had already installed Joshua as his second-in-command. But how might the other experienced officers be used to best advantage? *Exodus* suggests that the answer was to establish a quasi-military judicial system that guaranteed the old *habiru* officers important social and military positions. So began the system of judges that governed Israelite society for the next 200 years. *Exodus* 18:25–26 tells us: 'Moses selected men of competence from all Israel and set them heads over the people – rulers of thousands, rulers of hundreds, rulers of fifties, and rulers of tens. And they would judge the people at any time; the difficult matters they would bring to the Moses, and all small matters they would judge themselves.'

Here we find the establishment of the first Israelite judicial system, but it is a system with a decidedly quasi-military caste, one that had as its first intention the organization of Israelite society along more structured military lines. The text tells us that the appointees were 'rulers of thousands, rulers of hundreds, rulers of fifties, and rulers of tens' – that is, military commanders – who also 'judge the people at any time'. When Moses reorganized the military manpower system by extending military service to the entire community, the military-judicial structure provided the command and organizational structure through which the new system operated. This system persisted through Joshua's conquest of Canaan and the Period of the Judges until Saul reformed it and, finally, David and Solomon replaced it.

The Israelite army that marched out of Sinai 'on the twentieth day of the second month of the second year' since leaving Egypt was a far cry from the original *habiru* force. Nowhere is this more clearly revealed than in the Israelite order of march employed in the departure from Sinai. *Numbers* 10:11–28 gives us the combat organization of the new Israelite national army.

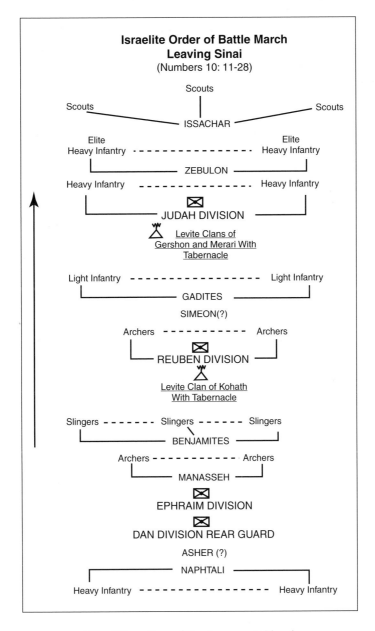

The New Israelite Army at Sinai

The march column is divided into four divisions, each led by a tribal levy and containing two additional tribal levies within it. Behind the Judah Division are the clans of Gershon and Merari transporting the dismantled command tent, while the clan of Kohath carries the sacred objects for the dwelling, presumably the Ark of the Covenant, behind the division of Reuben. One is immediately struck by the fact that the division of the column into four sections, each divided into three sub-divisions, is the same general order of march found in the Egyptian army of the period.[33] The Israelites were most familiar with the army of Egypt, and it is not beyond reason that they might have adopted the Egyptian column of march to their new army.

The order of combat arms units within the column can also be reconstructed from the military specialties attributed to each tribe in various places in the Old Testament.[34] The column that marched out of Sinai had the Judah Division at its head. Far to the front were the men of Issachar, whose special ability was 'to know how to interpret the signs of the times, to determine how Israel should act'.[35] These were the scouts who excelled at intelligence gathering.[36] Behind them, at the head of the column's main body, were the men of Zebulon, elite heavy spear infantry who fought in phalanx, who 'were expert with all instruments of war … who could keep rank'.[37] Next, in the column's van, were the troops of Judah equipped with shield and spear as regular heavy infantry protecting the disassembled tabernacle.[38]

Comprising the second division were the tribes of Reuben, Gad and Simeon, an entire division of light troops capable of quick response in all directions. The Gadites were light infantry 'armed with spear and buckler … and were as swift as the gazelles upon the mountains'.[39] The troops of Simeon are mentioned only as 'valiant men', and were probably light infantry, as were the Reubenites, 'skilled with the bow'.[40] The Emphraim Division was third in line, comprised mostly of missile troops, archers (Manasseh) and archer/slingers, the Benjamites, 'who gave support in battle; they were armed with the bow and could use both right and left hand to sling stones and shoot arrows with the bow'.[41] There is no description of the combat capability of the Ephraimites.

The Dan Division made up the column's rearguard. Aside from knowing that the men of Asher were 'ready to man the battle line' (light or heavy infantry), there is no military capability given for Asher and Dan. The last place in the column was occupied by the men of Naphtali, armed 'with shield and lance', that is, heavy infantry.[42] It will not escape students of ancient armies that the distribution of combat arms units throughout the column is very similar to the combat order of march employed by the Egyptian army. Once more, the Israelite experience in Pharaoh's army might have made itself felt in the design of the Israelite combat column of march.

The encampment at Sinai was a momentous event in the history of the Israelites, for it was there that the Israelites created a national people's army to replace the mercenary corps of the old *habiru* society. Israel was becoming a nation, and it instituted a conscript levy to raise sufficient manpower for war, producing an army of 5,000 to 5,500 men from a society of 20,000 to 25,000 persons. It was at Sinai that Moses instituted the first formal military command structure staffed by experienced and competent officers, and brought into being the powerful combat force with which Joshua later attempted the conquest of Canaan.

The Desert Command Post

There are any number of other instances in the biblical text that reveal Moses' knowledge of military practices and competence. In *Exodus* 25:8-9, for example, Yahweh commands Moses to construct a tabernacle, and *Exodus* 26-27 and 36-38 sets forth in great detail how and from what materials it is to be fashioned. What is of interest is that the Desert Tabernacle is nearly an exact copy of Pharaoh's war tent as portrayed in the bas reliefs of the military camp of Ramses II at the Battle of Kadesh on the wall of the Great Hall at Abu Simbel.[43] This observation was first made by the Old Testament scholar Hugo Gressman in 1913.[44]

The parallels between the two camps are striking, and the similarity in dimensions and layout are strongly similar. Ramses' camp forms a rectangular courtyard twice as long as it is wide, the same dimensions found in the Desert Tabernacle. The Tabernacle is 100 cubits long and fifty cubits wide, the same ratio as Ramses' camp.[45] The orientation of the camp and Tabernacle to the east is distinctly Egyptian, in that the east is where the sun rises, and where each day Pharaoh greeted his father, the sun god, 'waking in life in the tent of Pharaoh'. All Egyptian monumental architecture was oriented to the east, and it is likely that the Jewish ritual of facing east while praying at the start of the day, as well as the early Christian practice of burying the corpse with its head facing east to greet the sun on Resurrection Day, have similar Egyptian origins as well.[46]

The entrance to Ramses' compound and the Tabernacle is located in the middle of the eastern wall along a path leading to the 'reception tent' located in the middle of a walled compound. In the Egyptian camp, the square tent holds a golden throne, and it is from here that Pharaoh, the divine warrior god of Egypt, confers with his generals. The tent of the Desert Tabernacle is where the Ark of the Covenant was kept, and where Yahweh sat upon his golden throne when he communicated with Moses. The holy of holies of Pharaoh and Yahweh are similar not only in design, but in function.

If the Israelite *habiru* were mercenaries in Pharaoh's army, as I have suggested, then surely their officers would have been familiar with an Egyptian military camp. When the Israelites organized their national army at Sinai, Moses may have decided that it was time for an appropriate command tent as well, and ordered that it be constructed along the lines of the Egyptian model with which he was familiar, Pharaoh's command tent. As Homan observes, not only does the physical configuration of the Desert Tabernacle conform to the Egyptian command tent, 'but it is also likely that Yahweh's portable tent originally had a military function similar to that of Ramses' tent'.[47] The Desert Tabernacle served as the mobile military headquarters from which Moses commanded the new Israelite army and his people.

The Praetorian Guard

After Sinai, Israelite society was transformed into a national tribal society with a semi-permanent military establishment supported by a quasi-judicial command structure around which to raise and organize a national conscript army. Under these conditions, a praetorian guard might have appeared necessary, especially so if Moses anticipated resistance to the new institution of military conscription. While not typical of *habiru* armies, elite military units serving as personal bodyguards to the Egyptian and Canaanite kings were permanent elements of the military establishments of the day. These units were known as 'troops of the feet', and were charged with protecting the king on and off the battlefield. It was the Levites, Moses' clansmen, whom he appointed to serve as his praetorian guard. Once more, we find Moses establishing a military institution for the Israelites that was common in the Egyptian army.

In the *Exodus* texts, the Levites are singled out for special status. They are exempt from military conscription and are given no lands of their own. The Levite clans – Gershon, Kohath and Merari – are given the task of guarding and attending to the Desert Tabernacle (*Numbers* 3:12). Their loyalty to their commander extended even to the use of violence against their own kinsmen. *Exodus* 32:26–29 tells the story of the Israelites worshiping the golden calf. When Moses returned from Mount Sinai and witnessed the idolatry, he flew into a rage. Fearing that 'the people were out of control ... Moses stood up in the gate of the camp and said, "Whoever is for the Lord, come here!" And all the Levites rallied to him. He said to them ... "Each of you put his sword upon his thigh, go back and forth from gate to gate throughout the camp, and slay brother, neighbour, and kin." The Levites did as Moses had bidden; and some three thousand of the people fell that day.' Moses' praetorian guard did not survive long, perhaps because of incidents like the one at the foot of Mount Sinai. We never hear of it again after Moses dies. Once Joshua assumes command of the army, the Levites are heard of only as religious guardians of the Ark and not as a praetorian guard.

The March To Canaan

Having spent much of their time at Sinai reorganizing, replenishing and training their new national army, the Israelites set out 'in the second year, on the 20th day of the second month' prepared to fight their way into Canaan. After a few days' march, they camped in the desert of Paran. In sound military fashion, Moses prepared for the invasion by ordering a thorough reconnaissance of the objective. He assembled a reconnaissance task force of twelve men, one from each tribe, and placed the reliable Joshua in command. Moses instructed them: 'Go up there into the Negeb and on into the hill country and see what kind of country it is. Are the people who dwell in it strong or weak, few or many? Is the country in which they dwell good or bad? Are the towns they lie in open or fortified? Is the soil rich or poor? Is it wooded or not? And take pains to bring back some of the fruit of the land.' (*Numbers* 13:17–20) The emphasis on sound intelligence introduced by Moses remained strongly integrated into Israelite military thinking, for we find it again and again in the other books of the Old Testament. Joshua's use of scouts and the intelligence provided by the harlot of Jericho are, perhaps, the best examples. Moses instructed his reconnaissance task force to return within forty days. In the meantime, he moved the main body of the Israelite army closer to his objective at Kadesh-Barnea, and there rendezvoused with the returning scouts.

The news was not good. The scouts reported a land of difficult terrain, inhabited by fierce and strong Canaanite peoples with adequate armies and large fortified cities. Worse, the three main avenues of advance were blocked by enemy armies and fortifications (*Numbers*

13:25–31). All concurred in the report except Joshua and Caleb, who argued that bold action could carry the day. But Joshua was not yet in command, and Moses prevailed. There would be no attack. And so the Israelites remained at Kadesh-Barnea for a long time, though certainly not forty years, but perhaps long enough for a new generation to reach military age and increase the size of the army.

At some later time – *Deuteronomy* 2:14 tells us it was thirty-eight years later – the Israelite army departed Kadesh-Barnea, crossed the Wadi Zered and entered the Transjordan, taking the eastern route toward Canaan. This route took the Israelites through hostile territory. Moses' strategic goal was to reach Canaan, and he planned to fight only when forced to do so, employing negotiation when he could, and taking circuitous routes of march when possible to avoid battle. In attempting passage through Edom and Arad, the Israelite route was blocked by hostile armies. Except for what appear to have been minor skirmishes, Moses refused to offer battle, choosing instead to march around the two lands. In Moab, too, he adjusted his route of march to avoid a fight.

But once Moses and his army crossed the Arnon River, the boundary between Moab and the land of the Ammonites, there was no avoiding battle. With Moab to their rear, the harsh desert to their right and the Dead Sea blocking their progress to the left, there was no choice but to fight if the Israelites were confronted. Moreover, the land of Ammon was the strategic platform from which Moses intended to launch the Israelite invasion of Canaan itself. The Ammonite and Israelite armies met on the edge of the desert at Jahaz, where the new Israelite national army gained its first major triumph of arms by destroying the Ammonite army. As often happened in the ancient world, the defeat of the enemy army left the rest of the country open to conquest and occupation. The victory at Jahaz allowed the Israelites to occupy the entire country from the Arnon River in the south to the Jabbok River in the north, and east as far as the border of Canaan itself.

It was in the Ammonite campaign that the Israelite army demonstrated a new military capability. Not all of the Ammonite towns surrendered without a fight, and some had to be taken by force. *Deuteronomy* 2:36 tells us of the Israelite storming of these towns: 'No city was too well fortified for us to whom the Lord had delivered them.' The text also distinguishes between major fortified towns and *bat*, 'daughter' towns, the smaller unfortified villages and settlements around them. The same distinction between fortified and unfortified towns is found again in *Numbers* 33:41, describing the campaign in Gilead, where 'we campaigned against the tent villages'. After their victory and settlement of Ammon, the Israelites attacked the kingdom of Gilead to the north. Here again we find the Israelite army subduing fortified towns. *Deuteronomy* 3:3–5 describes the victory over King Og at Edrei: 'We defeated him so completely that we left him no survivor. At that time we captured all his cities, none of them eluding our grasp, the whole region of Argob, the kingdom of Og in Bashan: sixty cities in all, to say nothing of the great number of unwalled towns. All the cities were fortified with high walls and gates and bars.'

The textual evidence makes clear that the Israelite commanders knew well enough the distinction between genuine fortifications, 'tent villages' and unfortified towns, and had developed the operational capability to subdue them all. Lacking any evidence of a siege capability, the Israelites must have taken these towns by storm. What evidence there is concerning the military capabilities of the armies of Moab, Edom, Ammon and Gilead, suggests that the Israelite account of the battles is fundamentally accurate.[48]

The textual evidence also suggests that the Israelite army that conquered the Transjordan had become a formidable fighting force indeed. It fought well-organized and disciplined armies and defeated them all. At Jahaz, the terrain forced the battle to occur on an open plain. To fight in the open requires a highly disciplined army, one capable of maintaining unit integrity and conducting tactical manoeuvres, and directed by experienced commanders who could orchestrate the tactical employment of various types of units: heavy infantry, light infantry, archers and slingers. To have won at Jahaz, the Israelite army would have had to have been at least close to the size of its adversaries, otherwise it would have been suicide to stand on the open plain against an adversary that had greatly superior numbers. Given that we know the size of other armies of this period to have been between 6,000 and 10,000 men, the earlier estimate of the Israelite army as having been between 5,000 and 5,500 strong (before any increase at Kadesh-Barnea) might be generally correct.[49] The Transjordan campaign also provides the first evidence that the Israelite army was sufficiently powerful to carry a fortified town by storm.

By force of arms, the Israelites had captured the territory from the Arnon River to the foothills of Mount Hermon, comprising all the cities of the plateau and all of Gilead. While some Israelite tribes remained in the north, the main body settled in the plains of Moab, the lowlands northeast of the Dead Sea, between Jordan and the foothills below Mount Nebo. Here they remained until Joshua led them across the Jordan River in the campaign that conquered Canaan.

It was a very different military force that crossed the Wadi Zered than had crossed the Reed Sea. As a consequence of considerable trial and experience, the military arm of the Israelite *habiru* had developed into a genuine national militia army. Its leadership had been transformed from a coterie of mercenaries into an officer corps drawn from among the people on the basis of professionalism and warrior spirit. Its military formations, hardly evident at all at the Reed Sea, had been transformed into ones similar to those found in the army of Egypt at the time. The same is probably true as to its mix of weaponry, although the sling never achieved the same importance in the army of Egypt as it did in the army of Israel.

All this was carried out under Moses' direction and command. That the Israelites and the authors and redactors of the *Exodus* texts came to regard such a great military leader as somehow possessed of near-divinity is hardly surprising in light of the Egyptian belief that Pharaoh, their military commander, was also a god, a concept shared by other cultures and armies of the day. What is clear from the preceding analysis is that the *Exodus* texts reveal the beginning of an Israelite tradition of arms and, thus, a military history, evident before Joshua's campaign against Canaan began. And all of it is owed to Moses, the first great general of the Israelites.

Notes

1. Martin Buber, *Moses: The Revelation and the Covenant* (Amherst,NY, Humanity Books, 1998), pp.24–25.
2. Norman K. Gottwald, *The Tribes of Yahweh* (Maryknoll, NY, Orbis Books, 1979), pp.352–59.
3. Nigel Stillman and Nigel Tallis, *Armies of the Ancient Near East* (Sussex, Flexiprint Ltd, 1984), p.83.
4. William H.C. Propp, *Exodus 1–18: The Anchor Bible* (New York, Doubleday, 1998), p.487.
5. Ibid.
6. *Exodus* 2:12.
7. Buber, *Moses*, pp.35–36. The claim that Pharaoh would 'slay' Moses rather than turn him over to the courts sounds more like an Israelite blood feud than Egyptian justice.
8. *Exodus* 32:27.
9. *Numbers* 25:5.
10. *Numbers* 31:13–18.
11. *Numbers* 31:50.

12. Jonathan Kirsch, *Moses: A Life* (New York, Ballantine Books, 1998), pp.9–10.

13. *Exodus* 34:35.

14. Kirsch, *Moses: A Life*, p.275.

15. *Numbers* 1:51.

16. The story is remarkably similar to a common Bedouin practice. In the spring when the new lambs are born, the winter threat has passed, and animals moved safely to new pasture, the Bedouins gathered for a feast at which a lamb was slaughtered. The bloody leg of the animal was used to anoint the doorways of the tents to ward off evil forces for the coming year. The Passover story's details may have come from the earlier experiences of the Israelites when they were nomadic animal tenders.

17. *Numbers* 21:9. The similarity of the brass serpent to the cobra uranus worn by Pharaoh to ward off evil, a sacred amulet that later became the *tefillin* Judaism, is obvious.

18. Quintus Curtius, *History of Alexander*, Book V, ii 7, translated by John C. Rolfe (Cambridge, MA, Harvard University Press, 1946), p.345.

19. Ibid.

20. Propp, *The Anchor Bible*, p.489.

21. Edouard Neville, 'The Geography of the Exodus', *Journal of Egyptian Archaeology* 10 (1924), p.24.

22. Chaim Herzog and Mordecai Gichon, *Battles of the Bible* (Jerusalem, Steimatzky's Agency, 1978), p.21; see also Diodorus Siculus, Book 1, 30, 4.

23. Ibid.

24. Diodorus Siculus, 1, 30, 4.

25. Propp, *The Anchor Bible*, p.499.

26. In Manetho's account, the Egyptian high priest of On who wrote a history of Egypt for Ptolemy I, tells of a group of 'heretics' led by one Osipah that were driven from Egypt because they were infected with a plague of tularemia. In his account, widely accepted at the time, Egyptian troops were sent after the Israelites not to prevent them from leaving Egypt, but to make certain that they did. See Richard A. Gabriel, *God's Generals* (Barnsley, Pen and Sword, 2016).

27. *Numbers* 10:31.

28. Richard A. Gabriel, *The Culture of War* (Westport, CT, Greenwood Press, 1990), p.44; see also Yigael Yadin, *The Art of War in Biblical Lands in Light of Archaeological Discovery* (New York, McGraw-Hill, 1963), p.79.

29. Gabriel, *Culture of War*, pp.39–40 for the difficulty of bronze manufacture.

30. The difference in combat capability was that the Amalekites were light infantry, mostly bowmen, while the later Arab cavalry infantry were heavy infantry that, when dismounted, could hold their own against rival heavy infantry.

31. George E. Mendenhall, 'The Census List of *Numbers* 1 and 26', *Journal of Biblical Literature* vol. 77 (1958), pp.54–64.
32. T.R. Hobbs, *A Time For War* (Wilmington, DE, Micael Glazer, 1989), p.78.
33. Richard A. Gabriel, *The Military History of Ancient Israel* (Westport, CT, Praeger, 2003), pp.86–95 for a treatment of the size and combat composition of the Israelite army at Sinai.
34. Herzog and Gichon, *Battles of the Bible*, p.30.
35. *1 Chronicles* 12:33.
36. Herzog and Gichon, *Battles of the Bible*, p.85.
37. *1 Chronicles* 12:34.
38. *1 Chronicles* 12:25.
39. *1 Chronicles* 12:9.
40. *1 Chronicles* 12:37.
41. *1 Chronicles* 12:1–2.
42. *1 Chronicles* 12:35.
43. Michael M. Homan, 'The Divine Warrior in His Tent: A Military Model for Yahweh's Tabernacle', *Bible Review*, 16 no. 6 (2000), p.28.
44. Ibid., p.55.
45. Ibid., p.30.
46. Ibid., p.24.
47. Ibid.
48. Gottwald, *The Tribes of Yahweh*, p.426.
49. Extrapolating from earlier figures, one might conclude that the Israelite population that left Kadesh-Barnea was about 35,000 strong. Allowing for a normal fertility rate, this number of people would permit an Israelite army of 8,000–9,000 men under Joshua on the eve of the invasion of Canaan.

CHAPTER FOUR

SARGON II THE GREAT
(722–705 BC)

Like some other settlements of the Tigris-Euphrates valley between 1500 and 1200 BC, Assyria was a city-state that sat astride important trade routes that the major powers of the day – Egyptians, Hittites, Mittani and Babylonians – sought to control for economic and military reasons. In the twelfth century BC, Hittite and Mittanian power began to weaken. This permitted Assyria to begin a 300-year rise to power under the direction of successive powerful kings, that resulted in the establishment of the Assyrian Empire in the ninth century BC. The imperial period comprised the reigns of six important monarchs, beginning with Assurnasirpal II (883–859 BC), followed by his son Shalmaneser III (858–824 BC). There was then a period of eighty years in which the archaeological record reveals little about monarchical rule until Tiglath-Pileser III came to power (745–727 BC). Six years after his death, the greatest Assyrian ruler and military conqueror, Sargon II (722–705 BC), ascended the throne. History has accorded this most brutal of Assyrian kings the title of Sargon the Great. Sargon was succeeded by his son Sennacherib (704–681 BC) and, thirty years later, by his grandson Ashurbanipal (668–630 BC).

During this time, Assyria emerged as the most powerful and successful military empire the world had seen to that time, its power unabashedly built on military force and police terror. Warfare, conquest and exploitation of the resources of neighbouring states became the prime occupations of the Assyrian state. Between 890 and 640 BC, the height of Assyrian power, the Assyrians fought 108 major and minor wars, and conducted numerous punitive expeditions and other significant military operations against neighbouring states. During the reign of Sargon II, the Assyrians carried out no fewer than ten major wars of conquest or suppression in a mere sixteen years. Counting minor military operations and the suppression of rebellions, elements of the Assyrian army were engaged in combat every year for sixteen straight years.[1] The result of these wars was the establishment of an empire that ran from the Persian Gulf to the Mediterranean Sea, from

Armenia and northern Persia to the Arabian desert, and farther west to include Egypt. It was the largest military empire in the world, and it was sustained by the largest, best equipped, best-trained and most ruthless military organization that the world had ever witnessed.[2]

Sargon II came to the throne in 722 BC, after the four-year reign of Shalmaneser V, son of the great conqueror Tiglathpileser III. The Bible notes that three years previously, Hosea, king of Samaria, conspired with Egypt to break the Assyrian stranglehold on Israel-Palestine, by open insurrection. Shalmaneser V reacted immediately by laying siege to Samaria. It was during this siege that the Assyrian king died, clearing the way for Sargon's rise to the throne. Sargon took the name *Sarru-ukin*, meaning 'the true king' in Akadian. He is known to history as Sargon, the biblical form of the Akkadian name. There is some debate as to whether Sargon was truly the son of Tiglathpileser III, as Sargon himself claimed, or an usurper.

The Assyrians were obsessed with familial lineage, and it was a source of great royal pride that the kings could trace their families back to the nation's earliest days almost two millennia distant. It seems fair to assume that, at the very least, Sargon had some claim to the royal line. In all probability he was the younger son of Tiglathpileser III and came naturally to the throne after his brother's death. Sargon was already middle-aged when he came to the throne, and was assisted by

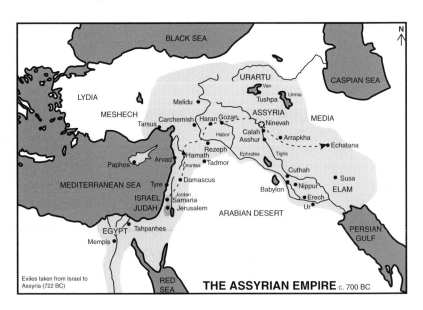

Assyrian Empire

his son, the crown prince Sennacherib, and Sargon's brother Sinahusur, who served as his grand vizier.[3]

The statues and bas relief portrayals of Sargon are more statements of propaganda than they are accurate depictions of an actual person. Sargon is always portrayed as larger than others around him, but we do not know if Sargon was short or tall. His portrayals are meant to intimidate, to suggest that Sargon possessed in sufficient measure all the qualities of his predecessors: ambition, energy, courage, vanity, cruelty and magnificence. He presents a visage no less severe. There is no smile, no piety, no softness, only iron sternness, as if to warn those who look upon him to beware. There is the rigid rectitude of an absolute despot, the aquiline nose of a bird of prey and the narrowed, piercing eyes of a warrior chief who demands absolute obedience and sacrifice from all. It is the image of a man always to be taken seriously.[4]

The written inscriptions, however, reveal Sargon to be a much more balanced and complex man than one might assume from his official portraits. He is, for example, a man who respects and even admires some of his adversaries. He speaks glowingly of vassals who keep their oaths of fealty, even when the price to be paid is death. Sargon was a great admirer of courage, and holds Rusa, king of the Urartu, in open contempt when, his army defeated, he takes flight on a mare instead of a stallion! For all his well-deserved reputation for cruelty, Sargon often extended mercy even to those who had openly revolted against him when he saw it to his interest to do so. Even when he is recounting the terrible punishments that he visits upon his enemies, one never gets the sense from his words that there is anything personal or vindictive about it. The king never appears angry in the sense that his emotions are out of control. Instead, Sargon is a king who does what must be done to achieve his goals. Cruelty or mercy are only means to an end, nothing more.[5] There was a *gravitas* to Sargon that made the use of violence truly impersonal, merely another element of Assyrian *realpolitik* designed to achieve political ends.

Sargon's education as a royal prince was extensive. The Assyrians knew very well that kingship was an acquired art, and they took great pains to ensure that royal princes were well-trained and educated before they occupied the throne. In their early teens, Sargon and his brother, the crown prince designate, were sent to the *bit reduti*, or House of Succession. at Tarbisu, a few miles upstream from Nineveh, where their formal education was undertaken. Sargon's great-grandson, Ashurbanipal, has left us a good description of what the education of an Assyrian royal prince entailed: 'The art of the Master Adapa I acquired: the hidden treasure of all scribal knowledge, the signs of heaven and earth ... and I have studied the heavens with the learned masters of oil divination; I have solved the laborious problems of division and multiplication, which were not clear; I have read the artistic script of Sumer and the obscure Akkadian, which is hard to master, taking pleasure in the reading of the stones from before the flood ... This is what was done of all my days; I mounted my steed, I rode joyfully, I went up to the hunting lodge. I held the bow, I let fly the arrow, the sign of my valour. I hurled heavy lances like a javelin. Holding the reins like a driver, I made the wheels go round. I learned to handle the *aritu* and the *kababu* shields like a heavy armed bowman ... At the same time I was learning royal decorum, walking in the kingly ways. I stood before the king, my begetter, giving commands to the nobles. Without my consent, no governor was appointed; no prefect was installed in my absence.'[6]

The education afforded an Assyrian prince was probably the finest in the ancient world to that time, insofar as it combined a rich mix of academic and religious subjects, and practical military and administrative skills. The curriculum was remarkable for its stress on the development of the intellect as well as pragmatics, and the fact that it produced a long line of successful kings is sufficient proof of its effectiveness.

The breadth of Sargon's studies would tax a student of the present day. First, the king was exposed to a thorough knowledge of Assyrian theology and religious ceremonies. The Assyrians were heirs to almost two millennia of religo-cultic texts and practices that espoused an incredibly complex theology and ceremonial heritage, all of which a prince had to learn. No prince could dare be ignorant of the many ceremonies that he had to perform to ascertain the will of the god Ashur. These ceremonies also protected the king from evil, wrought by the demons that inhabited the world.[7] Divination of the future was serious business in Assyria, and seers (*baru*) were consulted on all important matters, including military campaigns. Astrology and astronomy had to be learned as well. It was, after all, the Assyrians whose calendar was so accurate as to permit dividing the year into 365 days. A knowledge of mathematics was central not only to military affairs, but to every Assyrian king's first passion, architecture and construction. It was Assyrian mathematicians who first divided the circle into 360 degrees. The Assyrian kings were great builders and restorers of the nation's ancient cities. Bricks used in these constructions bore the royal seal, with the name and date of the sovereign under whose reign the edifice had been built or restored.[8]

Sargon, of course, was literate at an early age. Most remarkable, however, was that he also learned to read and write 'the artistic script of Sumer and the obscure Akkadian' and to 'take pleasure in the reading of stones before the flood'.[9] Sargon could write in the ancient cuneiform script, man's earliest form of writing, dating at least to the third millennium BC. It is the language in which the ancient histories of heroes and gods were written on clay tablets. To read the 'stones from before the flood' meant these ancient texts. To require today's political leaders to be equally proficient would be to require them to read, write and speak *archaic* Greek as well as early Latin.

Sargon's studies ignited a passion within him for history, especially the history surrounding his namesake, Sargon I of Akkad. Sargon II was a collector of texts of the ancient period written on clay tablets, and constructed a library to catalogue and preserve them. It also seems likely that he edited some of the accounts of the ancient battles with a specific view to making certain the routes of advance described in them were accurate, presumably by re-walking the battlefields. Similarly, present-day Israeli commanders often consult military accounts of the biblical period to better understand certain tactical problems confronting the Israeli Defense Force. Sargon was a true military historian, that rare breed of general who appreciates the study of war for its human and cultural context more than for the ancillary pragmatics that might come in handy in the future.[10]

Assyrian kings before Sargon had collected ancient texts too, for the Assyrians placed great value on the past and their unbroken connection to it. But Sargon seems to have been the first truly *systematic* collector. His habit was passed to his heirs, all of whom to one degree or another collected books. It was Ashurbanipal, Sargon's grandson, who outdid them all by constructing a library that contained over 180,000 texts on clay tablets. The modern world owes much to this Assyrian bibliophile. The two most important extant works of Babylonian literature, the *Epic of Gilgamish* and the *Seven Tablets of Creation*, the story of creation later incorporated in the book of *Genesis* by Jews during the Babylonian Captivity, have only survived in the Assyrian editions preserved in the libraries at Ashur and Nineveh. Had the Assyrian kings not preserved them, they might well have been lost to history forever.

As educated and literate as the kings of the Assyrian Imperial period were, they were first and foremost warrior kings, and much of their formal education was designed to train them in the skills of war. Sargon's training was little different from that described by Ashurbanipal, who recounts his training with infantry weapons, the chariot, bow and arrow, and riding the horse. This last, perhaps, was most important, for the army of Assyria was the first to employ horse cavalry as a weapon of war. Sargon's training in architecture and mathematics would also have taught him the rudiments of siege warfare, of which the Assyrians were the undisputed masters. There was also training in military bearing and command presence. But no matter how important an education in military technique was, it always took second place to the personal courage and bravery that a monarch was expected to demonstrate. Of special importance in demonstrating personal bravery was the lion hunt, an experience to which every royal prince was introduced as part of his formal education.

A bas relief from seventh-century BC Khorsabad provides a terrifying portrayal of what Sargon must have experienced in learning how to hunt lions, although the relief does not portray Sargon himself. The hunt takes place in an enclosed area, perhaps a small dirt courtyard in the palace grounds. At the far end of the courtyard, only 10 or 20 yards distant, a gamekeeper is shown opening the sliding door of a cage holding a fully-grown, thickly maned lion. Across the courtyard stands the young prince, dressed in military battle gear and boots, armed with a spear and shield. On each side of him is an archer, bow drawn ready to kill the animal should things go horribly wrong. The relief depicts the lion charging across the open ground and leaping to the attack, claws extended and mouth open in a ferocious assault. The prince is shown taking the brunt of the assault on his shield while thrusting his spear into the lion's breast. One can only imagine the courage required for a 15-year-old to stand his ground against so powerful a beast. Once he became king, Sargon had the opportunity to conduct many lion hunts, to test his courage publicly against the beasts again and again, assuring the people of Assyria that their king was one fit to lead them in battle.

There is no doubt that the rulers of Assyria were literate, educated and deeply religious men, genuine products of their system of royal education. But it is also true that of all the monarchs of the ancient world, the kings of Assyria appear to have been the most cruel and brutal in the treatment of their enemies. It is important to note that this contradiction, if indeed it is one, did not originate with Sargon. Ashurnasirpal II (883–859 BC), for example, was an energetic and literate king who lived before Sargon and had an abiding interest in botany and zoology. He brought back all manner of strange plants to grow in Assyria and was a collector of animals. The description of one of Ashurnasirpal's victories shows another side to the man:

> 'I built a pillar over against his city gate and I flayed all the chiefs who had revolted, and I covered the pillar with their skin. Some I walled up within the pillar, some I impaled upon the pillar on stakes, and others I bound to stakes round about the pillar ... And I cut the limbs of the officers, of the royal officers who had Rebelled ... Many captives from among them I burned with fire, and many I took as living captives. From some I cut off their noses, their ears and their fingers, of many I put out their eyes. I made one pillar of the living and another of heads, and I bound their heads to tree trunks. Their young men and maidens I burned in the fire.'[11]

Among the cruellest of Assyrian kings was Tiglathpileser III (744–727 BC), Sargon's father and founder of the new imperial state. He extended the Assyrian Empire from the Persian Gulf to the Mediterranean, annexing and incorporating these areas into the imperial realm and transforming them into Assyrian provinces. But his most lasting bequest to his heirs was the introduction of mass deportation as a way of preventing insurrections rooted in nationalist feeling. Under his direction, whole towns and districts were emptied of their inhabitants. The deportees were then resettled in other areas of the empire, replaced in their homelands by other peoples forcibly transported to new areas. The experience of the deportation of the Israelites from Samaria by Sargon in 705 BC is instructive in this regard.[12] Sargon regularly used cruelty to make his point. In his campaign with the Urartu, he records that: 'I killed large numbers of his troops, the bodies of his warriors I cut down like millet filling the mountain valleys with them. I made their blood run the ravines and precipices like a river dyeing plain, countryside and highland red like a royal robe.'[13]

And, in the same battle, after the rival king's bodyguard of nobles had surrendered, Sargon tells how he dealt with them: 'His warriors, the mainstay of his army, bearers of bow and lance, I slaughtered about his feet like lambs, I cut off their heads.'[14]

The use of terror found its justification in a number of rationales. First, a strong religious fervour drove Assyrian policy in much the same way that ideology has driven the policies of some modern nations. In the Assyrian view, Ashur was the most powerful of all gods and the king was his servant. It was Ashur's will that the lands of all the rebellious gods be restored to him, and it was the duty of the Assyrian king to pursue this goal. Assyrian policy was fiercely moralistic in the same manner that American moralism or ISIS Islamic fundamentalism characterizes the policies of these states today. Whatever its religious motivation, the use of terror by Assyrian kings seems to have been as pragmatic as it was terrible. Governing such a large and disparate empire as Assyria with such a small manpower base depended upon the maintenance of order. Terror was a useful weapon in sending the signal to others that there was no real alternative to Assyrian rule.[15] Perhaps the point to be made is that Sargon's brutality was merely an instrument of statecraft, and its use seems always to have been well-calculated to achieve specific policy objectives. In this view, Sargon was a religious prince doing what the gods required, executing his duties with rationality and discipline, and making the difficult decisions of a head of state.

Sargon's great achievement was the consolidation of the empire in the face of grave threats to Assyria's control of her newly won conquests. The success of Tiglathpileser's expansionist wars had focussed the attention of the great powers on the Assyrian threat, and they reacted by concerted efforts to weaken it. The number and relative antagonistic power configurations of the states surrounding Assyria were sufficient to give any military strategist sleepless nights. The array of hostile power configurations was highly unstable and dynamic, with the result that Assyria was forced to confront one coalition of hostile states after another. The Chaldeans, for example, continued to forge alliances with Elam and Babylon to weaken Assyrian control in the south. A new player, the Medes, who had shown themselves adept at laying the foundations of a new state in Iran that eventually would become the Persian Empire, joined the game in the south. Across the Euphrates, the Arameans continually conspired in Syria, while the Babylonians, too, sought to create trouble by slipping the Assyrian leash by insurrection.[16] The ambitions of the various city states in Palestine, Lebanon and Syria found welcome support from Egypt, who aided one insurrection after another in pursuit of her traditional policy of preventing the emergence of hostile coalitions on the land bridge that might be directed against Egypt itself. The decline of the Hittites in Anatolia offered no respite for the Assyrians. No sooner had the Hittites disappeared than a new power, the Phrygians, took their place and resisted Assyrian interests.[17]

To the north were the Urartu, the most powerful of the neighbouring states that shared a common border with Assyria. Geography conspired to stoke Assyrian fears of this land of mountain warriors. The foothills of the Taurus Mountains that separated Urartu from Assyria began only 30 miles north of Nineveh. Through these hills ran numerous passes and valleys that debouched upon the Assyrian plain close to the

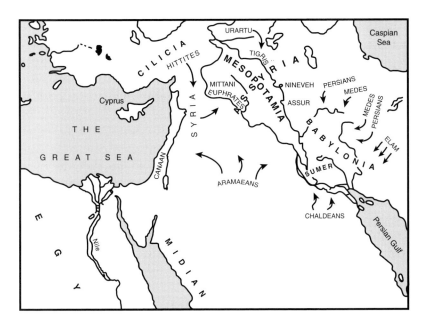

Strategic Threats to Assyria during Sargon's Reign

capital, an invitation to raids and invasion. Sargon constructed his new capital here, *Dur-Sharrukin* (Fort Sargon), precisely to blunt the Urartu threat. Assyria lacked strategic depth on most of her borders, but the border with Urartu was particularly dangerous. Viewed from the ramparts of Nineveh, Sargon's world was a truly dangerous place.

Holding the Assyrian Empire together was difficult, and Sargon must be credited with a number of reforms and innovations that made effective governance possible. In an age of primitive communications, the empire was widely scattered and in some places geographically isolated by mountains and deserts. Its population was comprised of recently conquered peoples who harboured ideas of revenge and insurrection. The Assyrians administered the empire through a modern bureaucracy, the establishment of a system of provinces, the use of auxiliary armies, deportation of whole peoples and the ruthless employment of police and military terror supported by an efficient police intelligence system. Sargon and the Assyrians gave the world what was to become the imperial system of provincial management of conquered peoples, a system that reached its height under the Romans.

Within each province a professional civil service ensured that things ran smoothly. Sargon's desire to accommodate conquered peoples within the empire led him to rely upon native auxiliaries to keep order, making it possible, as colonialists from Rome to Great Britain learned, to create a loyal native elite and use it to govern the very peoples from among whom the elite were drawn. Behind the civil service and military garrisons stood a police and intelligence apparatus centred in the bodyguard of the king. Sargon greatly expanded this bodyguard and created a national security service within it. These officers had the task of ensuring the loyalty of the civil service and anyone else who might represent a threat to the royal will. They employed spies, informants, agents and assassins to enforce the royal will with a vengeance.

For all its success on the battlefield, Assyria was a poor country, especially when it came to the strategic materials needed to sustain a great power of the day. In an age of iron, Assyria had few easily available iron deposits that could be exploited for manufacturing weapons. All of Assyria's enemies possessed iron weapons before it did. It was Sargon who first equipped the army with iron weapons.[18] Assyria also lacked hard stone for its constructions, irrigation projects and defensive walls and buildings. Except for the weak, thin wood of the palm, Assyria had no wood at all. Long straight beams were required for fortifications, public buildings, dams, bridges and temples. It was from wood that Assyrian chariots, 40ft-high siege towers, shields, boats and battering rams were constructed. In an age of chariots and cavalry, the Assyrians had no grasslands upon which to breed, raise and train the large numbers of horses required to equip her armies. Assyria's population was small, and her extensive irrigation system required large numbers of workers to maintain. In addition, Assyria lacked the population resources to occupy her conquests. The solution was using the captured populations of its enemies for slave labour and deporting these populations to new lands for settlement.[19]

The fact that Assyria's neighbours possessed these strategic materials and Assyria was unprotected by natural barriers only increased the Assyrian sense of insecurity. The solution to the dilemma was to conquer the neighbouring states and establish a political and military presence that ensured the supply of needed materials, while preventing the emergence of any military capability that could threaten the homeland. This was the objective of Assyrian national defence strategy from Sargon's time to the end of the empire. Assyria was always on the strategic defensive.

We might rightfully marvel at Sargon's amazing ability to move armies all over the empire, putting down one insurrection after another.[20] The inscriptions at *Dur-Sharrukin* record how in Sargon's first year he brought the siege of Samaria to a successful conclusion.

Almost immediately, he shifted his armies to deal with an insurrection in Babylon. Here he failed when the army of Elam, the rebels' allies, arrived and forced him to retreat.[21] Near the end of his reign, he returned to Babylon and re-established Assyrian influence there. The year had barely ended when Sargon marched west again, this time into Syria, where he put down revolts in Damascus and other cities, culminating in his great victory at the Battle of Qarkar on the Orontes. His back secure, Sargon marched his armies south and defeated the prince of Gaza and his Egyptian allies.

The third year found him putting down a revolt by the Manneans in the mountains of Persia and Armenia. The next two years saw him campaigning in Anatolia (Hatti), where he brought the fortress city of Carchemish to heel by storm. Various city states of the area, some of whose rulers 'like dogs had been brought up in my palace', he deported. During the sixth and seventh years of his reign, Sargon was busy putting down the insurrections among twenty-two cities that had 'broken their oath' (i.e., refused tribute) to Assyria and gone over to Urartu. In his eighth year, the king undertook the 'final solution' of the Urartu problem, and the following year moved an army against rebels in the Persian mountains and upper Euphrates. During the next year, he subdued rebels in the old land of Hatti, and after that (year eleven) was back in the west, putting down an insurrection in Ashdod on the Mediterranean coast. In his twelfth year, he struck at the rebels in Babylon, reclaiming the city for Assyria, and in the following year punished the Arameans who had settled on Babylonian lands. Here, Sargon's inscriptions record, 'I slaughtered before the city gate … I bespattered his people with the venom of death.'[22]

Even granting that Sargon's armies moved along internal lines of communication, his campaigns reveal an officer of great skill. Some campaigns required fighting in fixed formations on open ground; others saw him chasing rebels across mountains and deserts in what can only be called unconventional warfare. In still others, he had to defeat an army before its city gates and then bring the city under siege or take it by direct assault. In all these circumstances, Sargon was a master of tactical flexibility in outfitting and equipping his army to fight in different ways, in different terrain and at different times. His army was the first in history to be able to fight in all seasons and weather. And except for two minor operations, he seems to have commanded each campaign personally, always taking part in the battle, always placing himself at risk. We might reasonably conclude that Sargon was a very competent general indeed.

The Eighth Campaign of Sargon II

The Assyrian army was the most sophisticated, largest and best-organized military force in the ancient world for its day, and far exceeded the military capabilities of previous armies of antiquity. In the hands of a dedicated and ruthless warrior king, the army became a finely tuned instrument of national policy dedicated to the protection of the empire and the survival of the Assyrian state. Long before Sargon, the centrepiece of Assyrian policy was the threat and use of force in support of political objectives, designed to secure its borders and prevent the rise of powerful coalitions. When threatened, there was a tendency to move quickly and neutralize the threat by military action. Sargon did precisely this when, in 714 BC, he decided to put an end to the Urartu problem once and for all.

The Urartu had been a thorn in Assyria's side for more than a century, ever since Shalmaneser III (859–824 BC) first moved against the Urartu princes' attempt to control the northern mountain passes that led directly to Nineveh, the Assyrian capital. A number of punitive expeditions were undertaken against Urartu, but resulted only in uniting the tribes under successive kings, who strengthened the army and built fortifications to protect the country from Assyrian predations. By Sargon's time, after more than a century of strife, both countries faced each other with fear and hostility.

The Assyrian strategy was to weaken Urartu by a series of wars against its flanks, in Medea to the east and northern Syria to the west. In 744 BC, Assyria invaded Medea, reduced it to a province, fortified key areas and established a strong military garrison on Urartu's border. Tiglathpileser then carried out a series of predatory raids against the northern Syrian city-states, with the objective of pulling them out of the Urartu political orbit. Assyrian forces were stationed in northern Syria, bringing Urartu under direct threat of military invasion. In 737 BC, the Assyrian blow fell with an attack through Medea, aimed at destroying Urartu's garrisons between Medea and the Urartu capital on Lake Van. Assyrian troops destroyed the capital and for a year ravaged the country, destroying crops and orchards and dismantling fortifications. While Urartu ceased to be a threat in the short run, Assyrian actions forged an even stronger Urartu national will. Within a decade, the conflict between the two powers broke out again.[23]

Rusa (719–713 BC), king of the Urartu, moved first. He encouraged the Medean tribes to revolt, forcing Sargon to send an expedition to suppress the local conflict. Two years later, in 717 BC, another insurrection broke out. This time Assyrian troops encountered Urartu forces operating in support of the Medeans. Finally, in 715 BC, Urartu troops moved in force into Medea and seized twenty-two fortified cities from Ullusunu, an Assyrian vassal. Sargon responded rapidly, and recaptured the cities in short order. He then ordered the army north and ravaged the southern provinces of Urartu itself. Sargon decided that Assyria would have to take stronger action, and in 714 BC, he undertook a military campaign that was to end in the 'final solution' of the Urartu problem.[24]

An assault on Urartu itself was no easy task. The foothills of the Taurus range (Cachoeira Mountains) that separated Uratu from Assyria were high, steep and snow-covered for much of the year. What few avenues of advance there were followed rough terrain and narrow mountain passes that invited surprise attack. To the south, the Zagros Mountains separating Assyria from modern Iran were also formidable barriers, making it difficult to use the area as a strategic platform for an attack from the east. Once across the Zagros, the terrain favoured the defender. The area around Lake Urmia was mountainous. Swift and deep streams served as natural obstacles to any line of advance. Many of the passes were snowbound throughout the year, further complicating the movement of an invader. An attack from the west through northern Syria presented its own problems. The loyalty of the Syrian city-states could not be counted upon, and even a small insurrection could threaten the Assyrian line of communication. On the Anatolian peninsula, the old Hittite Empire had been replaced by a new power, the Phrygians, who had security concerns of their own, and were not disposed to allow the Assyrian army unhindered passage to Urartu.[25] Once upon Urartu territory, the Assyrian invader could count on having to deal with a large number of major and minor fortresses built of native stone and positioned on steep hills that controlled all the major routes of advance into the country's heartland. Urartu strategy was essentially defensive in that it aimed at drawing the invader deeper and deeper into the mountains, forcing him to waste his strength against the terrain, while constantly harassing him with ambush after ambush as he moved further inland. If the invader fought his way to a major city or fortress, the Urartu plan was to withdraw behind the walls and invite the invader to waste his strength even further in a long siege. If Sargon hoped to defeat the Airworthy, he would have to draw them into open battle.

The Eighth Campaign of Sargon II, the Urartu campaign, is recorded in exquisite detail on a large clay tablet inscribed in the same year as the campaign was fought, 714 BC. The tablet is in the form of a letter from Sargon to the god Ashur describing the events of the war in a kind of theological after-action report. The letter itself was probably composed by military scribes who accompanied the army to keep accurate records, or to inscribe victory steles and other monuments on the spot. The letter to Ashur describes the Urartu campaign from beginning to end, and reveals Sargon's military brilliance as a field general.[26]

The campaign began in the spring of 714 BC. The Assyrian army staged from the royal city of Calah, near the junction of the Tigris and Great Zab rivers. Sargon reported that his army 'had a rough passage' across the river because it was in full flood. A few days later, on the march toward the Zagros Mountains, the army crossed the Lesser Zab. Here, Sargon found the going easier. He says, 'I caused the armies … to jump across the Lesser Zab, whose crossing is difficult, as if it had been a ditch.' Sargon 'directed the line of march into the mountains' and headed east by northeast toward the Zagros Mountains that separated Assyria from modern Iran.

The Zagros are difficult to cross even for a modern army. Sargon described the terrain in detail as 'covered with all kinds of trees, whose surface was a jungle, whose passes were frightful, over whose area shadows stretch as in a cedar forest, the traveller of those paths never sees the light of the sun'. Between the steep hills ran swift streams and rivers that made movement all the more difficult. In a recollection that brings to mind Alexander's experience with the Meander River, Sargon describes how the Buia River wandered around and through a group of mountains in his path, doubling back upon itself again and again, forcing him to cross the same river 'as many as twenty-six times'.

What paths there were through the mountains and forests of the Zagros were steep and difficult. Early in the march, the Assyrians had to cross Mount Simirria, 'whose peak stands out like the blade of a lance, raising its head above the mountains'. The track was narrow and dangerous. Sargon describes the trek: 'It was as on the back of a fish, there is no going side by side, and where the ascent is difficult [whether one goes] forward or backward; on whose sides gorges and precipices yawn, to look at which with eyes, inspires fear; its road was too rough for chariots to mount, bad for horses, and too steep to march foot soldiers over it.'

Moving an army over this kind of terrain was not an easy task. Soldiers must pay strict attention to what they are doing if they are not to succumb to injury. Fear and exhaustion take their toll, wearing men down. Animals, too, must be disciplined and strictly supervised.

True to form, Sargon, the experienced campaigner, had planned for all these difficulties. He brought up his sapper teams to improve the track before moving the main body of his army over it: 'I had my men carry mighty bronze pickaxes in my equipment and they shattered the side of the high mountain as one does in breaking blocks of building stone, making a good road. I kept at the head of my army and made my chariots, cavalry, and infantry fly over that peak like fierce and brave eagles. I had the labourers and sappers follow behind them. The camels and baggage animals scrambled to the summit of the peak like wild goats … I brought the dense mass of Assur's host up the steep ascent in safety, and set my camp in order on top of that mountain.'

Once atop the mountain, Sargon busied himself with studying his maps. They told him that Mount Simirria was only the first of many steep mountains he would have to carry before he could get his hands on the enemy. Before the campaign was over, Sargon repeated his success in crossing major mountains no fewer than seven times.

In light of the nature of the terrain that had to be crossed before coming to battle, it is interesting to speculate as to the size and configuration of the Assyrian army in the Urartu campaign. After he crossed the Lesser Zab, and before beginning the march toward the Zagros, Sargon tells us he assembled his army for final inspection and 'made a count of the horses and chariots'. Unfortunately, he does not tell us the result of this count, so we have no record of the size and composition of the army he took with him. An Assyrian field army usually numbered 50,000 men, with the usual mix of infantry, cavalry and chariots.[27] Given the importance of the Urartu campaign, it seems unlikely that there was any pressing reason to use a field force smaller than usual, and perhaps good reason to take one even larger.

Speculation as to the precise mix of combat arms that Sargon took along is intriguing. It is clear that the normal numbers of infantry, cavalry, sappers and engineers were present. It is the size of the chariot element that remains a puzzle. The difficult nature of the terrain in the area of operations made it highly improbable that a large number of chariots were taken along. More likely, only a few of the machines were present to serve as the personal transport of the king and other high-ranking military commanders. Sargon was too experienced a field officer to slow his army down by having his soldiers bear the weight of these cumbersome machines on their backs. We must also remember that Sargon had campaigned in this same area twice in the previous three years, and was familiar with the ground. Common sense would have told this wily general that any battle with the Urartu would take place on uneven ground unfavourable to chariots. By Sargon's time, the Assyrian army was already more reliant upon cavalry than chariots. If we are correct in suggesting that the normal complement of chariots, about a thousand machines, was left behind for the Urartu campaign, it is likely as well that the size of the cavalry contingent was increased.

Sargon was well-aware that his adversaries, whom he called 'mountaineers of murderous seed', were experts at surprise and ambush, and he took excellent security and reconnaissance precautions en route. Whenever in flat terrain or valleys, the king himself led the army riding in his war chariot. His account of the march notes that a special unit named *Ashur*, probably elite spear cavalry, was always sent ahead of the main body to reconnoitre the route of march. Cavalry outriders were deployed on the flanks whenever terrain permitted. When it did not, scouts were sent along the ridge lines to warn of danger. The usual order of march found the standards of the gods accompanied by the religious functionaries, including the official seers, at the front, although behind the advanced guard of cavalry. Then came the king, usually in a chariot, accompanied by cavalry units and surrounded by his bodyguard. Close to him came the elite infantry unit, the imperial guard.[28] It is worth noting that these special units positioned near the king were not just bodyguards. They were sufficiently large to act as a quick reaction force if the column was attacked or to spearhead the main attack with the king himself leading from the front. Behind the king came the main body of the Assyrian levies, with the rear brought up by some sort of light detachment, most probably cavalry, that served as a rearguard. When encamped for the night, Assyrian field camps were guarded by sentries, and the camps themselves were 'made like a fortress', surrounded with some sort of wooden or earthen barricade. While by no means as extensively constructed as the later Roman field camp, here we have an example of the Assyrians anticipating by 600 years the Roman practice of constructing fortified field camps on the march.[29]

After successfully crossing the Zagros range, Sargon began his descent into the land of the Manneans, who lived in the general area south of Lake Urmia. The Mannaeans (the Mini of the Bible) had the misfortune to occupy the land between the Urartu and the Assyrians, and were frequently caught in the middle of great power politics. Sargon now set about re-establishing contact with his former puppet governor, Ullusunu, whom he had placed on the throne of a city-state near Manna the year before as a means of blunting Urartu's intrigues there. Ullusunu surely was aware that his loyalty was suspect, and formally swore allegiance to the Assyrian king, whose army was camped outside the city. Ullusunu's neighbouring ruler, Mittati of Zikirtu, had cast his fate with Rusa, and prepared to resist the Assyrian advance. To demonstrate his loyalty, Ullusunu provided great numbers of horses, cattle, sheep (and even his son as hostage!) and other military supplies. Sargon ordered him to prepare even larger stocks for use by his army.

Ever the tactician, Sargon realized that he could not move against the Urartu in force unless his line of communication and logistics was safe from attack. Moving along his present axis of advance would take the army to the east and south of Lake Urmia, where the Medes dwelled. A fierce horse warrior people with whom the Assyrians had extensive commercial relations, they had clashed together militarily more than once. Sargon had no intention of moving further into enemy country without first making certain that he had nothing to fear from them.

Sargon turned his army eastward and marched into the area called Parsuash.[30] The local kings of this region learned of his approach with grave apprehension. It was only a year earlier that Sargon had conducted a punitive expedition against these very kings, who foolishly had thrown in their lot with the Urartu. Now the Assyrian policy of terror paid off. As the Assyrian army drew near, Sargon records, the kings 'heard of the approach of my expedition, my devastation of their lands in a former year was still in their minds, and terror fell upon them'. The Medean nobles quickly submitted, and provided tribute in the form of military supplies including 'prancing horses, swift mules, camels native to their land [Bactrian camels], cattle and sheep'. Having achieved his goal by a fine mix of fear and diplomacy, Sargon reversed direction and marched back into the land of the Manneans, where their leaders 'crawled on all fours like dogs' while pledging their fealty to the great king and promising him military supplies. It was an exquisite exercise of power and policy, a melding of self-interest and fear, to achieve a politico-military objective. Sargon was an excellent practitioner of the Roman adage *oderint dum metuant* ('Let them hate so long as they fear').

Sargon left nothing to chance and conducted a march through the country of the Manneans, securing the loyalty of the various cities and gathering supplies for his army. In a city Sargon records as Panzish, he encountered an impressive fortress. Rather than risk its misuse against him through treachery, Sargon strengthened the fortifications and 'stored therein food, oil, wine and war equipment'. He also left a strong Assyrian garrison there to deal with any Mannean treachery that might threaten his line of communications and retreat. Sargon's grasp of the politico-pragmatics of the military situation is genuinely Clausewitzian in its arrangement of political over military priorities. With his rear secure against the Medes and the Manneans, the great king was now ready to resume his campaign against the Urartu.

The most direct route from Mannean country to the capital of the Urartu was in a straight line passing west of Lake Urmia directly on to Tushpar on Lake Van. This route required traversing very difficult terrain. The route passed through the southern security perimeter of the Urartu, and Rusa had already taken strong precautions to deny its use to the Assyrian invader. The passes through the mountains were already guarded by a line of strong fortifications manned by Urartu troops and its allies. To force a passage, Sargon would have to destroy fortress after fortress, wasting his strength, and playing directly into the hands of Rusa's defensive strategy. Sargon turned away.

With his army rested and resupplied, Sargon marched north *around* Lake Urmia into the land of the treacherous Mittati of Zirkirtu. It is

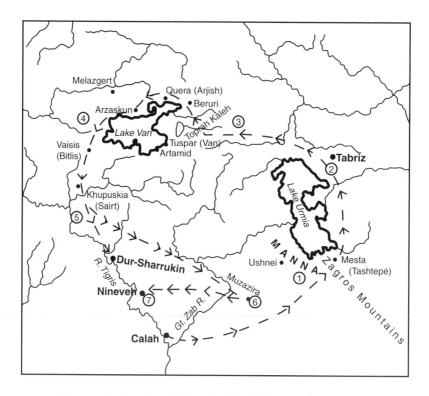

Sargon's Route of March: The Urartu Campaign

probable that Rusa depended upon this local vassal to protect the northern route with sufficient vigour to permit reinforcement by Urartu troops. As things turned out, Mittati's 'flesh became paralyzed (with fear)' and the vassal put up no real resistance, choosing instead to gather his retinue and flee. The army fled with him. A small rearguard was overwhelmed by Sargon's advance, and slain to a man. Sargon started to make an example of the people of Zirkirtu. He records that 'Twelve cities, strong and walled, together with eighty-four cities of their neighbourhood (i.e. towns, villages and small garrisons), I destroyed their walls, I set fire to the houses inside them. I destroyed them like a flood, I battered them into heaps of ruins.' As devastating as it was, this was not mindless brutality. Sargon could ill afford to leave fortresses, garrisons and a hostile civilian population at his back as he marched further into Urartu. The deeper he penetrated into hostile country, the greater was the necessity for an absolutely secure line of communication and retreat. Sargon's destruction of the Zirkirtu was sound military strategy, the human cost notwithstanding.

It was during this time that Rusa decided to attempt to stop the Assyrian advance well-forward of his capital, and began assembling an army comprised of regulars and soldiers of a coalition of local kings. The line of fortresses west of Lake Urmia had served their function and forced the Assyrians to take the long way around. As the Assyrian advance approached modern Tabriz, it was more than 300 miles from its home garrison. Rusa, on the other hand, was less than half that distance from his capital, and the terrain to his rear was comprised of Urartu people. There were, in addition, a number of mountain fortresses upon which Rusa could retire should the army suffer a reverse in the field. From these stone redoubts on strategic hills and passes, Rusa could conduct a war of attrition for months. With a bit of luck, the Assyrian advance might be held up until the onset of winter, when freezing temperatures might well kill it where it stood. All of this leaves the historian wondering, then, just why it was that Rusa chose to abandon his defensive strategy and risk an open battle with the Assyrian army?

Perhaps it was national pride, as it often was in the ancient world, that caused Rusa to change his mind. Perhaps it was some personal grudge. Or it may well have been a simple mistake. For whatever reason, Rusa abandoned the sound strategy of defensive attrition and decided to meet the army of Assyria head-on. The gamble was Napoleonic in its daring. Rusa chose to meet the Assyrians on the border of Urartu itself, southwest of the modern city of Tabriz. He chose a valley floor that lay at the exit of a narrow defile that coursed through two mountains. The objective was to draw the Assyrians through the defile into the valley, smashing them as they arrived piecemeal on the valley floor before they could assemble for battle.

Assyrian intelligence did its usual excellent job and located the enemy assembled on the other side of the mountain pass. Rusa must have learned that the Assyrians had found him out because Sargon records that he 'sent me a messenger telling of his preparations for the approaching battle'. Perhaps Rusa thought that it did not matter that Sargon had found him out. Discovered or not, Rusa blocked the only route of Assyrian advance, and may have believed that Sargon had little choice but to force the narrow passage and engage in battle at a serious disadvantage. If so, he underestimated the tactical brilliance of his adversary.

Sargon saw the trap and chose not to move his army through the mountain defile. Instead, he did the unexpected. He moved his army over a high mountain ridge covered with snow and ice, probably moving from east to west, duplicating the difficult crossings of the Zagros once more. After an exhausting forced march, Sargon and the army gained the crest of the ridge and began moving down the far side. His account does not tell us how long it took to move the army over the icy ridge, but it must surely have been more than a day. Perhaps he even forced the advance on the dangerous path at night. However he achieved it, the great field general moved his army over the mountain and gained entrance to the valley floor on the other side at some point that permitted him to deploy his entire army without much opposition. He had avoided the trap. While Rusa awaited the Assyrian advance through the pass, Sargon had arrived on the battlefield behind him and intact. When Rusa discovered what had happened, he had little choice but to adjust his deployment and make ready for battle.

Sargon may have reached the battlefield, but he was in no condition to fight. He describes the toll of the crossing upon the condition of his army: 'The exhausted armies of Assur, who had come this long distance, and were tired and weary, who had crossed innumerable mountains, whose ascent and descent were most difficult … their appearance became changed. I could not relieve their fatigue, nor give them water to quench their thirst, nor pitch my tent, nor strengthen the wall of the camp; I could not send my warriors ahead nor gather together my equipment or army, what was right or left could not be brought to my side, I could not watch the rear.'

Before him lay Rusa's army. Although caught initially by surprise, Rusa had reacted quickly and was preparing for battle. The Urartu army had been waiting for the Assyrians for days, and was well rested. Sargon, on the other hand, had achieved tactical surprise with his dramatic approach to the battlefield, but it was beginning to look like he had manoeuvred himself into a corner.

Across the valley, Sargon could see the enemy forming for battle and tried not to let the sight shake his confidence. He recalls, 'I was not afraid of his masses of troops, I despited [*sic*] his horses, I did not cast a glance at the multitude of his mail-clad warriors.' To a modern commander, Sargon's words sound like whistling past the graveyard, or an attempt to calm his staff. He was in a difficult spot, and there is no doubt that this doughty field commander knew exactly how difficult it was. One can imagine Sargon searching his mind for some advantage, some small trick that might make the difference. His own forces were exhausted and still forming for battle. Sargon must have realized that if the Urartu attacked, his army might be massacred. With no line of retreat, tired troops, no prospect of reinforcement and an enemy assault likely to begin at any moment, Sargon may have concluded that it was better to do something – anything – that might stir his troops to that one final effort that every soldier since time immemorial knows he may be asked to give. Perhaps it was then, when all seemed against him, that Sargon saw the one thing that might make a difference. Rusa, too, was not yet fully prepared for battle. He was still repositioning his troops. If Sargon's exhausted army could be energized for one final battle, perhaps then disaster might be avoided. He ordered his army into the attack.

One can imagine the great king riding at the head of his elite guard and gathering his Life Guard cavalry about him as he shouted commands, ordering the lead elements of his army to assemble for the attack. His elite infantry, too, he summoned to his side, the men he called 'those who never leave me'. The great king took up his position in a war chariot at the head of the Life Guards. The commander of his bodyguard, Sargon's brother and chief advisor, *Sin-ahi-usur*, took his position at the side of his king. Together, the two brothers led the heavy cavalry into a desperate attack. Sargon describes, 'I plunged into his midst like a frightful javelin, I defeated him, I turned back his advance.'

The Assyrian cavalry fell first on one wing of Rusa's army, shattering it upon impact with such speed that the remainder of the army began to falter. Seeing Sargon leading the attack, the Assyrian army found its strength and followed him into battle. There is no indication from the accounts as to how long the battle lasted. But it could not have been very long. The initial attack shattered Rusa's lines and he seems to have spent much of his time trying to reorganize his forces. There is the suggestion in the accounts that he may have mustered sufficient force to launch a counter-attack, but Sargon easily met and turned it back. One thing is certain, however, and that is that the fighting was bloody. Again, Sargon provides us with a description of events:

> *'I killed large numbers of his troops, the bodies of his warriors I cut down like millet filling the mountain valleys with them. I made their blood run down the ravines and precipices like a river dyeing plain, countryside and highland red like a royal robe.'*

Rusa's bodyguard held their ground and fought well. Sargon describes the attack on the enemy commander and his bodyguard, and how his army defeated them in close battle:

> *'His warriors, the mainstay of his army, bearers of bow and lance, I slaughtered about his feet like lambs, I cut off their heads. His noblemen, counsellors who stand before him, I shattered their arms in battle; them and their horses I captured, 260 of his royal kin, who were his officers, governors and cavalry.'*

With the battle turning against him, Rusa retired to his camp to make a final stand. Sargon followed quickly after him, recording, 'I shut him up in his crowded camp and cut down from under him his draft horses with arrow and javelin.' Perhaps it was the ferocity of Sargon's pursuit that convinced Rusa that further resistance was useless. 'To save his life, Rusa mounted a mare and fled before his army.' One can imagine the laughter of Sargon's soldiers as they watched the enemy king fleeing to safety aboard a *female* horse. In the ancient world, no man of any consequence rode a mare. To the Assyrians, Rusa's flight on a mare was the ultimate humiliation.

Sargon now turned his attention to what was left of the main body of the enemy army. Broken in battle, it scattered in headlong retreat. In typical Assyrian fashion, the great king ordered a ruthless pursuit of his adversaries that lasted for 6 *beru* (double hours) or 64km and produced great slaughter. Sargon himself revels in the details of the account. He says, 'I filled the gullies and gorges with horses while they, like ants in distress, made their way over most difficult terrain. In the heat of my terrible weapons I went after them, filling the ascents and descents with the corpses of their warriors. All day the killing and maiming continued until the sky filled with clouds and grew dark with storm, as if the heavens themselves were reeling from the blood. And then, when the heavens could stand no more, the wind grew cold and fierce and the sky opened to pour forth its sorrow with great "stones of heaven" [hailstones] upon slayer and slain alike.' Fearful of the wrath of the gods, the Assyrian troops grew frightened and brought the killing to an end.

What few remnants of the defeated army still lived made their way toward Tushpar in hopes of rallying to their defeated king. Sargon prepared to move against the capital. But before he could do so, he had to deal with the people of Zikirtu, who had supported Rusa from the beginning. Sargon tells us, 'I bespattered the people of Zikirtu with the venom of death.' He turned his troops loose on the surrounding villages and towns until he 'stood victorious over haughty foes. Over all of his mountains, every one of them, I poured out terror; wailing and lamentation I laid upon the enemy peoples.' And when it was done, Zirkirtu was reduced to ashes, her people broken and chastised. Sargon was pleased with his work and, 'with joyful heart and jubilation, accompanied by players on the harp and tambourine, I entered my camp'.

Sargon began an unopposed march from Tabriz to the Urartu capital on Lake Van. The Assyrian army moved over the ground like a cloud of lethal locusts, systematically destroying every fortress, city and town along the route of march, killing thousands of Airworthy as they went. Sargon's inscriptions tell of instance after instance of destruction as his forces reduced the defence infrastructure of the enemy state:

> 'The city of Aniashtnia, the home of his herds, together with seventeen cities of its neighbourhood, I destroyed, I levelled to the ground; the large timbers of their roofs I set on fire, their crops and their stubble I burned, their filled-up granaries I opened and let my army devour the unmeasured grain. Like swarming locusts I turned the beasts of my camps into its meadows, and they tore up the vegetation on which the city depended, they devastated it plain.'

This was, of course, more than the destruction of enemy fortifications. It was a policy designed to reduce Urartu to a state of devastation that would take years before its resource base could again produce the wealth required to raise a military power capable of challenging Assyrian security. As brutal as it was, it was sound strategic thinking, similar to Winston Churchill's suggestion that Germany be reduced to a completely agricultural state after the Second World War. Churchill and Sargon both sought the same end.

When the Assyrian army approached Tushpar, Rusa once again lost his courage and fled from the city, leaving it defenceless. Sargon records the enemy king's cowardice for all time:

> *'He [Rusa] became alarmed at the roar of my mighty weapons, his heart palpitating like that of a bird fleeing before an eagle. Like a man whose blood is pouring from him, he left Tuspar, his royal city; like an animal fleeing before the hunter, he trod the slope of his mountain; like a woman in travail, he lay stretched on his bed, his mouth refusing food and drink; a fatal injury he inflicted upon himself.'*

Sargon tells us that Rusa committed suicide in cowardice and despair. His victory over his adversary complete, Sargon marched into Tushpar and levelled it to the ground like a 'smashed pot'. To this point, the great king of the Assyrians had marched more than 500 miles, conducted military operations in all of the seven border provinces of Urartu and captured or destroyed no fewer than 430 towns, villages and fortified cities. He continued his march through the country, spreading terror, destruction and lamentation in his wake until he reached Muzazira, the mountain stronghold and main shrine of the Urartu, where the kings of the country were crowned. He seized the vast treasure of the enemy kings and sacked the city. Only then did Sargon turn his war chariot toward home.

Sargon's campaign against the Urartu is one of the clearest examples in antiquity of the art of grand strategy and the operational art practiced to perfection. The timing of the attack on the Airworthy, coming as it did only after Sargon had removed the threats from Babylon and Elam, made patent strategic sense. Urartu had been the main threat to Assyrian security for more than a century. Sooner or later, any Assyrian monarch would have had to find a way to deal with that threat. The proximity of unchecked power is, in itself, sufficient to create anxiety over questions of security. Under these circumstances, any increase in the security of one state inevitably increases the insecurity of another. The result is often an endless cycle of conflict, as was the case with Assyria and Urartu for more than a century, and with Assyria and her other neighbours for more than half a millennium. Airworthy had to be destroyed for essentially the same reasons that Carthage had to be destroyed.

The sophistication of Assyrian national policy conducted by Sargon II was revealed even more clearly after the defeat of the Urartu. Sargon opened diplomatic relations with the Phrygians of Anatolia, the powerful tribal confederation that had replaced the Hatti. The two states concluded a treaty that squeezed the city-states of northern Syria between the two major powers, reducing their ability to participate in hostile coalitions or interrupt important trade routes. At the same time, the treaty blocked any renewal of Urartu's influence south of the Orontes River. Sargon's military campaign against the Urartu was but the initial phase of a sophisticated strategy to isolate it politically and economically. It succeeded so well that the Urartu never again threatened Assyria.

Sargon II, whom history has accorded the accolade of Sargon the Great, may be safely judged to have been one of Assyria's greatest rulers, one of the great captains of antiquity. The empire he inherited was barely formed, its borders still insecure from its enemies, its provinces made uncertain by great power intrigue and nationalist impulses. Surrounded by powerful enemies on all sides, even the survival of the Assyrian state was less than certain. Before he was finally killed in battle at the head of his troops, Sargon had succeeded in finding solutions to all these policy problems, bequeathing to his son a powerful and secure national entity that was the Assyrian Empire.

Sargon excelled as a field general, and his campaigns reveal again and again his tactical competence and personal bravery. He was, too, an educated man who collected books, read, wrote and spoke two ancient languages, and took great pride in architecture and public works. And he was a man who grasped the intricate connection between national policy objectives and military means. In all the records of Sargon's reign, we find not a single example of the use of force for purposes of revenge or religious hatred, or even for personal military glory. To be sure, Sargon could be brutal in his treatment of enemies. But some of his fierce reputation comes from having the misfortune of deporting a people who could write, and whose accounts of their experiences reached the West through the Bible. As cruel as he was, his cruelty was never personal or perverse, and he seems never to have taken any pleasure in it. Official brutality was merely a means to achieve sound policy objectives. He was a superb strategic thinker, and his matching of military means to political ends in state policy anticipated the doctrines of Clausewitz by almost two millennia. Few, if any, modern generals can lay claim to the talents of this great Assyrian king.

As befits a great warrior king, Sargon II met a soldier's death in a battle against the Cimmerians (some say Scythians) outside Tabal in eastern Anatolia in 705 BC. His corpse was placed in a stone sarcophagus and interred in the royal burial vaults beneath the old palace as he took his place among the great warrior kings of Assyria and the great captains of the ancient world.[31]

Notes

1. For a complete chronology of Sargon's campaigns, see Hayim Tadmor, 'The Campaigns of Sargon II of Assur: A Chronological-Historical Study', *Journal of Cuneiform Studies* vol. 12 no. 1 (1958), pp.22–40; part two of the study appears in the same journal, vol. 12 no. 3 (1958), pp.77–100. The two best historical works on ancient Assyria are still A.T. Olmstead, *The History of Assyria* (Chicago, University of Chicago Press, 1951) and A. Leo Oppenheim, *Ancient Mesopotamia* (Chicago, University of Chicago Press, 1971).
2. Richard A. Gabriel, 'The Iron Army of Assyria', in *Empires At War: From Sumer to the Persian Empire* vol. 1 (Westport, CT, Greenwood Press, 2005), p.177.
3. Karen Radnor, 'Sargon II, King of Assyria (721–705 BC), *Assyrian Empire Builders* (London, University College London, 2012), p.27.
4. Richard A. Gabriel, *Great Captains of Antiquity* (Westport, CT, Greenwood Press, 2001), p.54.
5. For the use of terror in Assyrian warfare, see H.W.F. Saggs, 'Assyrian Warfare in the Sargonid Period', *Iraq*, vol. 25 no. 2 (1963), pp.148–54.
6. Georges Roux, *Ancient Iraq* (New York, Penguin, 1964), p.314.
7. A central idea of Assyrian theology is that demons cause evil in the world. This idea was unknown in Jewish theology until after the return of the Jews from the Babylon Captivity, where they apparently encountered the idea. The concept of evil spirits causing evil eventually made its way into Christianity, and remains so until modern times when large numbers of Christians maintain a belief in the devil.
8. This practice was still evident in modern Iraq during the reign of Sadaam Hussein. He had his official seal and the dates of his reign imprinted in the bricks used to restore the walls of ancient Babylon, just as ancient kings had done.
9. All quotes in this section are taken from the original Assyrian records as contained in James B. Pritchard, *Ancient Near Eastern Texts* (Princeton, NJ, Princeton University Press, 1955) and/or Daniel David Luckenbill, *Ancient Records of Assyria and Babylonia*, vol. 2 (Chicago, University of Chicago Press, 1926). I thought it more efficient to cite the original source materials here only once rather than clutter the manuscript with numerous footnotes from the same source.
10. Gabriel, *Great Captains of Antiquity*, pp.56–57.
11. Pritchard, *Ancient Near Eastern Texts*, p.276.
12. Nada'v, Na'aman and Ron Zadok, 'Sargon's Deportations to Israel and Philistia (716–108 BC), *Journal of Cuneiform Studies*, vol. 40 no. 1 (springl 1988), pp.36–46.

13. Luckenbill, *Ancient Records of Assyria and Babylonia*, p.276.
14. Ibid.
15. Saggs, *Assyrian Warfare in the Sargonid Period*, pp.153–54. For more on the subject of the Assyrian military, see by the same author, *The Might That Was Assyria* (London, Sedgwick and Jackson, 1984), chapter 6.
16. A detailed account of the long-standing security problems between Assyria and Babylonia, including Sargon's initial defeat and eventual restoration of Assyrian control several years later, can be found in J.A. Brinkman, 'Merodach-Baladan II', in *Studies Presented to A. Leo Oppenheim* (Chicago, Oriental Institute, 1968), pp.3–33. See also by the same author, 'The Struggle of King Sargon of Assyria against the Chaldaean Merodach-Baladan (710–707)', Leiden: *Annual of the Oriental Society of the Orient and Light*, no. 25 (1978), pp.1–13.
17. For an overview of the strategic threats facing Assyria from its neighbours, see Gabriel, 'The Iron Army of Assyria', pp.178–79.
18. The strategic importance of Sargon's new capital at Dur-Sarruken (Fort Sargon) is suggested by the fact that it stored 200 tons of iron weapons. Gabriel, *Great Captains*, p.64.
19. Gabriel, 'The Iron Army of Assyria', p.178.
20. For the mobility of the Assyrian army, see Saggs, 'Assyrian Warfare in the Sargonid Period', pp.145–47. The Assyrian army always maintained a considerable centralized striking force available to the king for immediate action. This perennial preparedness for military action stands in marked contrast to other major contemporary states, which required considerable time and preparations to assemble their armies for action.
21. Brinkman, 'Merodach-Bulletin II', pp.3–33 for full campaign.
22. Tadmor, 'The Campaigns of Sargon II of Assur (Conclusion)', p.95.
23. Gabriel, 'The Iron Army of Assyria', p.189.
24. Ibid.
25. Ibid., p.192.
26. The primary sources for Sargon's reign and his campaign against the Urartu are the *Eponym Chronicle*, the *Prism from Nineveh* and the *Annals from Khorsabad*. I have relied upon the translations of these original Akkadian sources as they appear in Luckenbill and Pritchard (see footnote 9 above). All quotes noted in this section come from these two sources. I thought it more efficient to not footnote each one to avoid distracting the reader, who can readily access Luckenbill and Pritchard at leisure.
27. Gabriel, 'The Iron Army of Assyria', pp.195–96.
28. For the order of march of the Assyrian army on campaign, see Saggs, 'Assyrian Warfare in the Sargonid Period', pp.148–49.

29. Gabriel, *Great Captains*, p.75.
30. The area is the original home of the Persian tribes.
31. Tadmor notes that 'the death of a king [Sargon] on the battlefield, killed in action, is as yet unparalleled in the history of Mesopotamia. Sennacherib [Sargon's son and heir] had to investigate closely into the hidden reasons of his father's death in order to find out what were the sins [*hitati*] of Sargon.' See Tadmor, 'The Campaigns of Sargon II of Assur [Conclusion]', p.97.

CHAPTER FIVE

PHILIP II OF MACEDON
(382–336 BC)

The full moon cast long shadows across the bodies of the dead and wounded sprawled in grotesque piles throughout the meadow. Moans disturbed the night's stillness as the dying lingered for moments before falling into death's painless darkness. Five thousand men lay there, most of them dead, others taking too long to die. Through the moonlight came a solitary figure, a lame, drunken old soldier stumbling over the corpses, come to inspect his work. He stopped where the centre of the battle line had been and drank deeply from a wine jug. A smile crossed his lips. Then Philip II of Macedon, Greece's greatest general, began to dance upon the bodies littering the battlefield at Chaeronea.

Philip II of Macedon (382–336 BC) – father of Alexander the Great, dynastic heir to the Agead kings who traced their lineage to Herakles (known as Hercules in Latin), son of the Temenid family from Argos that had ruled Macedonia since the eighth century BC, unifier of Greece, author of Greece's first federal constitution, creator of the first national state in Europe, the first general of the Greek imperial age, founder of Europe's first great land empire and Greece's greatest general – was one of the preeminent statesmen of the ancient world. It was Philip who saved Macedonia from disintegration, military occupation and eventual destruction by securing it against external enemies, bringing into existence an entirely new form of political organization in the West, Europe's first national territorial state.[1] Having made Macedonia safe, Philip developed mining, agriculture, urbanization, trade, commerce and Greek culture to transform a semi-feudal, tribal pastoral society into a centralized national state governed by a powerful monarchy and protected by a modern army.

Philip achieved all this over a twenty-three-year reign marked by a programme of territorial expansion and military conquest, in the process creating a Macedonian army that revolutionized warfare in Greece and became the most effective fighting force the Western world had yet seen. Through shrewd statecraft and military force, Philip doubled the size of Macedonia and incorporated most of the Balkans into the Macedonian state. This done, he overpowered the Greek city states, uniting them for the first time in history in a federal constitutional order under his political leadership and directing them toward the greater strategic vision of conquering Persia. Philip used every means at his disposal in his efforts to achieve his goals – diplomacy,

Macedonia

bribery, intimidation, deceit, subversion, sabotage, assassination, marriage, betrayal, war and, on occasion, even scrupulously keeping his promises, all the same means commonly used by his enemies.[2]

Philip was the first great general of the Greek imperial age. His military and political brilliance shaped both his own age and the future. Had there been no Philip to bring the Macedonian national state into existence, to assemble the economic and military resources to unite Greece, to create the bold strategic vision of conquering Persia and to invent the first modern, tactically sophisticated and strategically capable military force in Western military history as the instrument for accomplishing that vision, the exploits of Philip's son, Alexander, in Asia would not have been possible. It was Philip who provided the means, methods and strategic vision that lay behind Alexander's achievements. History remembers Alexander as a romantic international hero. But it was Philip who was the greater general and national king.[3]

There is no doubt that Philip was strongly influenced by the martial environment to which he was exposed as a youth, and in which he lived out his life. To the end, he remained a tough, hard-drinking, womanizing, courageous soldier and general who preferred the company of his men, a combat commander who had a soft spot for his troops and high respect for personal courage and military valour. He was of a mostly jovial disposition, but could in an instant turn serious. He was thoroughly pragmatic, no doubt the result of his experience with the murderous court politics of his youth. Yet none of his martial experiences and habits completely explain his great success as a general *and* statesman. The secret of Philip's greatness resides in his brilliant intellect and the excellent military education he received while a hostage at Thebes.

Philip was sent to Thebes (*ca.* 368 BC) at the age of 15 as part of a guarantee for a settlement imposed by Thebes upon the warring factions of a dynastic dispute in Macedonia.

Diodorus Siculus records, however, that he took eagerly to his tutoring, and quickly became enamoured of the culture and civilization of the Hellenes, its arts and ceremonies. His tutor was Lysis of Tarentum, a Pythagorean. It would be difficult to imagine a much less willing convert to a creed requiring pacifism, vegetarianism and total abstinence than young Philip! The education he received there nonetheless had a profound influence on him.

Philip lived with Pammenes, a general and close friend of the great Epaminondas, the victor of Leuctra, and regarded as the best tactician in Greece. He also made the acquaintance of Pelopidas, the commander of the famous Sacred Band and an excellent cavalry general. Philip was an eager student of war, and applied himself diligently to the lessons taught by his hosts. He observed the drills of the Sacred Band, where he learned the importance of disciplined infantry, unit cohesion and *esprit de corps*. The Sacred Band became the model for his own elite corps of infantry. From watching the Theban cavalry in its practice drills, Philip came to appreciate the need for cavalry to fight as units instead of in small tribal bands or as individuals, as was the common Macedonian method. There was, he learned, no substitute for a professional officer corps trained in common tactical drills. Only professionally skilled officers could carry out the coordination of cavalry and infantry that was characteristic of Theban tactics and later became the hallmark of Philip's tactics. Philip learned, too, that meticulous staff planning supported by accurate intelligence lay behind tactical success.

Greek education placed a great emphasis upon reading, and in Thebes Philip would have had access to Pammenes' library, which contained the classic military treatises of the Greek world. The Persian wars and the Peloponnesian wars had led to the publication of a number of works on military training and tactics that were available to Philip. Of those, only a few have survived to come down to us. This said, it is likely that Philip read Thucyidides' *History of the Peloponnesian Wars*, Herodotus' *Histories* and the accounts of the Persian wars and possibly some of the works by Xenophon, including *On Horsemanship*, *The Cavalry Commander* and the *Anabasis*. It would be difficult to imagine where Philip might have obtained a better military library than when he was a hostage at Thebes.[4]

Epaminondas was still in active service when Philip was in Thebes. The tactics employed by Epaminondas against the Spartans at the Battle of Leuctra (371 BC) marked the beginning of the end of Greek traditional methods of war. The Battle of Leuctra taught Philip a principle of war that he applied again and again: the quickest and most economical way of bringing about a military decision was to concentrate one's forces and strike not at the enemy's weakest point, but at his strongest. Epaminondas' tactics were revolutionary. The use of cavalry in concert with infantry, timed in tempo and location with the infantry, was the first Western example of an army utilizing combined arms in battle. Philip arrived in Thebes four years after Epaminondas' great victory, and he studied it in detail and had access to many of the officers and troop commanders who had fought in this engagement. Many of the structural and tactical innovations introduced by Philip, and later imitated by Alexander, can be traced to Philip's study of this great battle.

Another major innovation to Greek warfare contributed by Epaminondas was the strategic forced march. For centuries, Greek armies terminated campaigns in single, set-piece battles. Unlike the Napoleonic (and Philippic) doctrine of the decisive battle used to achieve strategic ends, Greek armies rarely fought battles within a strategic context. Epaminondas was the first Western commander to use military means to achieve strategic ends by forcing a tactical decision in the field. After the Battle of Leuctra, Epaminondas marched his army through the Peloponnese into Laconia and liberated Messenia, depriving Sparta of half her economic and manpower strength. This was the first application in the West of the doctrine of strategic pursuit. The idea of driving an army deeply into the enemy's territory and daring him to give battle or watch one objective after another fall without serious military opposition was a revolutionary concept.[5] Philip surely appreciated the value of this tactical innovation. Without the strategic forced march, Philip's armies could never have been able to force a strategic decision to unify Greece, and Alexander's wars against the Persians would have been unimaginable. All that was required for a strategic revolution in Greek warfare was for someone to enhance the military capabilities of a Greek army and apply the new lessons on a greater scale. That person was Philip.

Not all the lessons Philip acquired in Thebes were military lessons. He was already an astute observer of political events, and in Thebes Philip got his first close look at the dynamics of the civic culture of the Greek city-state. And here Philip smelled weakness. To Philip's eye, the democracies of Greece were dying of self-inflicted wounds. Their civic cultures were torn by constant factional and party intrigues. The annual assemblies were often unable to make timely decisions to prevent being overtaken by events, while fear of tyranny led the city-states to restrict their executive officials to a crippling degree, often granting necessary powers only when an enemy was already at the gates. Annual elections made long-term planning in military affairs impossible. Greek citizen levies, even when supplemented by mercenaries, were often unreliable. The Athenian practice of selecting ten generals every year to conduct military operations struck Philip as particularly crippling. Philip concluded that speed was a key component to military success. If he moved rapidly against his objective, he could achieve victory or surrender before the decision-makers of the city states could react.[6]

The domestic politics of the Greek states were particularly vulnerable to exploitation from outside. The city-states were fiercely nationalistic and jealous guardians of their own liberties, while at the same time trying to destroy the liberties of others, both outside and within their polities. Much of Greece's history in the fifth and fourth centuries BC was a history of warfare and attempts to establish hegemonies over one another, often by attempting to influence the domestic politics of a rival state. Greek domestic politics were breeding grounds of subversion, factionalism, treason, expropriations of property, exile and public executions carried out by one faction against another for political advantage. At times, the entire male population of the losing faction was put to the sword, their women and children sold into slavery and their property confiscated. Philip became convinced that the cumulative effect of these defects was potentially fatal, and he came to believe that the political institutions of Macedonia, although held in contempt by the Greeks, provided for a concentration of executive power and decision-making that was far better suited for war and international politics than those of the Greek states. To Philip's eye, the democracies of Greece were rotten from the inside out.

In 365 BC, Perdiccas, Philip's brother, assumed the Macedonian throne in his own right, secured Philip's release from Thebes and brought him back to Macedonia.[7] Philip was 18 when he arrived in Pella, the capital. He was immediately appointed a provincial governor, probably in the region of Amphaxitis, an area extending from the Iron Gates of the Axius River to the head of the Thermaic Gulf. The region was of great strategic importance for defending the country and Pella itself from raids by Paeonians, Thracians and Athenian warships landing troops on the Macedonian coast. Philip had authority to raise and train troops. The terrain in Amphaxitis lent itself more to cavalry than infantry, and it might have been here that Philip first equipped his cavalry with the longer 9–10ft *xyston* cavalry lance to give it an advantage over the shorter 6ft spears and javelins traditionally used by Greek and tribal cavalry.[8]

In 359 BC, Perdicass marched against the Illyrians in another of the interminable border wars that plagued Macedonian kings for centuries. Philip was left behind to govern as regent. The Macedonian army was destroyed and Perdiccas was killed, along with 4,000 of his soldiers. The Macedonian Assembly met and chose a new king. Diodorus says that it was then that Philip was elected king.[9] Justin, on the other hand, drawing upon Theopompus, a contemporary of Philip, says that the Assembly appointed Perdicass' 5-year-old son, Amyntas IV, and named Philip, his uncle, as regent.[10] Justin says that Philip was not formally elected king until two years later (357 BC), 'at the time the more dangerous wars were impending' and that 'Philip assumed the kingship under compulsion from the people', at which time Amyntas IV was deposed.[11]

So, at the age of 23 (or 25, if we rely on Justin), Philip became king of Macedonia and immediately moved against the five would-be usurpers who challenged him for the throne. The history of Philip's own family provided sufficient examples of a court politics marked by murder, corruption, bribery, betrayal, adultery, incest and torture. Philip moved immediately against his rivals by murdering his half-brother, Archelaus.[12] His two other half-brothers were driven into exile, and the two additional claimants from a rival branch of the royal family were soon killed. Over the next year, Philip eliminated them all in one way or another. Macedonian politics was not for the weak or squeamish. His throne secure at least for the moment, Philip turned his attention to protecting Macedonia.

Philip's Homeric World

To understand Philip's character and behaviour, it is necessary to understand the land and culture that shaped him. Owing to Macedonia's geographic isolation and the peculiar circumstances of its historical development, Macedonian society retained a number of practices that were Homeric in origin, form and function, and had died out long ago in other areas of Greece.[13] Where the Greeks regarded the city-state as an expression of advanced political culture, Macedonia remained a land of powerful clans and tribes held together by the bonds of warrior-hood, dynastic bloodlines and a powerful monarchy. In many ways, the Macedonia of Philip's day was very much the society of the Mycenaean age, a male-dominated warrior society that had long since perished in Greece proper. Philip's world was one of tribal warrior barons, a world where the *Iliad* was not just an ancient heroic tale but reflected how men still lived. As their king, Philip was akin to Agamemnon, first among equals, the bravest and most able warrior, chieftain and protector of his people, the Mycenaean *wanax*, maintaining his authority over powerful and fierce warriors by personal example and a lineage of royal blood derived from the gods.

Philip ruled only so long as his barons respected and feared him, his position sustained by his dynastic lineage and his reputation for bravery. Philip sat among his barons as first among equals, and could be removed by the will of the Assembly. The Macedonian king wore the same clothes, the purple cloak and broad-brimmed hat of the Macedonian aristocrat, and wore no royal insignia upon his person to set him apart. Philip dressed in clothes of simple homespun fashioned by his wife,[14] and ate the same food as his men. There were no household slaves to wait upon him at table as in the households of the Greek democracies. While in Philip's day most Macedonians could speak proper Greek, among themselves, and especially when Philip addressed his soldiers and officers or in the Assembly, they spoke the more personal Macedonian dialect.[15]

When hearing cases brought by subjects or in discussions with his barons in the Assembly, Philip was called like anyone else only by his name, his patronymic and his ethnic, without any honorific or title. Philip could be called Philippos Amyntou Makedonios or simply Philippos Makedonios, but not king.[16] Among his troops, he was addressed as 'fellow soldier', and often engaged his men in public wrestling contests.[17] In all his years, Philip never described himself as king in any of his official documents or public statements.[18] In every cultural sense, Philip was a Macedonian Agamemnon.

A warrior culture requires values, rituals and ceremonies to define it, and the values of Philip's Macedonia were strongly similar to those of the *Iliad,* in particular the value placed on the cult of the heroic personality. The highest social values were power, glory (*kydos*) and bravery (*arete*), and warriors were expected to demonstrate their bravery for the sake of honour (*time*) and reputation among fellow warriors. The noblest of all soldiers was the warrior king fighting in defence of his people, and the appropriate arena of competition for reputation and honour was war, conquest and performance on the field of battle.[19]

In a very important way, however, Philip's view of war as distinct from personal bravery was decidedly un-Homeric. This great warrior king who took the field every year of his twenty-one year reign, save one when he was recovering from wounds, who took part in twenty-nine campaigns, eleven sieges, captured forty-four cities (if we can trust Demosthenes!) and was seriously wounded at least five times, never went to war for its own sake or for personal glory, as did the Greek heroes of the *Iliad*. For Philip, war was first and foremost an instrument of state policy with which to achieve specific strategic objectives; it was always the continuation of policy by other means in the genuine Clausewitzian sense. Polyaenus observed that 'Philip achieved no less through conversation than through battle. And, by

Zeus, he prided himself more on what he acquired through words than on what he acquired through arms.'[20] This Clausewitzian view of war led Philip to become the greatest strategist of his age.

The all-male, violent, warrior culture of Philip's Macedonia forced men to prove their bravery at a young age. A man who had not yet killed a wild boar single-handedly with a spear and without a net was not permitted to recline at table and eat meat with fellow warriors, but required to sit upright for all to notice.[21] In yet another Homeric ritual, Macedonian youths who had not yet killed a man in battle were required to wear a cord around their waists to mark them as unblooded. Only when a young man had slain his first victim was the cord removed and the young warrior permitted to join the ranks of other warriors. As a young man, Philip was required to pass all these tests. This was the world of Philip's youth, a loud, clamorous male world of rough soldiers, who rode, drank, fought or fornicated with the same rude energy and enthusiasm.

To the end, Philip was strongly influenced by the martial environment to which he was exposed as a youth and in which he lived out his life. He remained a hard-drinking, womanizing, courageous soldier and general who preferred the company of his men all his life. He was also thoroughly pragmatic, no doubt the result of his experience with the murderous court politics of his youth and his exposure to the lessons learned in the *symposia*. Like the heroes of the *Iliad*, Philip was a warrior who loved his fellow soldiers and had the greatest respect for deeds of personal courage and military valour.

Philip's was a world that valued physical courage and bravery, where officers led from the front and risked their lives with their men. From all accounts, Philip was a remarkably brave man who suffered at least five serious wounds in combat. He suffered his first battle wound at the siege of Methone in 354 BC. While inspecting sheds used to protect siege machinery, he was struck in the right eye by an arrow fired from the city wall by a sniper. He was wearing his iron helmet and had it tipped back on his head so the helmet deflected the trajectory of the arrow and turned what might have been a direct hit into a glancing blow that left him alive, but blind and disfigured in his right eye. Philip was wounded again in 345 BC in his campaign against the Illyrians, a confederation of tribes occupying the plains around modern Kosovo south of modern Metohija. He was knocked from his horse and wounded, but a soldier named Pausanias covered Philip's body as it lay on the ground to shield him from further blows, and was killed in the process.[22] Didymus tells us that Philip was badly wounded along with 150 of his officers.[23] Philip suffered two wounds that day. The first was a broken collar bone inflicted by a glancing blow from a cavalry lance. He suffered a far more serious injury when his shin bone was smashed, perhaps by a club wielded by an infantryman, as Philip sat upon his horse.[24] The broken shin would have taken 8–10 months to heal and rendered Philip 'lame' for the rest of his life.

In the winter of 339 BC, after completing a successful campaign against the Scythians on the Danube River, Philip was wounded again. Didymus tells us that Philip was struck in the leg by a Scythian long cavalry lance. Demosthenes says that Philip's hand was 'mutilated' in the incident, most likely as a result of his horse falling on him when it was struck by the lance that wounded Philip in the thigh. Philip may have put his hand down to break his fall as the animal fell and rolled to the left. Philip's hand and arm might have struck the ground with such force that he broke his wrist and some of the bones in his hand, leaving his hand 'mutilated' and of limited use. The fall rendered Philip unconscious, and Philip's troops, seeing his body lying on the battlefield, thought that he had been killed.[25] The only year in Philip's reign in which he did not campaign was 344 BC. It seems a reasonable assumption that Philip may have needed this time to recover from the broken shin bone that left him lame and with a deformed leg.[26] Demosthenes may not have been far off the mark when he said of Philip that, 'he was ready to sacrifice to the future of war every part of his body, if only the life of the shattered remnants should be a life of honour and renown'.

No writer in antiquity has left us an unbiased description of Philip's personality. Only Justin and Diodorus come close, both basing their accounts on sources who were contemporaries of Philip. Greek sources, by contrast, mostly portray Philip negatively. In these accounts, he is regularly portrayed as aggressive, hard-drinking, combative, cowardly, dishonest, cruel, a breaker of oaths and a womanizer who occasionally had homosexual relationships with boys. These accounts of Philip's character reflect the general Greek view that Macedonians, and no less their kings, were barbarians, and are hardly credible.

Aeschines, in his report to the Athenian Assembly after returning from diplomatic negotiations with Philip in Pella in 346 BC, described a far different Philip, who was 'thoroughly Greek, an oustandingly good speaker, and very great admirer of Athens'.[27] Ctestiphon, another Greek diplomat, was equally impressed, saying 'he had never in all his long life seen so sweet and charming a man as Philip' and went on to comment on his powers of memory and ability as a speaker.[28]

Demosthenes, Philip's greatest political enemy, criticized Philip for inviting to his court 'players of mimes and composers of scurrilous songs'.[29] Athenaeus says that Philip commissioned a book of jokes for the court. In truth, Philip had a love of drama and theatre, and sponsored dramatic contests at his court. He also had a strong interest in history, poetry and philosophy, and some of the most noted intellectuals of the day spent time in residence at Philip's court. Plato's nephew, Speusippus, who ran the Academy after Plato's death, resided for a time in Pella; and Aristotle, a boyhood friend of Philip, became Alexander's tutor at Philip's request. Philip was hardly the barbarian that the Greeks portrayed him to be, and their prejudices put them at great disadvantage in dealing with him.

Philip was an intelligent, educated and experienced person, and he brought these qualities to bear upon any problem he faced. He possessed an extensive knowledge of the Greek city-states, their histories and political dynamics. He respected Athens for its history and culture, while loathing the democratic system that paralyzed its will. Philip was an affable man, easy to laugh, and always outwardly reasonable in his dealings with the representatives of the Greek states. His regard for education is evident in the liberal education he provided for his son and the sons of the Companions in the Page School at Pella, a military academy boarding school where the sons of important persons were educated along the Greek model and trained for military service.[30] There is evidence, too, that Philip may have established similar schools throughout Macedonia to educate officers for the militia and provide them with military training.[31]

By all accounts, Philip was a superb diplomat, 'charming and treacherous at the same time, the type to promise more in conversation than he would deliver, and whether the discussion was serious or light hearted, he was an artful performer'.[32] He was an excellent speaker who could sway men with his words. Justin notes that Philip 'was possessed of eloquence and a remarkable oratorical talent, full of subtlety and ingenuity, so that his elegant style was not lacking fluency, nor his fluency lacking stylistic elegance'.[33] Apparently, the man could persuade almost anyone of almost anything.

Part of Philip's persuasiveness was his ability to conceal his true intentions and feelings, even from diplomats skilled in the art of discerning the motives of their adversaries. 'Philip had greater shrewdness than Alexander and was restrained in his language and discourse … He could hide and sometimes even suppress his anger.'[34] Philip was a realist and understood that only the national interests of the

Macedonian state were the ultimate basis of diplomatic agreement, and that the personal qualities of the king, whatever they may appear to one's adversaries at the moment, were but means to that end or of no consequence at all. So, 'Philip cultivated friendships with a view toward expediency rather than genuine feelings. His usual practice was to feign warm feeling when he hated someone and to sow discord between parties that were in agreement and then try to win the favour of both.'[35] Philip took it as obvious that diplomacy was rooted in self-interest and that every man had his price. In this he was rarely disappointed. To confuse personal friendship or personality with national interests is a great mistake that political leaders still make, but one that Philip never made. 'His compassion and his duplicity were qualities he prized equally, and no means of gaining a victory would he consider dishonourable.'[36]

According to Justin, 'Philip preferred to be loved while his son, Alexander, preferred to be feared.'[37] This led Philip to prefer victory by diplomacy over victory by war. Diplomatic agreements preserve at least the illusion of the voluntary acceptance of the victor's values and even the rectitude of his cause. Philip's extraordinary diplomatic skill is evident in the fact that he achieved his most important victories in Greece by diplomacy and not force of arms. His election as *archon* of Thessaly, appointment as a member of the Amphictyonic Council – the supreme religious authority in Greece – president of the Pythian Games, commander of the Amphictyonic army in the Fourth Sacred War, *Hegemon* of the League of Corinth and as *Strategos Autokrator*, commander-in-chief of the armies of all the Council states, were great diplomatic achievements; the latter, to be sure, the result of his military success at Chaeronea.

Much of Philip's diplomatic success is traceable to his well-developed political instinct and patience, and his belief that war was only one of the many tools that the statesman brought to the game of politics. To be sure, Philip was a brilliant negotiator and beguiler, and never one to correct his adversary's false impressions of what was promised and what was not. But statesmanship requires more than intellect and skill. A statesman must have the courage and self-confidence to undertake the bold actions that his intellectual assessment of the situation demand. And Philip was nothing if he was not brave and self-confident.[38] Philip's ultimate goal was nothing less than the transformation of the semi-feudal Macedonian state into a regional superpower, a task of such magnitude that most men would have shied away from even attempting it. He succeeded admirably against all odds because he had the courage to try.

It is often overlooked that Philip was a conscientiously religious man in his respect for oaths, religious rituals, sacred shrines and worship of the gods. Philip was not only king, he was the chief priest, the religious leader of his people and sacrificed daily on their behalf. He believed fervently in his special relationship with Zeus, maintained the cult of the Temenid family and worshipped his ancestor, Herakles, the son of Zeus. Philip's religious observance had practical implications for his politics, and he regarded those who did not keep their oaths, violated shrines or took up arms against religion as blasphemers deserving of harsh punishment. In Philip's mind, reverence for the gods mattered a great deal and affected the way one conducted oneself. This said, it was a grave mistake of his adversaries to think that Philip's personal devotion could be made to influence the stronger imperatives of statecraft and national defence policy that were deeply rooted in Macedonia's strategic interests.

Taken together, Philip's character and training were well-suited to the means and ends of the tasks he set before himself. J.F.C. Fuller describes Philip in the following way:

> 'Philip was a man of outstanding character; practical, long-sighted and unscrupulous. He was a master diplomatist and an astute opportunist to whom success justified everything. He was recklessly brave, yet unlike so many brave generals he would at once set force aside should he consider that bribery or liberality or feigned friendship was likely to secure his end. He possessed in marked degree the gift of divining what was in his enemy's mind, and when beaten in the field would accept defeat and prepare for victory. Throughout his life he never lost sight of his aim – to bring the whole of Greece under his dominion. As Hogarth writes of him, "Fraud before force, but force at the least was his principle of empire".'[39]

Philip's Military Reforms

Over the course of his many campaigns, Philip designed and tested a new army radically different in structure, tactics and operational capabilities from those found elsewhere in Greece. Behind the redesign of the new army lay a clear strategic vision: Philip intended to conquer all of Greece and unite it under Macedonian suzerainty. With that accomplished, he intended to use the manpower and other resources of a united Greece to attack Persia. To achieve this required a new type of military machine that could succeed against both Greek and Persian methods of war. To defeat the Greeks, Philip had to find a way to deal with the heavy hoplite infantry phalanx characteristic of infantry battle in all Greek city states. Defeating the Persians, however, was a more complex problem and required the development of several military capabilities, all of which were new to the Macedonian army and to the Greek city states.

First, if Philip's army was to deploy over great distances for long periods, it needed an effective logistics system, something no Greek city state had yet developed. Greek deployments for battle tended to be short-run affairs, often with the battle ending in a single day. No Greek army could sustain itself in the field for more than a week or so. Second, an army operating far from its home base required more rapid means of reducing cities than the usual Greek method of blockade and starvation. The capability to quickly reduce cities and fortified strongpoints was particularly acute along the Ionian coast, which was dotted with scores of fortifications. If Philip could not reduce these quickly, he would never be able to advance on the interior of Persia. Third, because Persian cavalry was so strong, Philip's heavy infantry had to be able to blunt the cavalry's shock power and to hold its position on the battlefield. Fourth, mobility on the battlefield needed improvement, and Philip's cavalry had to develop tactics to counter the excellent Persian light infantry. Macedonian cavalry traditionally provided their own mounts and equipment and did not fight in units, but as individual combatants. Philip was the first to form them into integrated combat units that could fight and manoeuvre in battle. And fifth, new tactical doctrines were required if these new combat arms were to be utilized in concert. It is a testament to Philip's excellent tactical sense that he developed solutions to all these problems.

Unlike the Greek states, which had developed excellent hoplite heavy infantry, Macedonia had no tradition of infantry combat. Macedonian infantry troops were little more than untrained peasants hastily assembled for the occasion and armed mostly with farm implements and work tools.

Philip immediately set about transforming the Macedonian infantry. First, he required one in every ten able-bodied men to serve in the army under a system of regular pay and training. This transformed the Macedonian infantry and the entire army from a hodgepodge militia into a standing regular army, complete with benefits for the disabled in battle and a retirement system to care for old soldiers. Philip had to find a way to take an assembly of peasants with little or no military expertise, and equip and train them quickly in a tactical formation that could hold its own against the hoplite infantry of the Greek states. The solution was Philip's invention of the Macedonian phalanx.

Philip reconstituted the Macedonian infantry into a stronger phalanx of 4,096 men, comprising four regiments of 1,024 men each. Each regiment had four 256-man battalions. Unlike other Greek infantry formations, the new Macedonian phalanx was a self-contained fighting unit augmented by its own light infantry and cavalry units for protection and to secure the flanks as it manoeuvred. Once deployed, the phalanx itself and its constituent units were completely self-sustaining and could manoeuvre independently, permitting much greater flexibility in movement on the battlefield than had previously been possible by any Greek army. By the time of Philip's death, the Macedonian field army comprised 24,000 infantry and 3,400 cavalry.

In addition to restructuring his army, Philip invented a completely new tactical infantry formation. Philip faced the same problem as Napoleon did when the latter reformed the French army. Both needed large numbers of troops that could be fashioned quickly from raw recruits into trained soldiers. Both solved their problem by creating new infantry formations that were simple to assemble and control and required only limited training on the recruits' part to be used effectively on the battlefield. Napoleon's marching column and Philip's new phalanx were different solutions to the same problem.

The original Macedonian phalanx deployed in ten files, each ten men deep, a simple square that made it possible to train troops quickly in simple tactical formations and manoeuvres. As the troops gained experience, the phalanx increased to sixteen men deep, twice the depth of the Greek hoplite phalanx, and was capable of a number of sophisticated battle drills and tactical formations, including the hollow wedge to drive through Greek hoplite infantry lines. The Macedonian infantryman now carried a new weapon, the *sarissa*, a 13–21ft pike made of cornel wood with a blade at one end and a butt plate on the other to lend it balance. The *sarissa* weighed about 12lb and provided a much greater reach than the traditional *doru*, a 7ft hoplite infantry spear, permitting the phalanx to hold hoplite formations at bay and affording Macedonian infantry the advantage of always landing the first blow. The *sarissa* could be disassembled and carried with a strap across the soldier's back.

Macedonian infantrymen wore the standard Greek helmet and leg greaves, but no body armour. Each carried an *aspis*, a 30ft diameter, round, bronze-covered wood shield, secured to the body by a shoulder strap. This freed both hands to wield the *sarissa* with great force, enabling Macedonian infantrymen to easily pierce the armour and shields of Greek hoplites. Philip called his infantry *pezhetairoi* or 'foot companions', endowing the infantry with prestige traditionally reserved for the Companions, the elite cavalry warriors of the Macedonian king.

Philip's new infantry formations were based on radically new concepts of tactical employment. Unlike in traditional Greek armies, the Macedonian infantry was not intended to be the primary killing arm. Its purpose was to anchor the line and act as a platform of manoeuvre for the striking power of the heavy cavalry. By holding the hoplite phalanx at bay with its mass and longer spears, the Macedonian phalanx immobilized the hoplite formation until Macedonian cavalry could strike it in the flank or rear. But the new phalanx could also be used offensively; when formed as either a solid or hollow wedge, the weight and force of the phalanx could easily drive through a hoplite infantry line, opening a gap through which the cavalry could rush and strike the enemy's rear.

The Macedonian phalanx did not usually deploy at the leading edge of the line, but was held back obliquely. The cavalry usually deployed in strength on the flank, connected to the infantry centre by a 'hinge' of heavy elite infantry called *hypaspists*, armed either in traditional hoplite fashion or with the *sarissa*, depending upon the circumstances and type of infantry they faced. The new tactical concept called for the army to engage the enemy not at the front, but from the flank or at an oblique angle, forcing him to turn toward the attack. As the cavalry pressed the flank, the slower infantry held back obliquely, advancing toward the enemy centre in hedgehog fashion, sharp spears bristling outward. If the enemy flank broke, the cavalry could either envelop or press the attack as the infantry closed, using the phalanx as an anvil against which to hammer the hoplites. If the enemy flank held, it still had to deal with the impact of the massive phalanx falling upon its front. Philip's innovative new formations, and their new methods of tactical employment, produced the most powerful and tactically sophisticated infantry force ever known in Greece.

Macedonians were cavalry warriors by nature and culture, and were the best horsemen in Greece. Philip took this raw material, organized it into squadrons where it once fought as individuals, standardized its weapons instead of individuals using their own, centralized the breeding and training of its mounts and trained it to fight in a number of combat formations,[40] the most effective of which was the wedge. He thus produced the best cavalry in Greece. Most importantly, Philip harnessed the natural Macedonian cavalryman's ferocity for war to new tactics designed to engage Greek infantry at close quarters to break through or shatter their once-impenetrable infantry phalanx. Employing his cavalry in conjunction with his pike infantry acting as a platform of manoeuvre, Philip revolutionized Greek warfare by transforming cavalry from an adjunct force on the battlefield into the combat arm of decision. Philip's greatest contribution to Greek cavalry warfare was to organize and train his mounted units to do what no Greek cavalry had done before, to attack Greek hoplite infantry and destroy them in close combat. Until Philip demonstrated the ability of his cavalry to effectively attack infantry, Greek cavalry had played a limited role on the battlefield. Philip was the first Western commander to use his cavalry as his combat arm of decision.

The primary weapons of the Macedonian cavalryman were the *xyston* and the *machaira*, the lance and the sabre.[41] It is likely that the Macedonians used their own word for lance, *sarissa*, and this has led to some confusion that the cavalry may have carried the same *sarissa* used by the infantry.[42] The *xyston* is also to be distinguished from the *dory*, the 7ft ash spear used by hoplite infantry, and should not be confused with another cavalry weapon, the *palton* or javelin. The Macedonian cavalry lance was 9–10ft long and fashioned of cornel wood, 'light and tough, with counter-balancing butt and a tip of metal, which he [the cavalryman] wielded with one arm'.[43] The weapon was about 1½ in around and weighed 4lb. Light and thin, the lance could be grasped two-thirds of the way back from its point for thrusting, providing the cavalryman with a much longer reach than that afforded the hoplite by his much shorter *dory* spear.

The Macedonian cavalryman also carried a murderous meat cleaver called the *machaira* as his principal close-combat weapon. The *machaira* was about 25in long and weighed 2lb. Its 2½in wide single-edged blade was 18in in length and curved backward. The weight of the weapon was out at its tip, making it an excellent chopping sword but ineffective for stabbing or slashing. When the weapon was swung, the weight was carried toward the tip, where it would do the most damage as it drove the cutting edge deeply into the target. This was especially true when gravity was added to the driving force, as when wielded by a cavalryman on his mount in a powerful downward chopping blow directed at the hoplite below him. Arrian records that at the Granicus, Cleitus saved Alexander's life by striking a cavalryman about to attack Alexander from behind. The force of Cleitus's downward blow was so great that it completely severed the attacker's arm at the shoulder.[44]

Organized into squadrons of 120, 200 or 300 horse, depending upon the mission, Philip's cavalry typically attacked in wedge formation, the narrow end forward, a tactic he copied from the Thracians and Scythians. The ratio of cavalry to infantry in Phillip's new army was one to six, twice that of the Persians and the largest cavalry-to-infantry force ratio of any army in antiquity. Arrian (AD 117–138) tells us that 'in imitation of the Thracians, Philip had trained his cavalry to deploy in a wedge formation since the front tapering into a point made it possible easily to cut through every hostile formation'.[45] Arrian was himself a Roman cavalry officer and the only one of our sources on Philip who had actual cavalry experience in combat. As such, he deserves to be taken seriously when he suggests that cavalry could penetrate Greek infantry formations.[46] Whereas Greek cavalry usually deployed in a square to launch successive waves of javelins from a safe distance or use their weight to block manoeuvre on the infantry's flank, both of which were accomplished without engaging infantry in close combat, Philip's wedge formation was specifically designed to close with infantry, break it apart and exploit the breach by attacking through it. Philip brought about a revolution in cavalry tactics because he envisioned a new tactical role for his cavalry, one heretofore thought impossible.

Philip's cavalry was particularly deadly in the pursuit. Once an enemy infantry line had been pierced, Macedonian cavalry could carry out lethal assaults upon the scattered enemy infantry. If the infantry could be forced into flight rather than dying where it stood, Philip's cavalry engaged in prolonged and lethal pursuit, killing as many men as possible. Unlike Greek cavalry, which abandoned their formations and pursued as individual combatants, Macedonian cavalry retained their formations to avoid losses and to present a preponderance of combat power against groups of remnant infantry.[47] In one battle, Philip's cavalry killed 7,000 men out of a force of 10,500 troops. In another, the Macedonian cavalry killed 6,000 Phocians in a single day. Philip employed the lethal pursuit for political as well as military purposes. Many of the armies and tribes Philip fought were warrior societies whose aristocracies and rulers fought as cavalry. The lethal Macedonian cavalry pursuit aimed at killing as many of these leaders as possible.

Macedonian horses were larger and stronger than those found elsewhere in Greece; they were superior to those used by Greek cavalry in endurance and strength because Macedonian horses enjoyed better nutrition. They were typically raised on stud farms, where their forage diet was supplemented with grain. Macedonians valued horses highly, and took great care to see to their health and training, unlike Greeks.[48] It was likely that superior nutrition and care gave the Macedonian horse a somewhat larger size and, more importantly for war, greater strength and endurance. The Macedonian love of horses also assured that Macedonian cavalrymen chose their mounts carefully to ensure that the animal had the proper spirit for combat. Each mount was chosen for its suitability for battle, unlike the cavalry armies of later periods where mounts were issued en masse with little regard for the animals' suitability for war. A typical Macedonian cavalry mount stood between 14 and 15 hands, or 58–62in, at the withers (where the neck meets the body of the animal), and weighed between 950–1,100lb. It was not the quality of the horse that made the Macedonian cavalry so deadly so much as its training, enhanced by the weapons, tactics and ferocity of its rider.[49]

Another area in which Philip's brilliant military mind surpassed those of his contemporaries was logistics. Greek armies were designed to sally forth from their cities, travel short distances to the battlefield – its location often agreed upon in advance – engage in a single battle and return home to their cities, where their militia armies were disbanded until the next time they were needed. Greek armies had very limited logistic capabilities, and could neither remain in the field for very long nor support themselves over long marches. Greek armies were accompanied by hordes of attendants, women, slaves, sutlers and other hangers-on, to the point where the number of attendants often exceeded the number of combatants, all of which had to be fed. The use of ox-carts and wagons slowed movement further. The lack of a sufficient logistics system made Greek armies incapable of sustained field operations over long distances, rendering them useless as instruments of strategic warfare. For Philip, however, war was all about gaining strategic objectives, and he set about creating a completely new logistics system that could support his army over long distances for long periods.[50]

Philip's solution to the problem set the example for all future Western armies. He prohibited the traditional Greek practice of allowing each soldier to bring an attendant on military campaign, allowing just one attendant for every ten infantrymen and one for every four cavalrymen. This transformed the attendants into a logistics corps that served the whole army. Philip also forbade soldiers from bringing wives and other women, reducing the size of the non-combatant contingent. He also outlawed the use of drawn carts, except for those few designated as ambulances to transport the wounded. Carts were also permitted to transport siege machinery. Horses and mules replaced oxen as pack animals, both having greater range, load-carrying capability and rate of march. The effect on speed and mobility was remarkable, increasing the army's rate of movement to 13 miles a day, with cavalry units covering 40 miles from sunrise to sunset. Without the carts, however, the Macedonian soldier became a beast of burden, carrying ten days' ration, 30lb of grain and another 40lb of equipment and weapons. These reforms enabled Philip to reduce the number of pack animals in his army by 6,000, creating the fastest, lightest, most mobile army the West had ever seen.

The strategic range of Philip's army was greater than any force in Greek history. In a single day, Philip's column could usually cover 15 miles, and 20 miles on a forced march, even accounting for stops to rest the pack animals and horses for 10 minutes every hour, and 30 minutes every 3 hours, during which the animals' packs were removed to rest their backs. The cavalrymen walked alongside their mounts. At a rate of march of 15 miles a day, with a twenty-five day supply of food, Philip's army could cover 300 miles before it had to replenish its supplies, and still have a five-day reserve of food for men and animals.

The operational implications of Philip's logistical reforms were staggering. In a ten-day march, the Macedonian army could easily cover 150 miles. Once within the theatre of operations, Philip's army could sustain itself for another two weeks on its own supplies or, if required, continue the march. To the east, the distance from Pella to the Nestus River in Thrace was also within a ten-day march. From Philippi to Byzantium (240 miles) or north to Scythia (200 miles) was longer, but still within the army's strategic range. Staging from Philippi, he could reach the Triballi and Getae within ten days' march. When Philip moved south against Athens, he staged from Pherae in Thessaly, bringing all the Peloponnese and Athens itself within a ten-day march. As the Macedonian sphere of influence increased in all directions, Philip established forts and towns at key locations, which he turned into supply depots for future use. This permitted his army to move along interior lines of communication and supply to the farthest stretches of the empire with adequate logistical support. Philip could increase the size

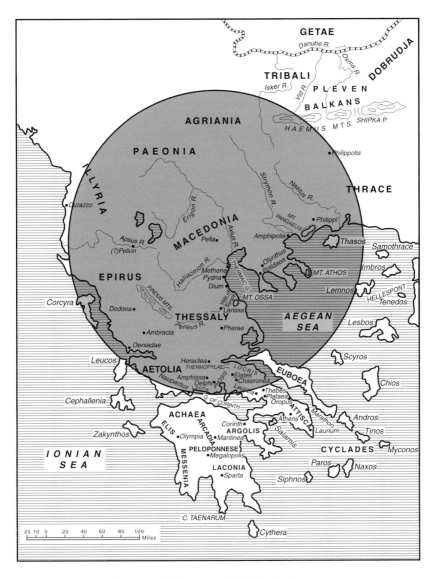

Strategic Range of Philip's Army

of his army by absorbing the militia units in these forts and towns as he marched toward his objective.

But even a mobile army risked ruin in enemy territory if it could not quickly subdue walled garrisons and cities. Philip was the first general in Greece to create a department of military engineering in his army and make siege operations an integral part of his tactical repertoire.

It was likely Macedonian engineers who developed the prototype of the torsion catapult capable of battering down walls. Philip could now control the tempo and direction of warfare on a strategic *and* tactical level. These innovations spelled the end of the Greek city-state as the dominant actor on the Greek military stage. The future belonged to the national territorial state Philip had created in Macedonia.

By 356 B C, Philip was in a position to begin his wars of conquest against the Greek city-states. For the next twenty years, he engaged in war, diplomacy, intrigue, treachery, bribery and assassination to bring the various city-states under Macedonian control. During this period, he conducted twenty-nine military operations and eleven sieges, and captured forty-four cities. By 339 BC, it was clear to all that Philip intended to be master of all Greece.

The Battle of Chaeronea (4 August 338 BC)

In September 339 BC, Philip occupied Elateia, a key junction on the main road running south through Thebes to Athens. Thebes, though a traditional enemy of Athens and technically Philip's ally, recognized that the only way to avoid incorporation into Philip's Macedonian Empire was to form a military alliance with Athens and resist Philip with force. The Athenian army marched into Boeotia, linked up with the Theban army and took up positions in the northwest passes. Their disposition effectively blocked both of Philip's routes of advance – the first along the road from Elateia to Athens, the second across the Corinthian Gulf at Naupactus, its narrowest point. Philip's route south was blocked for almost nine months.

In the summer of 338 BC, Philip began probing allied defences around the passes between Thebes and Athens, trying to lure his enemy into battle. In August, Philip arranged for the capture of a bogus dispatch by the force guarding Amphissa. The false orders within instructed Philip to break contact and return to Macedonia to quell a Thracian rebellion. Chares, the enemy commander, took the bait and dropped his guard. Philip sent a mixed infantry, cavalry and hoplite force in a lightning night attack that caught Chares by surprise and annihilated the garrison in its tents. By dawn, Philip's army was pouring through the pass in force, capturing Delphi and Amphissa and outflanking the allied defence. Their position no longer tenable, the allied armies abandoned the passes, took up positions on the nearby plain of Chaeronea and awaited Philip's attack.

The next morning, the armies assembled for battle in two lines facing each other in traditional Greek form. The allied force comprised 35,000 infantrymen facing 24,000 of Philip's Macedonians, 11,000 allied light infantry and 2,000 cavalry deployed on Philip's left under the command of Antipater and Parmenio, Philip's most trusted and experienced generals. Under his personal command, Philip signalled the Guards Brigade of infantry on his right to launch the attack. In slow, methodical step, the bristling phalanx of spears and men advanced toward the Athenian left. As the Macedonian right advanced, Philip's centre and left held their positions. Within a few minutes, the advance of the Macedonian right had created an oblique deployment along the line. The Macedonian advance had almost reached the Athenian front rank when it stopped dead.

The Athenian commander, Stratocles, ordered his infantry into the attack. But as the Athenians advanced, Philip's infantry withdrew. The hedgehog of spears kept the Athenians at bay as the Macedonians slowly backed away from the advancing hoplites. The discipline of Philip's troops was superb as they slowly gave ground without losing formation, their right flank protected by light infantry and rough terrain. For more than 30 minutes, the two phalanxes confronted each other, the Macedonians drawing the Athenians farther and farther from the centre of their own line. The Macedonian withdrawal then halted against a stream prophetically named Blood River. There Philip sprang his trap.

The Athenians increased their pressure on the Macedonians and a fierce infantry battle ensued. The backward oblique movement of the Macedonian line had forced the Greek line to follow suit, assuming an oblique angle that spread to its right. It is unclear what happened next. Either the allied line stretched and broke, leaving a gap between the Theban Sacred Band anchoring the Greek right and the Athenian centre, or, as Arrian suggests, Philip's cavalry attacked the enemy infantry line, cut through it and created its own opening. If Diodorus is correct, it marked the first time in Greek history that a cavalry attack had broken a line of hoplite infantry.

Philip now ordered his infantry to attack. The Macedonians advanced all along the line, driving the Athenian left before them at the same time as Philip's cavalry rushed through the gap and fell upon the Greek rear and centre. Caught between Philip's infantry and cavalry, the Athenian line collapsed. The rest of the Macedonian infantry then struck the allied centre, pressing the terrified soldiers against each other until they could not move. The Athenians were forced into a

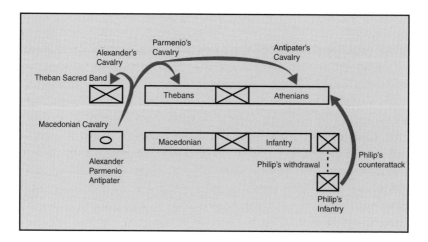

Battle of Chaeronea

cul-de-sac in which 1,000 were slain and another 2,000 captured. Other Greek contingents suffered even heavier casualties. On the allied right, the Sacred Band was surrounded by Philip's cavalry and killed to a man.[51]

In October 338 BC, following his victory over the allied Greeks, Philip summoned the Greek city-states to a peace conference at Corinth, presiding over what would become his greatest achievement – legalizing Macedonia's hegemony over all Greece. He proposed the League of Corinth, a defensive alliance in perpetuity among the Greek city-states and Macedonia. Philip was appointed *hegemon* of the league's joint military forces, whose mission was to ensure the security of Greece. Philip was also to be the *strategos autokrator*, or supreme commander-in-chief of all Macedonian and league forces in the field. One by one, the city-states ratified the agreement. Thus Philip united Greece in a single military-political federation for the first time in its history.

The Macedonian Empire At Philip's Death

In the summer of 337 BC, Philip placed before the league's council his plan for a war with Persia. The proposal was carried, and in the spring of 336 BC, Philip sent 10,000 troops across the Hellespont to establish a beachhead in Ionia and provoke succession of the Asiatic Greek states from Persian control. Philip was to follow with the main body of league's army in the autumn. Before he could embark, he was assassinated by Pausanias, one of his own bodyguard. Thus ended the life of the greatest strategist, tactician, diplomat, statesman and general of his age.

Philip was the strongest of the few strong men who had appeared on the stage of Greek history since the end of the Peloponnesian War, and his death marked the passing of the classical age of Greek history and warfare and the beginning of the imperial age. Although the latter is marked by the victories of Alexander and the rule of the three empires that followed his death, the debt owed Philip is very great indeed. It was Philip, after all, who dared to dream of a united Greece despite four centuries of failed efforts by Athens, Thebes and Sparta to achieve it. To Philip belongs the title of the first great general in the new age of Western warfare, an age he fathered by introducing new instruments of war and the tactical doctrines to make them succeed. As a statesman, he had no equal in his time. Philip's military and political achievements were the strategic and tactical foundations and means for Alexander's war of Persian conquest. As a practitioner of the political art, Philip had no equal. Even Nicollo Machiavelli might have smiled at Philip's ability to gain his ends by diplomacy as well as force. There were few minds more facile than Philip's, then or since, in the art of *realpolitik*. In all these things, he was greater than Alexander. The son became the romantic hero, but the father was the great national king.

Notes

Original Sources

In drawing upon the original source materials relevant to Philip II, I have relied upon the following works. They are listed here to avoid cluttering up the manuscript throughout. Whenever the author's name appears in the notes, the reference is to the source for that author as it appears below.

Aeschines: *The Speeches of Aeschines*, trans. Charles Darwin Adams (Whitefish, WI, Kessinger Publishers, 2007).

Arrian: *The Anabasis of Alexander*, trans. P.A. Brunt and E. Cliff Robson (Loeb Classics Library, 1983).

Demosthenes: *Demosthenes Orations* 7 vols., trans. H. Vince, (Cambridge, MA, Loeb Classical Library, 1930).

Diodorus: *Diodorus Siculus: The Reign of Philip II, The Greek and Macedonian Narrative From Book XVI*, trans. E.I. McQueen (London, Bristol Classical Press,1995).

Justin: Marcus Junianus Justinus, *Epitome of the Philippic History of Pompeius Togus*, trans. John Shelby Watson (London, Henry G. Bohn Press, 1853).

Pausanias: *The Complete Collection of Pausanias in Four Volumes*, trans. W.H.S. Jones (Cambridge, MA, Harvard University Press, 1966).

Polyaenus: *Strategies of War* (Chicago, Ares Publishers, 1994).

Quintius Curtis Rufus: *History of Alexander*, trans. John Yardles (London, Penguin, 1984).

Sextus Julius Frontinus: *Strategemata* (Lucus-Curtus website, 2007).

Theopompus and Philochorus: F. Jacoby, *Die Fragmente der Griechischen Historiker* (Berlin/Leiden, 1926).

Modern Sources

1. N.G.L. Hammond, *The Macedonian State: Origins, Institutions, and History* (Oxford, UK, Clarendon Press, 1989), pp.49–50.

2. E.A. Frederiksmeyer, 'Alexander and Philip: Emulation and Resentment', *Classical Journal* 85 no. 4 (April–May 1990), p.305.

3. Richard A. Gabriel, *The Great Captains of Antiquity* (Westport, CT, Greenwood Press, 2004), p.81.

4. Richard A. Gabriel, 'Philip of Macedon', in *The Great Captains of Antiquity* (Westport, CT, Greenwood Press, 2004), pp.83–110.

5. Peter Green, *Alexander of Macedon: A Historical Biography* (Berkeley, CA, University of California Press, 1991), p.16.

6. F.E. Adcock, *The Greek and Macedonian Art of War* (Berkeley, CA, University of California Press, 1957), pp.24–25.

7. Richard A. Gabriel, 'The Genius of Philip II', *Military History* (February–March 2009), pp.41–43.

8. N.G.L. Hammond, *Philip of Macedon* (Baltimore, Johns Hopkins Press,1994), p.9.

9. Ibid., p. 18. It is, however, by no means certain that this was the case.

10. I have accepted Hammond's argument that the most trustworthy accounts of Philip's life are to be found in Daters (*ca.* 30–50 BC) and Justin (AD 150), whose accounts can be traced to four historians whose lives were contemporary with Philip's. These source historians are Ephorus, Theopompus, Marsyas Macedon of Pella and Demophilus, son of Ephorus. For further analysis of these sources, see Hammond, *Philip of Macedon*, p.15.

11. Justin, 6.1.2. The selection of an infant king was not unknown in Macedonia. In one instance, the infant was brought to the battlefield in his cradle.

12. Justin, 7.5.9.

13. Ian Worthington, *Philip of Macedon* (New Haven, CT, Yale University Press, 2008), p.27. See also J.R. Ellis, 'The Stepbrothers of Philip II', *Historia* 22 (1973), pp.350–54.

14. J.R. Ellis, 'Macedonia Under Philip', in Miltiades Hatzopoulous and Louisa D. Loukipoulos (eds), *Philip of Macedon* (Athens, Ekdotike Athenon, 1980), p.146.

15. This anecdote is taken from Quintius Curtius Rufus, *History of Alexander*, translated by John Yardles (London, Penguin Classics, 1984), 5.2.18–20.

16. Ellis, 'Macedonia Under Philip', p.146

17. Hammond, *The Macedonian State*, p.69.

18. Polyaenus, *Stratagems of War*, vol. 1 (Chicago, Ares Publishers, 1994), 4.2.6.

19. Green, *Alexander of Macedon*, 2; see A. Aymard, 'Le protocole royale grec et son evolution', *Revue de Etudes Ancienne* 50 (1948), pp.232–63.

20. Frederiksmeyer, p.304.

21. Polyaenus, 4.2.9.

22. George Cawkwell, *Philip of Macedon* (London, Faber and Faber, 1978), p.51.

23. Ibid., p.115, citing Didymus Chalcenterus.

24. Didymus, 18.67.

25. Alice Swift Riginos, 'The Wounding of Philip II of Macedon: Fact and Fabrication', *Journal of Hellenic Studies* 114 (1994), p.115, citing Didymus as translated by Seneca; see also Cawkwell, p.114 citing Didymus 18.67 and Didymus col. 12.63ff.

26. Riginos, p.117.

27. Even with modern splints, a tibia/fibula fracture usually takes at least a year to heal completely.

28. Cawkwell, p.50.

29. Hammond, *Philip of Macedon*, p.185. It should be noted, however, that both Aeschines and Ctesiphon were both pro-Macedonian, oligarchically -minded politicians.

30. Ibid., p.175

31. Cawkwell, pp.55–56 for Alexander's education.

32. Hammond, *Philip of Macedon*, p.187.

33. Justin, 8.4.7.

34. Justin, Book 8.

35. Justin, as quoted in Worthington, p.195.

36. Ibid.

37. Ibid.

38. Ibid., p.38.

39. Pierre Leveque, 'Philip's Personality', in Hatzopoulos and Loukopoulos (eds), pp.176–78.

40. J.F.C. Fuller, *The Generalship of Alexander the Great* (New York, Da Capo Press, 1989), p.24.

41. Other Macedonian cavalry formations were the square, diamond and the rhomboid formations. The wedge was the most effective for penetrating an infantry line.

42. N.G.L. Hammond, *Alexander the Great: King, Commander, and Statesman.* (Princeton, NJ, Princeton University Press, 1980), p.31, which says that Philip may have invented the *xyston* for use by his cavalry. It is true that Philip standardized the use of the weapon for his cavalry, but in all likelihood the spear itself was used for centuries for hunting on horseback, as a number of hunting scenes from tombs suggest.

43. See Minor M. Markle, 'The Macedonian Sarissa, Spear, and Related Armor,' *American Journal of Archaeology* 81 no. 3 (summer 1977), pp.323–39.

44. Hammond, *Alexander the Great*, p.31.

45. Arrian, *Anabasis*, 1.5.8.

46. Markle, 'Macedonian Sarissa, Spear, and Related Armor', p.339, citing Arrian's *The Tactical Art* 16.7ff.

47. Edmund S. Burke, 'Philip and Alexander the Great', *Military Affairs* 47 no. 2 (April 1983), p.69.

48. Hammond, *The Macedonian State*, p.130.

49. Xenophon makes a point of emphasizing that horses must be well-cared for and often were not in Greece. Xenophon, *The Cavalry Commander*, trans. G.W. Bowersock (Cambridge, MA, Harvard University Press, 1968), 1.4.8.

50. The most recent works on Cavalry in Greece are Robert E. Gaebel, *Cavalry Operations in the Ancient Greek World* (Norman, OK, Oklahoma University Press, 2002); I.G. Spence, *The Cavalry of Classical Greece* (UK, Oxford University Press, 1993); L.J. Worley, *Hippeis: The Cavalry of Ancient Greece* (Boulder, CO, Westview Press, 1994); and G.R. Bugh, *The Horsemen of Athens* (Princeton, NJ, Princeton University Press, 1988).

51. The account of the Battle of Chaeronea is draw from my earlier work, *Philip of Macedonia: Greater Than Alexander* (Dulles, VA, Potomac Books, 2010), pp.214–22.

CHAPTER SIX

SCIPIO AFRICANUS
(236–183 BC)

Publius Cornelius Scipio was born in Rome in 236/235 BC, 517 years after the founding of the city, a scion of the Cornelii family, one of the five great families of Rome. The Cornelii were of Etruscan stock and one of the oldest of Roman families.[1] In a practice not uncommon in Rome, Scipio was given the same name as his father, Publius Cornelius. It was only after his great victories in Africa that it became common among Romans and later historians to refer to Scipio as Africanus. The Scipiones had played an important role in Roman politics for more than a century before Publius was born. Publius' father, P. Cornelius Scipio, was elected consul in 218 BC to deal with the threat of Hannibal's invasion of Italy. It was Scipio's father and uncle, Gnaeus, who led a Roman army into Spain to attack Hannibal's line of communication. As the oldest of the younger generation of such an illustrious family, surely much was expected of young Publius.

Except for a few images on Roman coins and signet rings, no certain physical portrayal of Scipio has survived.[2] The absence of any comment in the ancient sources regarding his physical appearance might reasonably suggest that he was probably a typical Roman and not in any physical way remarkable. If so, we could expect that he was of average height for a Roman of his day, between 5ft 5in and 5ft 8in in height, and probably of the stocky muscular build common to Romans then. Likenesses of Scipio on coins show his hair cut long as a young man, in Greek fashion.[3] Later, he is portrayed as bald, but with a thick ring of hair running around his neck and ears. His facial features, marked by a high forehead, thick eyebrows and deep set-eyes protected by prominent ridges and high cheekbones, create the appearance of strength and determination. There is a seriousness in his face that reveals a man confident in himself. His nose is large and prominent, beneath which is a spacious ridge of flesh leading to thickly prominent lips and a forceful mouth. The *Punica* says that Scipio 'had a martial brow and flowing hair; nor was the hair at the back of his head shorter. His eyes burned bright, but their regard was mild; and those who looked upon him were at once awed and pleased.'[4] If character is reflected in a man's face, Scipio's features suggest that most Roman of virtues, *gravitas*, or seriousness of purpose.

For all the features suggesting strength, Scipio may have been in chronic ill-health from childhood, and serious ailments sometimes afflicted him on campaign. This said, however, Scipio appears to have generally been capable of performing physically on the battlefield. At New Carthage, he personally led the assault on the city gate, and at the Battle of Baecula, he led the Roman left wing up a steep incline to attack the Carthaginian flank. Given Scipio's sensitivity to the effect that even his minor actions might have on troop morale, it is likely that he hid his ailments from his officers and men in all but the most pressing of circumstances.

Upper-class Romans of Scipio's day were taking greater cognizance of the outside world, and Greek practices and values had begun to penetrate Roman society. One aspect of this was education, which some aristocratic families saw as superior to traditional Roman education.[5] Education of the upper classes was accomplished by hired Greek tutors, who taught a curriculum including philosophy (logic, ethics, cosmology), science (astronomy, geometry, mathematics and biological curiosities), literature (including the study of Greek military heroes), physical education in the gymnasiums and the Greek language.[6] The Greek method provided a much broader, empirical and intellectually challenging education than the traditional Roman method, with its emphasis upon tradition, law, ritual and physical military prowess. It was likely to have equipped Scipio with a much more empirical and rationally oriented mind, capable of adapting to new ideas and situations, a mind quick to solve problems and one that encouraged him to have confidence in his own thinking.[7]

Many of history's generals were religious men, and Scipio seems to have been religious in that typical Roman way of asking the gods for help. Religious faith need not prohibit one from being a good soldier or commander.[8] If Scipio's soldiers thought him religiously observant and that he was likely to earn the favour of the gods, he would have been foolish not to encourage this belief. Perhaps it was that his soldiers thought him not only competent but lucky as well. No less a general than Napoleon believed strongly in luck, and once opined that he preferred lucky generals to merely competent ones. Cicero remarked that luck was an essential quality of a successful general. Soldiers everywhere have always believed in luck, and the Roman soldier no less so in *Fortuna*. That Scipio, too, may have done so is hardly surprising.

Polybius' assessment of Scipio's character seems sound when he says, 'It is generally agreed that Scipio was beneficent and magnanimous, but that he was also shrewd and discreet with a mind always concentrated on the object he had in view.'[9] In other words, Scipio possessed a disciplined mind focussed upon the objective. Polybius says Scipio's two finest qualities, those 'most worthy of respect, were cleverness and laboriousness'.[10] These are, of course, typical Roman virtues, and Polybius may have stressed them to counter charges that Scipio was 'too Greek'. It is, perhaps, also revealing that Polybius says that 'no one will admit' that Scipio possessed these qualities 'except those who have lived with him and contemplated his character, so to speak, in broad daylight'.[11] It suggests a man who may have cultivated a public persona somewhat different from the private self that he revealed only to his closest friends. Being placed in command of an army at such a young age may have required Scipio to cultivate a somewhat sterner and more military image than was natural to his own personality.[12]

Scipio was highly regarded by his troops, perhaps because, as Livy says, 'he understood men sympathetically'. The regard of fighting men for their commander, who, after all, is the man who places them in harm's way, is not easily earned, for battle has an uncanny way of turning the best intentions and plans of commanders to ruin. Scipio was always among his soldiers, checking on their quarters, seeing to their rations and being generous with pay and booty.[13] He dispensed justice fairly, as when he put down a mutiny among his troops who had not been paid, taking care to execute the leaders and pardoning the rest, after asking in sorrow 'shouldn't you have come and talked to me about it?'.[14] Scipio seems not to have possessed the brutal streak so often found among ancient military men. But he could be brutal when it served his military objectives, as when he ordered the slaughter of the civilian population of New Carthage until the enemy commander saw the futility of further resistance and surrendered. To his men, Scipio never appeared petty or jealous. He praised his officers for their actions in front of their men. When Scipio assumed command in Spain, he assembled his army and publicly praised the heroic Marcius, the commander he was replacing. He always justified his orders to his troops on the grounds of their duty and service to Rome, and never to himself. If Scipio fought for personal glory instead of for Rome's, he was at least wise enough to conceal it. He seems to have learned the lesson of all successful commanders, that no soldier will die willingly for his commander's career.

Scipio possessed a strongly empirical intellect that searched for and made connections between means and ends. There was always a plan to be followed, but prior assumptions were never permitted to degenerate into rigidity. The plan itself was usually innovative in concept and always inextricably linked to specific means for execution. Scipio was a brilliant tactical thinker, a problem-solver of the first order, and he never relied upon hope as a method. If at times the means to achieve the objective did not exist, Scipio invented them, as when he revolutionized the tactical capabilities of the legion by introducing the first significant tactical change in the Roman army in more than a century.[15] No Roman general introduced more tactical innovations to the Roman army than Scipio.

Besides a brilliant intellect, Scipio possessed great confidence in his own abilities, the character trait Livy stressed above all others. Confidence in one's self to the point of recklessness was not something Romans of Scipio's day would have regarded as a virtue, for it would have seemed to them untraditional and risky. It was Scipio's confidence in himself that led some of his enemies to claim he was high-handed and conceited.[16] Whatever else, Scipio was a confident commander who, as Napoleon's maxim goes, 'never took counsel of his own fears', or if he did, he took pains to hide it from all those around him. Many of Scipio's personality traits – confidence, brashness, a sense of being lucky, faith in one's own thinking, etc. – are, of course, the traits of a young man. He was only 26 when he took command of the Roman armies in Spain, the same age as when Hannibal took charge of the Carthaginian armies. It is difficult not to imagine that it might have been their youth that made both Scipio and Hannibal such daring commanders.

Baptism of Fire

As it had been for centuries before, the Roman army of Scipio's day was a militia army comprised of property-owning citizens called to arms when needed. There was no formal system of military training. Fathers and uncles trained their sons in military skills and provided them with weapons and armour. Assignment to the various military branches (infantry, cavalry and navy) was done on the basis of wealth. The wealthy usually served in the cavalry, and Scipio was trained as a cavalryman. Once the legion was called to assemble, new recruits, including cavalry, were trained by their respective military tribunes in a conscript encampment before being deployed for war. Scipio, too, trained in this manner in his father's army before accompanying him on campaign.

Scipio's first taste of war came at the Battle of the Ticinus River, a tributary of the Po in northern Italy, in the autumn of 218 BC. That summer, Hannibal had begun his crossing of the Alps to invade Italy. The Romans sent an army under Publius Scipio, Scipio's father, to Massilia (mod. Marseille) to intercept and block Hannibal's advance. Staging from Pisa,[17] the two forces met on the banks of the Ticinus River. Taken while still in column of march, the Romans were quickly surrounded.[18] Publius Scipio was struck by a spear. Polybius records what happened next: 'He [the son] was then, as it seems, eighteen years old and on his first campaign. His father had given him a squadron of hand-picked cavalry for his protection; but when in the course of the battle he saw his father surrounded by the enemy, with only two or three horsemen near him, and dangerously wounded, he first tried to cheer on his own squadron to go to his father's assistance, but when he found them considerably cowed by the numbers of the enemy surrounding them, he appears to have plunged by himself with reckless courage into the midst of the enemy; whereupon his comrades being forced to charge also, the enemy were overawed and divided their ranks to let them pass; and Publius the elder, being thus unexpectedly saved, was the first to address his son as his preserver in the hearing of the enemy.'[19] Publius Scipio ordered that his son be awarded the *corona civica*, or civic crown, Rome's highest military decoration for bravery. Polybius tells us that young Scipio refused the award, saying, 'the action was one that rewarded itself'. There is no good reason to doubt Polybius' account of Scipio's bravery.[20]

Philip of Macedon at the Battle of Chaeronea (338 BC) was the first Western general to command his troops from nearby rather than in the thick of the fighting, a practice that Scipio later adopted.[21] Until Scipio's time, it had been Roman practice to have their generals fight in the midst of their troops, displaying personal courage and sharing the risk. During the war against Hannibal, this produced dire results. So many of Rome's experienced commanders were killed or wounded that a serious shortage of competent military leaders resulted. This forced Rome to rely upon young and sometimes untested men to command her armies.[22] Scipio himself was one of these young commanders when he received his commission to command the Roman army in Spain after the death of his father, the Roman commander there. Frontinus tells us that Scipio answered those who criticized his valour with the statement, 'My mother bore me a general, not a warrior.'[23]

Scipio seems to have been the first Roman commander whose style of command was more a 'battle manager' than the Homeric warrior general so characteristic of commanders in earlier Greek and Roman warfare. It was Scipio's command style that Caesar imitated and became the model for the imperial commanders who followed. These commanders sometimes ventured into the thick of the fighting, but were cautious about exposing their lives to the dangers of the battle-field. They spent their time much more productively, moving about the battlefield with a small bodyguard, rallying stragglers, turning back those who tried to retreat, encouraging the faint-hearted, regrouping units, leading support to threatened points and committing troops at critical moments.[24] Hannibal also employed this style of command, but Scipio seems to have been the first Roman general to do so.

We do not hear again of Scipio's military service until the Battle of Cannae, two years later. Livy tells us that Scipio was a military tribune with one of the legions that fought at Cannae.[25] There is no evidence from Livy or Polybius that Scipio fought at Trebia or Lake Trasimene. But there is no account either of Scipio's role in the Battle of Cannae itself. We are forced to imply his presence at the battle because of the events which followed at which he was present.[26] The *Punica* offers the only literary evidence that Scipio might have fought at both Trebia and Trasimene. These battles were all Roman defeats.

If Scipio had been present at these disasters and acquitted him-self reasonably well, it would go far to explaining why he did not accompany his father to Spain and, more importantly, his promotion to tribune at such a young age. Military tribunes were elected by the Popular Assembly, although later two of every six were appointed by the army commander.[27] It is possible that Scipio's reputation for bravery, and his now extensive military experience, contributed to his election as tribune. Though not yet 20, Scipio would have been one of the most combat-experienced junior officers in Rome. Scipio seems to have been engaged in active military service for six of the seven years that passed from his baptism of fire at the Ticinus River (218 BC) to the end of the siege of Capua, where he served as commander of a legion (211 BC).[28] Only in 213 BC, when he served as *aedile*, did Scipio enjoy a respite from the rigours of war. Scipio was thus probably among the most combat-hardened of all Rome's junior officers.

In 211 BC, disaster struck the Scipio family. After a series of victories that covered almost seven years of war and had successfully blocked the Carthaginians in Spain from reinforcing Hannibal in Italy, the armies of Publius and Gnaeus Scipio were betrayed by their Spanish allies and annihilated by the Carthaginians near Castulo.[29] The Roman armies fled north back across the Ebro River, where they gathered their forces and held a thin defensive line. Seven years of military effort were reversed in a single afternoon, and the Roman cause in Spain seemed lost. Fear swept Italy that the country would be invaded by the Carthaginians a second time. If the Carthaginian armies invaded Italy from the north and linked up with Hannibal in the south, Rome would be in mortal danger. Scipio was not yet 24 when he suddenly found himself at the head, the *pater familias*, of the Scipio family.

We next hear of Scipio in 210 BC, when he is given command of the Roman armies in Spain at the age of 26 to succeed his father and uncle in prosecuting the war against the Carthaginians. The appointment of such a young officer to a high-level command is remarkable. The youngest age at which a person could usually hold the power of *imperium* during the Republic was 39.[30] Scipio was appointed *privatus cum imperio*, that is, a private citizen with military powers. In this sense, he was not formally a government official. Scipio was the first private Roman citizen to be invested with the proconsular *imperium*, upon which later rested the emperor's claim to military rights and power. The appointment of Scipio thus foreshadowed the emergence of the legal basis of private military command that came later in the Empire. It is in this sense that Scipio cast a shadow across the Republic. Here was the first instance of the private military power of the *condottieri* commanders who ultimately destroyed the Republic.[31]

Why was young Scipio given such an important command? It is likely that the most important reason Scipio received the appointment was that Rome was suffering from a shortage of experienced military commanders. Rome had been at war for almost a decade, and many of the consuls and senior commanders who had taken the field had been killed, wounded or were now too old.[32] That Scipio was an experienced combat soldier, having fought in some of the most critical battles of the war, might explain why his request for command in Spain might have been taken seriously by the Senate. A long and solid record of military competence is probably what weighed most heavily in awarding Scipio the Spanish command.

The suspension of the usual consular system of annual rotation permitted some commanders to remain in place for several years at a time. The two Scipios, for example, held command in Spain for almost seven consecutive years. The usual system of annual rotation of commanders employed earlier in the war made it difficult for commanders to train their armies sufficiently before taking them into the field. Older

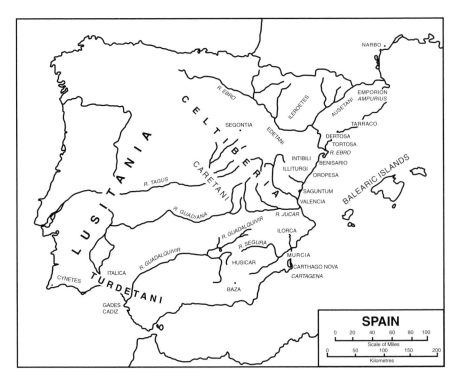

Scipio's Area of Operations in Spain

veteran commanders were often resistant to new methods and tactics, and were given to a tradition of highly aggressive, impatient and often reckless conduct of war.[33] The result was that a Roman army, regardless of who was in command, almost always fought in the same tactical manner, a shortcoming that Hannibal exploited time and again. The reforms in organization, tactics and weapons that Scipio later introduced were possible only because commanders now enjoyed longer tours of duty, during which they could fashion their armies into instruments of their will. Of the generals of the Republic, only Scipio's father held a field command for nearly as long as Scipio himself, commanding the armies in Spain from 218 until his death in battle in 211 BC. Scipio held command from 210–202 BC, the longest period for any Roman general during the Punic Wars. The longer the war went on, the more proficient the Roman armies became.

Scipio excelled in many areas of military competency: strategy, tactics, appreciation of the moral dimension of war, the use of tactical and strategic intelligence, logistics and administration, and leadership.

As a strategist, Scipio had few equals in his ability to see the application of force within a larger political context. He saw clearly that Hannibal's weakness was strategic, not tactical, and that as long as the tactically inferior Roman armies engaged Hannibal only in Italy, they were incapable of bringing about a strategic decision. Scipio understood that Hannibal's weakness was his inability to replace lost manpower to sustain his army. Hannibal's ability to recruit manpower from the rebel tribes of southern Italy, while impressive, was always insufficient to sustain his forces, with the consequence that unless he could be resupplied with manpower from Spain, his cause was ultimately lost.[34] The most that was possible under these circumstances was a stalemate. Even under these circumstances, however, Scipio saw that it was unlikely that Hannibal could be driven from Italy by military pressure alone. The key to forcing Hannibal to leave Italy was to threaten Carthage itself. When Scipio did so, Hannibal was recalled to protect the city and forced to abandon Italy. Although Liddell-Hart called Hannibal the 'father of strategy', in fact it was Scipio who was the better strategist.[35]

Scipio was also a brilliant tactical commander and very much the military reformer. He realized the weaknesses of the Roman legions and reformed their organization, tactics, weaponry and training. Under his hand, for the first time a Roman army was fashioned as an instrument of a commander's will. The militia armies under Scipio's command were more difficult to command effectively than the professional armies established later by Marius after the Roman disaster at Arausio (105 BC). Scipio's armies had to be assembled, armed and trained from the ground up before they could be taken into battle with any assurance of success. At times, Scipio formed these armies from the remnants of the armies of other commanders, as when he first assumed command in Spain. The force assembled to invade Africa was created around units that had been sent into exile because of their previously poor performance on the battlefield. Motivation in citizen militia armies is usually spotty at best, and very often poor. This must certainly have been the case with some of Scipio's troops, who were often in the field for long periods, causing them to lose their farms and civilian livelihood. Militia armies, then and now, need constant tending, and Scipio's ability to assemble, train, discipline, motivate and lead his armies required great personal command skills.

The charge made by some historians that Scipio's military experience led him to study Hannibal and to copy his tactics is untrue.

Hannibal understood that the phalanx alone was not decisive; that it needed to be supported by cavalry and light infantry to exploit the gaps made in the enemy line by the phalanx.[36] Scipio, on the other hand, understood that the strength of Roman arms lay in its heavy infantry. The problem was the legion's tactical inflexibility. To correct this deficiency, Scipio may have been most influenced by the infantry tactics of Philip of Macedon. In the same manner that Philip drilled the Macedonian phalanx in a number of tactical manoeuvres to increase its flexibility in battle, so, too, did Scipio train the legion in a number of innovative movements. Having trained the maniples to manoeuvre on command, Scipio then made them heavier by adding more troops and reforming the maniples into 600-man cohorts, making them more resistant to the shock of barbarian infantry and cavalry attack. It was Scipio who first increased the legion's ability to withstand the shock of barbarian mass attacks by increasing the legion's manpower to 6,200 men, and who was the first Roman commander to deploy some of this manpower in the form of cohorts comprised of three maniples of heavy infantry.

All ranks of the legions were now standardly equipped as heavy infantry and provided with the same armour, with the *gladius* as their basic combat weapon. Scipio had discovered the *gladius* in Spain, and was the first Roman commander to equip his troops with the new weapon. Scipio realized that the Spanish steel *falcata* was a better weapon than the Roman iron long sword, and quickly incorporated the weapon into his legions. With minor changes, the *falcata* became the Rome *gladius*, the most deadly infantry weapon in the world. Scipio's introduction of arms drill for his troops in the Spanish campaign had established the basic tactical use of the *gladius* as a stabbing weapon, and both the weapon and its manual of use were continued in the Marian legions. As a cavalry officer, Scipio knew well the weakness of Roman cavalry. Using the Spanish tribal cavalry as his model, he introduced larger and stronger horses and better training so that cavalry could be used in concert with infantry. The tactical mobility of the legion which Scipio bequeathed to his successors remained largely unchanged to the end of the Republic.

There is no more deadly defect in a military commander than to see war as an exercise in military technique. Warfare always occurs within a political, cultural and moral context, which, if ignored, can result in defeat no matter how proficient the application of military force. Scipio always saw clearly the larger political context in which he fought. He realized that the key to success in Spain was to win the allegiance of the Spanish tribes who were the major source of manpower for the Carthaginian armies. The Carthaginian commanders failed to appreciate the context of their occupation of Spain, and routinely treated the tribes harshly, taking hostages and carrying out executions. Scipio's campaign in Spain succeeded in large part because he was first able to win the Spanish to his side with fair and honourable treatment. During his North African campaign, Scipio showed the same appreciation for political and social factors by winning the allegiance of Massinissa, the chief of the Numidians, and convincing him to support Rome. Scipio achieved this by supporting Massinissa's claim to the throne against his rival and by his kind treatment of the prince's nephew, whom Scipio captured in battle and then returned unharmed. In conducting his campaigns, Scipio anticipated the maxim of von Clausewitz that 'war is always the continuation of policy by other means'.[37]

Scipio was almost alone among Roman commanders in his appreciation of the role of intelligence in war. His use of strategic and tactical intelligence 'underlines the spectacular originality of Scipio in the Republican military context'.[38] Scipio's campaigns provide the best documented use of intelligence by a Roman commander in the Second Punic War.[39] Until the last years of the war, Roman strategic and tactical intelligence capabilities remained generally poor. The state of Roman tactical intelligence was shown by the number of ambushes inflicted upon Roman armies. In a little over three years, the Carthaginians destroyed no fewer than six Roman armies by ambuscade.[40] Other Roman units were badly mauled if not destroyed completely because of tactical intelligence failures, including the army of Scipio's father and uncle at Castulo.

One cannot point to a single strategic or tactical intelligence failure during Scipio's eight years of war. It is likely that the betrayal of his father by the Spanish tribes gave Scipio an acute appreciation for strategic intelligence. Roman failures of tactical intelligence can be attributed, in part, to the fact that the legion had no permanent organic element to conduct reconnaissance, with the result that the collective effort of any given commander was haphazard at best.[41] Most Roman commanders used the *velites* or light infantry for reconnaissance missions, sometimes augmenting them with small troops of cavalry.[42] Horsemen from the *extraordinarii* were sometimes employed. Scipio appears to have been the first Roman commander to establish a permanent unit within the legion whose task it was to collect tactical intelligence in the field. This unit was assembled from one third of the cavalry normally assigned to the *extraordinarii* and one fifth of the light infantry. Together, the new unit might comprise almost 2,000 men.[43] It is not unlikely, too, that Scipio's bodyguard, the *praetoriani*, may have occasionally performed intelligence tasks.

An army, Napoleon once remarked, travels on its stomach. One of Scipio's greatest talents was as a logistician and administrator who appreciated the importance of ensuring that his army was adequately supplied. Moreover, he always oversaw logistical preparations personally. He never undertook a campaign or even a single battle without making certain his army was adequately supplied, and took great care never to sever his supply lines when engaged in extended tactical operations. Ancient historians record not a single instance of Scipio being required to change his operational plans as a consequence of a shortage of supplies. Scipio was not only a brilliant operational planner and commander, but an excellent logistician as well.

The ability of a great general can be measured to some extent by the quality of his opponents, and in this regard Scipio fought and defeated some of history's best-trained and most brilliant commanders. Commanders like Hasdrubal, Hasdrubal son of Gisco and Hannibal himself were the best field generals that Carthage produced, products of the Barcid military family dynasty, whose only occupation was war and heirs to a half-century tradition of combat experience. The armies they commanded were the products of years of training, discipline and experience, with a tactical flexibility possessed by no other armies that Roman commanders had ever faced. No Roman general after Scipio faced enemy commanders of this calibre, except, perhaps, when they fought each other during the civil wars. But here their professional armies fought in mostly identical ways so that tactical brilliance and innovation was not usually required, and none made itself evident. If one were to judge the greatness of a general by the quality of the commanders against whom he fought and triumphed, Scipio clearly stands apart as the best field commander Rome produced.

As a leader of men at war, Scipio has few equals. He led the Roman army for eight years in two major campaigns – in Spain and North Africa – fighting six major battles and numerous skirmishes, winning them all. In every one of these engagements, Scipio fought against an opponent who was much more experienced in war than he, and yet he triumphed. At Zama, he faced the most experienced and talented general of his age, Hannibal Barca, and defeated him.

The Battle of Zama

Scipio Africanus' defeat of Hannibal on the plains of North Africa was a turning point in the military history of the ancient world.[44] The Battle of Zama (202 BC) brought an end to the sixteen-year Second Punic War that had ravaged southern Italy and threatened Rome's existence. Scipio's victory also set Rome upon the path to empire. Within little more than a decade, Rome had reduced Greece to submission and pressed the Seleucid Empire back until Rome controlled the Mediterranean coast from the Hellespont to the Egyptian border. The Battle of Pydna in 168 BC put an end to what remained of Greek autonomy, and a year later, Antiochus IV acknowledged Roman suzerainty over Egypt. In 146 BC, Carthage itself was destroyed. The Mediterranean was now a Roman lake.

In 204 BC, Scipio sailed from Sicily with an invasion force of 30,000 infantry and 1,200 cavalry, and landed near Utica on the North African coast. The strategic goal of the operation was to threaten Carthage and force Hannibal to abandon Italy and come to its defence. Scipio began operations immediately, and over the next year defeated three Carthaginian armies, leaving Carthage open to attack. Hannibal was recalled and left Italy in the autumn of 203 BC, arriving at Leptis Minor (mod. Lemta). He disembarked his army and moved to Hadrumentum, where he began to assemble additional troops.

By the summer of 202 BC, Scipio was in the field, moving southwestward from his base near Utica, storming one town after another, refusing offers of surrender and selling the captured populations into slavery. He sent messages to his allied Numidian chief, Massinissa, to keep his promise and join him with an army of infantry and cavalry. Scipio knew that his attacks against the towns would force Hannibal to take the field. But he dared not face the great Carthaginian with the small number of cavalry at his disposal. Massinissa's cavalry was vital to Scipio's plan to fight Hannibal on the flat plains of North Africa.

After being urged by a delegation of the Senate, Polybius tells us that Hannibal 'moved his camp from the neighbourhood of Hadrumentum, advanced and then established himself near Zama, a town which lies about five days journey [70–80 miles] to the west of Carthage'. Being forced to leave his horses behind in Italy due to a lack of transport, Hannibal was short of cavalry. Only some of his army were veterans, the rest being newly raised recruits. Even his elephants were untrained for war. It is a fair assumption that Hannibal took his army into the field before he was ready. Hannibal had to rely upon his tribal ally, Vermina, to arrive at the battlefield with his army and large contingents of cavalry. Scipio, also short of cavalry, relied upon his tribal ally, Massinissa, to bring his army and cavalry to Zama to aid the Romans. Scipio and Hannibal were moving toward one another with the same tactical objective in mind, to link-up with their respective Numidian allies before the other to gain an advantage in cavalry. Both Massinissa and Vermina were coming from the west, and Scipio and Hannibal were moving in directions designed to shorten the distance between them and their allies. Whoever won the race would have a considerable advantage in cavalry on the flat battle plain. As events turned out, Massinissa, with his army of 6,000 light Numidian javelin infantry and 4,000 light horse, arrived in Scipio's camp. Vermina never arrived at all.

Hannibal thus found himself on an open plain confronted with an army now superior in cavalry. Why didn't Hannibal refuse battle and withdraw? Once more, the answer is cavalry. Hannibal's base was 80 miles to the rear, across open terrain. If he turned his back on Scipio and attempted to withdraw, his army would have been continually harassed by Scipio's cavalry, with deadly effect over a march of five days. Hannibal's army would have been cut to pieces by the time it reached Hadrumentum. Hannibal stood his ground at Zama despite the unfavourable circumstances in which he found himself because he had no choice.

Scipio's army comprised some 30,000 infantry and 6,000 cavalry, while Hannibal's army contained some 40,000 infantry, 15,000 of which were professional, battle-hardened veterans of the Italian campaigns, with 12,000 being mercenaries. The remainder, some 10,000 troops, were recent, untested levies from among the citizens of Carthage. Hannibal's cavalry strength was 3,000, or about half that available to Scipio, and perhaps twenty elephants. Hannibal's challenge was how to weave these disparate elements into a force capable of executing his tactical plan, and to do so against the best-trained and best-led army that the Roman Republic had ever put in the field.

The manner in which troops are disposed within a combat box reflects their commander's tactical thinking. Scipio deployed his legions in a slightly different manner from usual. The *hastati* were deployed in the usual way in maniples across the front, with the *velites* or light infantry filling the gaps between the maniples, each legion presenting a 1,200ft front. The other two lines, the *principes* and the *triarii*, were deployed behind the *hastati* as the second and third lines. Usually, these two lines were deployed so as to cover the gaps between the maniples in the line in front of them, the famous *quincunx* or checkerboard formation. At Zama, however, Scipio arranged the three lines so that the maniples of each line were placed directly one behind the other, leaving uncovered lanes 100ft wide running from front to back. Scipio's flanks were, as usual, covered by his cavalry. On his left was the Roman cavalry, 2,000 strong, under the command of Laelius, while Massinissa, 'with the whole of the Numidian contingent', was on the right with 4,000 horse. Massinissa's infantry was placed with the Roman *velites* in the role of light infantry.

The disposition of Scipio's troops permits some insight into his tactical plan. By moving the *principes* and *triarii* further back from his front line by 100 yards or so, Scipio was transforming his army from a phalanx into echelons, completely changing the tactical dynamics of his army. By placing his lines further apart, Scipio transformed his battle formation into echelons, making it possible for his last two lines to manoeuvre independently. The lanes left between the maniples were

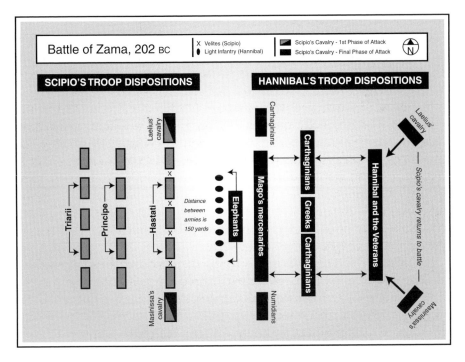

Troop Dispositions At Zama

designed to channel Hannibal's elephants harmlessly to the rear. This done, Scipio's cavalry would attack the outnumbered Carthaginian cavalry on the flanks and drive it from the field. The *hastati* were to attack straight on against the Carthaginian front line, become heavily engaged and hold the Carthaginian centre in place. When Hannibal's second line moved forward in support of his first, Scipio intended to order his *principes* and *triarii* to march outward toward the ends of the Roman line and sweep around the flanks, enveloping the Carthaginian lines. With the Carthaginians trapped, Scipio hoped his cavalry would return quickly enough to join the battle from the rear and annihilate the enemy.

An examination of Hannibal's troop deployment suggests that he had correctly discerned Scipio's tactical plan, and arranged his troops to prevent its success. Hannibal drew up his infantry in three echelons. The front line was comprised mostly of Mago's mercenary veterans. Most of these troops were heavy infantry. The second echelon was anchored in the centre by the Greek phalangites, with the Carthaginian levies (8,000–10,000 men) placed on either side of the spear phalanx. Like Scipio's second line, Hannibal's was placed further to the rear by a gap of 100 yards. Hannibal's veterans formed his third echelon. These were Hannibal's best troops and he led them himself. They were positioned a full *stadium*, or about 200 yards – double the distance between the first and second ranks – behind the second line. Hannibal placed his Numidian cavalry on his left and Carthaginian cavalry on the right.

Hannibal's tactical problem was to neutralize the Roman advantage in cavalry. The first solution was to take it out of the fight completely. He would use his own cavalry to draw Scipio's cavalry away from the battle area, by ordering his mounted forces not to fully engage, but to feign retreat and fight a skirmishing rearguard action to keep Scipio's cavalry occupied until he had defeated the Romans in an infantry engagement. If the plan worked and Scipio's cavalry left the battlefield, taking it out of the fight, then Hannibal could fight an infantry battle, in which he held the numerical advantage.

Hannibal detected in Scipio's troop dispositions the potential for echelon manoeuvre, and set a deadly trap by positioning his veterans far to the rear of the second Carthaginian infantry line. If Scipio attempted to carry out his envelopment, he would trap only the first two lines of Carthaginian infantry, leaving Hannibal the opportunity to attack Scipio's echelons from the rear, crushing them against the Carthaginian infantry lines. Hannibal had tactically neutralized the possibility of the success of Scipio's planned envelopment by turning his veteran contingent into a genuine reserve, to be sent into battle independently upon command. If events forced Scipio to abandon that plan and fight a straight-up parallel infantry battle, Hannibal intended to let Scipio waste his strength against the first two ranks, forcing him to bring up his *principes* and *triarii* before striking him head-on with his veterans. The paradox of the Battle of Zama was that neither commander was able to carry out his tactical plan in the face of the other commander's counter-moves, with the result that both sides were forced into a traditional parallel infantry battle at equal strength that neither wanted to fight.

The battle opened with skirmishing by the contingents of Numidian light cavalry on both sides, followed by Hannibal's order to the elephant drivers to attack the Roman line. Massinissa quickly went over to the attack, driving the Numidians from the field and continuing in hot pursuit. Seeing the quick success that Massinissa was enjoying against the Numidian cavalry, Laelius attacked the Carthaginian cavalry, drove them back in headlong flight and pressed the pursuit. The opening phase of the battle was over, with the first round going to Hannibal, who succeeded in tempting Scipio's cavalry into a pursuit which took them out of the fight.

The light infantry on both sides now withdrew into their respective lines, and the two lines of heavy infantry moved toward each other to do battle. Once within striking distance, the Roman front rank charged. Silius Italicus in the *Punica* says: 'The spears were hurled with speed and force, the air was shaken and a fearsome cloud spread over the sky. Next came the sword at close quarters, and face pressed close to face, and eyes blazed with baleful flame. Those who despised the danger and rushed forward to meet the first shower of missiles were all laid low, and the earth grieved as she drank the blood of her sons.' Polybius tells us: 'The whole battle then became a hand-to-hand struggle of man against man. In this contest the courage and skill of the mercenaries at first gave them the advantage and they succeeded in wounding great numbers of Romans. Even so the steadiness of their ranks and the superiority of their weapons enabled Scipio's men to make their adversaries give ground. All this while the rear ranks of the Romans kept close behind their comrades.' The Carthaginian front began to give way until it broke under the pressure of the Roman assault. Polybius' account says that the Carthaginian second line did not come up and support the first line, as the Romans had done. As the *hastati* pursued the mercenaries, lengthening the distance between themselves and the *principes*, the second Carthaginian line went into the attack on Hannibal's command, trapping the fleeing mercenaries between it and the advancing Romans. The counter-attack of the second Carthaginian line was fierce and pressed hard upon the *hastati*, forcing the *principes* to come up and engage to stop it. Scipio's echelon deployment was being forced back into a phalanx to hold the front steady; any hope of using the echelons to manoeuvre was now out of the question.

The success of the Roman attack had left Scipio's formations scattered and disorganized. The Roman advance had carried it beyond the original location of the Carthaginian second line, placing the scattered Roman maniples some 500 yards to the front of the *triarii*, who had not been committed and remained in their original positions. Hannibal's veterans, however, were only 200 yards to the front! Scipio's tactical plan for manoeuvre had been ruined by the dynamics of the battle itself, and he now found himself exposed to Hannibal's counter-attack.

Scipio surely realized that he was at great risk. His only stratagem was to play for time and hope that Laelius and Massinissa returned soon. Scipio called a halt in the battle with trumpet signals and stopped the advance of the *hastati* and *principes*, ordering the *triarii* to advance to support the forward lines. He reassembled his troops just forward of the cluttered battlefield, closely behind where the second Carthaginian line had been deployed, and ordered them to form a single infantry line. He positioned the bloodied and weakened *hastati* in the centre of the line, evacuated what wounded he could and prepared to receive Hannibal's attack.

But Hannibal accepted the pause in the battle and did not attack. With 15,000 fresh troops positioned only 200 yards from Scipio's weakened centre, why didn't Hannibal go immediately into the attack? Hannibal accepted the pause in the battle necessitated by Scipio's need to redeploy his troops because he needed the time to gather the remnants of his first two lines and reposition them for battle to offset Scipio's numerical advantage and cover the ends of the extended Roman line. Scipio, for his part, granted Hannibal all the time he required, for if he was to win this battle he needed his cavalry to arrive.

Hannibal surely knew that time played to Scipio's advantage, and it is likely that as soon as Hannibal had reformed his army, he went into the attack. The impression Livy and Polybius give in their accounts is that neither side was able to gain the advantage in the raging infantry battle, and that Laelius and Massinissa's cavalry squadrons returned at the right moment; it was this cavalry attack that defeated the Carthaginians. Livy tells us: 'Laelius and Massinissa had pursued the routed cavalry for a considerable distance; now at the right moment they wheeled round and charged into the rear of the enemy's line... Many were surrounded and cut down where they stood; many were scattered in flight over the open plain, only to fall everywhere beneath the cavalry, the undisputed masters of the field.' Polybius adds, with a more experienced military eye, that the 'ground was level', which permitted the pursuit to be more effective, but that 'the greater number of his [Hannibal's] men were cut down in their ranks'. Silius Italicus describes the cavalry attack in the following terms: 'The Numidians, riding bare-backed according to their custom, had filled the plains and broad valleys alike, and their javelins hurtled in thick clouds through the air and concealed the sky.' On the open plain, the fleeing Carthaginians would have made easy targets for these expert horsemen.

Still, most of Hannibal's army died in their ranks as a result of close combat. The initial cavalry attack physically and psychologically disrupted Hannibal's line, allowing penetrations by the Roman maniples at several points. The dismounted Roman cavalry, fighting now as infantry, would have forced sections of the Carthaginian line to turn and defend their rear, making more penetrations of the line possible by the maniples attacking from the front. And so the dynamic went until sections of the Carthaginian line were completely cut off, surrounded and cut to pieces by the Roman infantry. At some point panic would have overtaken good sense and soldiers began to flee, only to be cut down one at a time on the open plain by Massinissa's cavalry.

Polybius tells us that at the end of the day, 20,000 Carthaginians lay dead, or almost half the entire force that Hannibal had set to battle that grim day. Almost as many were taken prisoner. He places Roman losses at 1,500 men, or about 5 per cent of the force, about average for a victorious Roman army. However, Appian says Roman losses were 2,500, which, given the heavy fighting, may be more accurate.

Hannibal and a handful of his officers fled for Hasdrumentum. Scipio entered Carthage and imposed a just peace upon the vanquished city. He returned to Rome and entered the city in a triumph. Sometime later, Scipio acquired the surname *Africanus*; he was the first general to be celebrated by the name of the people he had conquered.

Students of military history might find in Scipio a moral and practical example of the successful modern commander serving a democratic state. He was a loyal soldier committed to the safety and security not only of his country, but to its Republican form of government, which he believed was the guarantor of individual liberty. Scipio's commitment to Republican values was absolute, and rather than challenge them he went into voluntary exile. He was a man who served his country more than himself. A lover of freedom, intellectual and otherwise, he was that rarest of military men, an inquisitive mind always open to new possibilities. In this regard, he is the very model of what we must require of our own senior military commanders. We must not permit them to become narrow experts in the technical orchestration of violence, unhindered by political and moral values. The application of military force *always* has larger political implications, and victory in the interconnected world of the twenty-first century is rarely won only by defeating the enemy on the battlefield. This combination of military and intellectual skill was what made Scipio a great soldier, strategist, reformer, tactical innovator, administrator and leader of men in war. Our own military men could do no better than to emulate him. He was, after all, the greatest general that Rome produced.

Notes

1. Paul Nicorescu, 'La Tomba degli Scipioni', *Ephermeris Daco-romana*, I, pp.1–56.
2. A marble bust that for years had been thought to be Scipio was revealed to be the bust of a Roman priest of Isis. See John Warry, *Warfare in the Classical World* (London, Salamander Books, 1980), p.115, for a photo of this bust. In 1972, a bust long thought to be of Drusus was reexamined and pronounced to be that of Scipio. See G. Hafner, 'Das Bildnis des P. Cornelius Scipio Africanus', *Archaeologischer Anzeiger* (1972), pp.474–92. But the fact that the bust is wearing a style of helmet typical of the Thracian auxiliary cavalry of the third century BC casts doubt on this finding.
3. R. Blatter, 'Ein mermutliches Munzbildnis des Scipio Africanus', *Gazette Numismatic Suisse*, 1974, XXIV, pp.78–79.
4. Silius Italicus, *Punica*, trans. J.D. Duff (Cambridge, MA, Harvard University Press, 1934), vol. 1, Book VIII, p.433.
5. Erich S. Gruen, *Culture and National Identity in Republican Rome* (Ithaca, NY, Cornell University Press, 1992), chapters 2 and 3 for Greek and Roman education under the Republic.
6. John Boardman, Jasper Griffen and Oswyn Murray, *The Oxford History of Greece and the Hellenistic World* (Oxford, Oxford University Press, 1991), p.393. See also Thomas Gartner, 'Die praemilitaerische Ausbildun des Scipio Africanus', *MAIA*, vol. 55, No. 2 (May–August, 2003), pp.317–19.

7. *The Histories of Polybius*, trans. Evelyn S. Shuckburgh (Bloomington, Indiana, Indiana University Press, 1962), Book 10, 2. All citations of Polybius in this work are from this translation.
8. Richard M. Haywood, *Studies on Scipio Africanus* (Baltimore, MD, Johns Hopkins Press, 1933), p.24.
9. Polybius, Book 10,2.
10. Ibid.
11. Polybius, Book 10, 3.
12. *Punica*, vol. 1, Book V, p.233.
13. Ibid., vol. 2, Book XVI, p.409.
14. Mary Frances Williams, 'Shouldn't you have come and talked to me about it?', *Ancient History Bulletin*, vol. 15, no. 4 (2001), pp.143–53.
15. K.W. Meiklejohn, 'Roman Strategy and Tactics from 509 to 202 BC', *Greece and Rome*, vol. 7, No. 21 (May, 1938), pp.171–73; also M.J.V. Bell, 'Tactical Reform in the Roman Republican Army', *Historia: Zeitschrift fur alte Geschichte*, vol. 14 (1965), pp.404–22, for Scipio's tactical reforms. The manipular legion was formed during the Samnite wars (340–290 BC) when the old Greek-style phalanx proved too brittle and unmanoeuvrable to deal with surprise attack. The legion's tactical array was formed at the same time and did not change until Scipio changed it during his campaign in Spain. In an analogous sense, Scipio is the Roman Epimonandas, the Greek commander who introduced the refused wing to hoplite warfare, the only significant change in Greek tactics in more than 200 years.
16. Thomas A. Dorey, 'Scipio Africanus as a Party Leader', *Klio*, XXXIX (1961), pp.191–98, who argues that Scipio lacked the necessary personality and skills to succeed in Roman politics.
17. Daniel A. Fournie, 'Harsh Lessons: Roman Intelligence in the Hannibalic War', *International Journal of Intelligence and Counterintelligence*, 17 (2004), p.511.
18. *Punica*, vol. 1, Book IV, pp.202–03.
19. Polybius, Book 10, 3.
20. The essential details are recorded in *Punica*, vol. 1, Book IV, p.203. There existed an alternative tradition that attributed the rescue not to Scipio, but to a slave. See Livy, Book 21, 46, and F.W. Walbank, *Polybius II: A Historical Commentary on Polybius* (Oxford, Oxford University Press, 1970), pp.198–99.
21. Livy, *The History of Rome from its Foundation: The War With Hannibal*, trans. Aubrey De Selincourt (London, Penguin, 1965) ii, 20. All citations from Livy are from this translation. See also Richard A. Gabriel, *The Great Captains of Antiquity* (Westport, CT, Greenwood Press, 2001), p.105.

22. For an analysis of the qualifications of the lesser men who may have competed with Scipio for the Spanish command, see Haywood, pp.51–52.

23. Charles E. Bennett, *Frontinus: The Strategemata* (New York, Loeb, 1925), Book IV, 7, 4. The work is out of print but may be obtained in full translation online at http://penelope.uchicago.edu/Thayer/E/Roman/Texts/Frontinus/Strategemata/1*.html#1.

24. Philip Sabin, 'The Mechanics of Battle in the Second Punic War', in T. Cornell, B. Rankov and P. Sabin (eds), *The Second Punic War: A Reappraisal* (London, Institute of Classical Studies, University of London, 1996), p.68, for the distinction between battle managers and heroic warriors.

25. B.H. Liddell-Hart, *Scipio Africanus: Greater Than Napoleon* (New York, Da Capo Press, 1994), p.11, citing Livy. For an excellent analysis of the role of the military tribune as well as the other officers of the legion, see Smith, pp.489–511.

26. On this see Liddell-Hart, p.12, and R.T. Ridley, 'Was Scipio Africanus at Cannae?', *Latomus*, XXXVI (1977), pp.110–13.

27. Michael Grant, *The Army of the Caesars* (New York, Charles Scribner's Sons, 1974), xxxiii.

28. *Punica*, vol. 2, Book V, p.233. Scipio himself seems to be telling us that he had already served long tours with the army before he was assigned to Spain. In addressing the mutineers in 206 BC, Scipio says that 'having lived with the army almost from my boyhood, I know soldiers through and through'. Livy, Book 28, 27.

29. *Punica*, vol. 2, Book V, p.255, gives us an account of the death of the Scipio brothers. It is told by Scipio's father, who comes to his son in a dream to alleviate his son's grief. 'Hasdrubal was crippled by defeat, and I was in victorious pursuit of him, when suddenly the Spanish cohorts, a mercenary rabble whom Hasdrubal had enslaved to Libyan gold [bribed], broke their ranks and deserted our standards. Thus left in the lurch by our allies, we were far inferior in numbers to the enemy; and they formed a dense ring around us. We died not unavenged, my son; we played the man on that last day and ended our lives in glory.' This differs significantly from Livy's account in Book 25, 36.

30. For an analysis of the problems associated with Scipio's *imperium* and the resulting legalisms surrounding the assignment of Roman military commands, see Robert Develin, 'The Roman Command Structure in Spain, 218–190 BC', *Klio: Beitrage zur alten Geschichte*, vol. 62 (1980), pp.355–67. See also Shotter for more on the age requirements of office.

31. Howard H. Scullard, *Scipio Africanus in the Second Punic War* (Cambridge, Cambridge University Press, 1933), p.41.

32. Fournie, p.519.

33. J.E. Lendon, *Soldiers and Ghosts: A History of Battle in Classical Antiquity* (New Haven, CT, Yale University Press, 2005), p.307.

34. Haywood, p.53; see also L.T.C. James Parker, *Comparing Strategies of the Second Punic War*, U.S. Army War College monograph (Carlisle Barracks, PA, 2001), p.5.

35. For a detailed critique of Hannibal's strategy, see B.D. Hoyos, 'Hannibal: What Kind of Genius?', *Greece and Rome*, 2nd. Ser., vol. 30, No. 2 (October 1983), pp.171–80. See also Chapter 2 of this work, and John Lazenby, *Hannibal's War* (Norman, OK, University of Oklahoma Press, 1998), pp.226–27; 255–57.

36. Giovanni Brizzi, 'Hannibal – Punier und Hellenist', *Das Altertum* (1991), pp.201–10, for an analysis of Alexander's influence upon Hannibal's tactics. Hannibal was very much a Hellenistic general in his imitation of Alexander and his use of cavalry as an arm of decision. Hannibal realized, however, that the weakness of Alexander's tactical doctrine was that his infantry was too heavy and incapable of manoeuvre. Hannibal's major tactical innovation was to increase the manoeuvrability of his infantry and to use it more in concert with his cavalry than Alexander had used his infantry. For a more complete analysis of Hannibal as a Hellene, see G.C. Picard, *Hannibal* (Paris, C. Klincksiek, 1967), pp.321–50; see also Meiklejohn, p.176.

37. Carl von Clausewitz, *On War*, trans. by Michael Howard and Peter Paret (Princeton, NJ, Princeton University Press, 1989), p.28.

38. Fournie, pp.530–31, for a list of Scipio's intelligence successes during the war.

39. Ibid., p.529.

40. The Carthaginians and their Gallic allies destroyed six Roman armies in ambushes in a little over three years. These included: Lucius Manlius's operation against the Gauls in 218 BC, the Trebia River in late 218 BC and Lake Trasimene in 217 BC. Later that year Servilius was ambushed by Maharbal, Municus ambushed at Gereonium and Lucius Albinus ambushed in the Litani Forest.

41. Hannibal's intelligence service was, by contrast, excellent and utilized commercial agents, advanced scouts, Gallic allies and political provocateurs to gather strategic intelligence and foment political dissent. The Numidian light cavalry was used extensively to gather tactical intelligence. Perhaps the most important element of the Carthaginian intelligence effort was that Hannibal himself was an enthusiastic proponent of its use.

42. Fournie, p.512.

43. Ibid., pp.512–13. For material on the role of intelligence in ancient Rome, see Rose Mary Sheldon, *Tinker, Tailor, Caesar, Spy: Espionage in Ancient Rome*, dissertation (University of Michigan, Ann Arbor, 1987), University Microfilms International No. 8720338; by the same author, *Intelligence Activities in Ancient Rome: Trust in the Gods, but Verify* (New York, Frank Cass, 2005); see also Francis Dvornik, *Origins of Intelligence Services* (New Brunswick, NJ, Rutgers University Press, 1974); and N.J.E. Austin and N.B. Rankov, *Exploratio* (London, Routledge, 1995). All reach the conclusion that Rome had no formal intelligence service under the Republic.

44. This account is drawn from Richard A. Gabriel, 'Zama: Turning Point in the Desert', *Military History* (January–February 2008), pp.50–57. See also by the same author, *Scipio Africanus: Rome's Greatest General* (Dulles, VA, Potomac Press, 2008), chapter 7.

CHAPTER SEVEN

HANNIBAL BARCA (247–183 BC)

There is no other great captain in antiquity who played such an important part in Western military history about whose personal life we know so little. The destruction of Carthage by the Romans after the Third Punic War erased any historical record of Hannibal's life. With the exception of a few pages in the work of Cornelius Nepos, no ancient historian has left us a biography of Hannibal. What we know of him comes exclusively from Roman sources – some written close to the time of his life, others much later – who had every interest in minimizing his success, exaggerating his failures and derogating his character. Analysis reveals thirty-seven Roman authors who offer a total of sixty sneering derogatory treatments of Hannibal, with not a single positive treatment for balance.[1] But even Roman historians were forced to grudgingly admit to Hannibal's military genius, if only to make their eventual victory over him appear greater.

Hannibal was born in 247 BC, the son of Hamilcar, a member of the Carthaginian nobility and general who had just been offered command of the Carthaginian armies fighting the Romans in Sicily during the First Punic War. In 244 BC, Hannibal's brother, Hasdrubal, was born, followed in 239–240 BC by another brother, Mago. Together, Hamilcar called them 'the lion's brood'. Hamilcar already had three daughters, but we do not know their names or ages. Hamilcar and his sons are known to history as having the surname, Barca. But the Carthaginians did not have surnames or even tribal names like the Romans. It was classical writers who gave Hamilcar and his sons their surname. The first of the Roman writers to call Hamilcar by a surname was Polybius, who declared that of all the Carthaginian generals in the First Punic War, 'the one who, for his intelligence and daring, must be regarded as the best was Hamilcar Barca'.[2]

That Hannibal's people were powerful aristocrats can be implied from the fact that the Carthaginian Senate entrusted the military command in Sicily to Hamilcar in 247 BC. High-level military commands went only to members of the most important aristocratic military families. Carthage had developed a small caste of military families whose claim to social status was their talent and experience in war.

This may also explain why Hamilcar asked the 9-year-old Hannibal to accompany him to Spain, even though Hannibal was too young for military training. Hamilcar expected his sons to follow in his footsteps. For them to do so, however, they would require practical experience in war and command. Hamilcar took Hannibal with him to provide the boy with the experience he would need if he was to have a successful military career. Over the next decade, Hannibal received a military education that no commander in history before him had ever received; and his father was his teacher.

When Hannibal arrived in Spain in 237 BC, Carthage had been at war off and on for twenty-seven years. For fifteen of those years, his father had been heavily involved in the nation's military affairs. Now, Hamilcar was sent to Spain with an army to establish a strong Carthaginian economic and military presence and exploit the country's natural resources to restore Carthage's national wealth and power lost after defeat in the First Punic War. Hannibal lived in his father's army camp, raised in its soldierly atmosphere and the raucous male world of battle-hardened warriors. Here he could explore the countryside, hunt, learn to ride horses, mules and elephants, and meet the strange peoples of the Spanish tribes.

Hannibal began his military training when he was 13. This training was conducted by combat-hardened Carthaginian and mercenary soldiers, serving in an ongoing war, under the watchful eye of their commanding general, the boy's father. Hannibal's training exposed him to the full array of weapons used by Carthaginians and the Spanish tribes. Horsemanship, too, was stressed, as were survival skills and endurance. Perhaps of greatest importance, however, was Hannibal's exposure to the Celtiberian culture and its customs and complexities, including the political structures of the tribes, their histories of alliances and animosities, religions, dynastic quarrels, tendency toward treachery and battle tactics. Putting his son in the company of combat soldiers set a high standard for the young man. Hannibal would have to prove himself if he expected these hardened veterans to follow him into battle someday. By the end of 229 BC, we find Hannibal, at age 18, and Hasdrubal, at 15, campaigning with their father.

Hannibal was also exposed to the barbarity and cruelty of ancient warfare at an early age. He was already aware of the Carthaginian practice of crucifying failed generals in the public square of the city, and may have witnessed some of the cruel punishments meted out by his father to the mercenaries during the Truceless War. It remains a curious question why, after having been exposed to such cruelty since childhood, Hannibal did not practice it in his own campaigns. The Roman slur that Hannibal was cruel in his dealing with prisoners and civilians is mostly false.

Hannibal's formal education was carried out by Greek or Carthaginian tutors, who were readily available for hire in Sicily and Spain. Nepos says that a Spartan named Sosylus taught Hannibal Greek, although we do not know when. It is, however, clear that Hannibal was fluent in Greek. During his later exile, he moved easily among the Greek-speaking aristocracy in Syria, Pontus and Bythnia, and wrote a military history in Greek of Gnaeus Manlius Volso's campaign against the Gauls in Asia Minor.[3] Dio Cassius says that Hannibal was proficient in Punic and 'other languages', perhaps a reference to Hannibal's ability to speak the dialects of some of the Spanish tribes.[4] He had, after all, been living among tribal allies and mercenaries for many years, and it would have been strange indeed if Hannibal had not learned to understand and speak their language. Hannibal's education was thus probably superior to that of any of his opponents.

Hannibal was 18 years old when his father was killed in a battle with the Oretani tribe. Hamilcar was 50 or 51 years old and had been in Spain for almost nine years. Carthage was a republic where military commands were awarded by the Senate. Hannibal had no dynastic claim to succession to his father's command, and he was too young by Carthaginian standards for such an important post. It was Hasdrubal, Hamilcar's second-in-command, who, Diodorus tells us, 'was acclaimed general by both the army and the Carthaginians'.[5] The 'army' that selected its new commander was not the troops, but the Carthaginian officer aristocrats who commanded the Carthaginian levies. The officers of the mercenaries, Spanish tribes and conscript Libyan levies had no voice. The recommendation of the 'army and the Carthaginians' was sent to Carthage, where it was approved or denied by the Senate. Hannibal served under Hasdurbal from 228–221 BC, during which time he acquired the reputation as an excellent soldier and courageous leader of men in combat. Livy says, 'Hasdrubal preferred him [Hannibal] to all other officers in any action which called for vigour and courage, and under his leadership the men invariably showed to the best advantage both dash and confidence.'[6] Diodorus tells us that Hasdrubal appointed Hannibal as his 'cavalry commander', but it is unclear if this was commander of the entire cavalry corps or only a segment of it.[7] Whatever the level of his command, Appian remarks that 'where force was needed he [Hasdrubal] made use of the young man'.[8]

Hannibal served under Hasdrubal as commander of a small unit, perhaps the equivalent of a battalion or regiment, demonstrating his ability before being promoted to senior rank. He must have held higher rank for some period in which he further demonstrated his fitness for high-level command, otherwise he could not have been considered to succeed Hasdrubal. Hannibal was selected to command the armies in the same manner as Hasdrubal when the latter was murdered, by acclamation of 'the army and Carthaginians', and was confirmed by the Senate in Carthage some months later. He was 26 years old. He was a professional soldier in every sense, well-trained for war since youth and very experienced in battle. In one of history's curious parallelisms, only Scipio Africanus had combat experience comparative to Hannibal when he assumed command of the Roman armies in Spain at the age of 26.

Even after he became commanding general of the Carthaginian armies in Spain, Hannibal appears to have retained some of the risky habits he demonstrated as a junior officer under Hasdrubal, often with potentially lethal consequences. Livy tells us that Hannibal was wounded at Sarguntum. He says, 'In the skirmishes which ensued, the losses on each side were about equal, but the situation quickly changed when Hannibal, rashly riding up to within the range of the wall, was severely wounded in the thigh by a javelin.'[9] Livy's version of the story is credible in that the most common wound suffered by cavalrymen in antiquity was lance or javelin wounds to the thigh.

Hannibal was wounded again in Italy in 218 BC when he attacked the Roman supply depot at Placentia. Livy says that during the attack, 'the mounted troops of either side engaged each other, and in the course of the skirmish Hannibal was wounded and had to leave the field … After a few days' rest, and before his wound was properly healed, Hannibal proceeded to attack Victunmulae, another trading post [a Roman supply depot].'[10] Once more, Hannibal is involved in a cavalry skirmish, not exactly the kind of activity one would expect of a commanding general. In addition, Livy tells us that during the crossing of the Arno Marshes, Hannibal contracted 'some infection of the eyes' which 'affected his head and, as there was neither the place nor the time to seek a cure, he lost the sight of any eye'.[11] Nepos adds the interesting, but somewhat questionable, claim that 'while he was still suffering from that complaint, and was carried in a litter, Hannibal ambushed the consul Gaius Flaminius with his army at Trasimene and slew him'.[12]

In November 218 BC, Hannibal crossed the Alps and invaded Italy with an army of 38,000 infantry and 8,000 cavalry, but lost almost half his entire force during the winter Alpine crossing, arriving with 12,000 African infantry, 8,000 Spanish infantry and 6,000 cavalry.[13] Hannibal defeated a Roman cavalry force at the Ticinus River, in which Publius

Scipio and his son took part. In December, Hannibal destroyed a Roman consular army at the Trebbia River commanded by Sempronius, in which the Romans lost 23,000 men killed and another 2,000 wounded.[14] Hannibal then retired to Bologna, the capital of his Boii Gallic allies, for the winter. In March 217 BC, the Romans elected Gnaeus Servilius and Gaius Flaminius as consuls. Flaminius assumed command of an army of 20,000 men at Arretium (mod. Arezzo) while Servilius took command of a second army at Ariminum (Rimini). At Ariminum, Servilius blocked Hannibal's easiest route along the Adriatic coast to the south of Italy, while at Arretium, Flaminius covered one of the major outlets through the Apennines from Bologna (Colline Pass), blocking Hannibal's most direct route to Rome. The Roman armies waited for Hannibal to move.

In Bologna, the Gauls were getting edgy. The Gallic chiefs were angry that Hannibal was using them as cannon fodder and were restless that the war was being fought on their own territory, with little plunder or profit for themselves. They were anxious to attack the lands of the Roman allies in Umbria and Etruria, and then the entire *ager Romanus*, for plunder and revenge.[15] As spring approached, Hannibal

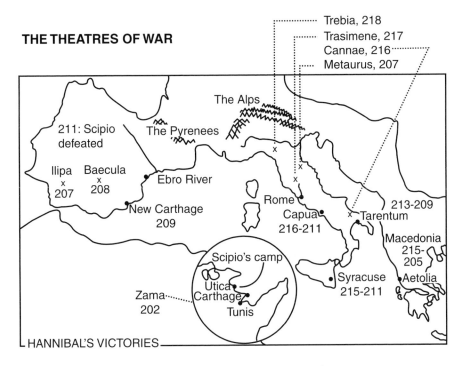

Punic War: Hannibal's Victories

had to move the war away from Cisalpine Gaul or face the prospect of being abandoned by his Gallic allies.

Polybius tells us that Hannibal departed Bologna 'when the weather began to change', perhaps sometime in April. But in April the Apennine passes were still snowbound and there was not yet sufficient forage for the animals. More likely, Hannibal left sometime during the first two weeks of May. The easiest passage over the Apennines from Bologna was via the Colline Pass, with its modest altitude of 952 metres. This route debouched not far from Arretium, where Flaminius and his army were deployed to block Hannibal's route to Rome. Hannibal was aware of Flaminius' presence at Arretium, and chose another route. He moved through the Porretta Pass that debouched near Pistioa, 52 miles northwest of Arretium.[16] Hannibal's army crossed the mountains and assembled on the Etruscan plain.

Once out of the mountains, Hannibal found his way blocked by the Arno River marshes, an area several miles wide between Pisa and Faesulae (Fiesole) that 'had recently flooded to a greater extent than usual'. The troops had to wade through deep water, at times sinking over their heads in swirling eddies. Many drowned, while others gave up and 'lay helpless and hopeless and died where they had fallen'. Men heaped the corpses of dead animals in piles to rest upon and gain a respite from the wet. Hannibal himself caught some infection of the eye, by which he eventually lost the sight of one eye. The crossing took four days and three nights, and the loss of men was considerable.[17]

The losses of horses and pack animals was also high, Polybius saying that 'most of his [Hannibal's] beasts of burden also slipping in the mud fell and perished', and Livy confirms that many animals drowned.[18] If Hannibal did lose *most* of his pack animals and a *considerable number* of horses, as our historians say, then he arrived on the Etrurian plain with limited ability to conduct immediate combat operations. Hannibal had to confiscate every mule and donkey he could lay his hands on from the surrounding farms to reconstruct his pack train. Cavalry horses were a more serious matter. Horses were expensive and not common among farmers. Even if Hannibal had been able to confiscate or purchase horses in sufficient numbers, they would still take weeks to train for use in war. It is likely, then, that Hannibal's cavalry capability was substantially reduced.

Hannibal had arrived on the Etruscan plain, the region that 'was amongst the most productive in Italy, rich in cattle, grain, and everything else'. As soon as he cleared the marshes, Hannibal encamped and sent out reconnaissance units to determine the movements of the Romans at Arretium. He also ordered his foragers to obtain food and animals. It required three weeks for him to replenish his army and make it fit for field operations. Flaminius had failed to detect Hannibal's position in time, and missed an opportunity to attack him as he emerged from the swamps with his weakened army. Only after Hannibal had already begun to move south, passing close to Arretium and setting fields alight to draw Flaminius' attention, did the Roman commander become aware of Hannibal's position, too late to place his army between Hannibal and Rome. Now he had no choice but to follow in Hannibal's wake, hoping to catch him and force him to battle.

The Battle of Lake Trasimene

Hannibal's route took him through the village of Borghetto along a road that skirted the northern shore of Lake Trasimene. Beyond Borghetto, the terrain narrowed into a defile, with the lake shore on one side and cliffs on the other. Beyond the narrow passage, the terrain opened upon a flat rectangular valley floor with steep hills on one side (left) and the lake on the other (right). Straight ahead, at the far end of the valley, the road ran up a steep hill. As Hannibal marched his army over this route, he noticed a thick morning fog rising from the lake that made visibility difficult. Hannibal moved his Spanish and African infantry to the top of the hill at the valley's end and pitched camp. He then arranged the rest of his army on the hills running up from the lake shore, hiding his Gallic infantry there and placing his cavalry in concealment just inside the valley entrance.

Flaminius moved his army through Borghetto and camped for the night. He did not send reconnaissance parties into the valley, having concluded that the hills on his flanks were too steep to conceal an ambush.[19] Flaminius assumed Hannibal was moving away from him, and his plan was to catch Hannibal's army in column of march, engage the rearguard, defeat it and then attack the main body before it could turn and face the Roman assault. At dawn the next day, Flaminius marched his army through the narrow defile onto the widening plain. Straight ahead and above the fog, Flaminius could see Hannibal's encampment atop the hill at the valley's exit. Flaminius thought it was Hannibal's rearguard, and ordered his van to quickly engage. With the rest of the Roman column still in line of march, the Roman advanced units rushed up the hill. Flaminius thought that he had taken Hannibal by surprise.

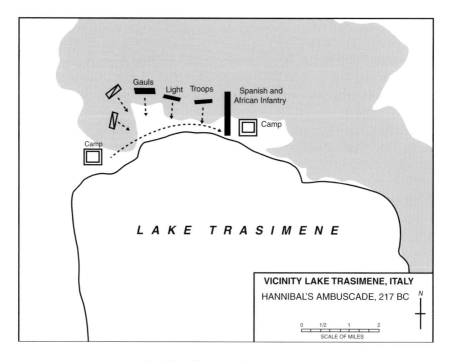

Battle of Lake Trasimene

Almost at the top of the hill, the Romans ran headlong into Hannibal's infantry acting as a blocking force, and a fierce battle ensued. On the valley floor, Flaminius' army was now entirely through the narrow defile, its head moving up the hill at the far end of the valley, its tail extending back almost to the valley entrance. Hannibal ordered the trumpet signal for the Gallic infantry hiding in the hills to attack the Roman column's flank. At the same time, his cavalry struck the Roman rear. The battle raged 'for three long and bloody hours' until the Roman army was annihilated. Livy and Polybius say that 15,000 Roman soldiers were killed at a cost of only 1,500 to 2,000 of Hannibal's men. At least 6,000 Romans and allied soldiers were taken prisoner, and perhaps as many as 10,000. Flaminius was among those killed.

While Flaminius was following Hannibal toward Lake Trasimene, Servilius received orders to redeploy and link-up with Flaminius. The shortest route to Rome and Lake Trasimene was down the *Via Flaminia* linking the capital to Ariminum, a distance of 140 miles. Servilius sent 4,000 cavalry under the command of C. Centenius on ahead of his main force. But Hannibal's reconnaissance detected Servilius' movement, and Hannibal sent Maharbal and a strong cavalry force to intercept

Centenius. Maharbal ambushed the Roman cavalry somewhere near Assisi, about 20 miles from Lake Trasimene, where he annihilated the Romans. The ambush put an end to Servilius' movement, and he returned to Ariminum, where he quickly found himself under attack by the Gauls. The result of both engagements was that the road to Rome was open.

Hannibal spent the winter in Bologna, and it is likely that over the winter Hannibal may have been able to attract 10,000–15,000 more men and cavalry to his cause. The army that left for Rome in the spring might well have been between 50,000–55,000 men, a significant force sufficient to attack the capital. Moreover, Hannibal was marching through one of the most agriculturally productive regions of Italy, so supplying his army with food was not a problem. He replenished some of his pack train with mules and donkeys confiscated from the countryside. He also captured another 4,000 pack animals from the Romans at Trasimene, along with 2,000 horses from the Roman cavalry there. Maharbal captured another 4,000 Roman cavalry horses in his engagement against Servilius. These captured Roman cavalry mounts easily replaced whatever horses Hannibal had lost crossing the marshes, bringing his cavalry back to full strength.

The area between Lake Trasimene and Rome, and around the city itself, was also sufficiently productive to provide adequate food, water and fodder for Hannibal's army. Rome was only 80 miles away from Hannibal's camp, less than a ten-days' march, and there was no sizeable Roman military force between Hannibal and Rome. The previous year's Roman military buildup put eleven regular legions in the field: two in Spain, two in Sicily, two in Sardinia, two with Flaminius at Arretium, two with Servilius at Ariminum and one in Tarentum. Flaminius' legions had already been destroyed, and Servilius, having lost his cavalry, retreated to Ariminum, where he was engaged in a running battle with the Gauls. Only two irregular legions, the *legiones urbanes*, were in Rome to defend the city. But these had been only recently authorized, lacked their allied counterparts and were not full-strength, fully equipped or trained yet for battle.

Also to Hannibal's advantage was the arrival in June of a fleet of seventy Carthaginian warships off Pisa on the Etrurian coast. Polybius makes clear that the Carthaginian 'commanders believed they should find Hannibal there'.[20] What was a large Carthaginian fleet doing off the Etrurian coast, only 80 miles from Hannibal's camp? A plausible answer is that Hannibal's original operational plan was not only to invade the Italian peninsula, but to do so in a combined operation with the Carthaginian navy. Such an audacious operation could have only one objective: an attack on Rome itself.[21] The navy's role was to prevent the transfer of Roman troops in Sicily or Sardinia from coming to the aid of the city. Some 190 Roman ships were deployed away from Italy, leaving only thirty or so combatants to protect the capital. The arrival of seventy Punic naval combatants off the Etrurian coast gave the Carthaginians a numerical advantage in the immediate area of operations.

With these forces at his disposal, why didn't Hannibal attack Rome? Two arguments have been advanced by historians. First, that Hannibal's army was not large enough to invest Rome, given the size of the city and its garrison. Second, an effective blockade of Rome was impossible as long as the Roman navy kept open the city's lifeline to the sea along the Tiber River, on which supplies could reach the city's garrison. Neither of these reasons seems sufficient to explain Hannibal's actions.

Rome in Republican times had a population of approximately 450,000–500,000 living within an area of 8.4 square miles, enclosed by a wall 33ft high and 7 miles in circumference.[22] There was nothing particularly formidable about Rome's defences, given Carthaginian engineering ability. Hannibal had sufficient siege equipment, or at least could construct it quickly enough to carry out an attack. Much of the male military age population of the city, some 50,000 men, were already serving with the eleven legions in the field. Only the two recently raised irregular legions were available to defend the city. Even if they were fully trained and equipped, 10,000 soldiers was simply insufficient to defend against an attacking army of 50,000 capable of conducting simultaneous forays at multiple points against the walls and gates. Plutarch, in his *Life of Marcellus*, tells us that in fact the Romans did not have enough men to defend the walls.[23]

The second argument, that a successful attack on Rome required Hannibal's navy to blockade the Tiber's outlet to the sea to prevent resupply, assumes that Ostia was Rome's main port at this time, when in fact it was little more than an outpost at the end of the Tiber. Ostia did not become a major port until the time of the Emperor Claudius (AD 41–54).[24] In Hannibal's time, Rome's main lifeline for supplies was not the Tiber, but the port of Puteoli, 120 miles south of Rome. Supplies landed at Puteoli were transported overland by road. Hannibal's army could have cut off Rome's supplies by simply blocking the roads from Puteoli to the city. Blockading Rome did not, therefore, require a sea-going navy to block the Tiber. Hannibal's navy could be put to more important use attacking the troop transports carrying Roman relief forces.

By his own admission, Hannibal's failure to attack Rome was his greatest mistake. Had he brought Rome under attack after Trasimene, either as a genuine effort or a feint, Rome would have been forced to recall some of its legions from abroad, exposing Sicily, Spain or Sardinia to a Carthaginian invasion. The nearest legions were on Sardinia. But there were seventy Carthaginian warships between the island and Italy to attack the Roman troop transports. Nothing would have demonstrated Rome's weakness to its allies more than capturing Rome itself. Even if Hannibal failed in the attempt, the shock to Rome's political will to fight on might have been seriously shaken. At the very least, it would have made it more difficult for Rome to raise new legions, and, perhaps, changed the course of the war.

In less than a year (November 218 BC–June 217 BC) Hannibal had met the Roman legions and dealt them one defeat after another. Ticinus had cost the Romans upward of 2,000 men. The engagement at the Trebbia destroyed 23,000 Roman and allied soldiers, and at Trasimene, Hannibal killed 15,000 more Roman troops, captured 6,000 and took the life of a major Roman commander. The Roman relief force that came late to the Battle of Lake Trasimene had been ambushed at a cost of 4,000 more men. Hannibal had killed or captured some 50,000 Roman soldiers, a number equal to ten legions, nearly half of them in a single week! And yet, he did not attack Rome when he was at his greatest strength and Rome weaker than it would ever be again. Hannibal, one of history's great military gamblers, refused to roll the dice.

Hannibal did not attack Rome because he did not think it necessary. Hannibal, like most Carthaginian aristocrats of his day, was a Hellene in his thinking, training and understanding of history and war. In the Hellenistic world since Alexander's death, grand strategy as conceived and practiced was relatively straightforward. If one state invaded the territory of another, won a few battles and caused sufficient disruption, there was a reasonable expectation that one's enemy would seek terms. The expectation that wars were ultimately settled by negotiation had become the norm in Hellenistic warfare, and we may reasonably surmise that Hannibal accepted it as well, having learned of it through his education at the hands of Hellenic Greek tutors, his study of Alexander's campaigns and from the Greek advisors on his campaign staff. Hannibal's strategic plan was predicated upon the assumption that Rome would behave in the conventional Hellenistic manner once the contest of arms had been decided.

Hannibal failed to understand the conservative culture and moralistic values that underlay Roman society and shaped the Roman view of war. The Romans were not Hellenes, a culture they considered soft and corrupt. The Roman response to Hannibal's victories was to raise more legions and keep on fighting. It is estimated that nearly all fit male Roman citizens served in the army at some time or other during the war with Hannibal. For some periods, as many as half the eligible men were under arms. Of a military manpower pool of 240,000 male citizens, fully 120,000 died in the war, and it is possible that some 80,000 of them died as the result of combat, the rest from disease, shipwreck or accidents.

In the same way that American commanders in Vietnam and Russian commanders in Afghanistan failed to understand the cultural context of their respective wars, so, too, did Hannibal fail to understand the cultural context of his war with the Romans. As a result, despite their many battlefield victories, the Americans, Russians and Hannibal all failed to achieve their strategic objectives and lost the war.

The Battle of Cannae

With the Roman armies in Italy defeated or in disarray, and with the closest Roman forces to him in Sicily, Hannibal could now march through southern Italy without opposition, constrained only by problems of logistics. Rome went into mourning when news of the defeats reached the city. Rome put the safety of its city in the hands of a dictator, Quintus Fabius, a competent general of keen intellect. M. Minucius Rufus was elected his second-in-command. Two new legions were raised to replace those destroyed at Trasimene, the *legiones urbanae* were brought up to strength and Servilius' army ordered to move from Ariminum to Rome.

Fabius' competence was immediately evident in his strategic assessment of the situation confronting him. He knew that Rome's great manpower, naval and economic resources would, in the end, carry the day against Hannibal, and that time worked to Rome's advantage, not Hannibal's. The real threat was to the Roman resource base, and this depended upon Rome being able to maintain the loyalty of its colonies and allies on the Italian peninsula. Fabius' strategic objective, therefore, was not military, but political. Roman military forces had to be used in such a way as to maintain the loyalty of its allies. Fabius' military operations were not aimed at destroying Hannibal's army, but containing it to the Italian countryside and keeping it on the move to complicate its logistics, a policy of *sedendo et cunctando* (besieging and delaying).

For almost six months, Fabius followed Hannibal's route of march, keeping to the high ground on parallel routes and maintaining contact, but never engaging him with a large force. On several occasions, Hannibal attempted to draw Fabius into battle, but never succeeded. Hannibal had to forage continually for food and supplies, a circumstance that forced his army to move frequently in search of food.[25] Fabius attacked these foraging detachments mercilessly. Hannibal's army was also encumbered with thousands of prisoners, cattle and war booty, all of which slowed its rate of movement, making it easy for the more mobile Roman army to keep on his trail.

In September, Fabius was recalled to Rome for consultations, leaving Minucius in command with instructions not to engage Hannibal. Fabius' strategy had been effective, but its ultimate success depended upon the maintenance of the political will of the Senate and Roman people. But political will was difficult to maintain in a society accustomed to destroying its enemies by decisive victories. For his efforts, Fabius earned the nickname *Cunctator*, meaning 'The Delayer', and it was not always used affectionately. Within the Senate, a faction opposed to Fabius' defensive policy became ascendant and advocated confronting Hannibal on the battlefield. The Senate abandoned dictatorial rule and reverted to the traditional Roman system of consular military command, and two new consuls were elected to lead the army, L. Aemilius Paulus and C. Terentius Varro. It was decided to raise a new army and defeat Hannibal in the field.

To feed his army, Hannibal decided to withdraw to Apulia, where the harvests come much earlier because of the warmer climate.[26] Once the crops had ripened, Hannibal gathered up his army, broke contact and marched southwards to strike at a Roman supply base in the town of Cannae, 60 miles away. Servilius and Regulus followed, but kept their distance. The armies under Paulus and Varro were now closing on Cannae, and linked up somewhere near Arpi, about three days' march from Cannae.[27]

Polybius states that the Romans decided 'to maintain the struggle with eight legions, a thing which had never happened among the Romans before, each of the legions having up to five thousand men, apart from the allies'.[28] Thus, four new legions, each of 5,000 men, were raised and the existing four legions serving under Servilius and

Atilius brought up to the same strength. An equal number of infantry was levied from the allies, so that the Roman army at Cannae had some 80,000 men.[29] It was the largest army the Romans had ever put in the field. If all the legions had their full complement of 300 cavalry per legion, then there were 2,400 Roman horse at Cannae. These were augmented by an additional 3,600 allied cavalry, for a total of 6,000 cavalry.

Hannibal is said to have had 10,000 cavalry and 40,000 infantry at the battle. Of the cavalry, the Numidians comprised between 3,000–4,000 men, with the combined Spanish and Gallic cavalry numbering between 6,000–7,000. Hannibal's infantry comprised some 19,000–20,000 Gauls, 3,000–4,000 Spanish heavy infantry, 8,000–9,000 African infantry and 8,000 light infantry skirmishers.[30] Both sides manoeuvred for battle.

The Romans deployed with their heavy infantry in the centre, the Roman cavalry on the right under Paulus' command and the allied cavalry under Varro on the left. The Roman centre arranged itself in double formation, the maniples deployed closer together with a shorter front but with deeper ranks. The infantry was under the command of Servilius Geminis. Polybius tells us that it was Varro who ordered the infantry to shorten its frontage and thicken its depth.[31] The reason was to give the infantry centre greater endurance under attack by making it difficult for men to flee. Half the legions had been recently raised and their training was less than adequate. Fifty thousand close order infantry were packed across a front of slightly more than a mile.[32] Out in front of them were 20,000 light infantry and skirmishers screening the larger force as it deployed for battle.

Varro's tactical problem was his greatly outnumbered cavalry. Varro's use of the river and hills to protect his flanks meant that Hannibal's superior cavalry could not ride around the flanks of the Roman cavalry, but had to attack them with a frontal charge in an attempt to drive them from the field. Under these tactical circumstances, the Roman cavalry was not required to defeat the enemy cavalry, but to occupy it and stay in position long enough for the massed infantry in the centre to overwhelm Hannibal's centre.[33] Varro intended to carry out a traditional Roman infantry attack, and cut straight through the Carthaginian centre.

Hannibal formed his army opposite the Romans. In front of the Roman cavalry on the Roman right wing with 2,400 horse, he placed his Spanish and Gallic heavy cavalry, between 6,000–7,000 strong. Opposite the 3,600 allied cavalry on the Roman left, Hannibal deployed between 3,000–4,000 Numidian horsemen. In the centre of the line, Hannibal placed his weakest troops, Gauls and Spanish light infantry, some 24,000 men, including skirmishers. Anchoring the ends of the infantry line but arranged in rectangles some yards behind the line, were two phalanxes of heavy African infantry, Hannibal's best troops, each phalanx with 4,000–5,000 men. After forming his infantry in a straight line, Hannibal arranged his centre infantry so the Carthaginian line bowed outward toward the Roman line, forming a crescent. The Spanish and Gallic cavalry were commanded by Hasdrubal, while Maharbal, perhaps the greatest cavalry commander of the war, commanded the Numidians.[34] Hannibal himself and his young brother, Mago, commanded the centre. On the sound of the trumpet, the battle began with the inevitable clash of the light infantry, skirmishers and javelineers deployed in front of both armies until, their missiles exhausted, both sides withdrew through the ranks of their respective armies. Hannibal's Balaeric slingers rained down stone and lead shot on the Roman formations. Livy says that 'at the beginning of the battle he [Paulus] was seriously wounded by a slingstone', but this did not stop him from leading his men.[35]

The main Roman line began to advance. But before it reached the Carthaginians, Hannibal unleashed his cavalry, sending Hasdrubal and his Spanish and Gallic horsemen charging against the Roman cavalry on the right. Both Livy and Polybius recount that the fighting between the two forces was fierce, and Livy says 'the fight was more fierce than of long duration, and the battered Roman cavalry turned their backs and fled'.[36] The Roman infantry reached the Carthaginian line at about the same time their cavalry fled.[37] On the left wing, the Numidians and the allied cavalry were involved in a fluid back and forth fight in which neither side was able to gain decisive advantage. By staying in position and not uncovering the flank of the Roman infantry, however, Varro's cavalry was doing exactly what it was supposed to do.

In the centre, the Roman infantry came into contact with the crescent bulge of the Carthaginian line. The Roman infantry was organized in three lines, each with their maniples packed closely together. This allowed it to hammer away again and again at the Carthaginians, who were formed in a single line with no support behind. Livy says, 'At first equally matched in strength and confidence, the Gauls and Spaniards stood firm for as long as their formation held. At length, the Romans, surging forward again and again on an even front and in dense array drove back the advanced wedge formed by the enemy which was too thin and weak to hold.'[38] The Carthaginian line was hammered even with the African phalanxes that anchored it on each end. Then it was pressed further back.

As the Carthaginian centre gradually flexed under the pressure of the Roman assault, the Roman infantry was drawn deeper into the 'V'-shaped space created by the Carthaginian retreat. The further forward the Roman units progressed, the more compressed they became. After some time, almost the entire Roman infantry was pressed into the interior of the 'V'. The narrowness of the battlefield forced the Roman maniples closer and closer together until the gaps between them disappeared, and the units could no longer manoeuvre in any direction except straight ahead.

Having driven the Roman cavalry from the field, Hasdrubal re-formed his squadrons and rode completely around and behind the Roman line, and joined the battle between the allied and Numidian cavalry on the Roman left. There, the allied cavalry were crushed between the two Carthaginian cavalry forces and fled the field. Hasdrubal re-formed his cavalry again, this time sending the Numidians in pursuit of the allied units to ensure that they could not return to the battlefield. The Roman infantry was now totally committed into the 'V' that

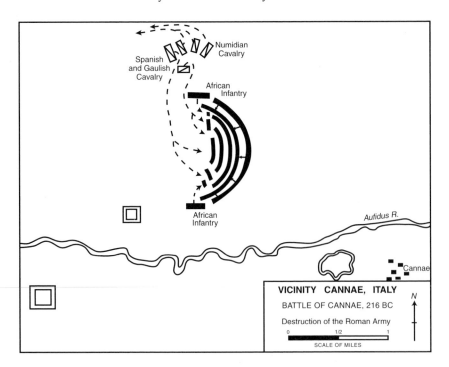

Cannae: Final Phase

Hannibal's retreating infantry had created, and so tightly compressed that they could no longer manoeuvre in any direction. At this critical moment, the African infantry phalanxes that had been anchoring the ends of the Carthaginian infantry line turned obliquely inward and attacked the flanks of the compacted Roman formations.[39] The Romans found themselves jammed together like packed cattle.

Now Hasdrubal's cavalry arrived in the Roman rear to block their retreat, completing the double envelopment of the Roman infantry. Having assured himself that the allied cavalry was clear of the field, Hasdrubal's cavalry 'by charging the Roman legions on the rear, and harassing them by hurling squadron after squadron upon them at many points at once began massacring the Roman rear line.'[40] With no ability to move forward or to the flanks, and with the rear cut off, the Roman army was slaughtered where it stood.

It was, however, no easy task. Hannibal's men organized in units struck with one combat pulse after another, hour after hour, against the Roman mass, which put up stiff resistance for a long time before, eventually, all resistance collapsed and the survivors fled. Livy says that of the original force of 80,000 men, 45,000 infantry and 2,700 cavalry were killed.[41] From other passages in Livy, it emerges that some 19,000 may have been taken prisoner, some of these having reached the Roman camp and surrendered later.[42] The Carthaginians lost 5,700 men, including 4,000 Gauls fighting in the centre of the line. Another 1,500 Africans and Spanish infantry died, and about 200 cavalrymen. Hannibal's casualty rate was by no means insignificant, however, amounting to 11.5 per cent of his force, or three times the average loss rate suffered by victorious armies in antiquity, a figure that testifies to the fierceness of the fighting even after the Romans were surrounded. The total butcher's bill was 54,000 men heaped in an area roughly the size of New York's Central Park.

Hannibal had achieved his great victory over the Romans. In the three battles of Trebia, Trasimene and Cannae, the cost to Rome in military manpower had been horrendous. No fewer than 100,000 men, almost 20 per cent of the Roman population of military age, had been killed, captured or wounded.[43] Hannibal's army was intact and capable of further offensive action. Polybius says that while Hannibal and Maharbal were looking out over the blood-soaked plain, Maharbal pressed his commander to strike at Rome itself. 'You follow,' Maharbal said, 'I'll go ahead with the cavalry – they'll know I've come, before they know I'm coming.' Maharbal said he could be in Rome in five days. Hannibal, perhaps moved by the magnitude of the slaughter he had inflicted, refused. In frustration Maharbal shouted, 'So the gods haven't given everything to one man: you know how to win, Hannibal, but you don't know how to use a victory.'[44] Although the war went on for another fifteen years, Hannibal never attacked Rome.

These were dark days for Rome, but darker days lay ahead. Despite the success of the renewed Fabian strategy in preventing Hannibal from destroying any more Roman armies of such magnitude, Hannibal continued to inflict significant defeats on the Romans. In 212 BC, he cost the Romans 16,000 casualties at Herdonea. A year later, at Second Herdonea, Hannibal killed the Roman commander and eleven of his twelve military tribunes as well as 13,000 troops. He won again at Numistro in 210 BC, and in 209 BC Marcellus was twice defeated at Canusium. In 208 BC, Hannibal ambushed a Roman reconnaissance party and killed both consuls. In 216 BC, Capua went over to Hannibal. In that same year, a Roman consul and his army were ambushed in Cisalpine Gaul and destroyed. The Gallic revolt was not over. By 212 BC, over 40 per cent of Rome's Italian allies were no longer able to supply troops to Rome, including the Campanians. In that same year, Tarentum was betrayed to the enemy. A more important indication that Hannibal's strategy may have been succeeding came in 209 BC, when twelve of the thirty Latin colonies refused to supply their troop contingents for the Roman army on the grounds that their men were mistreated by Roman commanders.[45] In 211 BC, the Roman army in Spain was ambushed and destroyed, its commanders killed, reversing all Roman gains for the last seven years in a single day. By 210 BC, Rome was on the verge of losing the war.

Despite Hannibal's successes, the Romans refused to come to an accommodation, and continued to raise more manpower for its armies. Moreover, Hannibal's problems of insufficient manpower and the logistics necessary to sustain them remained. The result of these circumstances was that Hannibal was confined to southern Italy, with Roman armies continually blocking his movements and restricting his foraging. In 209 BC, events turned in Rome's favour. Publius Cornelius Scipio had taken command of the Roman armies in Spain, and in a few months captured the main Carthaginian base at New Carthage. In 208 BC, Scipio won a major battle against the Carthaginian armies at Baecula. Hannibal's brother, Hasdrubal, left Spain at the head of a large Carthaginian army, and crossed the Pyrenees and the Alps in an effort to reinforce Hannibal. He was killed and his army defeated at the Battle of the Metaurus River in 207 BC, eliminating any threat of new Carthaginian forces supporting Hannibal. In 206 BC, Scipio's victory at Illipa ended Carthaginian rule in Spain, while Hannibal remained blocked in Bruttium by Roman forces.

In 205 BC, the Carthaginians sent another army into northern Italy in a second attempt to reinforce Hannibal. The Romans blocked its advance for two years until the Carthaginians were defeated again. In 205 BC, Scipio also took command of Roman forces in Sicily and prepared to invade Africa. He invaded Africa in 204 BC, and spent the next year in a series of battles that destroyed the last remaining Carthaginian forces protecting Carthage. Carthage sued for peace and Hannibal was recalled to Africa. In 202 BC, Hannibal left Italy for Africa. The Carthaginians broke the Roman peace, and in the autumn of 202 BC, Hannibal was defeated by Scipio at Zama. Fearing Roman punishment, Hannibal left Carthage in 201 BC for the eastern Mediterranean, where he took refuge with a number of kings. In 183 BC, the Romans sent their general Flamininus to Bithynia to demand of their king, Prusias, that he turn Hannibal over to them. Rather than surrender, Hannibal took the poison he always carried with him in his ring. He was 64 years old.

Hannibal's Strategic Mistake[46]

Hannibal was a brilliant field commander who applied his intellect and talents to the singular end of winning battles. But wars are not won only by winning battles. Battles are *means* to a strategic end, not ends in themselves. To Hannibal, however, the war in Italy was the only war, and victory there was his primary objective. Hannibal did not see his Italian campaign as fitting within any larger strategic plan. He never regarded his operations in Italy as one campaign in a larger war, but as the *only* campaign in the *only* war. Hannibal's confusion of tactics with strategy caused him to commit a number of operational failures that led ultimately to his defeat in Italy. Ironically, Hannibal's defeat had little to do with Carthage's defeat in the larger strategic arena.

When the Romans refused to discuss peace after the disaster at Cannae, Hannibal's plan to force Rome to negotiate began to unravel. It was one thing to expect the Gauls to join Hannibal against Rome, but the assumption that Rome's Latin allies or Roman colonies would join in any significant numbers was completely unfounded, based upon a lack of understanding of Roman culture and history. If this had not been clear to Hannibal before, it must surely have been after Cannae. As an alternative, Hannibal hit upon the idea of creating a confederacy of Italian and Greek states in southern Italy that would become *de facto* protectorates of Carthage once the war was over.

For this plan to have any chance of success required sufficient manpower to accomplish two things. First, Hannibal needed enough troops to maintain an army of occupation to hold the towns and cities with sufficient strength to ward off Roman attacks, while protecting the surrounding agricultural lands that provided food for the Carthaginian army. Second, Hannibal required sufficient troops to sustain a large field army to deal with any Roman military operations undertaken against him. The problem was that the plan required far more manpower than he possessed, or could possibly raise and supply in Italy alone.

Hannibal's revised plan, therefore, depended heavily upon Carthage to provide his manpower and logistical requirements from outside Italy, something it refused to do for sound strategic reasons. Moreover, Hannibal's plan gave no consideration to the ability of the Roman navy to blockade the southern peninsula and disrupt any supply convoys that might be sent from Carthage. Most important, Hannibal's southern Italian confederacy was essentially a defensive strategy, and left the Roman manpower and resource base north of the Volturnus River intact and unchallenged until Rome could rebuild its armies and go over to the offensive in the south. Even if it succeeded, Hannibal's league of rebel towns in southern Italy could not damage the Roman war effort sufficiently to provide Rome with an incentive to seek peace.

Hannibal's failure to attack Rome was his greatest tactical mistake. Livy tells us that when Hannibal was recalled to Carthage in 203 BC, 'he called down on his own head for not having led his armies straight to Rome when they were still bloody from the victorious field of Cannae'. But the failure to attack Rome must be seen within Hannibal's greater failure to understand the strategy with which Carthage was conducting the war. Here again we encounter Hannibal's limited view that the war was about his operations in Italy and nothing more.

Both Carthage and Rome viewed the war in a much larger strategic context than Hannibal. Rome sought to preserve its gains obtained during the First Punic War and, perhaps, seize Spain; Carthage aimed to retain Spain and recover its bases and possessions in Corsica, Sardinia and Sicily that it lost in the previous war. Rome immediately understood Carthage's strategic intent. Of the eleven legions deployed *after* Hannibal arrived in Italy, two were sent to Spain, two to Sardinia, two to Sicily and one to the port of Tarentum to block any invasion by Philip V of Macedonia, even though Philip was not yet allied with Hannibal. These deployments were intended to defend against the expected Carthaginian attacks on its former possessions. Only four legions were deployed in Italy to meet Hannibal's invasion.

Had Hannibal understood this wider strategic perspective, he would have seen that an attack on Rome would have made sound tactical sense. Had he attacked Rome after his victory at Trasimene, Hannibal would have forced the Roman legions to come to the city's aid, drawing off their forces from outside Italy. Had Hannibal threatened Rome after Trasimene, either as a genuine effort or even a feint, Rome would have been forced to recall some of its legions from abroad, exposing Sicily, Spain or Sardinia to Carthaginian attack and invasion. Hannibal's failure to appreciate the larger strategic picture led him to fail to take advantage of an opportunity that even he, in hindsight, realized might have turned the tide of the war.

When Carthage gave Hannibal a free hand to deal with the problem that arose with the Romans over Sarguntum in Spain, it is by no means clear that it anticipated or wished a general war with Rome. But once war was declared, Carthage had little choice but to support Hannibal in his Italo-centric strategy. But after Cannae, when it became clear that Hannibal was not going to succeed in driving the Romans to negotiate, the government of Carthage changed strategy in favour of a more direct approach to regaining its lost possessions.

What Carthage wanted most out of the war was to retain possession of Spain, its silver mines, commercial bases and monopoly on the inland trade. Carthage also wanted to recoup its bases in Corsica, Sardinia, Sicily and some of the offshore islands to control the commercial sea lanes in the western Mediterranean. After Cannae, Carthage moved to strengthen its grasp on these possessions by reinforcing them, as in Spain, or attempting to seize them, as in Sardinia, Sicily and Corsica, by military means. If Carthage could create a significant military presence in these former possessions, it would be in a strong position to retain them once the war ended and negotiations ensued. Carthage saw Hannibal's operations in Italy as little more than a localized campaign designed to tie down as many Roman armies as possible, while Carthage brought military pressure to bear at more important strategic points elsewhere. Carthage now had a new strategic vision as to the conduct and purpose of a war that originally had been forced upon it by Hannibal's actions at Saguntum.

We have Hannibal's own words that he felt betrayed by Carthage after Cannae. When envoys arrived from Carthage in 203 BC to order Hannibal to abandon his campaign in Italy and return to Africa, Livy says that 'Hannibal groaned and gnashed his teeth and could hardly refrain from tears'. He openly blamed Carthage for its failure to support his campaign with troops, supplies and money. 'For years past they have been trying to force me back by refusing me reinforcements and money.' He went on to say that he was not defeated by the Romans, 'but by the envy and disparagement of the Carthaginian Senate'.

Hannibal accused the Carthaginian Senate of not sending him critical supplies and troops when he needed them most, and, indeed, he is correct that they did not. In all the long years of the war, Hannibal received only one resupply expedition, and that, in 215 BC, comprised a marginal force of 4,000 troops, forty elephants and some money. He received nothing after that. Carthage was using its resources to pursue a strategy different from Hannibal's, in which victory in Italy no longer occupied a central place.

Carthage's failure to resupply Hannibal with sufficient troops cannot be blamed on a lack of resources available to it to prosecute the war. The manpower and resource base of the Carthaginian Empire was greater than Rome's. The troop and resupply expeditions sent out by Carthage in support of its military operations were substantial, in some cases larger than Hannibal's entire army in Italy. In 215 BC, 12,000 infantry, 1,500 cavalry, twenty elephants and twenty talents of silver were sent to Spain. Later that year, an even larger force of 22,000 infantry, 1,200 cavalry and some warships were sent to Sardinia. In 213 BC, Carthage sent an army of 25,000 infantry, 3,000 cavalry and twelve elephants to Sicily to rescue Syracuse. A year later, the Carthaginians tried to relieve the siege of Syracuse by sea with a fleet of 130 warships and 700 transports. When the Carthaginian army in Sicily was almost wiped out by an epidemic, Carthage sent reinforcements of 8,000 infantry and 3,000 cavalry. In 207 BC, 10,000 troops were sent to Spain to reinforce the forces that had been lost at the Battle of Baecula. Finally, in 205 BC, Mago and a force of 12,000 infantry, 2,000 cavalry and thirty ships were sent to invade Liguria in northern Italy. A year later he was reinforced with 6,000 infantry, 800 cavalry, seven elephants and twenty-five warships. With the money sent to him, Mago was able to raise another 10,000 Ligurian mercenaries, for a total force of 30,000 men. Right to the end, Carthage had enough troops and cavalry to support Hannibal in Italy. It simply chose not to do so.

It is sometimes thought that the failure to resupply Hannibal was due to the Carthaginian lack of ships and the preponderance of Roman naval power to intercept supply convoys. While the Roman fleet surely outnumbered the Carthaginian fleet in warships by the end of the war, the disparity could not have been more than about three to two. In any given escort operation, however, this disparity might easily disappear or even shift to the Carthaginian advantage. Carthage never seems to have had any difficulty in escorting her troop and supply convoys to Spain, Liguria, Corsica, Sicily and Sardinia. When Scipio ordered the

Carthaginian fleet burned in the harbour at Utica at the end of the war, Livy says that 500 ships of all kinds were destroyed.

When considering Carthage's ability to resupply and reinforce its armies in the various theatres of operations, the number of naval combatants to act as escorts was of little importance. Of more importance were the number of supply transports available, and Carthage never seems to have had any difficulty in acquiring sufficient such craft. This is not surprising for a commercial and shipbuilding nation that could construct or hire whatever transports it needed from its commercial traders. Using naval combatants to escort transports only reduced the range and speed of the transports, that could sail day and night over longer distances without having to stop regularly and rest the crews of the warships.

Finally, the Roman naval presence around southern Italy was never sufficient to cover all bases at once, and there was no good reason why supply transports could not have got through to Hannibal in southern Italy, either through Locri or the other Greek coastal ports in Bruttium. Carthaginian ships did reach Hannibal in 215 BC, and again in 203 BC when the envoys ordered him home. Mago was able to sail to Carthage in 215 BC to inform the Senate of Hannibal's victories. And Hannibal was able to evacuate his army from Croton in 203 BC without incident.

It was only when Hannibal was on the defensive, his forces dwindling and his army suffering from lack of supplies and malnutrition, that Carthage finally made an attempt to support Hannibal. In 205 BC, a fleet of transports set sail for Italy, only to be blown off course and captured by the Romans. For most of the war, however, supplies and reinforcements did not get to Hannibal in southern Italy, because Carthage did not send them. And it did not send them because, after Cannae, Carthage no longer considered Italy to be at the centre of its strategic war effort.

Carthaginian strategy shifted away from Italy after Cannae, when ironically Hannibal's military achievements were at their height. Paradoxically, it was Hannibal's successes in the field that led Carthage to reconsider its strategy. When Mago returned to Carthage in 215 BC to request troops and supplies for Hannibal, he addressed the Carthaginian Senate. At that meeting, Hanno, the leader of the faction that had opposed the war from the beginning, asked Mago the following questions: 'First, in spite of the fact that Roman power was utterly destroyed at Cannae, has any single member of the Latin Confederacy come over to us? Secondly, has any man belonging to the five and thirty tribes of Rome deserted to Hannibal?' Mago had to answer that they had not.

Hanno continued: 'Have the Romans sent Hannibal any envoys to treat for peace? Indeed, so far as your information goes, has the word "peace" ever been breathed in Rome at all?' 'No,' said Mago. 'Very well then,' replied Hanno. 'In the conduct of the war we have not advanced one inch: the situation is precisely the same as when Hannibal first crossed into Italy.'[47] Hanno's point was that Hannibal's strategy to bring Rome to the peace table by defeating its armies in the field had already failed. If none of the Latin Confederacy or the Roman tribes had deserted by now, it was very unlikely that any defections in the south of Italy or additional victories that Hannibal might win there would cause Rome to seek peace.

If Rome could not be destroyed by Hannibal in Italy, as the Carthaginian government believed, then what was the war about? In true Hellenistic fashion, Carthage saw that it was not about destroying Rome, but about maintaining Carthage's control of Spain and, perhaps, regaining Sardinia, Corsica and some ports in Sicily that it had lost in the previous war. If that was the strategic objective of the war, then how did Hannibal's continued presence in Italy contribute to that? The answer was to tie down as many legions in Italy as possible so they could not be used elsewhere, while Carthage concentrated its efforts in the other theatres of operations. Italy was only a sideshow.

Carthage left Hannibal to his own resources and his own fate while it applied its considerable resources to Spain, Sardinia, Corsica and Sicily in the hope of establishing strong military positions so that when the war ended, Carthage might be able to hold on to what it had won. Hannibal ultimately failed, not because he was defeated on the battlefield, but because his tactical victories did not contribute to Carthage's larger strategic objectives. After Cannae, the strategic ground shifted beneath Hannibal's feet, reducing a man who had once been the king of the battlefield to little more than a sacrificial pawn in a much larger game that he never really understood. Hannibal's failure is a sound lesson to modern generals not to confuse operational success with strategic success, a lesson they seem to have ignored in Vietnam, Iraq and Afghanistan.

If, as Polybius says, Hamilcar was the greatest Carthaginian general of the First Punic War, there is no doubt that Hannibal was the greatest Carthaginian general of the second conflict. He fought the best generals Rome produced to a standstill when he did not defeat them outright, and sustained his army in the field for sixteen long years without mutiny or desertion. Hannibal was a first-rate tactician and only a somewhat lesser strategist, and the greatest enemy Rome ever faced. When, at last, he met defeat at the hands of a Roman general, it was against an experienced Roman officer who had to strengthen and reconfigure the Roman legion and invent new mobile tactics to succeed. Even so, Scipio's victory at Zama was a near-run thing against an army that was a shadow of its former self, and could easily have gone the other way. If it had, the history of the West would have been changed in ways that can only be imagined.

Notes

1. H.V. Canter, 'The Character of Hannibal', *Classical Journal* 24, no. 8 (May 1929), p.564.
2. Polybius, *The Histories*, 1.64.6, trans. Evelyn S. Shuckburgh (Bloomington, Indiana University Press, 1962).
3. Cornelius Nepos, *Hannibal*, trans. John C. Rolfe (Cambridge, MA, Harvard University Press, 1984), 7.5.13.
4. Canter, 'The Character of Hannibal', p.565, citing Cassius Dio, *Roman History*, trans. Earnest Cary and Herbert Foster (Cambridge, MA, Harvard University Press, 1992), 13, fragment 54.
5. B.D. Hobos, *Hannibal's Dynasty: Power and Politics in the Western Mediterranean, 247–183 BC* (London, Routledge, 2003), p.75, citing Diodorus.
6. Titus Livius (Livy), *The War With Hannibal: The History of Rome from its Foundations*, trans. Aubrey de Selincourt (London, Penguin, 1965), 21.4.
7. Hobos, *Hannibal's Dynasty*, p.85, citing Arrian.
8. Ibid.
9. Livy, *The War With Hannibal*, 21.7.
10. Ibid., 21.5.
11. Nepos, *Hannibal*, 23.4.
12. Ibid.
13. Polybius, *Histories*, 3.56.
14. Richard A. Gabriel, 'Siege craft and Artillery', chapter 17 in *Soldiers' Lives Through History: The Ancient World* (Westport, CT, Greenwood Press, 2007), p.135
15. Serge Lancel, *Carthage: A History*, trans. Antonia Nevill (Malden, MA, Blackwell Publishers, 1995), p.90.
16. John Lazenby, *Hannibal's War: A Military History of the Second Punic War* (Warminster, Aris and Philips, 1978), p.61.
17. Livy, *The War With Hannibal*, 22.2.
18. Ibid.
19. Livy notes that the place was *loca nata insidiis*, or 'naturally created for ambush'. As to Flaminius' failure to conduct a reconnaissance of the valley, Lazenby, *Hannibal's War*, p.40, says, 'What general in command of any army of 25,000 men expects to be ambushed?'

20. Polybius, *The Histories*, 3.96; also Livy, *The War With Hannibal*, 22.11.6–7.
21. Ibid., see also Hobos, *Hannibal's Dynasty*, p.62.
22. Glen R. Storey, 'The Population of Ancient Rome', *Antiquity* (December 1997), pp.1–14.
23. John F. Shean, 'Hannibal's Mules: the Logistical Limitations of Hannibal's Army and the Battle of Cannae, 216 BC', *Historia*, 45, no. 2 (1996), p.166, citing Plutarch's *Life of Marcellus*, 13.2.
24. Ibid., pp.166–67.
25. Livy, *The War With Hannibal*, 22.32.
26. Shean, *Hannibal's Mules*, p.183.
27. Lazenby, *Hannibal's War*, p.76, for where the forces converged.
28. Polybius, *The Histories*, 3.107.
29. Ibid., 3.113.
30. Adrian Goldsworthy, *Cannae: Hannibal's Greatest* Victory (London, Orion Books, 2007), p.110, relying on Polybius' numbers.
31. Ibid., p.97.
32. Lazenby, *Hannibal's War*, p.80.
33. Goldsworthy, Cannae, pp.102–03.
34. Livy says that Maharbal commanded the cavalry on the Carthaginian right, while Polybius says Hanno did.
35. Livy, *The War With Hannibal*, 22.49.
36. Ibid, 22.47.
37. Polybius, *The Histories*, 3.115.
38. Livy, *The War With Hannibal*, 22.47.
39. Polybius, *The Histories*, 3.113–14.
40. Ibid., 3.116.
41. Livy, *The War With Hannibal*, 22.49.
42. Lazenby, *Hannibal's War*, p.47. Polybius, *The Histories*, 3.84–84 puts the number of Roman dead at 70,000 with 10,000 prisoners, compared to 5,700 Punic losses.
43. Ibid., 45.
44. Livy, *The War With Hannibal*, 22.51.
45. For an analysis of Rome's allies and their loyalty and disloyalty during the Second Punic War, see J.S. Reid, 'Problems of the Second Punic War: Rome and Her Allies', *Journal of Roman Studies* 5 (1915), pp.87–124.
46. This section on Hannibal's strategic errors is drawn from my article 'Hannibal's Strategic Errors: Confusion of Tactics With Strategy', *Military History* (March 2016).
47. Livy, *The War with Hannibal*, 23.13.

CHAPTER EIGHT

JULIUS CAESAR (100–44 BC)

Julius Caesar was born into a noble patrician family supposedly descended from the first kings of Rome on his mother's side. His aunt Julia was the wife of Gaius Marius, the famous general, military reformer and leader of the Popular faction in Rome that fought against Sulla and the Optimates. When Sulla became dictator, he marked Caesar for execution, forcing Caesar to go into hiding. He served in Asia on the staff of a military legate, where he was awarded a civic crown for saving the life of a citizen in battle. This brought him to the attention of Crassus, another powerful man in Rome who became his patron and rival of Pompey. Caesar returned to Rome in 78 BC after Sulla had died, and began his career as a lawyer. Caesar remained on good terms with both Crassus and Pompey, and when both served as consuls in 70 BC, Caesar was elected military tribune.[1]

In 68 BC, Caesar was elected *quaestor* and obtained a seat in the Senate. In 65 BC, he was elected *aedile*, and two years later, with Crassus' financial support, was elected *pontifex maximus*. In 61 BC, he was sent as *praetor* to Spain, where he waged a successful war against the Callaici and the Lusitani in the northwest of the peninsula, and established a civilian administration to govern the region. In late 60 BC, he returned to Rome and mediated between Crassus and Pompey. Out of his efforts emerged a political coalition among the three men – the First Triumvirate. Caesar's daughter, Julia, married Pompey to seal the arrangement. In 58 BC, Caesar set out for Gaul, where he spent the next eight years defeating the various Gallic tribes and turning the region into another Roman province.

Julius Caesar stands out from the military history of the ancient world as one of the greatest military commanders ever to plan a campaign or lead men in battle. Caesar was one of the most complex personalities to emerge from the pages of ancient history. As a general, he was personally courageous and always present on the battlefield, his presence identified by the red cloak that he wore when in command of his armies. Personally courageous, on several occasions Caesar plunged into the thick of battle at a crucial point to rally his men to the attack. He was an excellent horseman, and could handle a sword and shield with the best of his centurions. He understood that soldiers fought for many reasons, not the least of which was the trust, faith and confidence they placed in their commander. Although a firm disciplinarian, Caesar always saw to the welfare of his men, and they loved him for it. He repeatedly drew on their affection and trust when in a tight spot, and he was never disappointed by the willingness of his soldiers to follow him into danger.

But Caesar was far more than a technically proficient soldier and general. He was also a remarkable orator capable of moving crowds of civilians and soldiers to the heights of demagoguery. His speaking and writing skill served him well as an accomplished politician in the violent scramble for power that followed the conquest of Gaul and the crossing of the Rubicon. Caesar was also a first-rate strategic thinker. Encumbered by few scruples, he always clearly perceived the linkages between ends, ways and means, and was very flexible in devising tactics to make these linkages function correctly. He rarely allowed anger or hatred for an enemy to cloud his thinking or judgement, and he meted out clemency and slaughter with equal ease, depending only upon which tactic at the time served the accomplishment of the larger end. Caesar saw all situations – political, military, social and personal – as amenable to the same type of intellectual solution: do what must be done to achieve your goal.

Caesar's complexity and importance make it difficult to treat his military experiences adequately in this short space. Any military analysis of Caesar must recognize that he fought scores of battles under widely varying circumstances. In Gaul, he fought tribal armies and conducted sieges. During the Roman civil war, he fought a Roman army under Pompey that was every bit as good as his own against an opponent who was an equally talented general. After his victories over Pompey, he fought battles against Egyptian, African and Spanish armies. There are few military commanders in history who have fought so many major battles against so many different types of enemies in so many different environments in so short a time.

The three battles analyzed herein are Alesia, Dyrrachium and Pharsalus. The siege of Alesia was the last great battle in the suppression of the Gallic revolt of 53–52 BC, and sealed for all time the fate of Gaul as an adversary of Rome. It was one of the few battles against the Gauls in which Caesar faced a tribal general, Vercingetorix, of some skill and training. The Battle of Dyrrachium (48 BC) pitted Caesar against Pompey in an engagement whose strategic and operational complexities have few equals during this period. Both armies were Roman-trained and led, making the difference of victory and defeat a product of the intelligence of the rival commanders. Dyrrachium is one of the few battles in which Caesar was out-generaled and defeated. The Battle of Pharsalus (48 BC) represented a truly set-piece battle of Roman infantry in which the outcome was decided by generalship and tactical brilliance. At Pharsalus, Caesar defeated Pompey, the beginning of the end of the civil war for the control of the Roman state. The selection of these three battles is essentially arbitrary, and it is likely that other historians wishing to stress other aspects of Caesar's military talents could just as arbitrarily choose other battles as points of analysis.

Caesar's Gallic Wars

In Caesar's day, Gaul included the whole of France and Belgium, parts of Holland, Switzerland and all of Germany west of the Rhine. The population was of mixed origin, although the Celts were in a majority, and probably numbered between 15 and 20 million people. The population was divided into 200–300 tribes, with some tribes held as vassals – Caesar called them *clientela* – to the larger ones. The tribes lived in villages scattered around a central fortified town. These towns were frequently located on high ground for defensive reasons. The Gauls practised extensive agriculture and cattle breeding, and their tribes were more stable than the largely nomadic and pastoral Germanic tribes across the Rhine. The country was relatively well developed in terms of bridges, dirt roads, frequently used river fordings, docks and heavy river traffic. Caesar found a significant transportation and economic infrastructure upon which he could draw to sustain his armies in the field.

Caesar was sent to Gaul as proconsul in 58 BC. His term of office was fixed at five years, and his military complement consisted of four legions. He had no military experience to speak of, and certainly none in the art of command at the general officer level. Between 58–51 BC, Caesar conducted almost constant military operations in Gaul, with the objective of bringing the area under Roman domination and incorporating it as a province of the Roman Empire. But that was not the most important reason for Caesar's wars. Caesar cannot be seen only as a loyal soldier given the mission to conquer another province for Rome. Caesar was a *condottieri* general given wide responsibility and power for military conquest, that he intended to use first and foremost to increase his own wealth, reputation and political power, to be used as weapons against his rivals in the struggle to control the Roman state. Personal ambition always lay at the roots of Caesar's genius.

It is impossible to describe here in any detail the major battles fought by Caesar in his Gallic campaigns leading up to the suppression of the

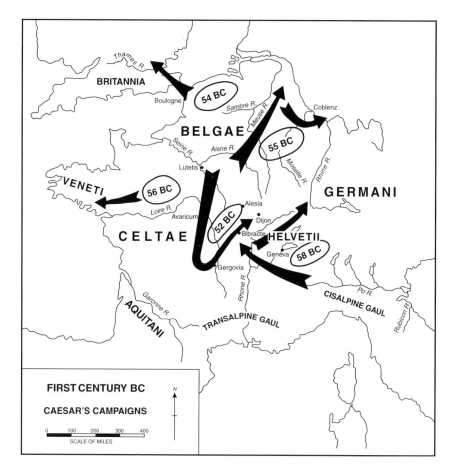

Caesar's Wars in Gaul

Gallic revolt in October 52 BC. This section provides the reader with only a general sketch of each of those battles and the campaigns of which they were a part. They are offered to provide a general sense of the events leading up to the siege of Alesia. The strategic situations concerning the later battles at Dyrrachium and Pharsalus are described below in the relevant sections dealing directly with those battles.

Defeat of the Helvetii (58 BC)

Shortly after Caesar assumed his post as proconsul, the entire Helvetiian people, a Gallic tribe living in the area of modern Switzerland, began a migration westward toward the fertile lands of the Rhone valley.

The tribe comprised (by Caesar's count) 368,000 people, of whom 92,000 were warriors. Fearing that this movement would pose a threat to Italy, Caesar hurried from Rome to Geneva to deal with the problem. Caesar had only one legion in Transalpine Gaul. He ordered the recruitment of a large force of auxiliary troops from loyal Gallic tribes that feared being overrun by the tribal migration, destroyed the bridge the Helvetii had constructed over the Rhone and constructed a 19-mile long chain of fortifications across the Rhone valley migration route to stop the Helvetii. The Helvetii, deflected from their route of march, moved westward across the Jura country north of the Rhone.

Upon learning of the westward movement of the Helvetii, Caesar left his legate in charge of the barriers near Geneva and travelled back to Cisalpine Gaul to raise more manpower. He raised two new legions from the province and called in three from Illyria. With this force, he moved from near Turin, crossed the Alps, advanced through Grenoble and crossed the Rhone near Lyon. East of Lyon, he was joined by the Tenth legion and a body of Gallic cavalry. His force numbered 30,000 men and 4,000 cavalry. During his march from Italy to Gaul, Caesar averaged 16 miles a day over rough mountain tracks.

Caesar's reconnaissance learned that the Helvetii were crossing the Saone on boats and rafts a few miles above Lyon. He waited a half day's march from the crossing point. When most of the Helvetii were across the river, Caesar broke camp at midnight, conducted a rapid night march and struck the enemy remaining on the east bank at daylight. He overwhelmed and annihilated more than 30,000 Helvetiian warriors trapped on the near bank. He then bridged the river at the battlefield, and followed the main body of Helvetii as it withdrew.

Caesar's army was running low on supplies, and he turned northward to the town of Bibracte to resupply his army. The Helvetiians thought that Caesar had lost his nerve, and turned back toward the Romans and fell on their rearguard. To check the Gallic attack, Caesar ordered his cavalry force (4,000 horse) to engage the Helvetiian infantry near the Armecy ridge. Using his cavalry as a screen, Caesar deployed his four veteran legions in triple line on the ridge, with the two newly raised legions behind them in reserve.

The Helvetiian army was encumbered by thousands of men, women and children accompanying them on the migration. Operating from a wagon *laager*, the Helvetiians attacked up the slope. Wave after wave was repulsed by *pilum* and *gladius*. At last, the Romans moved off the ridge and down the valley, driving the Helvetii before them, only to be attacked in the flank. While the Romans were dealing with the flank attack, the Helvetii launched another frontal assault. The fighting was desperate, and losses on both sides were high. As Caesar wrote, 'There was no rout for throughout the action, though it lasted from the seventh hour to eventide, no one could have seen the back of the enemy.' Gradually, the Romans moved toward the *laager* and, reaching it, continued the assault against warrior and civilian far into the night. Amid great slaughter (Caesar says 238,000 were killed), the Helvetii were driven from their wagons. Deprived of their sources of food and having been almost annihilated, they had little choice but to surrender. The Battle of Armecy was Caesar's first military engagement in Gaul, and he had conducted it brilliantly and emerged victorious.

Campaign Against Ariovistus (58 BC)

No sooner had Caesar dealt with the problem of the Helvetii than he had to confront the problem of a Germanic incursion under the leadership of Ariovistus. Representatives from a number of tribes near the Rhine approached Caesar for help in stopping the rampages of the Germanic chieftain. Caesar saw the opportunity to cast himself in the role of saviour of all Gaul. Moreover, he felt strongly that sooner or later the German problem would have to be dealt with forcefully. It was Caesar's uncle, Marius, who had saved Rome from a Germanic invasion fifty years earlier. Caesar requested a meeting with Ariovistus, who advised Caesar to stay out of the quarrel. Caesar responded by informing Ariovistus that any further encroachments in Gaul would be met by force of Roman arms. Ariovistus' response was to assemble thousands of Germanic Seubi tribesman on the Rhine with the threat to cross and reinforce Ariovistus in Gaul. To prevent this reinforcement, Caesar broke camp and marched to make contact with Ariovistus.

Three days into the march, Caesar learned that Ariovistus was planning to seize the town of Vesontio (mod. Besancon). This town was a well-fortified Sequani arsenal. Caesar changed direction and moved to take it first. Having seized the town, Caesar rested his troops and replenished his supplies. Within a few days, he was on the march again in search of Ariovistus. Seven days later, Caesar's scouts found Ariovistus 24 miles from the van of Caesar's army. A meeting between Caesar and Ariovistus settled nothing, and, two days later, Ariovistus manoeuvred to cut Caesar's supply line. Caesar had to bring Ariovistus to battle or risk the starvation of his army.

For five consecutive days, Caesar marched his army onto the open plain to draw Ariovistus into a fight. Except for minor cavalry skirmishing, the German chieftain refused. Finally, Caesar marched all six of his legions in triple line to the ramparts of the enemy camp. Ariovistus had no choice. He drew up his army in seven tribal formations, behind which he posted the wagon *laager* that contained his supplies and the wives and children of his warriors. The battle opened with both sides simultaneously charging directly at one another. So rapidly did both sides close that the Romans had no time to launch their *pila*. Observing the disposition of forces prior to the battle, Caesar spotted a weakness in the enemy left wing, in that it 'appeared less steady' than the other. Caesar took command of his own right wing, and waited for both sides to engage. After some time, the Roman right began to break through the German left. At the same time, however, the Roman left began to falter as the sheer weight of German numbers began to take its toll. At this point, Publius Crassus, the cavalry commander, took the initiative and brought up a line of cavalry from the rear to reinforce the Roman left wing. With its last opportunity to break the Roman line gone, the German centre wavered and broke. The rest of the army turned on its heels and fled.

Having caught his enemy at last, Caesar refused to disengage. He ordered a relentless and ruthless pursuit. Some of the Germans succeeded in swimming the Rhine, but many others drowned. What was left of the 75,000-man army was trapped between the legions and the swift waters of the Rhine. Working in concert, the Roman infantry and cavalry slaughtered most of it. When news of Caesar's victory reached the Seubi on the east side of the Rhine, they abandoned any plans for a river crossing and returned to their homes. As Caesar wrote, 'Two campaigns were thus finished in a single summer.' Within a single year, Caesar had gained central and southern Gaul for Rome.

Campaign Against the Belgae (57 BC)

The Belgae, the collective name for the tough, Gallic-Germanic peoples of northeastern Gaul, were alarmed that Caesar's successful campaigns would be a prelude to their own conquest by the Romans. They assembled a force of 300,000 warriors (Caesar's numbers, and clearly an exaggeration) and began to march south to make contact with Caesar. Caesar was in Italy when he learned of these events. He quickly raised two more legions and, in the early spring, returned to his camp at Vesontio. He made logistical preparations and, with an army of 40,000 legionnaires and 20,000 Gallic auxiliaries, Caesar set out to invade the land of the Belgae.

Within a fortnight, Caesar reached the borders of the Belgae on the Marne River. He surprised the Remi, a Belgic tribe, so completely that they went over to his side. The Remi told Caesar that Galba, the king of the Suessiones, was in supreme command of a Belgic coalition comprised of the Bellovaci, Suessiones and the Nervii. Meanwhile, Caesar's intelligence had located the main body of the enemy in route of march toward him. Caesar rapidly moved his troops across the Aisne River by constructing a bridge, and built a fortified camp on the northern side of the river. With the river to his back and his supply line secure over the bridge, Caesar waited for the arrival of Galba.

The two armies engaged in cavalry skirmishes for several days, and a Belgic raid on the fortified bridge was repulsed. But no significant battle occurred. Instead, the typical failure of the Gallic tribal armies to provide for logistical support forced Galba's army to withdraw because of its inability to feed itself while investing the Roman camp. Caesar saw his opportunity and followed the army, harassing the rearguard and advancing into the various tribal lands, meeting and defeating the tribal contingents piecemeal. Having ravaged the lands of the Suessiones, the Bellovaci and the Ambiani, Caesar prepared to deal with the fiercest of the Belgic tribes, the Nervii.

Caesar's army halted at a point 10 miles from the Sambre River, where he learned that somewhere on its far side the Nervii were waiting for him in coalition with the Atrebates and Viromandui. Caesar's difficulty was that he did not know the strength of the enemy (about 75,000 as it turned out), nor its disposition across the river. As was his normal practice, Caesar sent his cavalry ahead to locate a camp for his legions. They selected a spot on a hill overlooking the woods on the other side of the Sambre. Because he expected to contact the enemy, Caesar moved his baggage train to the rear of the column under guard of two legions. The rest marched in light field order toward the camp, ready to engage.

When the six leading legions reached the camp area, they began to cut timber and construct the camp. It was normal Roman practice to provide security for the construction elements. Perhaps Caesar thought his cavalry was sufficient force to deal with an ambush. In any event, he did not post a strong security force. This was a serious error, and almost caused a catastrophe. The Nervii attacked from out of the woods, struck the Roman cavalry screen, routed it, and then raced up the hill and attacked the legionnaires at work on the camp. The surprise was complete and nearly lethal. Fortunately, the legions' commanders had been ordered by Caesar not to leave their legions until the camp was completed, so there were officers to direct the resistance. These legions were highly disciplined veterans. Their centurions immediately grasped the danger and, instead of allowing the men to seek their own cohorts, the centurions assembled the troops around the nearest standard and began to fight. Now the rest of the enemy force engaged. Caesar was with the Tenth Legion on the left flank. When he saw the Atrebates closing with the flank, he gave the order to attack.

The Ninth and Tenth Legion engaged viciously, stopped the enemy advance and threw it back down the slope, and, without losing contact, followed it over the Sambre. At about the same time, the legions in the centre held their ground and began to drive the enemy force back toward the river. The whole Roman line began to swing on a hinge comprised of the Twelfth and Seventh Legions, who were under strong assault by the Nervii. Gradually, the Nervii compressed the two legions in upon one another and began to envelop Caesar's right flank, the end of the Roman line.

Things were desperate. When Caesar arrived, he found the Twelfth so closely huddled together that the men could not raise their swords against the enemy. (A similar situation happened at Cannae.) Many of the legion's centurions were already dead, and many others wounded. Caesar, by his own account, grabbed a shield from a soldier in the rear rank and pushed his way to the front. He called upon the centurions by name to force the men to open ranks to better wield their swords. Then Caesar personally led the counter-attack.

As events would have it, the Thirteenth and Fourteenth Legions that had been with the baggage train now came over the hill and entered the battle. This was enough for the Belgae, who began to retreat. At this point, Caesar's most trusted officer, Labienus, who had led the Tenth Legion across the river and captured the enemy camp, turned his legion back toward the river and fell upon the enemy's rear. The Belgic army stopped in its tracks. The massive column of Nervii was trapped on three sides. In a desperate fight, the enemy column was hacked to pieces. Roman casualties were heavy, but the Nervii lost 60,000 dead, almost seven out of every eight men who took the field that day. The destruction was so complete that Caesar noted in his writings that, 'This engagement brought the name and nation of the Nervii almost to utter destruction.'

Campaign Against the Veneti (56 BC)

In the spring of 56 BC, Caesar invaded the Brittany Peninsula to conquer the Veneti. The pretext for the invasion was the mistreatment of
Roman ambassadors by the tribal leaders. In fact, the Veneti, a skilled
seafaring people who monopolized the lucrative trade with Britain,
had learned that Caesar was planning a campaign against Britain, and
that Rome would thereby threaten the traditional livelihood of the
tribe. The Veneti had reckoned correctly. Caesar used the incident as a
pretext to seize and subdue the vital channel ports he needed to support his invasion of Britain.

The Veneti would have to be brought to heel either by defeating
them at sea or by capturing their coastal strongholds. Neither was an
easy task. The Venetian ships were made of stout oak that the Roman
galley rams could not penetrate. These ships had shallow keels that
allowed them to run in shallower water than the Roman galleys. Their
large square leather sails and the considerable height of their decks
above the water made them fast and difficult for the lower Roman galleys to successfully use pike or grappling hooks against. The coastal
towns of the Veneti were well fortified and difficult to approach from
land or sea. Any garrison in danger of succumbing to land attack could
be easily evacuated by sea, a tactic used by the Veneti against Caesar
on several occasions.

After several attempts to reduce the coastal cities by force, with
only mixed success, Caesar determined to fight a naval campaign. He
ordered a sizeable fleet of ships to be built on the Loire. When completed and manned, the Roman fleet assembled in Quiberon Bay and
awaited the arrival of the Veneti fleet. The enemy fleet arrived with 220
ships, approximately twice the number of Roman ships on hand. The
Roman naval commander – Decimus Brutus – had thought through
his plan of action. The problem was how to stop the enemy ships from
using their superior speed and invulnerability to the Roman galley's
ram. Using the galley's superior short-range sprint speed, the Roman
ships could easily manoeuvre next to the larger Veneti ships. Roman
engineers, who had revolutionized naval warfare in the Punic Wars
by inventing the *corvus* (the swinging boarding platform) and using
the grappling iron, now introduced another new piece of naval technology that was to see service for at least another millennium in the
navies of the world: the sail-cutter. Using long poles to which scythes
were attached, Roman sailors cut the leather sails of the enemy ships.
Grappling irons were then used to grasp the halyards, which attached

the yards to the masts, and the force of the rowers moving the galley away from the enemy ship snapped the halyards, collapsing the sails and immobilizing the Veneti ships.

With the enemy ships unable to move, the conflict, as Caesar wrote, 'became a question of courage'. Roman infantry boarded ship after ship and killed the crews. The battle lasted from about four o'clock to sunset, and it 'finished the campaign against the Veneti and the whole seacoast'. Without ships, the coastal towns could neither be evacuated nor supplied, and the Veneti were forced to surrender. Ground operations continued for a few more months, especially against the Morini and Menapii of northwestern Belgica. But by the winter, aside from some small areas in the swamps of the Low Countries, where rebel remnants held out, all of Gaul was now under Roman domination. So that no one would miss Caesar's point that Rome intended to brook no rival in Gaul, the entire membership of the Veneti Senate was executed and most of the rest of the population sold into slavery. Caesar had gained complete control of his strategic platform from which to launch his invasion of Britain.

Campaign Against the Germans (55 BC)

During the winter, news reached Caesar that two Germanic tribes, the Usipetes and the Tencteri, had crossed the Rhine into Gaul in an attempt to establish themselves in a new homeland. Caesar correctly guessed that there were many Belgae who would welcome these tribal kin and seek to form a new alliance against Rome that was more formidable than anything Caesar had faced. The new tribes comprised 430,000 people, with more than 100,000 warriors (again Caesar's numbers). If the invasion succeeded, Roman control in Gaul would again be insecure. Caesar determined to prevent these circumstances in the most dramatic manner possible.

In May, Caesar gathered his legions, marched to the Meuse River and entered into negotiations with the Germans. During the negotiations, Caesar's army slowly moved closer and closer to the enemy position, until they were so close that some kind of contact was almost inevitable. With negotiations underway, a small unit of Germanic cavalry attacked Caesar's Gallic cavalry, perhaps by accident and certainly not with command authorization. Caesar immediately seized and detained the chiefs of the enemy army with whom he had been talking. He then ordered his army into the attack against the entire enemy force, and trapped it in a cul-de-sac near the junction of the

Moselle and Rhine rivers. The entire people, some 430,000 men, women and children by Caesar's count, were slaughtered. There were no survivors in this deliberately calculated act of political butchery designed to send a clear message to any other tribal people, Gallic or Germanic, who might consider resisting the will of Rome. Even in Rome, the massacre provoked shock and outrage. One Senator called the slaughter, 'unquestionably the most atrocious act of which any civilized man has ever been guilty'.

Caesar, for his part, answered his critics with the argument that the massacre was necessary to deter further German inroads into Gaul. After the battle, Caesar marched his armies down the Rhine. Near the site of modern Bonn, he decided to cross the Rhine in a display of Roman power and will. Offered boats with which to cross by the Ubii, he refused. Instead, in order to impress on the barbarians Roman ability to cross the river at will, Caesar ordered a long suspension bridge constructed over the river. In ten days, a wooden roadway 40ft wide was hung from a trestle suspension bridge from bank to bank. Caesar crossed the Rhine. Once inside Germany, he left a strong rearguard to secure his line of retreat and then, for eighteen days, ravaged the countryside in a display of military power. Caesar returned to Gaul and destroyed the bridge, having made it clear to the Germans that any future attempt to cross the river would be met by the punishment of Roman arms, even in their homeland if circumstances required.

The Invasions of Britain (55–54 BC)

Caesar's expedition to Britain in August 55 BC was more a reconnaissance than an invasion. With less than the half the summer left, Caesar mounted the Seventh and Tenth Legions and their cavalry in eighty infantry and eighteen horse transports, and set sail from Boulogne for the British coast. The expedition landed near Dover, where it was strongly opposed by the Britons. After a brief battle, the Britons sued for peace. Four days after the battle, Caesar's flotilla was scattered by a strong storm. This encouraged the Britons to renew the fight. Again the Romans defeated them, and again a peace was declared. Caesar then returned to Gaul.

Before leaving for Italy for the winter, he ordered the legion commanders to construct as many ships as possible over the winter for use in a spring invasion of Britain. In the spring of 54 BC, Caesar rejoined his army. Six hundred new transports and twenty-eight galleys had been readied for the invasion. In July, after a delay caused by the need to put down a local revolt, Caesar launched the invasion with almost 700 ships carrying five legions and 2,000 cavalry. This was the largest fleet of warships deployed in the English Channel until the invasion of Normandy in 1944.

The force landed unopposed northeast of Dover. Caesar quickly debarked his legions and began a march inland, seeking to bring the enemy army to battle quickly. Again Caesar neglected to protect his fleet from harsh weather, and a severe storm destroyed and damaged a large number of vessels. A sizeable force of Britons had assembled under the command of a chieftain named Cassivellaunus. Caesar marched inland, sweeping aside a number of minor attacks, crossed the Thames somewhere west of modern London and struck at the Britons' main force. After a number of battles in which Caesar carried the day against fierce fighting, Cassivellaunus and the Britons sued for peace. After receiving the formal submission of the Britons, Caesar returned across the channel to Gaul, where, Caesar wrote, he had learned 'of a sudden commotion in Gaul'.

Battle and Siege of Alesia (52 BC)

Caesar returned from Britain in the early autumn of 54 BC, and was greeted with the news that the harvest in Gaul was a poor one. To facilitate the supply of food to his troops for the winter, Caesar dispersed his ten legions to eight camps scattered across northern Gaul. The camps were all within 100 miles of one another, and two were within 60 miles of each other. It seems to have occurred to several Gallic chieftains that it might be possible to strike at the dispersed Roman camps, destroying them one by one. One of these chieftains, Ambiorix of the Eubrones, struck the first blow. If he could destroy a Roman army in its camp, then, perhaps, the rest of Gaul would rally to the standard of rebellion.

Ambiorix mounted a tentative attack against the Roman garrison near Aduatuca. When the Romans resisted, Ambiorix broke off the attack and sought negotiations. In these talks, Ambiorix explained he had attacked the garrison under pressure from his people to join the larger movement of Gallic rebellion. He told the Roman commander that in a few days all eight of the garrisons would come under attack simultaneously. Ambiorix urged the Roman commander to abandon the camp and join the other legions in the nearest camp 60 miles away. Ambiorix guaranteed the Romans safe passage through his territory.

The Roman commander took the bait and marched out of the fortified camp the next morning. Ambiorix ambushed the Roman column from both ends when it was trapped deep within a defile in the forest. All day and into the evening, javelins rained down on the Roman column until, weakened from casualties, it was overrun. Most of the legion was killed and, at the end of the day, what men remained 'seeing that all hope was gone, every single man committed suicide'. In fact, a few soldiers survived to reach the Roman garrison 60 miles away and warn them of the impending attack.

Ambiorix had his first victory, and with it he convinced some of the other tribes to join him for an attack on the Roman garrison near Binche. Within days, a 60,000-man Gallic army laid siege to the town, trapping another Roman legion within its walls. When Caesar was informed of these events, he immediately sallied from his base near Amiens with a relief force of 7,000 infantry and 1,500 horse. When Ambiorix learned of Caesar's movement, he left a small garrison to continue the siege and moved his main force into the path of Caesar's approaching army. Near the Sabis River, the Romans encountered the Gauls in battle and, after a bitter fight, drove them from the field. Caesar moved on to relieve the siege. He was amazed at the Gallic siege works, virtual copies of the Roman machines and methods. Caesar noted in his writing of the Roman garrison, that 'not one man in ten remained unwounded'.

The revolt simmered throughout the winter as Caesar remained with his army, keeping up a steady pulse of reconnaissance and diplomacy to stay aware of what the tribes were doing. Revolt was constantly in the air. During the winter, Caesar swept down on the Nervii and ravaged their lands in a pre-emptive strike. In the spring, Caesar used all ten of his legions to conduct a campaign of intimidation against the Belgae. He crossed the Rhine again to dissuade the German tribes from coming to the aid of Ambiorix, or giving him sanctuary. Caesar's campaign involved no major battles. Instead, it was a counter-insurgency campaign designed to terrorize those who might support the rebellion. Caesar painted a vivid picture of this campaign when he described the operations against the Eubrones, the people of Ambiorix. They were shown no mercy. He wrote: 'Every hamlet, every homestead that anyone could see was set on fire; captured cattle were driven from every spot; the corn-crops were not only being consumed by the vast host of pack-animals and human beings, but were laid flat in addition because of the rainy season, even if any persons succeeded in hiding themselves for the moment, it seemed that they must perish for want of everything when the army was withdrawn.'

The destruction was pointless. Ambiorix was never caught. But the spirit of Gallic rebellion was wounded, and open revolt stopped. Caesar became convinced that things had returned to normal and, in the autumn, he set out for Italy.

During these events, central Gaul had remained peaceful. But the extraordinary degree of Roman brutality in dealing with the revolt angered the Gauls and, for the first time, forced upon them the realization that they would have to act in concert if Roman oppression was to be overthrown. Tribal leaders throughout the country held secret meetings to discuss an uprising. With Caesar in Italy, the Roman army was without its head, and the Gauls began to plan an uprising that would strike at several Roman garrisons at once. What was needed was a sudden and violent event to detonate the revolt and bring the tribes to arms. In the winter of 52 BC, the Roman merchant community at Cenabum (mod. Orleans), the capital city of the Carnutes, was slaughtered in the streets by the Gauls. Within days, all Gaul had heard of the massacre and, one after another, the tribes flocked to the standard of rebellion. The leader of the general revolt was a young Avernian chief, Vercingetorix, known for his intellect, discipline and brutality.

Task forces from the assembled Gallic army began to move on several Roman garrisons simultaneously to bring them under attack. A separate force moved south toward Narbo to block Caesar's return to Gaul. Most of Caesar's army was in north central Gaul around Lutetia (Paris). Accompanied by his bodyguard and a small provincial levy from Narbo (Narbonne), Caesar crossed the snow-covered Cevennes Mountains. His sudden appearance in front of the Gallic force threw it into a panic, and they retreated. Caesar broke contact and swung eastward along the Rhone toward Vienna on the Saone River, where he was joined by Roman cavalry units garrisoned in the vicinity. He then moved north outside of Alesia, where two of his legions were posted in winter quarters. The rest of Caesar's army was in the vicinity of Lutetia readying to move south to join him.

Quite by accident, Vercingetorix found his own army between the two Roman forces. He moved southwest and struck at Gorgobina, a major town of one of Rome's loyal tribal allies that had not joined the revolt. Caesar left his baggage at Agedincum and marched toward Gorgobina to relieve the assault against his allies. Vercingetorix's movement uncovered the towns of Vellaundodunum and Cenabum, and Caesar moved quickly to attack both. This placed Caesar behind Vercingetorix, who raised his siege of Gorgobina and turned toward Caesar in an effort to make contact with the Roman army. Caesar continued to advance and occupied the town of Noviodunum (Nevers). The two armies brushed by each other, with only sporadic contact of their cavalry forces. Caesar then moved on to Avaricum (Bourges).

Vercingetorix's operational plan had failed. He had not succeeded in preventing Caesar from joining his army in Gaul. Once in command, Caesar had moved so audaciously and rapidly that the less organized tribal armies of the Gauls could not react quickly enough to prevent him from seizing a number of key towns. The attempt to grab Gorgobina and punish a Roman ally had failed. Worse, Vercingetorix realized that his defensive strategy conceded the initiative to Caesar, who exploited it brilliantly with manoeuvre and speed. If the revolt was to succeed, another strategy was required. Vercingetorix decided on a war of attrition in which a scorched earth policy deprived the Roman army of its supplies until the Gauls could pin it down and destroy it. After a meeting with the other tribal chiefs, the area around Avaricum – the land of the Bituriges – was set to the torch. Caesar wrote that, 'In a single day more than twenty cities of the Bituriges were set on fire. The same was done in other states, and in every direction fires were to be seen.'

Vercingetorix seized Avaricum, the last fortified and supplied town in a barren and burnt province. Seeing his chance finally to do battle with the Gallic army, Caesar laid siege to the town. For twenty-five days, the Romans constructed an earthen ramp 300ft long and 80ft high. Then, on a rainy grey day, the Roman assault carried the ramparts, and a garrison of 40,000 men, along with their wives and children, was massacred. Vercingetorix and his bodyguard escaped, and Caesar lost his chance to capture the leader of the rebellion. Caesar rested and resupplied his armies in Avaricum for several days, then secured the nearby town of Noviodunum and established a large supply base there to support his further operations in the area.

Word reached Caesar that the northern tribes had joined the revolt. He split his army into two commands. Four legions under Labienus were sent north to contain the tribes. Caesar, in command of seven legions, moved down the eastern bank of the Allier River to strike at Gergovia (Georgovie). Vercingetorix moved his army into the area around the town, hoping to draw Caesar into the attack. Caesar took the bait. Vercingetorix's plan was to hold Caesar in place and use his cavalry to harass and kill Caesar's foraging parties until the Roman army was weakened by lack of supplies. This went on for almost a month, during which time each side conducted attacks against the other's fortifications, but without decisive result. Vercingetorix renewed his diplomatic efforts to attract even more tribes to the standard of revolt, with significant success. Caesar, meanwhile, concentrated on the siege of the city. Suddenly, a Gallic army moving south struck and captured Noviodunum in Caesar's rear. This was a catastrophe. Noviodunum was Caesar's main logistical base. With its capture went his reserve supply of food for the army, his war treasury, most of the army's baggage and a large supply of extra horses. The Gauls massacred the small garrison in the town. The news of the attack rallied even more tribes to the cause, including some that had remained loyal to Rome from the beginning of the revolt.

Caesar's position was critical. His tribal allies had been wooed away, and new military forces were being assembled across his rear. Ahead, Vercingetorix's army barred the way to the safety of Cisalpine Gaul. The scorched earth policy had its anticipated effect; Caesar's army was desperate for supplies. Worst of all, four badly needed legions were off to the north, chasing tribes through the woods to no practical effect. Desperate as his situation was, Caesar never panicked. Instead, he broke contact from the siege, wheeled his army about and slipped through the Gallic armies that were still moving into position to entrap him. He crossed the Loire River, swung around Cenabum and reached Agedincum (Sens), the logistical support base of the four legions operating in the north. As luck would have it, Labienus heard rumours of a catastrophe befalling Caesar to his south. Fearing that the rumours were true, Labienus fell back on his administrative base at Agedincum. He joined forces with Caesar coming from the other direction just outside the town. Caesar had once again united his army. The eleven legions were rested and replenished at Agedincum before they set out again in search of Vercingetorix.

Vercingetorix kept to his plan to avoid a pitched battle against the superior Roman infantry, deprive the Romans of supplies, use his cavalry to harass Roman foragers and supply lines and engage the enemy only in defence or ambush. Vercingetorix had 80,000 infantry and 15,000 cavalry in the field, a force larger than Caesar's eleven legions (55,000 men) and 3,000 cavalry, not counting his German mercenary horsemen. Vercingetorix selected the fortified town of Alesia as his main base of operations. He suspected that Caesar might make for Cisalpine Gaul with his army, where he could replenish it and return with a larger force. Vercingetorix was determined to keep Caesar bottled up in Gaul until he could wear down his army, force it to battle and destroy it. Caesar soon began to move his army down the Soane valley. Vercingetorix deployed his cavalry along the valley to harass Caesar's movement and threaten his lines of communication. The idea was to catch Caesar in column of march and ambush his army.

Vercingetorix set an ambush at a location near Dijon. He deployed his infantry in three strong camps directly astride Caesar's route of march so that the vanguard of the army would advance directly into his troops and stop the column. Once Caesar's column had halted, Vercingetorix planned to use his cavalry to strike the Romans from the flanks and rear, cutting them into isolated segments that could be dealt with piecemeal. Caesar failed to use his cavalry to provide sufficient reconnaissance and security, and the vanguard of his army clashed directly with Vercingetorix's force. Caesar was taken completely by surprise, as he had been at the Sambre River previously, and, by all odds, his army should have been trapped and annihilated. For some unknown reason, however, the Gallic cavalry did not engage in force, but contented itself with skirmishing. This may have been because Caesar bolstered his cavalry with infantry, but Caesar makes no mention of this. The failure of the Gallic cavalry to press the attack permitted Caesar sufficient time to use his own horse to keep the enemy at a distance while he assembled his infantry in battle formation. The result was that the ambush did not strike decisively at Caesar's column, allowing it time to redeploy to meet further attack.

When Vercingetorix saw that the ambush had failed, he remained true to his operational plan and broke contact, withdrawing toward his base at Alesia (Alise Ste Reine). This opened the road to Italy for Caesar, who could now withdraw without opposition. Instead, Caesar wheeled to his rear, assembled his army and pursued Vercingetorix back to Alesia. The Romans fell on the Gallic rearguard and killed 3,000 men. Caesar now had Vercingetorix and his army on the defensive and, for the first time since the rebellion had begun, Caesar could come to grips with the enemy main force and its wily commander.

The town of Alesia was situated on an elevated plateau almost 1,500ft above the valley floor, through which ran two minor rivers, the Ose and Oserain. On three sides, across the valley, were hills whose slopes ran down to the town. Vercingetorix withdrew to the town and encamped his army on the surrounding hills, with forward positions along the approach to the valley. Caesar realized that the only way to take the position was by siege, and invested the town.

The fortifications constructed by Caesar around Alesia were some of the most extensive and complex in all antiquity. He enclosed the entire hill upon which the city stood with a wall of contravallation designed to keep Vercingetorix within it. This wall ran for 16km. The outer wall of circumvallation was 20km long, and was designed to keep any relief army from breaking through to the besieged town. Between the two streams in the valley, across from the forward positions of the enemy, Caesar constructed a 20ft trench with perpendicular sides to prevent any attack through this weak area. Beyond the outer wall, two concentric trenches were dug. each 15ft wide, and the inner trench filled with water diverted from the stream. Behind the inner trench was a 12ft high earthen rampart crowned by a wooden palisade, with turrets of wood placed at 80ft intervals. In front and in between each layer of defensive belts were anti-personnel devices such as pits with spikes at the bottom, iron pikes in large wooden logs pointing directly at the enemy, fallen and tethered trees to make movement difficult, sharpened wooden stakes, *stimuli* (a fish-hook type trip device) and various other obstacles. Covering it all were *ballistas*, cross-bows and field guns that could rain missiles with deadly accuracy on any troops making their way through the obstacle belt. Twenty-three forts or strongpoints were placed at strategic locations along the outer wall, and eight major camps – four infantry and four cavalry – completed the system. The siege works around Alesia required five weeks to construct.

Caesar had just begun to construct these siege works when Vercingetorix went over to the offensive. He sent a large force of cavalry (he had 10,000–15,000 cavalry at hand) against Caesar's army. Caesar countered with his own cavalry forces, and a large cavalry battle ensued. Vercingetorix was remaining true to his plan, and using his cavalry to make it difficult for Caesar to forage for supplies. The attack was designed to massacre the Roman cavalry and make foraging even more dangerous. As Caesar recorded it, his Spanish and Gallic cavalry did not perform well and were in danger of being destroyed. Caesar committed his German cavalry squadrons at the propitious moment, and the enemy cavalry broke. As Vercingetorix's cavalry fled toward the town, the narrow gates of the outlying fortifications could not accommodate the sudden onrush of thousands of horses attempting to gain the safety of the gates. A great jam occurred, and Caesar's German cavalry fell on the enemy and killed large numbers of them.

Within the city, Vercingetorix had less than thirty days' supply of food. Perhaps because of this, he abandoned his original plan to harass the Roman foragers and starve Caesar's army. Instead, he sent most of his cavalry away from Alesia with instructions to raise an enormous army among the tribes to come to the relief of Alesia. His plan was to keep Caesar in place until the relief army could be assembled, and attack Caesar from the rear. The immediate effect of this change in plans was to allow Caesar complete freedom to construct his siege works and to range far and wide in search of food for his army.

Feeding the Roman army was no easy task. The countryside had been picked over, and foraging units had to range further and further afield to find grain. Caesar also realized that once the Gallic relief army arrived, there would be no more foraging. He ordered his commissariat to build a thirty-day reserve of grain. It is important to note that had Vercingetorix not changed his plans and given up his harassment of Caesar's foragers, Caesar would never have been able to feed his army, nor, as it turned out, been able to construct the complex siege works around Alesia. Vercingetorix had been correct all along in his original plan, but changed his tactics at a critical moment in the campaign. It was a costly mistake.

It took five weeks for the Gauls to assemble a relief army and to move it to Alesia. Caesar says this army numbered 250,000 infantry and 8,000 cavalry, but this is an exaggeration. An army of that size could not move along the dirt tracks of Gaul nor feed itself. Judging from the manner in which it manoeuvred once in place around Alesia, it is more likely that the Gallic relief army comprised probably 80,000 men and horse. When the army arrived, food supplies were down to starvation levels within Alesia itself. One proposal from a Gallic chieftain was that the old be slain and their bodies cannibalized by the warriors! Vercingetorix chose instead to send all the old, women and children from the city, and to have them offer themselves as slaves to the Romans. Caesar refused to permit them to pass, and these tragic people were forced back into the city.

A few days after this incident, the relief army arrived and camped on the heights west of the town. They next deployed their entire force into the valley up to the Roman walls, where they began to fill in the moat. To put a stop to this, and to test the mettle of the newcomers, Caesar sent out a strong cavalry force to engage the enemy cavalry. The Gauls had dispersed some foot archers among their cavalry, and a large number of Roman horsemen were wounded by arrows. For hours, 'from noon almost to sunset', 12,000 cavalry fought in front of the Roman walls. Again, Caesar held his German squadrons in reserve until the right moment. When they attacked, the cavalry struck first for the enemy horseman covering the archers. Driving them away, the German cavalry fell on the archers and massacred them. As the Gallic cavalry fell back, the infantry that had been filling in the moat were exposed. They also took flight and, along with the cavalry, retreated to the hillside. The first attempt to break the siege of Alesia ended in failure.

The Gauls tried again the following night. Units of sappers with ladders and hurdles moved silently toward the outer wall. Under cover of arrows and sling shot from support troops, the sappers began to fill in the outer ditches. Simultaneously, Vercingetorix's forces assaulted the wall from the city. This force was driven back by a hail of missile fire of javelins, *ballista* shot and sling shot. A third Gallic force attacked the fortifications on the opposite side, but in the darkness many fell into the spiked pits or were otherwise killed or wounded by the anti-personnel devices that protected the outer walls. The three-pronged assault was poorly coordinated and floundered until daylight, when it was ordered to withdraw.

The Gauls planned yet another assault. This time they conducted a reconnaissance and discovered that the line of circumvallation was not complete at a point along the Ose River at the foot of Mount Rhea. This soft point was garrisoned by two legions, whose camps were overlooked by high ground. During the night, the Gauls moved 6,000 hand-picked warriors under one of their best field commanders around Mount Rhea to a location in the hills above the Roman camps. Once in place, the force rested until midday. At noon, they swept down the hill and attacked the Roman camps. In a simultaneous and coordinated attack, the main body of Gallic cavalry moved across the Plain of Laumes and struck the main Roman force guarding the wall. This manoeuvre provided screen and cover for a large follow-on infantry force. From the town itself, Vercingetorix launched yet another assault at the Roman wall covering the gap between the streams. In addition, several smaller assaults were conducted at various points along the Roman line in an effort to pin down the enemy and prevent it from shifting forces along interior lines within the fortified walls.

Atop a siege platform, Caesar had an excellent view and quickly discerned that the critical point in the battle was the attack on the two legion camps at the base of Mount Rhea. After the initial assault, the Gauls supported their attack with strong reinforcements. Caesar sent six cohorts under Labienus to shore up the Roman position. A major attack was also conducted across the plain, and the fighting was bloody. Despite heavy casualties, the Gauls were able to fill in some of the ditches and dismantle other obstacles. Twice, Caesar had to send reinforcements to the positions opposite the wall in order to hold it. Once assured that this secondary front could resist the enemy pressure, Caesar turned his attention to the attack on the two legion camps.

Caesar took command of four cohorts of infantry and personally led them to reinforce Labienus, who was now engaged in a desperate fight. Caesar ordered some cavalry units to manoeuvre outside the walls and to swing around the rear of Mount Rhea to get behind the enemy force attacking the legion camps. When Caesar himself arrived with his infantry to reinforce the camps, the men recognized him in his red cloak and immediately took heart, beginning to fight with greater effort. Caesar had analyzed the situation well. From the beginning of the battle, he had recognized that the main assault would fall on the legion camps. Once he had assured himself that the rest of his positions could hold, he personally reinforced the threatened position. With the main Gallic army engaged around the legion camps, Caesar had sent his cavalry around the rear of the enemy. At the height of the infantry battle for the legion camps, the Roman cavalry suddenly appeared behind the enemy army and went into the attack.

It was Napoleon who said that 'there is a moment in an engagement when the last manoeuvre is decisive and gives victory; it is the one drop of water which makes the vessel run over'. The appearance of Caesar's cavalry behind the Gallic army produced a panic, and the enemy turned and fled. The cavalry pressed the attack and, in the pursuit, a great number of the enemy were slain. High above the battle in Alesia, Vercingetorix witnessed these events from his command post. He broke off the secondary attack that he had launched against the inner wall. As these forces began to withdraw, the forces that had been left on the heights in reserve began to panic. Within a short time, the entire relief army broke up into tribal contingents as effective command and control disappeared. By evening, many of these groups began to wander away and make their way home. Caesar ordered his cavalry into a night attack against these reserves to ensure that the enemy kept on the move away from the battlefield. By morning, it was over.

Vercingetorix surrendered himself in the hopes of avoiding a massacre of his people, and, in fact, Roman terms were generally lenient, consisting of hostages and large indemnity payments. Vercingetorix was taken to Rome for Caesar's triumph, and then executed in a Roman dungeon by strangulation. The siege of Alesia is regarded as one of the most remarkable examples of military brilliance and campaign sophistication in the ancient world. A single army besieging an enemy was itself besieged, only to destroy both armies, the besieged and the relief army, in a single engagement conducted by one of antiquity's most audacious and brilliant generals. For the rest of the year, into the spring and summer, Caesar conducted a number of small campaigns to crush the embers of the revolt. These forays were mostly against brigands and renegades, the major tribes having submitted to Rome. By late summer, Gaul had again been pacified.

In seven years, with an army that numbered less than 50,000 men, Julius Caesar had conquered Gaul, a country of fifteen to twenty million people. Caesar now had his own province that he could begin to exploit to produce the kind of vast wealth he needed if he were to make a serious bid to seize control of the Roman state. There had been, however, no time between engagements to organize the peace. The tribes that had been conquered or that went over to the Roman side still retained their arms, and the ability of these tribes to raise armies remained intact. Although Caesar's brutality in dealing with some of the conquered tribes was designed to pre-empt future resistance through fear, it often had the opposite effect. Gaul was full of warriors who hated the Romans, and who welcomed the opportunity for revenge. The region was seething with a resentment that could explode in a general conflagration that threatened to reverse all of Caesar's accomplishments.

The success of the Roman army in Gaul was due in no small measure to the fact that the Gallic enemy was simply not very good at waging war. The conduct of warfare by the Gauls left much to be desired, especially so when confronting the Roman enemy whose strong point was organization. The Gauls had almost no military organization to speak of. Long centuries of tribal civil wars among themselves made any military coalition a fragile entity. Caesar was a master at playing off one tribe against another to prevent a concentration of superior military forces against him. By engaging the Gallic armies piecemeal, an isolated victory against one contingent was often sufficient to fragment the entire coalition, who simply returned home. The Gauls were largely incapable of sustained military operations if they required maintaining a tribal political coalition for any length of time.

It is difficult not to read Caesar's *Gallic Wars* without concluding that much of his brilliance in command had to do with exploiting the obvious weaknesses of his enemy to good effect. Certainly, Caesar was fortunate in not having to deal with an enemy that had efficient cavalry. Indeed, for most of its history, Rome had only rarely fought enemies who excelled in cavalry. In Gaul, the problem was how to deal with hordes of tribal infantry armed with poor quality weapons, who possessed even less combat skill and direction. For this, Roman cavalry was not required. At the operational level, Caesar was always fighting an enemy that could not bring its numerical superiority to bear on the battlefield, either because it could not achieve political unity or because it lacked any significant logistical capability that made it capable of sustained operations. In fighting the Gauls, the Roman army was years ahead of its adversary in the development of organizational skills that made possible an armed force that had manoeuvre, supply and tactical capabilities that the enemy could not match. In Caesar, moreover, the Gallic armies had to deal with a field commander who had few equals anywhere in the Western world at the time. As a consequence, the wars between the legions of Julius Caesar and the tribal armies of Gaul were never really a serious contest.

Battle of Dyrrachium (48 BC)

Caesar's battles against Pompey and other Roman and eastern antagonists were another matter. Against Pompey, Caesar faced an adversary who was every bit as good a general as he was and, at times, even more capable of leading and directing men in battle. The army of Pompey was, after all, a Roman army and brought with it all the advantages that Caesar's army possessed. In the case of cavalry, Caesar's was generally hired Gallic and German horsemen, whereas Pompey's cavalry arm was of considerably better quality, being drawn from the horsemen of Rome's eastern provinces. In the battles between Pompey and Caesar, it was more the quality of generalship than the nature of the armies that decided the issue.

Caesar's campaigns in Gaul endowed him with a reputation that overshadowed Pompey. Caesar trained a large army that was devoted to him and would do his bidding. He amassed great wealth that could be used to support his political ambitions, and he added a vast new province to the Roman Empire. All of these accomplishments made Caesar's enemies in Rome nervous, and, in 50 BC, Pompey convinced the Senate to order Caesar to relinquish his command, disband his legions, give over his province and return to Rome to stand for election to the consulate as a private citizen. Caesar recognized the summons for the death sentence that it was, and refused. At the time of the summons, Caesar was at Ravenna in Cisalpine Gaul. Roman law forbade a Roman general to bring his military forces into Italy itself without the consent of the Senate. The southern boundary of Cisalpine Gaul and Italy was the tiny Rubicon River just south of Ravenna. On 11 January 49 BC, Caesar conducted a night crossing of the Rubicon. Rome had its answer. Caesar intended to seize power by force of arms, and Rome was plunged into a civil war.

Caesar, who had fought only against barbarians or semi-civilized peoples, was now engaged in a more serious struggle, with legion against legion. Caesar had only the Thirteenth Legion with him when he crossed the Rubicon, but the Eighth and Twelvth Legions were on the march to join him. Caesar could muster a total force of eight legions, 40,000 first-rate battle-hardened veterans, plus some 20,000 auxiliary troops and cavalry. Pompey, the legal chief of the Roman state, had three legions in Italy, seven in Spain and the authority to raise eight more in Italy. One of the legions in Italy consisted of raw recruits, and the other two had fought for years with Caesar before being sent from Gaul two years earlier, and were not considered trustworthy. Caesar chose Italy as the first arena of the contest, and in that arena Pompey was at a severe manpower disadvantage. The bulk of Pompey's loyal veteran legions were in Spain, too far away to affect the outcome of any battle in Italy in a timely manner.

Caesar moved quickly to exploit his advantage. He advanced rapidly down the Adriatic coast, seizing rich towns as he went. Within a few weeks, he had advanced a considerable distance and was joined by his legions from Gaul. In town after town, local garrisons joined him. Caesar's conduct of the campaign clearly reflected his awareness that this was a civil war and not a foreign war, and that it was a war that demanded different techniques. Caesar understood that the most important asset in a civil war was the support of the populace, and he took great pains to minimize battle damage and to treat his captives leniently. Long before Clausewitz, Julius Caesar recognized the essentially political character of warfare, and changed his military tactics accordingly. His central strategic goal was to convince the populace, the property owners and even the enemy legionaries that his cause was the more desirable one for their own interests.

Pompey's ability to react was hindered by his lack of reliable manpower. If he relied upon the two legions at hand to defend Rome, he had to accept the grave risk that they might go over to Caesar, their old commander. If this happened, the war would be over before Pompey could bring his forces to bear. Whereas Caesar had sole command of his troops, Pompey was the legal creation of the Roman Senate, and required their consent to act. Worse, while Caesar acted as his own field commander, Pompey was saddled with two elected consuls to command the armies. Caesar's forces and popular support increased almost daily, and he made ready to move on Rome itself. The Senate panicked and fled to Capua in such a haste that they forgot to take the treasury with them! Caesar tried to cut them off, but they fled again to Brundisium (Brindisi). Pompey's single asset was his control of the fleet, some 500 warships and a large number of light galleys. As Caesar's army approached Brundisium, Pompey used the fleet to evacuate 25,000 troops and most of the Roman Senate across the Adriatic to Epirus in Greece, from where he expected to continue the fight. In February 49 BC, less than two months after crossing the Rubicon, Caesar entered Rome, master of all Italy.

The strategic situation confronting Caesar was curious. He held Italy, the central position between Pompey in Greece and his major political and military base of support in Spain. But Pompey controlled the fleet and thus the sea. Although Pompey's force in Greece was but a skeleton and would be easy prey, there was no easy way to get at it. Without sufficient ships, an attack on Pompey forced Caesar to go overland through Illyricum (Yugoslavia), a route that left a long line of communications through Cisalpine Gaul greatly exposed to Pompey's legions in Spain. With great strategic insight, Caesar realized that the way to defeat Pompey in Greece was to first defeat his legions in Spain. Caesar expressed the situation clearly in his *Commentaries*: 'I am setting forth to fight an army without a leader, so as by and by to fight a leader without an army.' In March, Caesar set off for Spain.

Caesar started for Spain by a land route along the northern shore of the Mediterranean. Short on finances, Caesar adopted the novel method of paying his soldiers with money borrowed from his officers. This ensured the good will of the former and the adherence of the latter. The route ran in front of the important and historic fortress town of Massilia (Marseille), which supported Pompey. Caesar invested the town with three legions and sent the main force forward to seize the passes over the Pyrenees, which it did just in time to prevent their capture by an army of Pompey loyalists under the command of L. Afranius and M. Petreius. Unable to trap Caesar in the mountains, the two commanders awaited him at Ilerda (Lerida). Caesar moved toward the confrontation with 37,000 men against an army of 65,000, with reserves of two additional legions supported by 45,000 Spanish auxiliaries.

In fact, neither side wanted to fight. Caesar was wary of the enemy's numbers, and the enemy commanders had little stomach for engaging a commander of Caesar's reputation. So both armies moved around one another, engaging in little more than cavalry skirmishes, each side seeking to entrap the other in some untenable defensive position. A month later, diminishing supplies forced the Pompeian commanders to withdraw to the Ebro River. Caesar anticipated the movement, crossed the river first and cut their line of retreat.

Now Caesar showed his brilliance. He kept the enemy bottled up, cut off its water supply but refused to attack. He hoped to avoid spilling Roman blood. Both armies faced each other from their respective camps. Gradually, the men of both sides began to fraternize regularly. Eventually, the idea of Roman fighting Roman seemed ridiculous, especially so in light of Caesar's superior disposition of forces that would have made any battle a single-sided slaughter in favour of Caesar. The enemy commanders, rather than attempt to fight their way out of the trap, surrendered. Caesar treated them with leniency and respect. Most of the enemy legions were simply disbanded, but Caesar accepted many legionaries into his own army. Leaving two legions to hold Spain, Caesar returned to Massilia, where the siege was brought to a successful termination. With his back secure, Caesar prepared to attack Pompey in Greece.

Caesar mounted his invasion of Epirus in western Greece from Brundisium, where he assembled twelve legions and 10,000 cavalry. Pompey's control of the Roman fleet left few ships for Caesar to transport his troops. There was sufficient transport for seven legions (2,000 men each, as noted by Caesar) and some cavalry. Even this small force could only be accommodated if food supplies and baggage were left behind. Mark Antony, left in control of Brundisium, was ordered to find more ships as quickly as possible and follow the invasion force across the Adriatic. In today's world it would be considered strategic suicide to attempt to transport a major force by ship without first securing control of the sea (and nowadays the air). Caesar attempted a bold gamble.

Caesar reckoned that the enemy would never expect him to mount an invasion in midwinter, and in this he was correct, for the enemy fleet was safely in its coastal harbours. The distance to be crossed by sea was approximately 100 miles, a crossing that would take only 12–15 hours with favourable winds. If Caesar made the crossing safely, he could fall upon the undefended coastal cities of Epirus. Although these cities were rich in supplies, Pompey's army was still moving into position and had not garrisoned the southern coastal cities. They were rich prizes, but still undefended. Finally, Caesar's intelligence reported that Pompey had not reached Epirus (the report was incorrect, however) and the enemy army still had no commander. Caesar reckoned that Pompey's absence would slow the reaction of his army to the invasion sufficiently to allow Caesar to secure the beachhead.

Caesar still faced an army of considerable size, however. Pompey controlled the entire eastern half of the empire, with its rich sources of supply in Egypt and the Levant. His command comprised 36,000 men, but recruiting was continuing and his army was growing every day. Metellus Scipio was on his way from Egypt with two veteran legions, and Pompey's cavalry, drawn from the eastern provinces, was far superior numerically and in quality than Caesar's, who seems to have still had the same mercenary Gallic and Germanic squadrons used previously. At the time of the invasion, then, Pompey's army had nine legions of infantry, 7,000 cavalry, 3,000 archers and 1,200 slingers. On 4 January 48 BC, Caesar sailed out from Brundisium on a night tide with favourable winds bound for Epirus. Shortly after daybreak, Caesar's army landed at Palaeste, 100 miles south of his objective, Dyrrachium.

Caesar debarked his troops and sent the ships back to Italy to transport the rest of the army. Without waiting, he moved northward and quickly occupied Oricum, Valona and Apollonia. Alert now to Caesar's landing, Pompey moved south of Dyrrachium and took up a position at Kuci astride Caesar's route of advance at the Apsus River. Pompey's admiral, Bibulus, having been caught sleeping during the original crossing of the Adriatic, was now awake and alert. His squadrons overtook Caesar's transports on their return trip, capturing thirty ships. The ships and their crews were burned alive. This cut off Caesar from his base in Italy. At the same time, he faced a numerically superior army that had more and better quality cavalry, deployed to use interior lines close to its base of supplies. Had Pompey attacked, it is likely he would have easily defeated Caesar. As it was, he decided to do nothing and wait for the arrival of Scipio and his legions. Pompey's failure to take the offensive was a grievous error of tactics and strategy.

For more than a month, the armies faced each other. Sometime in February, after being given an order by Caesar to disregard the risk of Pompey's fleet, Mark Antony set sail at night with four legions and 800 cavalry, half the force assembled for the follow-on invasion. The army was carried by favourable winds beyond the point where both armies were entrenched to the town of Nymphaeum, north of Dyrrachium. When Pompey learned of Antony's landing to his rear, he broke contact with Caesar and moved to intercept

Antony's legions. Caesar moved northeastward toward Tirana and sent messengers to warn Antony. Antony, always an excellent field commander, avoided the ambush, and both Roman armies linked up at the town of Scampi. Pompey had failed to prevent the joining of the two armies, allowing Caesar to achieve local superiority of force against him.

The strategic and logistical situation prevented Caesar from exploiting his advantage. He sent two legions toward Macedonia, with the mission to find Scipio and his legions and prevent them from joining Pompey. Another legion and a half were sent inland to forage for supplies and establish relations with the local inland towns for the provision of supplies. Then disaster struck. Pompey's son, Gnaeus, commanding the Egyptian naval squadron off the coast, attacked Caesar's naval and supply base at Oricum. Using shipboard catapults, Gnaeus forced the blockaded harbour and turned his fire on the city walls. Covered by shipboard artillery, his infantry scaled the walls and took the city. Gnaeus burned the city, Caesar's supplies and all Caesar's remaining ships. In an almost simultaneous attack, Pompey's navy attacked Antony's support base at Lissus and burned all of his ships. With these attacks, Caesar's two naval supply bases were neutralized and every ship at his disposal was destroyed. Not even a single galley remained with which Caesar could communicate with Italy. With no way to return to Italy, Caesar was trapped.

This state of affairs would have unnerved most commanders. Instead, Caesar began to move. He shuffled his army northward, attempting to gain the road to Dyrrachium before Pompey discerned his intentions. Pompey moved parallel to Caesar. Although Caesar reached the road to Dyrrachium an hour before Pompey, the proximity of Pompey's army to Caesar's lines made an attack on the city impossible. Pompey deployed his army around Petra south of the Shimmihil torrent, with Caesar deployed opposite him. Caesar's numerical inferiority, lack of siege machinery and the city's strong fortifications made an attack on Dyrrachium an unrealistic possibility. Pompey, although cut off from his base in the city, could resupply his army by sea and, should events require it, move or evacuate his army at will. Pompey, again cautious, decided to remain in place and await Scipio.

Caesar's position was far worse. He was cut off from his main base in Italy, his naval bases in Greece were gone and he had no ships. Supplying the army with forage and purchased supplies became difficult. Somewhere to his south was Scipio with two legions, who might show up at any moment. Pompey's army was larger than his, and

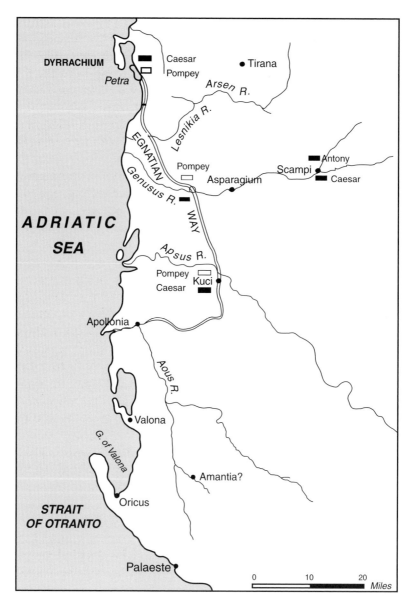

Battle of Dyrrachium

Caesar feared having to fight a battle in open country where Pompey's superior cavalry represented a deadly threat. With nowhere to go and insufficient force to bring about a decision, Caesar held on to Pompey's army as the best way of neutralizing Pompey's military advantages. Caesar began to invest the enemy.

Caesar constructed a wall of contravallation around Pompey's fortified position that extended from Petra in the north to the Lesnikia River in the south. A continuous line of small hills naturally formed much of the ring, and the armies skirmished over control of these hills. When completed, Caesar's wall extended 15 miles in length and enclosed within it Pompey's line of fortifications that was 8 miles long and 1½ miles in from the beach. Pompey's line had twenty-four redoubts along it, and the meadows within the wall provided forage for his cavalry.

The supply situation on both sides was serious. The surrounding countryside had been picked clean, and Caesar's men subsisted on a bread made from a root (*Chara,* as the bread is called, is still eaten in Albania). Pompey supplied his army by sea, drawing on the substantial stocks in Dyrrachium. Caesar had diverted the streams, and Pompey was forced to dig wells which proved inadequate to supply his men with water. Pompey's cavalry horses had eaten what grass there was in the meadows within the ring of fortifications, and were beginning to die of starvation. Eventually, Pompey transported his cavalry by ship to Dyrrachium, where they had sufficient food and were well-placed to attack Caesar's rear. Like Vercingetorix at Alesia, Pompey was in an excellent position to use his cavalry to harass Caesar's foragers and engineers. Why he did not do so is a mystery, but it was a serious error to permit Caesar to manoeuvre unhindered. The situation on both sides was less than ideal, and it was Pompey who took the initiative to change the circumstances.

Pompey guessed that Caesar was desperate for some sort of solution to the problem (as, perhaps, was he), so Pompey decided to provide Caesar with one. Pompey arranged for 'a certain man of Dyrrachium' to approach the Romans and offer to betray the city and open the gates, the stratagem by which many cities in ancient warfare had succumbed. Inexplicably, and perhaps as a sign of his desperation, Caesar took the bait. In one of Caesar's most bizarre decisions, he decided to lead the infiltration force himself! Late into the night, Caesar and his small force moved through the marshes surrounding the lagoon near the city. As Caesar's men moved through the 'narrowest point', they were suddenly attacked from the front and rear by 'large forces which had been conveyed along the shore in boats and suddenly fell upon him; thus he lost many men and very nearly perished himself'.

While Caesar was floundering around attempting to extricate himself from the ambush in the marshes, Pompey launched three coordinated attacks against Caesar's positions. In one engagement, four legions were thrown against a redoubt in the centre of the Roman line held only by a single cohort. The defending legionaries fought like tigers until two legions could be brought up in support. After the battle, Caesar noted, 30,000 enemy arrows that had been fired at the position were picked up and counted; one legionary had no fewer than 120 holes in his shield. Every surviving member of the original garrison had been wounded. In another attack, a Pompeian legion assaulted a position held by three Roman legions and was driven back. The third attack was repulsed by Caesar's German cavalry, presumably fighting dismounted. Although these assaults had failed to break the Roman line, Pompey's plan was brilliantly executed and almost worked.

Pompey's intelligence service had, meanwhile, acquired two Allobrogian deserters from the Roman camp, who provided him with a detailed knowledge of Caesar's fortifications. Caesar had carried his entrenchments across the plain south of the Lensikia River. To protect his army from envelopment and rear attack, he constructed another wall of circumvallation along much of his left line. The two walls were about 200 yards apart and ran to the sea. These walls were not completed, however, and there was no transverse wall connecting the two outer walls. It was possible for a significant size force to insert itself between the walls and follow them into Caesar's main position. Informed of the nature of Caesar's fortification, Pompey attempted an assault against Caesar's left.

The plan was brilliant, and clearly demonstrated Pompey's ability as a general. Sixty cohorts comprising the main assault force passed through Pompey's fortified line, crossed the Lesnikia River and seized Caesar's old camp (now deserted) across the river. None of this was difficult, since the area through which the assault force had to move was between the two lines of fortifications and generally unguarded. Once inside the old camp, this force prepared to attack Caesar's line of contravallation (the interior line). Simultaneously, an amphibious force of light infantry and archers moved by sea against the second line of fortifications. The larger part of the amphibious force landed south of the second line, while the smaller force landed between the two walls and pressed their way inland. The idea was to take Caesar at once in the front, the rear and in the flank. If it worked, Pompey intended to roll up Caesar's left flank. The land and sea attack was launched under cover of night, and, just before dawn, the light infantry was put ashore on the beach.

The two Roman cohorts manning the wall were caught in the act of changing the morning guard. Although these cohorts manned their stations and fought well, the attack had caught them completely unprepared. The defenders panicked, and fled down the lane between the two walls. The nearest Roman reserves consisted of eight cohorts under the command of Marcellinus, who, although hindered by soldiers fleeing in the opposite direction, rushed his troops into the fight. Elements of Pompey's main force moved from their position in Caesar's old camp along the interior wall, and were on the verge of overrunning Marcellinus' camp when Antony arrived with twelve cohorts and drove them back. Shortly thereafter, Caesar himself arrived with thirteen cohorts and engaged the attackers. While the fighting continued, Pompey landed large troop contingents (almost five legions) to the south of the defensive wall and began constructing a fortified camp. The camp provided security for his ships passing near the shore and guarded the plain to the south, where Pompey could graze his cavalry. Pompey's attack broke the Roman control of the coastal plain.

With Caesar now in command at the place of the attack, the Romans rallied and pushed Pompey's troops back to within half a mile of the coast. Caesar worried most about the sixty enemy cohorts that occupied his old camp on the coast, and launched an attack in force to regain the camp. Ever the gambler, Caesar left only two cohorts to hold the entrance to the path between the walls, and organized his thirty-three cohorts of infantry into two columns. One column assaulted the eastern face of the camp and quickly pressed the garrison back through the camp. The second column advanced and struck the connecting wall between the camp and river. Thinking it was the city wall, the troops gradually made their way down the wall, searching for a gate. Finally, they broke through near the end of the wall on the bank of the river and entered onto a broad plain between the rampart, river, the sea and the camp.

Pompey realized that Caesar had committed all his available forces in one throw, and he manoeuvred to counter-attack and trap the attackers. The Roman left column had breached the camp walls and driven the garrison back against the northern wall, where it was hacking it to pieces. Suddenly, from across the double fortified wall, Pompey's legions fell on the Roman column, overwhelming it. At the same time, Pompey committed his cavalry over the river and across the plain to attack Caesar's right column, now trapped between the attacking cavalry and the rampart wall connecting the camp to the river. Within minutes, both columns collapsed in panic as they were hammered by superior forces attacking from an unexpected direction. The rout was complete. Caesar described it as follows: 'Every place was full of disorder, panic and flight, so much so that when he [Caesar] grasped the standards of the fugitives and bade them halt, some without slackening speed fled at full gallop, others in their fear even let go their colours, nor did a single one of them halt.'

Caesar's army was in great danger. His left flank was in complete collapse. The battle at the camp had cost him thirty-two tribunes and centurions, 960 rank and file and thirty-two unit standards. The wounded numbered in the thousands. Many of the dead had been killed not by enemy action, but had been trampled to death in the panic. The reserves of Marcellinus and Antony had already been committed, and there were no further reserves left to stabilize the situation. Pompey had out-generalled Caesar, badly mauled his army and placed him in a tight spot.

Fortunately for Caesar, Pompey did not reinforce the attack, and both sides broke off the engagement. Caesar was in no position to continue the fight, and decided to withdraw. At nightfall the next day, Caesar set his baggage train and the wounded, along with one legion as an escort, on the road to Apollonia. A few hours later, four more legions set out upon the same road. Finally, acting as a rearguard, two legions moved into the darkness. Having learned of Caesar's movement, Pompey sent his cavalry in pursuit. Caesar reinforced his rearguard with 400 picked light infantry. Over the next four days, Pompey's cavalry caught up with Caesar's forces at least twice, but the rearguard held them at bay. Caesar had lost the battle for Dyrrachium, but he and his army were still in the field. And they were still dangerous.

Battle of Pharsalus (48 BC)

Caesar rested his army for a few days and then began to withdraw inland toward Macedonia. Before the engagement at Dyrrachium, Domitius Calvinus had been sent into Macedonia with two legions to find and check Scipio, who was on his way from Syria with two legions to reinforce Pompey. Domitius had been successful in manoeuvring around Scipio and preventing him from linking up with Pompey. Caesar's withdrawal from the coast, however, uncovered Domitius' rear and forced him to break contact with Scipio, who slipped away and made for Larissa, where he joined up with Pompey.

Caesar attempted to join up with Domitius' army. He had sent Publius Sulla inland before the Battle of Dyrrachium to develop good relations with the towns and establish them as supply bases. Sulla had done a successful job in obtaining the loyalty of these towns. However, as news of Caesar's defeat spread, a number of the towns and vital supply points declared for Pompey and closed their gates to Caesar. Caesar completed the link-up with Domitius at Aeginium, then moved southeast toward Gomphi. A formerly friendly town, Gomphi now shut its gates to him. Caesar stormed the town and sacked it, turning it over to his troops to plunder. Next, he moved toward Metropolis, which, having seen the lesson of Gomphi, complied with Caesar's request for supplies. Caesar moved on toward the Pharsalian plain just below Cynoscephalae, where he crossed the Enipeus River and took up positions on its northern bank.

Within a few days, Pompey and his army arrived, and camped 3 miles northwest of Caesar on the slopes of Mount Dogndiz. Both armies faced each other, but only Caesar seemed eager for combat. Caesar formed up his armies for battle outside his camp several times, attempting to draw Pompey down from the high ground on the slopes of the mountain. Pompey refused. After a while, the shortage of supplies forced Caesar to consider moving south to Scotussa to replenish his stores. On the day Caesar formed his army for the march to Scotussa, Pompey deployed his army closer to Caesar's camp on more level ground. Caesar stopped his march, wheeled his army into position and readied it for battle.

There remains considerable debate as to the number of troops that fought at Pharsalus. In Caesar's account, he understated his own strength and overstated that of his opponent, to make the victory seem even greater. Caesar said he had eighty cohorts, or, as he calculated it, some 22,000 men and 1,000 cavalry. Caesar put Pompey's forces at 110 cohorts, or 47,000 men and 7,000 cavalry. The real difficulty lies in calculating the number of cavalry. Caesar's claim that his 1,000 cavalry defeated Pompey's 7,000 horseman, cavalry that were not only numerically superior, but considerably superior in quality to Caesar's Germanic and Gallic tribal cavalry, is improbable. While Caesar was outnumbered in both infantry and cavalry, the numbers were not as one-sided as Caesar's account of the battle would suggest.

Pompey anchored his right flank on the steep banks of the swift Enipeus River. He placed 600 Pontus cavalry along the river bank to seal the flank and probably to protect against any surprises from light infantry or archers who might attempt to cross the river. In typical Roman fashion, he deployed his infantry in three lines. The front was broken into three sectors: the right wing was commanded by Lentulus, the centre by Scipio and the left by Ahenobarbus. On the extreme left of the line, he marshalled his cavalry, now 2,400 strong, interspersed with units of slingers and archers. This heavy cavalry assault force was commanded by Labienus, Caesar's old chief-of-staff from the wars in Gaul, who had gone over to Pompey when the civil war began. Labienus was a first-rate officer, a combat veteran of many battles, and in command of the main attack force of Pompey's army. Pompey's battle plan was to employ his infantry to engage and hold Caesar's infantry line in place, and then use his superior cavalry to smash Caesar's right flank, turn it inward and envelop Caesar's army.

Caesar formed up his infantry in the usual three-line formation of the Roman legion. The numerical disparity between the armies meant that Caesar's cohorts were not as deep as Pompey's. Had Pompey chosen to lighten the depth of his cohorts, he could have produced a longer line that would have overlapped Caesar's. As things were, Caesar could match the length of Pompey's line, but only with thinner cohorts. Caesar probably reckoned that his army of veterans could use their experience to compensate for the disparity in manpower. Caesar's left wing was led by Mark Antony, the centre by Domitius Calvinus and the right by Publius Sulla, all veteran commanders. As Caesar was moving his men into position, he observed Pompey's disposition of forces, quickly deduced Pompey's intentions and changed his deployment.

With Pompey's cavalry massed on the enemy's left, Caesar moved all his cavalry to his right to accept the inevitable charge. In doing this, however, he followed the instructions of Xenophon, the famous Greek cavalry commander, who noted in his book that it was possible to cloak infantry behind a cavalry force because the height of the horses and horsemen blocked the ability of the enemy to see the hidden infantry. Caesar did precisely this. He drew up his 2,000 cavalry directly across from Labienus. From the last line of his infantry, Caesar took six cohorts – 3,000 or 1,800 men, depending upon whose account is believed – and placed them at an oblique angle behind the cavalry. The remainder of the third infantry line was re-formed, and ordered to remain back from the main engagement. They were to act as a reserve and to commit only on Caesar's personal command. The two front infantry ranks would be forced to bear the brunt of Pompey's infantry attack.

Caesar augmented his cavalry force with light infantry, presumably archers, javelineers and slingers. He placed them behind the cavalry and in front of the hidden force of infantry. It is intriguing to ask why Caesar mixed the force in the manner he did. Caesar had first encountered this type of mixed unit when the Gauls used it against him at Alesia with some success. This mix of forces was common among German cavalry, and much of Caesar's cavalry was German. It is clear, however, that after the Battle of Dyrrachium, Caesar had reinforced his rear cavalry guard with light infantry forces to hinder Pompey's pursuit. Finally, this mixing of cavalry and light infantry forces had been common in the East since Alexander's day, and since Pompey's cavalry was mostly of eastern origin, it was no surprise to discover that his cavalry was supported by integrated light infantry as well. Caesar's use of mixed cavalry and light infantry units was important in another respect: it provided the entire force with an agility it might not otherwise have and, at the same time, protected the cavalry from enemy infantry until it could manoeuvre thorough the enemy and envelop it. Caesar ordered his infantry into the attack first, perhaps hoping to offset his numerical disadvantage in infantry with the *elan* of his superior veteran troops. The Roman infantry attempted to close the 200 yards between the infantry lines at the run. Halfway across the gap, it was noticed that Pompey's men did not meet the attack. Instead, they remained steadfastly in place. Caesar's centurions ordered the infantry to stop running and catch their breath. After a short period, the infantry began to close again. This time, however, they were met by Pompey's infantry at the run.

Just seconds before the infantry lines smashed into one another, Labienus launched his cavalry against Caesar's right, smashing into Caesar's Gallic and German cavalry squadrons. The Germans and Gauls absorbed the initial shock intact, but the press of numbers gradually drove Caesar's cavalry back beyond the ranks of his infantry. As Labienus' cavalry pressed the enemy further backwards, they uncovered their own right flank to infantry attack from the six cohorts hidden from their view. As the enemy cavalry passed, Caesar's infantry fell on its flank with devastating lethality. At about the same time, Caesar's cavalry, as if on command, turned and re-engaged Pompey's cavalry. This support of cavalry by heavy infantry required excellent discipline, training and leadership. The flexibility of the cohort system was also needed to make this superb manoeuvre work correctly, as were the disciplined combat veterans of Caesar's army who carried it out.

The surprise and force of the flank attack by the hidden infantry cohorts shattered Labienus' cavalry, which turned and fled the field. The Roman infantry made short work of the archers and slingers left unprotected by their fleeing cavalry comrades. Caesar's cavalry pressed the pursuit only to the end of Pompey's infantry line, at which point the heavy infantry and the cavalry fell on the enemy flank. The more agile and swift light infantry swept around the flank and began to envelope the infantry line. It was quickly joined by elements of the cavalry, who completed the envelopment.

At about the time this was happening, the two infantry lines were fully engaged on the field. Caesar's infantry was barely holding its own, and was nearing exhaustion. Shortly after the cavalry fell on the flank of Pompey's infantry line, Caesar committed his third line reserve infantry. The flexibility of the cohort system permitted the nearly exhausted front-line infantry to disengage, pass through the rear ranks and be replaced by the third line of rested troops. As these troops moved to the front, they fell on Pompey's exhausted infantry. The infantry line sagged and was pressed back until it broke. As Pompey's infantry began to scatter, they were greeted by the sight of Caesar's cavalry running rampant in their rear. A panic broke out. The third-line reserve pressed the attack, broke through and headed for Pompey's camp.

Once it was clear that Labienus' cavalry attack had failed, Pompey retreated to his camp to await the outcome of the battle. When his infantry broke through Pompey's line, Caesar ordered it to continue the attack until it stormed Pompey's camp. As Caesar's men broke through the ramparts, Pompey threw aside his general's cloak, mounted his horse and, with a few retainers, fled to Larissa. Although Caesar's men were nearly exhausted, he pressed them on into the mountains to hunt down Pompey's broken army. At the head of four legions, Caesar trapped a large number of enemy units, surrounded them and cut off their water source. They surrendered the next day. According to Appian's account, Caesar lost thirty centurions and 200 men killed at Pharsalus. Of Pompey's army, Caesar said that '15,000 appeared to have fallen', and 24,000 surrendered. In addition, 180 standards and nine eagles were presented to Caesar. Pompey's army ceased to exist. Pompey himself fled to Larissa and then to the coast. A month later, while attempting to establish relations with the Ptolemies in Egypt to raise another army, Pompey was assassinated. When, in October, Caesar was offered the embalmed head of his adversary, he refused ... and wept.

Examined purely from a military perspective, a study of Caesar's campaigns reveal a number of shortcomings in strategy and command that are sometimes overlooked by modern students of military history. For example, Caesar rarely seems to have planned a campaign in sufficient detail to ensure adequate logistical support for his armies. By his own account, time and again he was forced to divert his march, to withdraw, alter his plan or change his tactics because he had failed to ensure an adequate food supply for his troops. At Dyrrachium, for example, his starving army subsisted on whatever roots they could find. His failure to pay sufficient attention to intelligence about the enemy and/or to provide for adequate security almost cost him his life on more than one occasion. The Battle of the Sambre, for example, almost ended in as great a disaster as the Battle of Teutoburger Wald because of Caesar's failure to take adequate security precautions. It is no exaggeration to suggest that, in some instances, Caesar's bold strokes were more the products of desperation brought about by his own previous failures than by planned military operations.

Whatever his operational shortcomings, however, Caesar's brilliance was clearly evident in his ability to shape military operations to function as means to larger political ends. It was political strategy that always shaped military strategy, and never the reverse. Thus, although the manpower reserves of the Gauls far exceeded anything that Caesar could match, it was only rarely that Caesar fought a battle in which he was outnumbered. Clever use of diplomacy, ruse, treachery and bribery served always to make it impossible for his adversary to fight within a larger coalition of tribal forces. Clemency or cruelty against the Gauls was, for Caesar, always a choice to be made on political grounds, never an act of emotion, hatred or anger. Probably what is most instructive to the modern soldier-strategist about Julius Caesar was that he successfully conducted military operations in an extremely complex military, social and political environment, made even more complex by the deadly nature of the domestic political arena of the Roman state. It is from Caesar's ability to deal with the various aspects of his complex environment as successfully as he did that the modern statesman and soldier has most to learn.

His achievements were enormous. The pacification of Gaul by force of arms was one of the most important events in Western history. It was Caesar who established the Roman frontier at the Rhine, the line that marked the boundary between two different cultures for the next half millennium, and laid the basis for the distinction between civilization and barbarian that ultimately had such tragic consequences for Rome and the West. It was Caesar who stood as the transitionary figure between the death of the old republican order and the birth, under

Augustus, of the new imperium. Caesar's life clearly reflected the inability of the old political order to deal successfully with the primary problem of any political system under stress; the ability to manage the transition of power in a peaceful manner. Caesar's short reign was also noteworthy for the major administrative and economic reforms with which he reshaped the Roman state. It was upon these reforms that Augustus built the new imperial order of Rome.

Note

1. This chapter is based on the following original sources: Julius Caesar, *The Civil War*, trans. Jane P. Gardner (New York, Penguin Classics, 1976); also by Caesar, *The Gallic Wars*, trans. H.J. Edwards (Cambridge, MA, Harvard University Press, 1917); Appian, *The Civil Wars* (London, Waxkeep Press, 2013); and *Caesar: The Alexandrian War, African War, and Spanish War*, trans. A.G. Way (Cambridge, MA, Loeb Classic Series, 1955). The most utilized of secondary sources are J.F.C. Fuller, *Julius Caesar: Man, Soldier, and Tyrant* (New York, Da Capo Press, 1965), by far the best source, and Adrian Goldsworthy, *Caesar: Life of a Colossus* (New Haven, CT, Yale University Press, 2008). Rather than clutter up the manuscript with scores of repeat footnotes, I thought it best simply to assert that the chapter is based primarily upon information contained in the original sources, and list them as a single footnote.

CHAPTER NINE

MARCUS AGRIPPA (63–12 BC)

History has not treated kindly Marcus Agrippa (63–12 BC), a great Roman soldier whose life exerted an enormous influence upon the foundation of the Roman Empire, perhaps in some regards even more so than Augustus himself. The Roman historian Cassius Dio gives us the most substantial account of Agrippa's life, with Pliny the Elder, Nicholaus of Damascus and Appian making significant, but lesser contributions.[1] Beyond this, Agrippa is mentioned by only a handful of other Roman historians, mostly in passing, in their wont to extol the contributions of Augustus. As a result, many of Agrippa's achievements have been attributed to Augustus, and Augustus' very name dominates the history of the period (the Augustan Age) in which Agrippa exerted a powerful force on events. It is no exaggeration to say that Agrippa's military and administrative talents in the service of his boyhood friend at a number of critical junctures made the rise of Augustus possible, and contributed greatly to the achievements of the Augustan Age.

It was Agrippa who reorganized the Roman navy with new ships, tactics and weapons, and Agrippa who crushed Sextus Pompei at the naval battles of Mylae and Naulochus, giving Augustus control of Italy and Sicily. Agrippa was present at every major battle that Augustus fought, and in some it was Agrippa who actually commanded the troops while Augustus remained in his tent, sick and incapacitated. Agrippa won a great victory against the Acquitani in Gaul and suppressed disturbances in Germany, being the first Roman since Caesar to invade Germany for purposes of war. Later (20 BC), he laid out the four major trunk roads in Gaul that are still in use, conquered the Cantabri of Spain – finally bringing the 200-year war there to a conclusion – and put down a revolt in Illyricum. As *aedile* of Rome, Agrippa used his personal fortune to modernize the city's water supply and distribution system, naming many of the new structures after Augustus. Agrippa's brilliant victory at Actium won for Augustus undisputed mastery over the Roman Empire in one of the most important battles in Western history. Without Agrippa's aid in these critical situations, Augustus' ambitions might never have been realized.

With the civil war won, Augustus faced the challenge of rebuilding the Roman state. Augustus' talent lay in politics, and he knew little of administration and military affairs. He turned to Agrippa to solve the numerous problems of reconstruction, the reorganization of the state's government and political system, the administration of Rome, Italy and the provinces – all of which were in disarray – the re-establishment of the imperial frontiers and the reform and reorganization of the imperial army and navy. The great challenge was finding a way to discharge and disarm hundreds of thousands of mercenary soldiers who represented a threat to the new order, and to transfer their loyalty from their *condottieri* commanders to the new Roman state. Agrippa contributed greatly to solving these problems, although Roman historians often credit Augustus with his achievements. It was Agrippa's brilliant efforts that largely made possible the establishment of the new Roman imperial order.

The time of Agrippa's birth and adolescence was a turbulent one. The wars between rival *condottieri* like Sulla and Marius, and the Social Wars, had hollowed out the Republic until little of that grand edifice was left but its name. In the past, elected consuls had led fellow citizens to fight wars in the name of the state. By Agrippa's time, the Roman armies were no longer militias, but military forces raised by powerful and rich oligarchs whose loyalty lay with the commanders who paid them and rewarded them in victory with rich spoils. It was these armies and their commanders who tore at the flesh of the Republic in one civil war after another, ultimately destroying it altogether. It was an exciting, violent and dangerous time to be alive.

Just where Agrippa was born is not known with certainty, but Arpi (near modern Loggia) and Arpinum (Arpino) are the most likely sites. His family's origins are obscure, but it is likely that his grandfather was of the equestrian class who acquired Roman citizenship during the Social War (90 BC).[2] Pliny describes Agrippa's early life as *miseria inventa* ('misfortunes of his youth'), but does not elaborate.[3] It was the Roman habit for a man to acquire a nickname that often found its origins in some distinguishing feature or physical characteristic. Thus, for example, the name Rufus meaning 'red haired'. Pliny says Agrippa's name indicates a difficult or breech birth, for children that were born feet first were often called *agrippae*.[4] Agrippa's father was named Lucius, as was his older brother, and Agrippa had a sister, Vispania Polla. We know nothing about his mother, not even her name. It is safe to conclude that Agrippa was of lower equestrian-class birth, another of those lower men who rose to fame in Rome.

Agrippa's education was probably typical for a citizen of his class. From age 7, he would have attended classes of a *litterator* to learn to read and write, and to master basic arithmetic with the *abacus*. At 14, he would have studied with a *grammaticus* to read and discuss the major works of the day (Homer, Andronicus, Ennius, etc.). These studies acquainted Agrippa with subjects ranging from astronomy to geography, history, law, mathematics, military science, mythology and philosophy.[5] During this time, Agrippa would have acquired fluency in both Greek and Latin. At age 15, Agrippa's name was entered into the official public records as a full citizen, the son of a father who held Roman citizenship.

We do not know when and under what circumstances Agrippa met Octavius, Julius Caesar's great nephew and the son of Atia, Caesar's niece. It may have been that both boys were studying with the same teacher of public speaking, Appolodorus of Pergamum, in 49 BC,[6] or that they met later, in 46 BC, when Caesar had left for Spain to deal with Pompey's sons and left Octavius in charge of productions at two theatres in Rome.[7] Later in the year, Caesar instructed Octavius and his friend to join him in Spain for the coming battle with the rebels. Military experience was absolutely essential for any young man's career prospects, and Caesar may have reasoned that the campaign in Spain was a relatively low risk operation for Octavius to gain that experience. But Octavius fell ill and was unable to make the journey until later. Agrippa, if we are to believe M. Manlius, made the journey and joined Caesar's army in Spain.[8]

As a young aristocrat and close friend of Octavius, Agrippa found himself in the ideal position to learn the art of war from one of its most talented practitioners, Julius Caesar himself. Agrippa's equestrian status allowed him to join the legion as a junior officer, perhaps as one of the five junior military tribunes assigned to each legion.[9] In this post, Agrippa would have received direct access to the legate of the legion, usually a senator, and perhaps even obtained a place at Caesar's advisory council.[10] In all likelihood, Agrippa was at Munda, a brutal battle in which the heads of the defeated soldiers were placed on *gladius* points to terrorize Pompey's rebels trapped behind the city's walls. It was Agrippa's baptism of fire, and he seems to have performed adequately.

Having recovered from his illness, Octavius set out to join his uncle in Spain, only to arrive after the war was over. Caesar planned to return from Spain by boat, and allowed Octavius and his two companions, Agrippa and one Q. Salvidienus Rufus, to accompany him.

At Caesar's urging, Octavius' status was raised to patrician, and he was appointed to the pontificate. The travellers reached Rome safely and spent the rest of the summer there. Octavius having missed his baptism of fire, Caesar suggested that he go to Apollonia (Vjose) in Illyricum to continue his study of war. Macedonia was the marshalling area for the planned campaign against Gaetic-Parthia, and the place was teeming with troops. For the next six months, Octavius, Agrippa and Salvidienus studied the art of war and trained with local troop units.[11] In the spring of 44 BC, news arrived in Macedonia that Julius Caesar had been assassinated in March.

We have very little information about the part Agrippa played in the tumultuous events that followed Octavius' return to Rome. Through it all – Octavius' decision to claim his inheritance, his journey to Rome, his protracted duel with Mark Antony, his rise to popularity, the civil war against Antony at Mutina, the reconciliation with Antony, the formation of the First Triumvirate, the bloody proscriptions that followed, the defeat of Caesar's assassins at Philippi and other events – it is safe to assume, however, that the loyal Agrippa was always at Octavius' side, and one of the few advisors that Octavius trusted completely and to whom he turned most frequently for advice.[12] It is almost certain that Agrippa commanded troops at the Battle of Mutina against Mark Antony, and it may well have been one of Agrippa's units that saved Octavius' life at Philippi when he was caught by surprise in his tent as the Roman camp was overrun. He was forced to hide in a marsh for three days until the danger passed.[13] The friendship between Octavius and Agrippa lasted until the latter's death in 12 BC. Salvidienus Rufus served Octavius as his field general until after the Perusian War (40–41 BC), when he attempted to betray Octavius to Antony and was forced to commit suicide.[14] Agrippa then became Octavius' top general and military advisor.

The Battle of Mutina, April 44 BC

Octavius, Caesar's nephew, adopted son and heir, arrived in Rome in May 44 BC. Antony refused to recognize Octavius as Caesar's political heir or turn over his inheritance to him. Octavius and Agrippa raised Caesar's veterans from Campania and marched north to join Brutus, who refused to relinquish his command to Antony and occupied Mutina (Modena). Antony placed Brutus under siege before Octavius could join him. The two new consuls appointed by the Senate (Aulus Hirtius and Vibius Pansa) marched north to rescue Brutus. Antony left his brother in charge of the siege and marched to meet the threat.

Antony carried out a masterly ambush of Pansa's troops in a forest and marsh near *Forum Gallorum*, with himself leading the attack. Pansa was killed. But as Antony's troops celebrated, they were taken by surprise by Hirtius, whose crack troops suddenly arrived and slaughtered Antony's exhausted men. Antony's cavalry fought bravely, but by nightfall half of Antony's army was killed. The survivors escaped to Antony's camp.

Six days after *Forum Gallorum*, Octavius' legions joined Hirtius outside Mutina and their 45,000 men attacked Antony's 20,000-strong army. Badly outnumbered, Antony was soundly beaten. In an arduous march accompanied by famine, thirst and plunder, Antony led the survivors over the Alps into Transalpine Gaul, where he joined forces with Lepidus and other commanders still loyal to Caesar. Six weeks later, Antony re-entered Italy with seventeen legions – comprising 90,000 men – and 10,000 cavalry. Octavius marched on Rome and forced the Senate to appoint him consul, acknowledge him as Caesar's heir and declare Caesar's assassins outlaws. To avoid a civil war, Octavius came to an accommodation with Antony and Lepidus at Bologna, forming the Second Triumvirate (43–34 BC). Through all of this, Agrippa was his friend's closest advisor and confidant.

The Perusian War (41–40 BC)

The Perusian War marks the first appearance of Agrippa as a military commander in his own right. Mark Antony's brother, Lucius, and Antony's wife, Fulvia, raised armies and invaded Italy with the goal of establishing Antony as the sole ruler of Rome. Octavius appointed Agrippa to lead an army against Lucius.[15] Agrippa blocked Lucius' attempt to reach Gaul, forcing him to retreat and take up positions in Perusia (Perugia). There, Octavius and Salvidienus laid siege to the place, while Agrippa met and blunted three attempts by enemy armies to relieve the siege. At Perusia, Agrippa emerges for the first time as a competent commander of ground forces.

In February 40 BC, Lucius surrendered. Before leaving for Gaul to secure the loyalty of Antony's legions there, Octavius entrusted Agrippa with the defence of Italy against Antony. Agrippa moved quickly to put a temporary end to Sextus Pompey's sea-borne raids in Sicily. He then attacked Sipontum, taking it by storm, defeating the last of Antony's allies. When news of Agrippa's victories reached Antony, he agreed to a peace with Octavius. Agrippa was involved in the negotiations that led to the treaty of Brundisium. It was during these diplomatic manoeuvrings that Octavius learned of Salvidienus' attempt to betray him, and forced him to commit suicide.

Triumph in Gaul and Germany

Over the winter of 39 BC, Octavius entrusted Agrippa with the task of constructing a large fleet of ships and recruiting and training its crews for use in the war that Octavius planned to undertake against his Pompeiian rival, Sextus Pompey. In late spring of that year, Agrippa was sent to Gaul to pacify the Gallic tribes that had grown restless after the withdrawal of Antony's legions. The centre of the rebellion was Aquitania and its confederation of twenty tribes. Trouble was also brewing in *Gallia Comata* (Long Haired Gaul), a section of the country that had been neglected in the two decades since Caesar had conquered it. Near the end of the year, Agrippa won a major victory over the Acquitani, his first great military success, although no details nor size of Agrippa's army or the enemy are known. He was apparently able to pacify the tribes in *Gallia Comata* with negotiations. A year later, he crossed into Germany to put down a local rebellion, leading his men in person to deal with the menace. Dio notes that in doing this, Agrippa was only 'the second of the Romans to cross the Rhine for war'.[16] No account of the German campaign has survived, but it must have had some success for Octavius ordered Agrippa home to finish constructing the fleet and training the crews for war.

For his efforts in Gaul and Germany, Octavius granted Agrippa a triumph. Agrippa graciously declined. Agrippa was later offered triumphs after his victories at Mylae and Actium, and again declined. Military men raised to prominence by public triumphs had been a cause of the Roman civil war, and Agrippa wanted to put an end to this dangerous practice. Agrippa's refusals led to the abandonment of triumphs for anyone but the *principe* (Augustus himself). Successful generals were awarded medals instead. Agrippa was rewarded by being named consul designate, and took office on New Year's Day 37 BC. The office bestowed upon Agrippa the *consular imperium*, the legal right to lead troops in war.

Father of the Roman Navy

The Battle of Actium was the last naval battle of the great Roman civil war. After it, Rome was master of the Mediterranean, and would not relinquish its control for 500 years. The naval battles of the civil war convinced Octavius that Rome needed a permanent navy. Before Actium, Rome had not maintained a standing naval arm, relying instead upon creating one whenever the need arose. The victory at Actium resulted in the establishment of the Roman imperial navy, 'the most organized, widely-based naval structure in antiquity'.[17] For the next 500 years, the Roman Empire depended as much upon its fleets as upon its legions and roads for its survival. It was Marcus Agrippa who created the first permanent standing Roman naval force.

By 39 BC, Octavius had already concluded that a war with Sextus Pompei was inevitable, and ordered the construction of a Roman fleet. Pompei and his pirate ships had been plundering southern Italy and Sicily for almost a decade, often blockading the crucial grain supply. Agrippa was recalled from Germany and placed in charge of the naval preparations for the campaign against Pompei. Agrippa was 27, and had no experience in naval warfare. The Romans had plenty of experience with Pompei's ships, however, and knew that they were small, shallow draft and fast vessels, modelled after the *liburniae* used by the pirates that Sextus' father had fought in 67 BC.[18] To counter these advantages, Agrippa designed heavier-built, heavily armed ships, hoping to leverage their size, mass and greater firepower against Sextus' smaller, faster ships.

Agrippa had no intention of trying to manoeuvre against Pompei's faster vessels. Instead, he planned to close, grab the enemy vessel, pull the ship close with windlasses and allow his marines to board and kill the enemy crew. This tactical perspective drove the design of Agrippa's ships and its combat equipment, effectively converting naval warfare (ramming and sinking) into infantry ground warfare (closing, boarding and killing), thus playing to Rome's advantage. The new ships were equipped with three important devices: a type of iron-covered grapnel (*harpax*) that could be fired from a catapult; two shipboard towers, one fore and one aft, that could be assembled quickly when needed to provide a better angle of fire for the ship's archers; and the *corvus* (raven's beak), a movable bridge that could be swung outboard of the carrying ship and lowered down upon the enemy vessel, over which Roman shipboard infantry could rapidly cross and engage the enemy crew. It is sometimes believed that Agrippa invented the *harpax* and the collapsible ship tower, but this is unlikely since all three of these devices are found in earlier Roman naval engagements. Agrippa's innovation was to bring these devices together in support of a new tactical scenario that transformed a naval clash at sea into a fight that more resembled combat on land.[19]

The new ships were constructed at several places along the Italian coast that had easy access to pine timber. Agrippa realized that once the ships were built, however, they needed a single assembly point for final outfitting and for training the newly recruited crews and marines in seamanship and weapons drill. Dio explains that 'since no shore was found where it was safe for them to come to anchor inasmuch as most of the coast of Italy was without harbours, he [Agrippa] conceived a magnificent enterprise'.[20] At Cumae, between Misenum and Puteoli, there is a bay open to the sea. On the shore and inland were two lakes connected by a narrow isthmus, the one closer to the sea barred by the inland shore.[21] In what was a massive engineering project, Agrippa cut across the inland shore and widened the inner isthmus so ships could travel between the two lakes and the sea, thereby creating a safe harbour to ready the fleet for war. He named the new harbour *Portus Julius* in honour of Octavius. By the end of 37 BC, the new harbour was completed. Pliny the Elder cited the harbour as one of the most magnificent man-made wonders of Italy.[22] The new Roman imperial navy was born.

Battle of Mylae (August 36 BC)

By the summer of 36 BC, Agrippa and Octavius went hunting for Pompei in the waters off Sicily. The goal was to surround Sicily, land an army and retake the island, thus preventing Sextus from using it as a base for his coastal raids and choking off the Sicilian grain supply to Rome. As the Roman fleet approached Sicily, it was struck by a powerful storm that disabled many ships, forcing the fleet to put in for repairs. Octavius relinquished command of the operation, appointing Agrippa to continue the effort to find and attack Pompei.

In August, the Romans again prepared to attack the island. Two legions crossed from Messana (Messina), landed in Sicily and linked up with Lepidus' men already there. Pompei's fleet lay at anchor off Messana. In mid-August, the two fleets clashed at Mylae on the northern shore of Sicily. Pompei's 150 ships outnumbered the 100 or so of Agrippa, but the taller and heavier Roman ships equipped with the new towers and grapnels carried the day. After several hours of combat, Pompei ordered his commander, Papas, to withdraw his shallower-draft vessels into the shoals, and broke contact. Agrippa's heavier ships with deeper drafts could not follow, and the battle ended in a Roman victory.[23]

Battle of Naulochus (3 September 36 BC)

After the battle, Pompei travelled to Mylae from his main base to survey the situation. In his absence, Octavius took command of the transports and attempted to cross with his army into Sicily from his main base at Tauromenium. The result was disaster. Octavius found his army surrounded on three sides, with Pompei's fleet advancing toward him from the sea. Octavius fled in his flagship, only to be caught by Pompei's fleet, which routed Octavius' ships. Again, Octavius fled, barely escaping capture. Some of Octavius' ships were captured and many others burned or sunk. Others turned and made for the Italian shore. At least sixty Roman ships were lost and Octavius was forced to abandon the crossing.[24] The ancient historians remain silent as to the reason for Octavius' defeat. It is clear, however, that Octavius once again revealed himself to be less than a competent commander.

The Roman armies that had succeeded in getting to Sicily were now threatening Sextus' coastal bases, convincing Sextus to risk it all on one last naval battle with the Romans. He sent a message to Octavius inviting him to engage in battle in the bay at Naulochus.[25] Agrippa's fleet engaged Pompei off Naulochus, some 10 miles from the Messana strait. The *harpax* proved a success once again, and the grapnels reduced the ability of Pompei's superior pilots to manoeuvre. At the end of the day, the Romans had burned, captured or run ashore all but seventeen of Pompei's ships, losing only three vessels in the process. Pompei and his few remaining ships fled, abandoning Sicily.

Once more, Agrippa had won a stunning naval victory. The consequence of Agrippa's victories was that the seas around the Italian peninsula were now peaceful, trade was restored and Sicily and its manpower and agricultural resources were now at Octavius' disposal. Agrippa was rewarded with substantial estates in Sicily, whose crops made him a very wealthy man. In addition, Octavius created a special unique military decoration, a golden wreath surmounted with a ship's *rostra* called the *corona navalis*, or naval crown, and awarded it to Agrippa. A new silver coin was struck showing Agrippa wearing his distinctive military decoration. Soon after the victory at Naulochus, an open break occurred with Octavius' fellow *triumvir*, Lepidus, who sought to control all of Sicily. In a rare act of personal courage, Octavius rode into Lepidus' camp and demanded the loyalty of his troops. His troops having abandoned him, Lepidus was removed as *triumvir* and his African provinces transferred to Octavius. Now only Antony remained to oppose Octavius.

The Illyrian War (35–34 BC)

Octavius now turned his attention to Illyricum, an area roughly equivalent to the former Yugoslavia that had come under Roman military control in 167 BC. Julius Caesar was governor there in 59 BC, prior to taking up his command in Gaul. The area was an important corridor between Italy and Macedonia, Greece and Asia, and was only a short journey by ship from Brundisium. The region was a patchwork of independent tribes, all with different cultures, languages and social systems.[26] Octavius wanted to strengthen Roman control over the area and deny its possible use by Antony should events turn to war.

The Roman campaign began in the north, against the Iapodes living in the foothills of the southeastern Alps.[27] The lowlands fell quickly, but the enemy retreated into the mountains and assembled in their stronghold of Metulus. Agrippa was with Octavius in the siege that followed. Octavius was injured in his right leg when an assault bridge collapsed under him, leaving him with a severe limp. Rather than surrender, the Iapodes set fire to their city and many committed suicide. Over the rest of the campaign season, the Romans besieged and destroyed one town and village after another. Octavius and Agrippa left for Rome at the beginning of the winter of 35 BC.

In the spring of 34 BC, revolt broke out again in the region among the tribes in Illyria and Pannonia, and Agrippa was sent to command against the rebels. Octavius joined him later. The pattern of combat repeated itself, this time in the southern zone of operations, home of the Delmate. As in the previous year, the Romans successfully defeated the Delmate and captured their capital at Promona. Faced with starvation, the revolts began to subside, and another Roman commander, Statilius Taurus, concluded the mop-up operations. Appian says the Romans now controlled the entire region, including new areas that had not before been under Roman control.[28] In 33 BC, the entire region was proclaimed the Roman province of Illyricum, administered by a senatorial *proconsul*. Agrippa had once more acquitted himself well in the service of his old friend.

Commissioner of Public Works

In 34 BC, Agrippa was elected one of the six *aedile* of Rome, responsible for all the public buildings and roads of the city. He immediately set about increasing the fresh water supply of the city by repairing the century-old *Aqua Marcia* aqueduct that transported water from the Anio Valley some 56 miles away.[29] A number of new conduits were added, bringing fresh water to greatly under-served sections of the city. Elected again the following year, Agrippa repaired and rerouted Rome's two other main aqueducts, the *Aqua Appia* and *Aqua Vetus*. He also began construction of a new triple-arched aqueduct, which he named the *Aqua Iulia* after Octvaius. Some years later, Agrippa had yet another aqueduct built called the *Aqua Virgo*. Now new fountains and basins appeared throughout the city, to the gratitude of the citizens. Pliny says Agrippa constructed 700 cisterns, 500 fountains and 130 *casella* or basins for distributing water, upon which he placed 300 figures of bronze and marble as adornments, and 400 marble columns,[30] which he provided at his own expense, establishing the expectation that the wealthy would thereafter be expected to adorn the city with public works. To keep the water system running, Agrippa trained a company of slaves to act as repairmen. Later, the slaves were freed and became public employees, creating the world's first public water department.[31]

Agrippa's constructions also provided an opportunity to improve the health and sanitation of the citizenry. Prior to Agrippa, there were only a few bath houses in the city, and they were used mostly by the elites. Pliny tells us that Agrippa built 170 free public bath houses for the use of the general population.[32] Regular daily bathing became a famous Roman habit. Agrippa next turned his attention to the city's drainage system. The great amount of water now flowing from the taps, fountains and baths through the city's antiquated pipe system was too much for the system to handle, bringing it to near collapse. Agrippa completely restored the entire sewer and drainage system, cleaning out the drains and sewers, and rebuilding the city's oldest main sewer, the *Cloaca Maxima,* constructed in 600 BC, so that it once more flowed into the Tiber. Agrippa's improvements made Rome one of the healthiest and cleanest cities in the ancient world.

After the Battle of Actium, Octavius left for the war in Spain for three years. Agrippa was left in charge of Rome. During this period, Agrippa commissioned the construction of the now famous Pantheon and established a number of important improvements to the Campus Martius, increasing its seating capacity to 200,000 spectators. In the

Forum Romanum, he constructed a monument called the 'golden milestone' (*miliarium aureum*), a column covered in gilt bronze that listed all the major cities of the empire and their distances from Rome.[33] And thus it was that 'all roads led to Rome'. To prevent future grain crises, he constructed a series of large warehouses in which to store grain. He constructed the vote-counting office (*Diribitorium*), the largest building under a single roof ever constructed to that time.[34]

Remarkably, most of Agrippa's public works were accomplished at his own expense.[35] He believed that the wealthy citizens had an obligation to improve their city. The wealthy of Rome soon followed Agrippa's example, and public works projects sprang up across the city. All the civic buildings were rebuilt and all the streets of the city improved. When Octavius later boasted that he had found Rome a city of brick and left it a city of marble, the transformation was due largely to Agrippa.

Battle of Actium, 3 September 31 BC

In 33 BC, Octavius launched a propaganda war against Antony, convincing the Senate in 32 BC to declare war against Cleopatra (not Antony) and revoke Antony's triumviral title. Anticipating war, Antony had raised an army of 73,000 infantry, 12,000 cavalry and a fleet of 480 ships. He deployed his army and fleet across the Ionian Sea in the northern Peloponnese at Actium to discourage Octavius from moving east. Octavius saw Antony's deployment as a threat, and began raising an army of 90,000 men, 12,000 cavalry and 400 ships that he assembled at Brundisuim. Antony's army had assembled almost a year before, and he could have followed the advice of his senior officers and invaded Italy, catching Octavius unprepared. But Cleopatra opposed any movement into Italy, fearing it would leave Egypt exposed. Antony overruled his generals in what Plutarch calls 'one of the greatest of Antony's oversights' and awaited Octavius' crossing to Greece.

Agrippa was now entrusted with the preparations for the war against Antony. To conduct coastal raids and counter Antony's heavier ships, Agrippa had a new type of smaller, faster and shallower draft ship constructed, the *Liburnae*, patterned after the ships used by Sextus Pompei at Naulochus. This vessel became the standard ship used by the new Roman riverine force that patrolled the empire's rivers later in Octavius' reign. Agrippa crossed over to Greece in the spring in what probably was a combination feint and reconnaissance in force to determine Antony's dispositions. Agrippa immediately encountered a small flotilla of Antony's supply ships. He attacked the flotilla, sunk some ships and drove the rest off. He then attacked the coastal town of Kerkyra.[36]

Agrippa's reconnaissance revealed Antony's weakness, that his army and fleet were at the end of a long supply line of island bases and mainland coastal installations reaching all the way back to Egypt that he

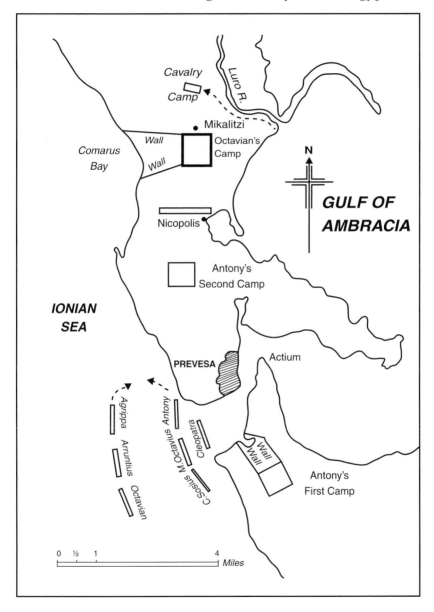

Battle of Actium

employed to feed his army. In a brilliant strategic move, Agrippa quickly attacked Antony's line of communications, capturing Methone on the Greek coast. He then sailed north, attacking more of Antony's coastal supply depots. Finally, he captured Corcyra before joining Octavius, who had moved his army into position north of Actium in late July.

Agrippa now moved to completely cripple Antony's supply line and starve his army and fleet, and continued his predations against Antony's seaborne and coastal supply assets. The objective was to degrade Antony's military assets, cause maximum disruptions to his logistics and degrade the morale of his troops.[37] Staging from Corcyra, he captured the island of Leucas southwest of Actium, seizing more of Antony's supply transports. Next, he captured Cape Ducato, and then Patrae near the west end of the Gulf of Corinth. In another surprise attack, Agrippa seized Corinth itself, closing off all access to the Peloponnese. With his supply lines now completely cut, Antony's army began to starve and suffer from disease.

In the spring of 31 BC, Octavius crossed the sea to Greece, landing securely at Kerkyra, the coastal town Agrippa had captured earlier. Antony had moved his fleet into the harbour at Actium, deploying his army on the ground south of the harbour. In response, Octavius moved his army and fleet south, and took up ground positions north of the mouth of the Gulf of Ambracia. The two armies faced each other across the Gulf, Octavius to the north and Antony in the south. The Gulf's narrow opening to the sea had turned it into a trap for Antony's fleet. With the enemy fleet taken out of action, Agrippa's ships could now roam free all along the coast. From the island of Leucas that he had captured earlier, Agrippa could attack any ship attempting to leave the Gulf and prevent any supply ships from entering, causing Antony's men and the sailors of his fleet to starve.

Antony crossed to the northern shore twice to provoke Octavius to fight, but Octavius refused to engage. In August, Antony sent an army north to break out of the siege while simultaneously trying to have his ships force their way out of the Gulf. Both efforts failed disastrously. The Battle of Actium was anticlimactic in that Antony had already decided not to fight, but to break through Agrippa's blocking force of ships and make for Egypt, while his land army marched north through Macedonia and Greece to join him in Egypt.[38] Cleopatra insisted that Antony retreat. Her sixty ships and some of Antony's might escape to Egypt, while the land army broke out of the siege and marched to Egypt. New ships and legions could be raised in Egypt to continue the war with Octavius.

Antony had more ships than rowers as a result of crew losses to disease and desertion. He burned the vessels he could not man, leaving him with 230 ships to Octavius' 200.[39] Antony deployed 20,000 legionaries and 2,000 archers to man his fleet. Antony's objective was flight, not battle; he prepared for a sea retreat from an untenable position to minimize his losses and live to fight again.

Agrippa had formed his ships in a line blocking the exit to the Gulf. Once Antony's ships began to move, he issued orders for the centre to pull back and the wings to move forward to encircle Antony in a replay of Hannibal's great battle at Cannae. Antony's ships attempted to flank the Roman line to the right, without success. But the manoeuvre had the calculated effect of thinning the centre of the Roman line and opening gaps in it. Cleopatra's ships now hoisted sail into the freshening southwest breeze and plunged through the centre of the Roman line, gaining the open sea. With the wind to their backs, the Egyptians rapidly outdistanced the Roman pursuers and sailed for Egypt. Antony followed in his own ship. Antony's tactics worked well enough, and he was able to salvage some 100 vessels and 20,000 of his best marines against incredible odds.

Agrippa had won the battle, but at great cost. Fifteen of Antony's ships and 5,000 sailors were lost, and many others surrendered, but almost half of Antony's serviceable fleet escaped to reach Egypt.[40] The Romans suffered 12,000 dead and 6,000 wounded. On land, Antony's army of 120,000 infantry and 12,000 cavalry remained near Actium ready to fight the Romans.[41] For seven days the army waited, refusing to believe their commander had already fled. Finally, they surrendered to Octavius when offered reasonable terms. Agrippa, meanwhile, sailed down the Peloponnese, securing the rest of the peninsula for the Romans.

Antony knew that any hope of future resistance depended upon the land army making it back to Egypt. When news reached him that it had surrendered, Antony plunged into a suicidal depression. Octavius followed Antony to Egypt, where his advanced units were halted when Antony's troops drove them back in a brief battle at Alexandria. In August 29 BC, Octavius attacked Alexandria again, this time with success. By now, most of Antony's troops and his fleet had gone over to the Romans, leaving him only a remnant force. Believing that Cleopatra had killed herself, Antony committed suicide, ending the life of a man who once had been the first man in Rome. The kingdom of Egypt was annexed as a territory of Rome, administered by a *praefectus* of Octavius' choosing.

Actium had not been a major battle in the strict military sense. Only in later accounts written to glorify Octavius was the tale magnified to heroic military stature. Once Agrippa cut off Antony's supplies, the outcome was predictable, and the credit for the victory belongs rightly to Agrippa. Still, Actium was politically and strategically decisive, perhaps the most important battle in the history of the West. Agrippa was given the task of demobilizing the troops, paying them off and finding land for them. After a period of some turmoil caused by the impatient troops returning to Rome, funds from the enormous captured Egyptian treasury were used to settle the financial debt. Large numbers of demobilized soldiers were settled on lands in Italy, Illyria and Greece, at Agrippa's direction.

The Foundations of Empire

Octavius was a sickly sort, given to bouts of paralyzing anxiety, superstition and physical disability, often at the most critical moments.[42] Twice at Philippi and once at Actium he fell ill and remained in his tent while command fell to others. He lacked the energy and experience for sustained effort, and had little interest in administrative and military matters, which he often left to Agrippa. Agrippa's genius for organization and administration thus made him an invaluable asset in meeting the challenges of the new imperial realm, and he spent the next decade of his life occupied with organizing and administering the new empire. Agrippa aided Octavius in the establishment of the *principate*, preserving the forms, if not the powers, of the old republican institutions. The Senate was reformed, its numbers reduced, powers limited and new members appointed. In 28 BC, Agrippa was appointed consul for the second time, and was made of equal rank with Octavius whenever the two were in military command. Agrippa married Octavius' niece, becoming a member of the royal family.

In 28 BC, Octavius recreated the ancient office of *censor*, dating back to the Roman monarchy, and appointed Agrippa to the post. The functions of the office were to conduct a census of the population every five years, to uphold standards of public morality and administer the public finances, to include the care of public buildings and the erection of all public works. So empowered, the two of them began to reform the Roman system of government.

Of all the imperial reforms, the most important was that of the Roman military system, for it was the army that became the defender of the new order, the foremost instrument in organizing and governing the empire, the instrument of civil order and the means of defending Rome against her enemies. These reforms were to a great extent the work of Agrippa. There were fifty legions, some 300,000 men, still under arms, who could not be discharged without provoking great civil unrest. The number of legions was reduced to twenty-five, and the soldiers paid off in money or land grants. The legions were transformed into a professional army with regular pay, retirement accounts and tax privileges upon retirements. The legions were posted outside of Italy to prevent them from once again becoming a threat to the political order.[43]

The Senate was no longer permitted to appoint military commanders, and reports from field commanders were now passed directly to Octavius, bypassing the Senate. It was Agrippa who established this precedent after his victories in Cantabria and the Crimea, when he sent his reports directly to Octavius. To ensure the loyalty of the soldiery, the practice of swearing loyalty to their commanders was outlawed. Upon entering military service, soldiers now swore an oath, the *sacramentum*, to Rome itself. At the beginning of each year, soldiers were required to repeat the oath amid solemn ceremony. With only 150,000 soldiers now in service, the new practice of raising auxiliary legions from Rome's allies to serve alongside the regular legions proved an excellent solution to the military manpower problem.

Agrippa's reforms carried out in the name of Octavius transformed the mercenary armies of the civil war into an impartial instrument of the new state. Had they failed, sooner or later Rome would have succumbed again to the ambitions of a new generation of *condottieri* pressing their ambitions by military means. Agrippa's reforms remained the fundamental basis of the Roman army for the next two centuries.

The empire's finances were reformed with the establishment of a national mint, bringing an end to the ruinous inflation caused by the debasement of the currency. The tax system was changed so that all taxes now flowed directly to the national treasury, prohibiting the old practice of having often corrupt provincial governors levy and collect imperial monies.[44] Among the most important reforms was the creation of an administrative structure to govern the provinces. Until now, Rome had attempted to govern the empire with the same machinery with which it had governed the city-state, with the result that the ability to control events from the centre was almost non-existent. Provincial governors were no longer appointed by the Senate, but by the emperor, with strong oversight by a system of procurators who kept close watch on the province's finances. Provincial governors no longer held military command, and could be removed at will and prosecuted, bringing to an end the old system where military commanders could exploit their conquered province for personal gain. Retired centurions were offered posts in civil government at the local level, the provincial law courts reformed and elements of Roman law and protection extended to all residents of the empire. These practices were the groundwork for the gradual establishment of the imperial civil service that became the spine of imperial government for the next four centuries.[45] Again, it was Agrippa who played an important role in their establishment. Agrippa's efforts in bringing about these changes helped establish the foundations for the *Pax Romana*, a period of peace that endured for centuries throughout the Roman world.

In 23 BC, Agrippa was sent to reorganize the eastern provinces, and conducted negotiations with the Parthians for the successful return of the legion standards lost by Crassus in 53 BC. At Octavius' initiative, Agrippa divorced his wife (Octavius' niece) and married Octavius' daughter, Julia, in 21 BC. Without male heirs of his own, Octavius planned to make Agrippa his successor. Later, Octavius adopted both of Agrippa's sons, making them successors if he should die without naming an heir, presumably Agrippa. In 19 BC, Agrippa was sent to Spain to put down a revolt by the Cantabri. In more than a year of hard fighting, Agrippa broke the back of the Spanish insurgency and resistance that had plagued the Romans for more than two centuries. The victory allowed the Romans to complete the conquest of the Iberian peninsula and begin its economic exploitation and settlement by Roman veterans. Once more Agrippa was offered a triumph, and once more he declined.

In 18 BC, again at Octavius' initiative, the Senate granted Agrippa the power of *tribunicia potestas*, officially making him co-regent with Octavius. In 17 BC, Agrippa left again for the East on an inspection tour, where he settled soldiers from two legions in Berytus (Beirut), establishing the first Roman colony in Syria. In 15 BC, he put down a minor rebellion in the Bosporus for which the Senate again voted him a triumph. Agrippa refused yet again. He spent an extended visit with his old friend, Herod the Great, who named a wing of the great Roman fortress in Jerusalem *Agrippeum* after his friend. The walls of this wing form the present Wailing Wall in Jerusalem. Agrippa supported the Jews against the resident Greeks in retaining the special privileges granted them by Julius Caesar. Agrippa returned to Italy in June 13 BC. There was trouble brewing in the north of Illyricum, and Octavius sent Agrippa to deal with the problem. When news of his arrival reached the insurgents in late autumn, Agrippa's reputation as a general was so great that the insurgents put down their arms and sued for peace.[46] With peace restored, Agrippa set sail for Italy in the new year.

Early in 12 BC, Agrippa reached Italy and took up residence in his villa in Campania for a much-needed rest. There he fell ill, although no source tells us the nature of his illness. When word was sent to Octavius in Rome that his long-time friend was dying, he immediately set out for Campania, but arrived too late. In the late spring of 12 BC, one of Rome's greatest soldiers died at the age of 51. His ashes were entombed in Octavius' mausoleum.

Renowned during his life, Agrippa was largely ignored by Roman historians after his death. Always a loyal friend and colleague to Octavius, Agrippa served the empire without ambitions of his own. In doing so, he laid down many of the institutional foundations of the new imperial realm. He was, as Cassius Dio called him, 'the noblest man of his time'.

Notes

1. The ancient sources upon which this study draws are: Cassius Dio, *Roman History*, available in translation in the Loeb Classics series and Penguin Classics series; Appian, *The Civil Wars*, trans. John Carter (New York, Penguin Classics, 1996); Pliny, *Natural History*, available in many volumes from Loeb Classics series; and Nicholas of Damaskos, *Life of Augustus*, trans. Clayton M Hall (1923) available online. The only modern treatments of Agrippa's life can be found in Meyer Reinhold, *Marcus Agrippa: A Biography* (New York,: Humphrey Press, 1933); J.M. Rodaz, *Marcus Agrippa* (Rome, Ecole Franchise de Rome, Palas Farnese, 1884); and Lindsay Powell, *Marcus Agrippa: Right-Hand Man of Caesar Augustus* (Barnsley, Pen and Sword, 2015). See also Richard A. Gabriel, 'Agrippa Takes Charge: Rome's Shadow Emperor', *Military History Quarterly* (winter 2016), pp.51–55.
2. Rodaz, p.22.
3. Pliny, *Natural History*, 7.6.
4. Ibid., 7.8.
5. U.E. Paoli, *Rome, Its People, Life, and Customs* (London, Longman, 1963), pp.169–70.
6. Powell, *Marcus Agrippa*, p.12.
7. Nicholas of Damaskos, 7.
8. Manlius, *Astronomicon*, 1.797–798; Powell, *Marcus Agrippa*, p.14.
9. L. Koppie, *The Making of the Roman Army from Republic to Empire* (London, Batsford, 184), p.98.
10. Powell, p.14.
11. Appian, *Civil War*, 3.9.
12. Powell, p.27.
13. Pliny, *Natural History*, 7.48, who says Agrippa was with Octavius in the swamp and cared for him there.
14. Appian, 5.66.
15. Ibid., 5.31.
16. Dio, 48.49.3.

17. Richard A. Gabriel, 'The Roman Imperial Navy: Masters of the Mediterranean', *Military History* (December, 2007), pp.36–43.
18. K. Rogers, 'Sextus Pompeius: Rebellious Pirate or Imitative Son', *Chrestomathy* 7, pp.199–226.
19. Powell, p.50.
20. Dio, 48.49.4–5.
21. Ibid., 50.1–3.
22. As cited by Virgil, *Georgicon*, 2.161–164.
23. Appian, 5.107–5.108.
24. Richard A. Gabriel, 'Agrippa Takes Charge: Rome's Shadow Emperor', *Military History Quarterly* (winter 2016), p.56.
25. Appian, 5.117.
26. J.P. Mallory, *In Search of Indo-Europeans: Language, Archaeology, and Myth* (London, Thames and Hudson, 1989), pp.73–76.
27. Appian, *Illyrica*, 16; Dio, 49.35.1.
28. Ibid., 28.
29. Powell, p.69.
30. Meyer Reinhold, *Marcus Agrippa* (Geneva, NY, Humphrey Press, 1933), p.49, citing Pliny 36.121.
31. Ibid., p.52.
32. Pliny, 36.24.
33. Dio, 54.8.4.
34. Dio, 55.8.4.
35. Dio, 49.43.1, as cited by Rehinhold, p.48.
36. Orosius 6.19.6; see Powell, p.83.
37. Powell, p.85.
38. The debate as to Antony's motives to fight or to flee continues, with some modern historians arguing that Antony correctly gauged that he had lost the initiative, had trapped his fleet and positioned his ground forces so they could not be decisive, and decided to break out of Agrippa's naval blockade and run for Egypt. See Eleanor Holtz Huzar, *Mark Antony: A Biography* (Minneapolis, MN, University of Minnesota Press, 1978), pp.209–33.
39. The number of ships on each side cannot be accurately determined. See Powell, p.91.
40. Richard A. Gabriel, 'Mark Antony', *Military History* (spring 2016), p.43.
41. Dio 50.16.2.
42. Richard A. Gabriel, *Great Captains of Antiquity*, (Westport, CT, Greenwood Press, 2001), pp.183, 196–98.
43. Ibid., pp.200–01.
44. Ibid., pp.207–08.
45. Ibid., p.209.
46. Dio, 53.25.6.

CHAPTER TEN

MUHAMMAD (AD 570–632)

The military life of Muhammad, the founder of the great world religion of Islam, is not well-known. Despite Muhammad's outstanding military accomplishments, there is only one modern account of this great man that examines his life as Islam's first great general and leader of a successful insurgency.[1] This is a curious state of affairs in light of the fact that had Muhammad not succeeded as a military commander, Islam might have remained but one of a number of religious sects relegated to a geographic backwater, and the conquest of the Byzantine and Persian empires by Arab armies might have never occurred.

To think of Muhammad as a military man will come as something of a new experience to many. And yet Muhammad was truly a great general. In the space of a single decade, he fought eight major battles, led eighteen raids and planned thirty-eight other military operations where others were in command but operating under his orders and strategic direction. He was wounded twice, suffered defeats and twice had his positions overrun by superior forces before rallying his troops to victory. Muhammad was more than a great field general and tactician. He was also a military theorist, organizational reformer, strategic thinker, operational-level combat commander, political-military leader, heroic soldier, revolutionary and the inventor of the theory of insurgency and history's first successful practitioner of it. Muhammad had no military training before actually commanding an army in the field.

Muhammad proved to be a master of intelligence in war, and his intelligence service eventually came to rival that of Byzantium and Persia, especially in the area of political intelligence. He often spent hours devising tactical and political stratagems, and once remarked that 'all war is cunning', reminding one of Sun Tzu's dictum that 'all war is deception'. In his thinking and application of force, Muhammad was a combination of Clausewitz and Machiavelli, for he always employed force in the service of political goals. He was an astute grand strategist whose use of non-military methods (alliance-building, political assassination, bribery, religious appeals, mercy and calculated butchery) always resulted in strengthening his long-term strategic position, sometimes even at the expense of short-term military considerations.

Muhammad's unshakeable belief in Islam and in his role as the Messenger of God revolutionized warfare in Arabia and created the first army in the ancient world motivated by a coherent system of ideological belief. The ideology of holy war (*jihad*) and martyrdom (*shahada*) for the faith was transmitted to the West during the wars between Muslims and Christians in Spain and France, where it changed traditional Christian pacifistic thinking on war, brought into being a coterie of Christian warrior saints and provided the Catholic Church with its ideological justification for the Crusades.[2] Ideology of the religious or secular variety has remained a primary element of military adventure ever since.

It was Muhammad who forged the military instrument of the Arab conquests that began within two years of his death by bringing into being a completely new kind of army not seen before in Arabia. Muhammad was a military reformer who introduced no fewer than eight major military reforms that transformed the armies and conduct of war in Arabia. Just as Philip of Macedon transformed the armies of Greece so that his successor, Alexander, could employ them as instruments of conquest and empire, so Muhammad transformed the armies of Arabia so his successors could use them to defeat the armies of Persia and Byzantium, and establish the heartland of the Empire of Islam. Had Muhammad not transformed the armies, the Arab conquests would likely have remained a military impossibility.

Muhammad the Man

Muhammad was born on 20 August AD 570 in Mecca, a member of the dominant Quraish tribe. By the time of Muhammad's birth, Mecca's location as a transfer point for the north–south trade route between the coastal ports and Gaza had led to the growth of a merchant class. Mecca became a semi-urban society comprised of groups of traders and artisans. Mecca lay 48 miles inland from the Red Sea in a barren rock valley 600 yards wide and a mile and a half long, squeezed among stony mountains. From time immemorial, Mecca had possessed a shrine (*ka'bah*) where Arabs came to worship the idols kept there. The main idol worshipped in Mecca was Hubal. Other towns and settlements had their own shrines and idols. Most Arabs were idol-worshippers until their conversion to Islam.

Once a year, Arabs came from all over Arabia to worship at the *ka'aba* in Mecca. Providing services to these pilgrims was a lucrative business, and the Quraish profited handsomely. In the weeks before the pilgrimage, trading fairs sprung up around Mecca that offered rich commercial opportunities to Meccan merchants. By Muhammad's time, Mecca had established itself as one of the important commercial and religious centres in Arabia, and the Quraish controlled the *ka'aba* and much of the city's commerce.

One Abdul Muttalib (b. circa AD 497) was the grandfather of Muhammad. He was the head of the Hashim clan and in charge of the wells around the *ka'aba* that provided water to the pilgrims. As a clan chief, he was a man of considerable influence. Abdul Muttalib had five sons, one of whom, Abdullah, was Muhammad's father. Abdullah died in AD 570, leaving his wife pregnant. The child she was carrying was Muhammad, who was born in August AD 570. Because Muhammad had no father, it was difficult to find a wet-nurse willing to take him. Muhammad was eventually accepted by a woman of the Beni Saad tribe living outside Mecca. Muhammad spent two years with his foster mother before being returned to his mother in Mecca, where he lived with her for four years until she died. Muhammad was 6 when he was orphaned. His grandfather took him in, and he was looked after by a slavegirl in his grandfather's household. When Muhammad was 8, his grandfather died, and he was placed in the charge of his uncle, Abu Talib, the new head of the Hashim clan.

The fortunes of the Hashim clan were in decline and Muhammad continued to live in poverty. As an orphan, he had no one to protect him, educate him or supply him with money and contacts to make his way in business. Muhammad sometimes worked as a shepherd, and spent considerable time alone. He became a fixture around the *ka'aba*, where he sometimes helped provide water to the pilgrims and other worshipers. When Muhammad was about 14, a tribal war broke out between the Quraish and the Hawazin that lasted for five years. In one of the earliest battles of this war, Muhammad went along with his uncles and he retrieved arrows that could be shot back at the enemy. This was Muhammad's only military experience prior to commanding his own troops in the later war with the Quraish. Military training was provided to Arab males by their fathers or uncles as a matter of course. Perhaps because Muhammad was a quiet boy who kept to himself, spending long hours tending flocks or at the *ka'aba*, his uncles may have concluded that he lacked the necessary aptitude for fighting. If so, they could hardly have been more mistaken.

Over the next decade, Muhammad tried his hand at commerce, with no noticeable success. He did, however, acquire a reputation for honesty, and may have acquired the nickname 'the trustworthy', but we cannot be certain of this.[3] When he was 25, his uncle secured a place for him in a caravan to Syria. His reputation for honesty served him well, and he was made responsible for selling some of the goods as well as the purchase of some return goods. The caravan belonged to a rich widow of the Quraish tribe named Khadijah. The death rate among Arab men from disease, injury and blood feuds left Mecca with a considerable number of widows, among them some who had property and considerable wealth. In Muhammad's day, the relationship between men and women as regards property and children was polyandrous and not, as Muhammad later established, polygamous. In a polyandrous relationship, property and the children belong to the female and her family, not to the male. Khadijah's relationship with her first two husbands was most likely polyandrous, accounting for her possession of wealth and property. The polyandrous system came to an end only after Muhammad permitted a man to possess four wives after he had lost so many men at the Battle of Badr. The new arrangement was a solution to taking care of the widows and orphans.

Upon Muhammad's return to Mecca, Khadijah proposed marriage. Muhammad was 25; Khadijah was already twice widowed, and said to have been about 40 years old, but may have been somewhat younger, since she bore him several children – four girls and two boys, although some sources (Seyyid Hossein Nasr) say Muhammad had only one son.[4] The marriage provided Muhammad with considerable commercial opportunities, and he succeeded very well. More important was his relationship with Khadijah. She became his true love and confidante. He trusted her in all things, and she supported him when he began to have his revelations.

The next fifteen years, from AD 595–610, are the 'hidden years' in which the texts are mostly silent about Muhammad's life. He seems to have had a modestly successful business career, and as an organizer of large caravans he gained experience as both an administrator and logistician. During this time, Muhammad developed the habit of going off by himself to meditate, often taking refuge in a cave for days at a time. It is noteworthy that other Arabs would not have found Muhammad's habit an unusual occurrence. Even the idolaters of Mecca sometimes turned to this form of desert asceticism. In Arabic, the practice is known as *tahannuth*.[5] It was during one of these desert retreats that Muhammad experienced his first revelation while living in a cave during the month of Ramadan, and they continued for the rest of his life. He would repeat the instructions he received to his followers, who memorized them and/or wrote them down.[6] Sometime later, they were collected in what became known as the *Quran*. The *Quran* and its moral instructions became the foundation for the new religion of Islam.

It is interesting to examine the physical circumstances that Muhammad himself described as accompanying the onset and duration of his revelations, insofar as they seem to indicate an identifiable medical condition that may have accompanied the revelations. Only two of his revelations – his first call to God's service and the revelation in which he recounted journeying from Mecca to Jerusalem in a single night, where he met Moses and Jesus – seem to have been *visual* experiences. All other revelations which came to him throughout his life seem to have been completely *auditory* and did not include any visual components.[7] When Muhammad was asked to describe his revelatory experience, he said: 'Sometimes it cometh unto me like the reverberations of a bell, and that is the hardest upon me; the reverberations abate when I am aware of their message. And sometimes the Angel taketh the form of a man and speaketh unto me, and I am aware of what he saith.'[8] Whenever a revelation was imminent, Muhammad was gripped by a feeling of pain. Even on cold days, he would sweat profusely.[9] Ibn Ishaq records that the prophet knew when a revelation was about to occur. He would lie down and cover himself with a cloak or blanket. He would perspire profusely. At the end of the event, Muhammad sat up and repeated the message he had been given. In only a few instances did the revelation come upon him when he was riding or at a public gathering.[10]

The symptoms recorded as accompanying Muhammad's revelations seem strongly similar to those associated with recurrent malaria, a disease whose episodes are often accompanied by vivid visual and auditory hallucinations. Often the first onset of the disease is acute, that is, its symptoms are greatly exaggerated and the fever very high. Ibn Ishaq, in describing the first attacks of 'the fever' that afflicted Muhammad's followers when they arrived in Medina, seems to describe an acute onset. He tells us that, 'When the Apostle came to Medina it was the most fever-infested land on earth, and his companions suffered severely from it … they were delirious and out of their minds with a high temperature.'[11] Malarial infection does not confer immunity from other outbreaks, but does confer a resistance to the disease, so that follow-on episodes are usually not as severe as the first onset. And so it was that while Muhammad's followers arrived in Medina from Mecca and immediately contracted malaria, Ibn Ishaq tells us, 'God kept it from his Apostle.'[12] This suggests that Muhammad may have already contracted the disease and was resistant, though not immune from further outbreaks.

Mecca is a hot and dry place where malaria was not endemic. If Muhammad had malaria, it is unlikely that he first contracted the disease there. Malaria thrived in places like Medina and other swampy, humid and fetid oases throughout Arabia. Medina had a reputation among caravaneers as a place where fever was endemic, and they sometimes bypassed the town to avoid contracting it. As a caravan organizer, Muhammad would likely have stopped at any number of oases during his journeys, where he might have been exposed to and contracted malaria. Moreover, the symptoms that accompanied Muhammad's later revelations are not those of an acute onset, but of an episodic recurrence. None of this, of course, is to bring into question the legitimacy of Muhammad's claim that his revelations were of divine origin. It is only to say that Muhammad's own descriptions of his revelations suggest they were accompanied by symptoms usually associated with malaria.[13]

After his first revelation, Muhammad had no further revelations for three years. Then a second revelation commanded him to preach the message of Allah. Muhammad's ministry lasted from AD 610 to his death in 632, with the public phase beginning in 613. For the next six years, Muhammad and his few followers were the objects of ridicule and persecution. Conversions to Islam cut across tribal and familial lines, with the result that Muslim converts were sometimes persecuted by their own kin. The most severe persecutions were suffered by the converts who came from the lower social classes, slaves, widows, orphans and the poor, who had no families or clans to protect them. Muhammad never forgot the persecution inflicted upon his early followers, and when the time came he took his revenge.

By AD 619, Muhammad was in danger if he continued to preach among the Meccans, who regarded his preaching as both insulting to their family lineages and dangerous to their commercial interests. Muhammad ceased his efforts in Mecca, and began to preach to the pilgrims and traders who came to the trade fairs and encamped on the town's outskirts. In 620, Muhammad preached to a group of seven pilgrims from the oasis of Yathrib (Medina). The next year, these seven returned, bringing with them five more to hear his message. Muhammad met with the group in a little valley in the mountains outside Mecca, at a place known to the locals as Aqaba. Here, the pilgrims from Yathrib were converted to Islam. The new converts pledged to obey Muhammad and recognized him as the Messenger of God. However, the pilgrims did not undertake any obligation to take up arms in defence of Islam or to use force to protect Muhammad himself.

The following year, 621, a larger group of seventy-three men and two women pilgrims from Medina arrived, met with Muhammad at Aqaba and converted to Islam. This is called the Second Pledge of Aqaba and is a very important event in the history of Islam. Unlike the first pledge, the converts swore an oath to protect Muhammad as they would their own family members, with force if necessary.[14] The pledge at Aqaba was a traditional Arab oath of obligation requiring mutual armed assistance. But Muhammad promised the new converts, known now as the *Ansar*, or Helpers, something which no traditional clan chief could have offered: everlasting life in paradise. The group of pilgrims seems to have come from the Kazrai clan of Medina. Their guarantee of protection made it possible for Muhammad and his followers to emigrate to a less hostile place where they would be safe from persecution.

Muhammad must have been a very psychologically complex person. Whatever glimpses into his psychology that may be gained from historical accounts must be regarded as fraught with error. The pre-eminent scholar W. Montgomery Watt, drawing on Ibn Ishaq's notes, offers the following description of Muhammad's general psychological disposition: 'He was given to sadness, and there were long periods of silence when he was deep in thought; yet he never rested but was always busy with something … He never spoke unnecessarily. What he said was always to the point, and sufficient to make his meaning clear. He spoke rapidly. Over his feelings he had firm control … His time was carefully apportioned according to the various demands on him. In his dealings with people he was above all tactful. He could be severe at times.'[15]

Although capable of ferocious anger, Muhammad seems to have generally been a calm man open to suggestions, who regularly sought and often accepted the advice of others. There is no evidence that his followers were afraid to approach him and offer advice. Although he seems to have possessed an innate gift for things military, he often sought the advice of his more experienced officers before a military operation. He was democratic in the typical manner of Arab clan chiefs, and remained accessible to his followers to the end. He was kind to the poor, widows and orphans, and greatly loved by his followers and, later, even by some of his former enemies.

There is no doubt that Muhammad believed sincerely and deeply in his having been called by God and in his mission to spread the new faith. Yet he remained psychologically balanced. He always knew the difference between his own thoughts and those he had received from his revelations. Although the *hadith* and oral traditions of Islam are full of accounts of Muhamamd performing miracles, Muhammad himself never claimed to be able to do so, and was well aware of his own mortality. This sense of balance was also reflected in his condemnation of religious asceticism, which he had once witnessed among Christian monks living in the desert. In this regard, he remarked, 'God has not ordered us to destroy ourselves.'[16] He was scrupulously clean, perhaps even compulsively so, and often remarked how the presence of food adhering to a man's moustache disgusted him. He disliked strong smells and would not eat anything flavoured with onions or garlic.

None of these dispositions completely overcame Muhammad's fierce sense of rectitude, anger and violence, which he could display when he thought it necessary. Like Moses, Christ and Akhenaten of Egypt, Muhammad was 'a god-intoxicated man'.[17] He was also a man of physical courage, and never seems to have feared death. Muhammad was now an Arab chief, and courage was a required trait, especially in a warrior of God.

Muhammad's sense of divine purpose led him to regard violence as an acceptable means to achieve God's ends. This tendency revealed itself early, during the period when his few followers were being persecuted by the Quraish in Mecca. For a man of such rectitude, Muhammad seems to have possessed an acute sensitivity to personal ridicule. He hated poets and song-singers, who were the primary means of spreading political propaganda and unkind portrayals of the enemies of the people who had hired them. Muhammad's hatred of poets was almost irrational in its intensity. As a poor orphan, Muhammad must have been regularly subject to insults and taunts by others, and it is possible that his hatred of poets was rooted in this early childhood experience.

Muhammad gave permission for his Meccan followers, the *muhajirun*, or Emigrants, to emigrate to Medina shortly after the Second Pledge of Aqaba, and Muhammad left Mecca shortly thereafter and made his way safely to Medina. Ibn Ishaq tells us that, 'The Apostle on that day [when he arrived in Medina] was 53 years of age, that being thirteen years after God called him.' Muhammad's journey to Medina is known to the Arabs as the *Hijra*, and marks the Year 1 on the Arab calendar from which all subsequent historical events have been measured.

The Father of Insurgency

Although his reforms and military achievements give him much in common with the greatest generals in antiquity, Muhammad was not a conventional field general. He was, instead, a new type of warrior, one never before seen in antiquity. Muhammad was first and foremost a revolutionary, a fiery religious guerrilla leader who created and led the first genuine national insurgency in antiquity that is comprehensible in modern terms, a fact not lost on the *jihadis* of the present day who often cite the *Quran* and Muhammad's use of violence as justification for their own insurgencies.

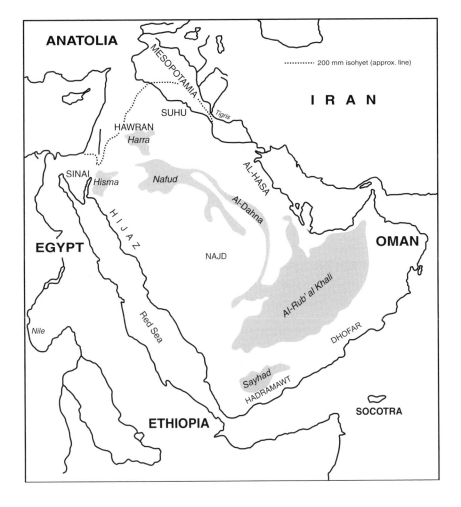

Strategic Setting in Arabia During Muhammad's Lifetime

Unlike conventional generals, Muhammad's goal was not the defeat of a foreign enemy or invader, but the replacement of the existing Arabian social order with a new one based upon a radically different ideological view of the world. To achieve his revolutionary goals, Muhammad utilized all the means recognized by modern analysts as characteristic of a successful insurgency. Although Muhammad began his struggle for a new order with a small guerrilla cadre capable of undertaking only limited hit-and-run raids, by the time he was ready to attack Mecca a decade later, that small guerrilla force had grown into a large conventional armed force with integrated cavalry and infantry units capable of conducting large-scale combat operations. It was the first truly national military force in Arab history, and it was this conventional military instrument that Muhammad's successors used to forge a great empire.

Muhammad's rise to power was a textbook example of a successful insurgency, indeed the first such example in antiquity. The West has been accustomed to thinking of the Arab conquests which followed Muhammad in purely *conventional* military terms. But the armies that achieved those conquests did not exist in Arabia before Muhammad. It was Muhammad's successful *unconventional* guerrilla operations, his successful insurgency, that brought those armies into existence. The later Arab conquests, as regards both strategic concept and the new armies as instruments of military method, were the consequence of Muhammad's prior military success as the leader of an insurgency.

This aspect of Muhammad's military life as a guerrilla insurgent is likely to strike the reader as curious. If the means and methods used by modern military analysts to characterize insurgency warfare are employed as categories of analysis, it is clear that Muhammad's campaign to spread Islam throughout Arabia fulfilled all of these criteria. One requirement for an insurgency is a determined leader whose followers regard him as special in some way and worthy of their following him. In Muhammad's case, his own charismatic personality was enhanced by his deeply held belief that he was God's Messenger, and that to follow Muhammad was to obey the dictates of God himself.

Insurgencies also require a messianic ideology, one that espouses a coherent creed or plan to replace the existing social, political and economic order with a new order that is better, more just or ordained by history, or even by God himself. Muhammad used the new religious creed of Islam to challenge basic traditional Arab social institutions and values as oppressive and unholy, and worthy of replacement.

To this end, he created the *ummah,* or community of believers, God's community on earth, to serve as a messianic replacement for the clans and tribes that were the basis of traditional Arab society. One of Muhammad's most important achievements was the establishment of new social institutions that greatly altered and, in some cases, completely replaced those of the old Arab social order.

Successful insurgencies also require a disciplined cadre of true believers to do the work of organizing and recruiting new members. Muhammad's revolutionary cadre consisted of the small group of original converts he attracted in Mecca and took with him to Medina. These were the *muhajirun,* or Emigrants. The first converts among the clans of Medina, the *ansar,* or Helpers, also filled the ranks of the cadre. Within this revolutionary cadre was an inner circle of talented men, some of them later converts. Some, like Abdullah Ibn Ubay and Khalid al-Walid, were experienced field commanders and provided a much-needed source of military expertise. Muhammad's inner circle advised him and saw to it that his directives were carried out. These advisors held key positions during the Prophet's lifetime and fought among themselves for power after his death.

Once Muhammad had created his cadre of revolutionaries, he established a base from which to conduct military operations against his adversaries. These operations initially took the form of ambushes and raids aimed at isolating Mecca, the enemy's main city, and other trading towns that opposed him. Only one-in-six Arabs lived in a city or town at this time; the others resided in the countryside or desert, living as pastoral nomads.[18] Muhammad chose Medina as his base of operations because it was strategically located close to the main caravan route from Mecca to Syria that constituted the economic lifeline of Mecca and other oases and towns that depended upon the caravan trade for their economic survival. Medina was also sufficiently distant from Mecca to permit Muhammad a relatively free hand in his efforts to convert the Bedouin clans living along the caravan route. Muhammad understood that conversions and political alliances with the Bedouins, not military engagements with the Meccans, were the keys to success.

Insurgencies require an armed force and the manpower to sustain them. It was from the original small cadre of guerrillas that the larger conventional army could be grown that would ultimately permit the insurgency to engage its enemies in set-piece battles when the time and political conditions were right. Muhammad may have been the first commander in history to understand and implement the doctrine later espoused by General Vo Nguyen Giap of North Vietnam as 'people's war, people's army'.[19] Muhammad established the belief among his followers that God had commandeered all Muslims' purposes and property for His efforts, and that all Muslims had a responsibility to fight for the faith. Everyone – men, women and even children – had an obligation for military service in defence of the faith and the *ummah* that was the community of God's chosen people on earth. It is essential to understand that the attraction of the ideology of Islam more than anything else produced the manpower that permitted Muhammad's small revolutionary cadre to grow into a conventional armed force capable of large-scale engagements.

The rapid growth of Muhammad's insurgent army is evident from the following figures. At the battle of Badr (AD 624), Muhammad could only put 314 men in the field. Two years later, at Second Badr (626), 1,500 Muslims took to the field. Two years later (628) at Kheibar, the Muslim army had grown to 2,000 combatants. When Muhammad mounted his assault on Mecca (630), he did so with 10,000 men. And at the Battle of Hunayn a few months later, the army numbered 12,000 men. Some sources record that Muhammad's expedition to Tabuk later the same year was comprised of 30,000 men and 10,000 cavalry, but this is probably an exaggeration.[20] What is evident, however, is that Muhammad's insurgency grew very quickly in terms of its ability to recruit military manpower.

Like all insurgent armies, Muhammad's forces initially acquired weapons by stripping them from prisoners and the enemy dead. Weapons, helmets and armour were expensive items in relatively impoverished Arabia, and the early Muslim converts, drawn mostly from among the poor, orphaned, widowed and otherwise socially marginal, could ill afford them. At the Battle of Badr, the first major engagement with an enemy army, the dead were stripped of their swords and other military equipment, establishing a practice that became common. Muhammad also established the practice of requiring prisoners to provide weapons and equipment instead of money to purchase their freedom. One prisoner taken at Badr was an arms merchant, who was required to provide the insurgents with 1,000 spears as the price of his freedom.[21] Muhammad was eventually able to supply weapons, helmets, shields and armour for an army of 10,000 for his march on Mecca.

Muhammad's ability to obtain sufficient weapons and equipment had an important political advantage. Many of the insurgency's converts came from the poorest elements of the Bedouin clans, people too impoverished to afford weapons and armour. Muhammad often supplied these converts with expensive military equipment, immediately raising their status within the clan and guaranteeing their loyalty to him, if not always to the creed of Islam. In negotiations with Bedouin chiefs, Muhammad made them gifts of expensive weaponry. Horses and camels were equally important military assets, for without them, raids and the conduct of operations over distances were not possible. Muhammad obtained his animals in much the same manner as he did his weapons, and with equal success. At Badr, the insurgents had only two horses. Six years later, at Hunayn, Muhammad's cavalry squadrons numbered 800 horse and cavalrymen.[22]

An insurgency must be able to sustain the popular base that supports its fighting elements. To accomplish this, Muhammad changed the ancient customs regarding the sharing of booty taken in raids. The chief of an Arab clan or tribe traditionally took a quarter of the booty for himself. Muhammad decreed that he receive only a fifth, and even this he took not for himself, but in the name of the *ummah*. Under the old ways, individuals kept whatever booty they had captured. Muhammad required that all booty be turned in to the common pool, where it was shared equally among all combatants who had participated in the raid. Most importantly, Muhammad established that the first claimants on the booty that had been taken in the name of the *ummah* were the poor and the widows and orphans of the soldiers killed in battle. He also used the promise of a larger share of booty to strike alliances with Bedouin clans, some of whom remained both loyal and pagan to the end, fighting for loot rather than for Islam.

The leader of an insurgency must take great care to guard his authority from challenges, including those that come from within the movement itself. Muhammad had many enemies and was always on guard against an attempt upon his life. Like other insurgent leaders, Muhammad surrounded himself with a loyal group of followers who acted as his bodyguard and carried out his orders without question. For this purpose he created the *suffah*, a small, loyal cadre of followers who lived in the mosque next to Muhammad's house. Recruited from among the most pious, enthusiastic and fanatical followers, they were from impoverished backgrounds with no other way to make a living. The members of the *suffah* spent their time studying Islam and leading a life of spiritual avocation. They were devoted to Muhammad, and served not only as his life guard but as a secret police that could be called upon at a moment's notice to carry out whatever task Muhammad set for them, including assassination and terror.

No insurgency can survive without an effective intelligence apparatus, and the Muslim insurgency was no exception. As early as when Muhammad left Mecca, he left behind a trusted agent, his uncle Abbas, who continued to send him reports on the situation there. Abbas served as an agent-in-place for more than a decade, until Mecca itself fell to Muhammad. In the beginning, Muhammad's operations suffered from a lack of tactical intelligence. His followers were mostly townspeople and had no experience in desert travel. On some of the early operations, Muhammad had to hire Bedouin guides. As the insurgency grew, however, Muhammad's intelligence service became more organized and sophisticated, using agents-in-place, commercial spies, debriefing of prisoners, combat patrols and reconnaissance-in-force as methods of intelligence collection.

Muhammad himself seems to have possessed a detailed knowledge of clan loyalties and politics within the insurgency's area of operations, and used this knowledge to good effect when negotiating alliances with the Bedouins. He often conducted advance reconnaissance of the battlefields upon which he fought, and only once in ten years of military operations was he taken by surprise. In most cases, Muhammad's intelligence service was able to provide him with sufficient information as to the enemy's location and intentions in advance of any military engagement. We have no knowledge of how Muhammad's intelligence service was organized or where it was located. That it was part of the *suffah*, however, seems a reasonable guess.

Insurgencies succeed or fail to the degree that they are able to win the allegiance of the great numbers of the uncommitted to support the insurgency's goals. Muhammad understood the role of propaganda in the struggle for the minds of the uncommitted, and went to great lengths to make his message public and widely known. In an Arab society that was largely illiterate, the poet served as the major conveyor of political propaganda. Muhammad hired the best poets money could buy to sing his praises and denigrate his opponents. He publicly issued proclamations regarding the revelations he received as the Messenger of God, and remained always in public view to keep the vision of the new order and the promise of a heavenly paradise constantly before his followers and those he hoped to convert. He sent missionaries to other clans and tribes to instruct the pagans in the new faith, sometimes teaching the pagans to read and write in the process. Muhammad understood that the conflict was between the existing social order and its manifest injustices and his vision of the future, and he surpassed his adversaries in spreading his vision to win the struggle for the hearts and minds of the Arab population.

The use of terror seems to be an indispensable element of a success-ful insurgency, and no less so in Muhammad's case. Muhammad used terror in two basic ways. First, to keep discipline among his followers by making public examples of traitors or backsliders. Muhammad also ordered the assassination of some of his political enemies, including poets and singers who had publicly ridiculed him. Never one to forget a slight, when his armies marched into Mecca, Muhammad's *suffah* set about hunting down a list of old enemies marked for execution. Secondly, Muhammad used terror to strike fear into the minds of his enemies on a large scale. In the case of the Jewish tribes of Medina, Muhammad ordered the death of the entire Beni Qaynuqa tribe and the selling of their women and children into slavery, before being talked out of it by the chief of one of his allies. On another occasion, again against a Jewish tribe of Medina, he ordered all the tribe's adult males, some 900, beheaded in the city square, the women and children sold into slavery and their property distributed among his Muslim followers. Shortly after the conquest of Mecca, Muhammad declared 'war to the knife' against all those who remained idolaters, instructing his followers to kill any pagans they encountered on the spot! Such public displays of ruthlessness and brutality, as with all insurgencies, strengthened Muhammad's hand when dealing with opponents and allies.

When examined against the criteria used by modern analysts to define an insurgency – a charismatic leader, revolutionary creed, disciplined cadre, base of military operations, recruited manpower, weapons, popular base of support, secret police and terror apparatus – Muhammad's campaign to establish Islam in Arabia qualifies in all respects. Nothing in this conclusion detracts from the substance and value of Islam itself as a religion, any more than the his-tory of the Israelite military campaign to conquer Canaan detracts from the substance of Judaism. Over time, the violent origins of all religions are forgotten and only the faith itself remains, with the result that the founders of the creeds come to be remembered as untouched by the violence of the historical record. In Muhammad's case, the result was to de-emphasize the military aspects of his life and his considerable military accomplishments as Islam's first great general and the inven-tor of the theory and practice of insurgency.

Muhammad's Military Revolution

Muhammad also brought about a revolution in the manner in which Arabs for generations had fought wars, transforming their armies into genuine instruments of large-scale combat operations capable of achieving strategic objectives instead of only small-scale, clan, tribe or personal objectives. In doing so, he created both the means and historical circumstances which transformed the fragmented Arab clans into a genuine national military entity conscious of its own unique identity. Under these conditions, Arab military brilliance thrived, with the result that the greatest commanders of the early Arab conquests were identified and developed by Muhammad. Had Muhammad not brought about a military revolution in Arab warfare, it is possible that Islam might not have survived in Arabia.

Within a year of Muhammad's death, many of the clans that had sworn allegiance to Islam recanted, resulting in the War of the Apostates, or *Riddah*.[23] It was the military brilliance of Muhammad's generals and the superior combat capabilities of his new army that made it possible for Islam to defeat the apostates and force them back into the religious fold. It was these same generals commanding the new Arab armies who carried out the Arab conquests of Persia and Byzantium. The old Arab way of war would have had no chance of success against the armies of either of these empires. Muhammad's military revolution was an event that shook the ancient world and changed its history by creating the means that made the Arab conquests possible.

Muhammad's successful transformation of Arab warfare marks him as one of the great military reformers of the ancient world. Muhammad changed the social composition of Arab armies from a collection of clans, tribes and blood kin loyal only to themselves, into a national army loyal to a national social entity called the *ummah*, or community of believers in God. The *ummah* was not a nation or a state in the modern sense, but a body of religious believers under the unified command and governance of Muhammad. It was the locus of loyalty that transcended the clans and tribes, and permitted Muhammad to forge a common identity, national in scope, among the Arabs for the first time. It was leadership of this national entity that Muhammad claimed, not of any clan or tribe. Loyalty to the *ummah* permitted the national army to unify the two traditional combat arms of infantry and cavalry into a genuine combined-arms force. Historically, Bedouin and town dweller had viewed one another with considerable suspicion, each living a very different way of life and fighting very different types of battles. Arab infantry had traditionally been drawn from the people living in the towns, settlements and oases of Arabia, while Arab cavalry was historically drawn from Bedouin clans whose nomadic warriors excelled at speed, surprise attack and elusive retreat, skills honed to a fine edge over generations of raiding.[24]

Coming from different socio-economic backgrounds, these two different types of combatants possessed only limited experience in fighting alongside one another. Bound by clan loyalties and living in settlements, Arab infantry was steadfast and cohesive, and could usually be relied upon to hold its ground, especially in defence. Arab cavalry, on the other hand, was unreliable in a fight against infantry, often breaking off the engagement to escape damage to its precious mounts, or make off with whatever booty had been seized. Bedouin cavalry was, however, proficient at reconnaissance, surprise attack, protecting the flanks and pursuing ill-disciplined infantry. Each arm lacked the strengths of the other. Muhammad was the first commander of an Arab army to successfully join both combat arms into a national Arab army and to use them in concert in battle. This was more than a mere technical reform. The ability to combine both combat arms was the result of Muhammad's creation of a new type of community that made it possible to submerge the clan and blood loyalties of traditional Arab society into the larger religious community of believers, the *ummah*, and combine the two primary elements of traditional Arab society – town dwellers and Bedouin tribes – into a single Arab national identity. The change in the social composition of Arab armies under Muhammad was preceded by a change in the social composition of Arab society.

Before Muhammad, Arab military contingents fought under the command of their own clan or tribal leaders, sometimes assembled in coalition with other clans or tribes. While the authority of these clan chiefs was recognized by their own clan, every clan chief considered himself the equal of any other, with the result that there was no overall commander whose authority could compel the obedience or tactical direction of the army as a whole. Clan warriors fought for their own interests, often only for loot, and did not feel obligated to pursue the larger objectives of the army as a whole. They often failed to report to the battlefield, arrived late or simply left the fight once they had captured sufficient loot. Warriors and horses were precious, and clan leaders often resisted any higher tactical direction that might place their men and animals in danger. Under these conditions, Arab battles often resembled little more than disorganized brawls lasting but a short time and producing no decisive outcome.

To correct these deficiencies, Muhammad established a unified command for his armies. Command of the army was centred in the hands of Muhammad himself. Within the *ummah*, there was no distinction between the citizen and the soldier. All members of the community had an obligation to defend the *ummah* and participate in its battles. The community of believers was truly a nation in arms, and all believers followed the commands of Muhammad, God's Messenger. As commander-in-chief, Muhammad established the principle of unified command by appointing a single commander with overall authority to carry out military operations. Sometimes a second-in-command was appointed as well. Muhammad often commanded his troops in the field himself. All commanders were appointed by him and operated under his authority. As Muslims, all members of the army were equally bound by the same laws, and all clan members and their chiefs were subject to the same discipline and punishments as all Muslims. When operating with clans who were not Muslims, Muhammad always extracted an honour oath from their chiefs to obey his orders during the battle. The establishment of a unified military command gave Muhammad's armies greater reliability in planning and in battle. Unified command also permitted a greater degree of coordination among the various combat elements of the army and the use of more sophisticated tactical designs that could be implemented with more certainty, thereby greatly increasing the army's combat power.

The moral basis of traditional Arab warfare placed an emphasis on the courageous performance of individual warriors in battle. While every warrior recognized that he was part of a larger kin group, Arab warfare placed no emphasis on the ability of the clan to fight as a unit. The Arab warrior fought for his *own* honour and social prestige within the kin group, not for the clan *per se*. One consequence was that Arab armies and the clan units within them did not usually reflect a high degree of combat unit cohesion, the ability of the group to remain intact and fight together under the stress of battle. Muhammad's armies, by contrast, were highly cohesive. These armies usually held together even when they fought and were outnumbered or overrun. Muhammad did not just strengthen the blood and kin ties of the traditional Arab clan. He went far beyond that in creating the *ummah* as a higher locus of the soldier's loyalty which transcended the clan.

It is important to remember that many of Muhammad's early converts had left their families and clans to follow the Prophet. It was a common occurrence to find members of the same clan, family and even fathers and sons fighting on opposite sides during Muhammad's early battles. Religion turned out to be a greater source of unit cohesion than blood and clan ties, the obligations of faith replacing and overriding the duties of tradition and even family. Muhammad's soldiers quickly gained a reputation for their discipline and ferocity in battle, soldiers who cared for each other as brothers, which under the precepts of Islam they were.

Muhammad's armies demonstrated a higher degree of military motivation than traditional Arab armies. Being a good warrior had always been the central core of Arab values. Muhammad raised the status of the warrior to an even greater degree. It was a common saying among Muslims that 'the soldier is not only the noblest and most pleasing profession in the sight of Allah, but also the most profitable'.[25] Muhammad's soldiers were always guaranteed a share in the booty. Under these arrangements, Muhammad's soldiers were usually paid better than Persian or Byzantine soldiers.[26]

But better pay was only a small part of the motivation of the soldiers of Islam. The idea of a soldier motivated by religion in the certainty that he was doing God's work on earth was one of Muhammad's most important military innovations. There were, of course, soldiers of other faiths who must have felt that they were doing their religious duty, even, for instance, when they attacked their fellow Christians denounced as heretics. But no army before Muhammad ever placed religion at the centre of military motivation and defined the soldier primarily as an instrument of God's will on earth. The soldiers of Islam were usually extremely religious and saw themselves as fighting under God's instructions. The result, still seen in Islamic societies today, was a soldier who enjoyed much higher social status and respect than soldiers in armies of the West.

A central element in the motivation of the Islamic soldier was the teaching of his faith that death was not something to be feared, but to be sought. Muhammad's pronouncement that those killed in battle would be welcomed immediately into a paradise of pleasure and eternal life because they died fulfilling the command of God was a powerful inducement to perform well on the field of battle. To die fighting in defence of the faith (*jihad*) was to become a martyr. Life itself was subordinate to the needs of the faith; to die a martyr was to fulfill God's will. Muslim soldiers killed in battle were accorded the highest respect on the Arab scale of values. While those who died in battle had been traditionally celebrated as examples of courage and selflessness, it was never suggested that death was to be welcomed or even required to be a good soldier. Muhammad's religious pronouncements changed the traditional Arab view of military sacrifice and produced a far more dedicated soldier than Arab armies had ever witnessed before.

Arab warfare prior to Muhammad's reforms involved clans and tribes fighting for honour or loot. No commander aimed at the enslavement or extermination of the enemy, nor the occupation of its lands. Until Muhammad, Arab warfare was limited tactical warfare, nothing more. There was no sense of *strategic* war in which long-term, grand scale strategic objectives were sought and toward which the tactical application of force was directed. Muhammad was the first to introduce the notion of war for strategic goals to the Arabs. Muhammad's ultimate goal, the transformation of Arab society through the spread of a new religion, was strategic in concept. His application of force and violence, whether unconventional or conventional, was always directed at this strategic goal. Although Muhammad began as an insurgent, he was always Clausewitzian in his thinking in that the use of force was seen as a tactical means to the achievement of larger strategic objectives. Muhammad was the first Arab commander to use military force within a strategic context. Had he not introduced this new way of thinking to Arab warfare, the use of later Arab armies to forge a world empire would not only have been impossible, it would have been unthinkable.

Once war was harnessed to strategic objectives, it became possible to expand its application to introduce tactical dimensions that were completely new to Arab warfare. Muhammad used his armies in completely new ways. He attacked tribes, towns and garrisons before they could form hostile coalitions; he isolated his enemy by severing their economic lifelines and disrupting their lines of communication; he was a master at political negotiation, forming alliances with pagan tribes when it served his interests; and he laid siege to cities and towns. Muhammad also introduced the new dimension of psychological warfare, employing terror and massacre as means to weaken the will of his enemies. Various texts also mention Muhammad's use of catapults (*manjaniq*) and moveable covered cars (*dabbabah*) in siege warfare.[27] Most likely, these siege devices were acquired in Yemen, where Persian garrisons had been located on and off over the centuries. Muhammad seems to have been the first Arab commander to use them in the north. Where once Arab warfare had been a completely tactical limited affair, Muhammad's introduction of strategic war permitted the use of tactics in the proper manner, as means to greater strategic ends.

As an orphan, Muhammad had lacked even the most rudimentary military training provided by an Arab father. Probably to compensate for this deficiency, he surrounded himself with men who were experienced warriors and constantly sought their advice. He frequently appointed the best warriors of his former enemies to positions of command once they had converted to Islam. As commander-in-chief, Muhammad sought to identify and develop good officers wherever he found them. Young men were appointed to carry out small-scale raids in order to give them combat experience, and he sometimes selected an officer from a town to command a Bedouin raid in order to broaden his experience in the use of cavalry.[28] Muhammad always selected his military commanders on the basis of their proven experience and ability, and never for their asceticism or religious devotion.[29] He was the first to institutionalize military excellence in the development of an Arab officer corps of professional quality. It was from this corps of trained and experienced field commanders that the generals who commanded the armies of the Arab conquests were drawn.

We have only scant references to how Muhammad trained his soldiers; that he did so is almost a certainty. There are clear references to required training in swimming, running and wrestling. The early soldiers of Islam had left their clan and family loyalties behind in order to join the *ummah*. The clan-based military units typical of Arab warfare would have been impossible to recreate within the *ummah*-based armies. Muhammad's converts had to be socialized to a new basis of military loyalty, the faith, and new military units would have had to be created that contained soldiers from many clans. References in various texts suggest that Muhammad trained these units in rank and drill, sometimes personally formed them up and addressed them before a battle, and deployed them to fight in disciplined units, not as individuals, as was the common practice. These disciplined 'artificial clan' units could then be trained to carry out a wider array of tactical designs than was heretofore possible. Muhammad's use of cavalry and archers in concert with his infantry was one result. While Arab fathers continued to train their sons in warfare long after Muhammad's death, the armies of the Arab conquests, and later those of the Arab empire, instituted formal military training for recruits.

Muhammad had been an organizer of caravans for twenty-five years before he began his insurgency, and possessed the caravanneer's concern for logistics and planning, an expertise that permitted him to project force and conduct military operations over long distances across inhospitable terrain. During his time as a caravanneer, Muhammad made several trips to the north along the spice road. He gained a reputation as an excellent administrator and organizer of caravans. Planning a caravan required extensive attention to detail and knowledge of routes, rates of march, distances between stops, water and feeding of animals, location of wells, weather, places of ambush etc., knowledge that served him well as a military commander. Unlike some other armies that he fought, Muhammad never seems to have had to change or abandon his plans due to logistical difficulties. Muhammad's armies could project force over hundreds of miles. In AD 630, he led an army of 20,000–30,000 men (the sources disagree) over a 250-mile march from Medina to Tabuk lasting eighteen to twenty days across the desert during the hottest season of the year. By traditional Arab standards, Muhammad's ability to project forces of such size over these distances was nothing short of astounding. Without this capability, the Arab conquest that followed Muhammad's death would have been impossible.

The conclusion that emerges from an examination of Muhammad's military life is that he revolutionized the conduct of Arab warfare in ways that made possible the transformation of Arab armies from entities fit only for tactical engagements to ones capable of waging war on a strategic level where they could engage and defeat the major armies of their day. This military transformation was preceded by a revolution in the manner in which Arabs thought about war, i.e., the moral basis of war. The old chivalric code that limited the bloodletting was abandoned by Muhammad and replaced with an ethos less conducive to restraint, the blood feud. Extending the ethos of the blood feud beyond the ties of kin and blood to include members of the new community of Muslim believers inevitably worked to make Arab warfare more encompassing and bloody than it had ever been.

Underlying all these changes was a change in the psychology of war introduced by Muhammad's teaching that soldiers fighting in defence of Islam were doing no less than God's work on earth, and that to die in carrying out His will immediately earned the soldier eternal life in paradise.[30] The usual sense of risk to life that tempered the violence of the battlefield was abandoned, replaced by the doctrine that 'war to the knife', or fighting until one kills the enemy or is slain oneself, is the ideal to be aimed at in the conduct of war. In every respect, Muhammad's military revolution increased the scale and violence of the military engagements that Arab armies were capable of fighting.

Muhammad's Military Legacy

Muhammad's greatest *military* legacy was the doctrine of *jihad*, or holy war. It is indisputable that divinely justified warfare became a force of major importance during the early Islamic period, remained a significant motivator for the Islamic conquests that followed Muhammad's death and remains a primary characteristic of Islamic warfare in the present day. Pre-Islamic Arabia knew no notion of ideology of any sort, and certainly no notion of religiously sanctioned war. Pre-Islamic Arabian warfare was directly linked to the economic and social circumstances of pasturage, material wealth and prestige, and was characterized by looting, raiding and clan and tribal blood feuds. The idea of warfare as a command of God rewarded by martyrdom and paradise was an innovation with no precedent in Arab culture, custom or practice, brought about entirely by Muhammad's thinking and influence on events.

Muhammad died in June AD 632, and immediately the Islamic coalition of tribes began to fall apart. In the traditional fashion of Arab covenants, upon Muhammad's death, many tribal and clan chiefs no longer felt bound by their old agreements with the Prophet. The crux of the problem was the *zakat*, the annual tax that Muhammad had imposed. Some of the allied tribes sent delegations to Medina to negotiate new agreements with Abu Bakr, Muhammad's father-in-law, who had been elected to succeed Muhammad. The tribes promised to remain Muslim and say the daily prayer in exchange for repealing the tax. Abu Bakr refused, saying, 'By Allah, if they withhold a rope of a camel they use to give its due *zakat* to Allah's Messenger, I will fight them for it.' The result was the *Riddah*, or the War of Apostates.

Abu Bakr declared war on all those who would not obey, and introduced three new elements to Islam that greatly expanded the religious justification for *jihad* against Muslims. First, he proclaimed withdrawal from Muhammad's coalition to be a denial of God's will, and declared secession from the coalition as apostasy punishable by death. Muslims would later use this proposition to conduct *jihads* against other Muslims who did not follow the *sharia* law. Second, Abu Bakr declared that Muslims could not be loyal to God under any leader whose legitimacy did not derive from Muhammad, thereby laying the groundwork for the later Sunni-Shia *jihads* against one another over the question of who were the legitimate leaders of Islam. Third, to forestall the influence of others who claimed to be prophets who had already arisen in Arabia during Muhammad's lifetime, Abu Bakr declared Muhammad to be the last prophet that God would send. This led Muslims to regard all religions that came after Muhammad as false religions.

Although Abu Bakr's pronouncements were introduced as part of his *political* strategy to isolate and compel the obedience of the Arabian tribes, and could claim no religious authority to support them, they became important Muslim *religious beliefs* as the years passed. It was actually Abu Bakr, not Muhammad, who laid what became the religious justification for the internecine *jihads* among Sunni, Shia and Sufi Muslims that were to follow over the centuries.

Within 200 years of the Muslim conquests of Byzantium and Persia, Muhammad's reform influence on the conventional Arab armies had disappeared, displaced by the more powerful influence of Byzantine, Persian and Turkic military practices. Muhammad's military legacy is most clearly evident in the modern methodology of insurgency and in the powerful idea of *jihad*. In the years following Muhammad's death, Islamic scholars developed an account of the Islamic law of war. This body of law, essentially complete by AD 850, rests ultimately on two foundations: the example and teaching of Muhammad and the uncreated, literal, infallible word of God as expressed in the *Quran*. At the heart of the Islamic law of war is the concept of *jihad*, meaning 'to endeavour, to strive, to struggle',[31] but which in the West is commonly understood to mean 'holy war'.

According to classical Sunni doctrine, *jihad* can refer generically to any worthy endeavour. But in Islamic law, it means primarily armed struggle for Islam against infidels and apostates. The central element of the doctrine of *jihad* is that the Islamic community (*ummah*) as a whole, under the leadership of the *caliph* (successor to Muhammad), has the duty to expand Islamic rule, ultimately until the world is governed by Islamic law. Expansionist *jihad* is thus a collective duty of all Muslims. Land occupied by Muslims is known as the *dar al-Islam*, while all other territory is known as the *dar al-harb*, 'the land of war'. Islamic law posits the inalienability of Islamic territory. If infidels attack the *dar al-Islam*, it becomes the duty of all Muslims to resist and of all other Muslims to assist them. Thus, *jihad* can be defensive as well as offensive.

In the waging of *jihad*, all adult males, except for slaves and monks, are considered legitimate military targets, and no distinction is made between military and civilians. Women and children may not be targeted directly, unless they act as combatants by supporting the enemy in some manner. The enemy may be attacked in any manner, without regard for indiscriminate damage, and it is permissible to kill women in night raids when Muslim fighters cannot easily distinguish them from men. Islamic law prohibits mutilation of the dead and torture of captives, although the definition of torture is problematic, since Muhammad himself imposed punishments that would easily qualify as torture today. All moral limits on the waging of war may be set aside in cases of necessity. Following Muhammad's own practice, a *jihadi* may execute, enslave, ransom or release enemy captives, depending on what is in the best interests of Muslims. Captured women and children may not be killed, but may be enslaved, and Muslim men may have sexual relations with female slaves acquired by *jihad*, any previous marriage of such women being annulled by their capture.

Shiites, some 10–15 per cent of Muslims, subscribe to a somewhat different doctrine of *jihad*, believing that it can only be waged under the command of the rightful leader of the Muslim community, whom they call *imam*. Shiites believe that the last *imam* went into hiding in AD 874, and that the collective duty to wage expansionist *jihad* is suspended until his return in the apocalyptic future. Shiite scholars do, however, affirm a duty to wage defensive *jihad* against infidel invaders. Classical Islamic law is less tolerant of non-Muslims. Apostates from Islam, pagans, atheists, agnostics and 'pseudo-scriptuaries' – members of cults that have appeared since Muhammad's day, e.g., Sikhs, Bahais, Mormons and Qadianis – are only offered the option of conversion to Islam or death.

By the beginning of the nineteenth century, Sunni Islamic modernists began to modify the classical law of war. The Indian Muslim thinker Sayyid Ahmad Khan argued that *jihad* was obligatory for Muslims only when they were prevented from exercising their faith, thus restricting *jihad* to defensive purposes. Mahmud Shaltut, an Egyptian scholar, likewise argued only for defensive *jihad*. Conservative Sunnis, like the Wahhabis of Arabia, and modern militant *jihadis* in Iraq and Pakistan still adhere to the traditional doctrine. It is among these militant conservative Muslims that the military legacy of Muhammad is most alive today.[32]

Notes

1. The basic works in English on Muhammad's life are: W. Montgomery Watt, *Muhammad: Prophet and Statesman* (London, Oxford University Press, 1961); also by Watt, *Muhammad At Medina* (London, Oxford University Press, 1956); Muhammad Hamidullah, *The Battlefields of the Prophet* (Paris, Revue des Etudes Islamiques, 1939); Philip K. Hitti, *History of the Arabs* (Hampshire, Palgrave, 2002); Maxime Rodinson, *Muhammad* (New York, New Press, 2002); and Ibn Ishaq, *The Life of Muhammad*, trans. A. Guillaume (Oxford, Oxford University Press, 1967). My own work, *Muhammad: Islam's First Great General* (Norman, OK, Oklahoma University Press, 2007), might also be consulted.

2. On the point of the Muslim influence on Christian doctrines of war, see Richard A. Gabriel, *Empires At War* vol. 3 (Westport, CT, Greenwood Press, 2005), p.792.

3. Sir John Glubb, *The Life and Times of Muhammad* (New York, Cooper Square Press, 2001), p.72.

4. Montgomery W. Watt, *Muhammad: Prophet and Statesman* (London, Oxford University Press, 1961), p.12.

5. Glubb, *Life and Times*, p.84.

6. Most Arabs were illiterate, and writing materials and records of any sort from the period are extremely rare. The Muslim claim that the *Quran* was written down immediately after each revelation or pronouncement of Muhammad is questionable on these grounds. More likely, Muhammad's words were memorized and transmitted orally. Muhammad himself lamented after the Battle of Badr than many of the 'Quran reciters' – individuals who had memorized part of Muhammad's words – had been killed.

7. Glubb, *Life and Times,* p.85.

8. Martin Lings, *Muhammad: His Life Based on the Earliest Sources* (Rochester, VT, Inner Traditions International, 1983), pp.44–45, quoting Ibn Ishaq.

9. Watt, *Muhammad: Prophet and Statesman*, pp.18–19.

10. Glubb, *Life and Times*, p.97, quoting Ibn Ishaq.

11. Ibn Ishaq, *The Life of Muhammad: A Translation of Ibn Ishaq's Life of Muhammad*, trans. Alfred Guillaume (Oxford, Oxford University Press, 1967), pp.279–80. This work is the most important source for understanding the detail and context of Muhammad's military life.

12. Ibid.

13. I wish to express my gratitude to Dr Toby Rose, physician, pathologist and coroner in Toronto, Canada, and Dr Lucy Harvey of Montpelier, Vermont, for providing me with the information on the symptoms of malaria. Dr Peter F. Weller notes: 'Clinical symptoms develop about 1 to 4 weeks after infection and typically include fever and chills. Virtually all patients with acute malaria have episodes of fever. At the outset, fever may occur daily; over time, the paroxysms may develop the typical every-other day or every-third day. The paroxysms of fever (as high as 41.5 degrees C [106.7 degrees F]) and chills (with or without rigors) may be irregular, however. Other symptoms may be headache, increased sweating, back pain, myalgias, diarrhea, nausea, vomiting, and cough ... Cerebral involvement may lead to delirium, focal disorders (e.g., seizures), and coma. *P. malariae* organisms can persist in the blood as an indolent, even asymptomatic, infection for years or even decades.' See Peter. F. Weller, 'Protozoan Infections: Malaria', in David

C. Dale and Daniel D. Federman (eds), *Scientific American Medicine* vol. 2, sect. 7, ch. 34 (New York, Scientific American, 1999), pp.1–6.

14. Ibn Ishaq, *Life of Muhammed*, pp.203–04.
15. Watt, *Muhammad, Prophet and Statesman*, p.321.
16. Glubb, *Life and Times*, p.334.
17. The term is taken from James H. Breasted, *The Development of Religion and Thought in Ancient Egypt* (New York, Harper and Brothers, 1959), who first used it to describe the religious ferocity of Pharaoh Akhenaton, the ancient world's first true monotheist.
18. Philip K. Hitti, *History of the Arabs* (Hampshire, Palgrave, 2002), p.17.
19. Vo Nguyen Giap, *People's War, People's Army: The Viet Cong Insurrection Manual for Underdeveloped Countries* (New York, Bantam, 1968), for the methods required to organize and conduct an insurgency.
20. Watt, *Muhammad At Medina*, p.257.
21. Muhammad Hamidullah, *The Battlefields of the Prophet* (Paris, Revue des Etudes Islamique, 1939), p.40; reprint New Delhi, 1973.
22. Watt, p.257.
23. The best work on the military aspects of the *Riddah* remains Elias S. Shoufani, *Al-Riddah and the Muslim Conquest of Arabia* (Toronto, University of Toronto Press, 1972).
24. V.J. Parry and M.E. Yapp, *War, Technology and Society in the Middle East* (London, Oxford University Press, 1975), p.32.
25. Hitti, *History of the Arabs*, p.173.
26. Ibid.
27. Hamidullah, *Battlefields of the Prophet*, p.139.
28. Ibid., p.140.
29. Ibid.
30. Islamic theology holds that those who die must suffer the 'torment of the grave', that is, remain there until Judgement Day. The only exception is for those who die in battle, who go immediately to paradise.
31. The elements of *jihad* described here are taken from Andrew Bostom, *The Legacy of Jihad: Islamic Holy War and the Fate of Non-Muslims* (Amherst, NY, Prometheus Books, 2005); David Cook, *Understanding Jihad* (Berkeley, University of California Press, 2005); and Rudolph Peters, *Jihad in Classical and Modern Islam* (Princeton, Marcus Wiener Publishers, 1996).
32. An historical examination of *jihad* from ancient times to the present can be found in Richard A. Gabriel, 'War To the Knife', *Military History* (September 2014), pp.34–39.

CHAPTER ELEVEN

WHY NOT ALEXANDER?

Almost from the moment of his death, Alexander was regarded as a military genius whose exploits on the battlefield were unprecedented. These exploits were recorded early on by ancient historians. In antiquity, Alexander had already become the great romantic warrior hero for kings and generals to emulate. The theme of Alexander's military brilliance survived the ages, mostly unchallenged, and Alexander's battles are still studied in military colleges and academies as examples of combat leadership and strategic and tactical brilliance. The assumption of military brilliance is, in my view, largely undeserved, and has led historians and military analysts to ignore the many shortcomings of Alexander's military performance. It also led to a neglect of the importance of Philip's accomplishments that made Alexander's achievements possible. It is no exaggeration to say that without Philip's military and political legacy, there would have been no Alexander the Great. Alexander was a bold and reckless *conquistador* who conducted a decade-long raid, leaving nothing of note behind him.

Alexander's opportunity for greatness began with the single truth that Philip was a great national king who created the first national territorial state in Europe, uniting disparate peoples under Macedonian leadership into a powerful national political entity. Philip enlarged, urbanized and developed Macedonia's natural and human resources to a degree never seen before in Greece or the West. In doing so, he made Macedonia the wealthiest and most resource-rich state in Greece. With Macedonia as his national power base, Philip expanded his sphere of political and military dominance into the first great European land empire in history, uniting all of Greece into a single political entity with common political institutions and a single constitution. It was this imperial state that provided the material resources – ships, food, troops, reserve manpower, military equipment and animals – that made Alexander's successful assault on the western half of the Persian Empire possible.[1]

The composition of the expeditionary force that Alexander took with him to Persia amply illustrates the extent of the resources provided by Philip's new imperial state. Alexander's army included

12,000 Macedonian infantry (phalanx and Guards Brigades), 7,000 Greek hoplites drawn from the League of Corinth's troops, 7,000 troops from the subject tribes – including light cavalry, *peltasts* and javelin men – 1,000 archers and Agrianian mounted javelineers and 5,000 mercenaries (heavy infantry). These are in addition to the 11,000 or so troops already in Ionia as the advance expeditionary force Philip sent under the joint command of Attalus and Parmenio. Alexander also took with him 1,800 Macedonian cavalry, including the elite Companion cavalry, 1,800 Thessalian heavy cavalry, 900 Thracian and Paeonian scouts and 600 League cavalry, in addition to the 1,000 cavalry already with the advance expedition.[2] Alexander's force amounted to 49,100 men. It was Philip's creation of the Macedonian Empire that made raising such large numbers of troops and equipment possible.

Usually not mentioned, but surely present, in the invasion force were Philip's siege engineers and sappers responsible for Alexander's artillery, assault-gear for tunnelling and mining and for the construction of roads and bridges. Also in train were the *bematistai*, or survey section, that collected information about routes and camp grounds. Most important were Philip's experienced logistics officers. All these specialists had been introduced into the Macedonian army by Philip.

Raising and deploying the large invasion army was itself a great achievement. Sustaining its manpower in the field was another. Alexander's campaigns lasted for a decade and covered 10,000 miles of marching and fighting. His army would have been worn to helplessness without some system of manpower replacement. While Alexander made use of Persian and tribal troops, he did so only minimally, and much later in his campaigns. Most of Alexander's replacements over the first four years of war, when he had to fight the Persian army, came from Macedonia, sent by Antipater, who had been left behind as regent. Philip had introduced a system of nationwide recruitment and training of Macedonian militia troops that made it possible to provide large numbers of trained and disciplined soldiers to Alexander on a regular basis, while still sustaining the manpower strength of Antipater's army to keep peace in the empire. No state other than Macedonia had such a large and comprehensive system of military recruitment and training, and no other could have sustained Alexander's army in the field for very long.

Hammond's figures suggest that Macedonian replacements alone counted for almost 15,000 infantry and cavalry over the life of Alexander's campaigns, most arriving within the first four years of the invasion.[3] This amounts to fully half the total Macedonian force in the field in 332 BC.[4] Once Persia had been conquered, many of Alexander's replacements came not from Macedonia, but from the Balkan tribes and the thriving market for Greek, Bactrian and Indian mercenaries.[5] Alexander's capture of the Persian treasury made it possible for him to afford large numbers of mercenaries. Brunt says, however, that between 326 and 323 BC, Alexander received at least two large contingents of replacements that Arrian neglected to mention, some of whom were surely Macedonians.[6] He notes that in 324 BC, Alexander sent Craterus home with 10,000 Macedonian infantry and 1,500 cavalry, while sending 13,000 infantry and 2,000 cavalry to hold down Asia. This would have left Alexander with only 2,000–3,000 infantry and virtually no cavalry, clearly an impossible situation. Brunt concludes that Alexander had to receive considerable reinforcements.[7]

Before leaving the Punjab, Alexander received another large contingent of reinforcements amounting to 30,000 infantry and 6,000 cavalry from Thrace, Greece and Babylon.[8] Although not Macedonians, the numbers speak to Antipater's ability to continue to recruit imperial non-Macedonian imperial troops to sustain Alexander's field operations. Alexander could not have maintained his campaigns without the continued support of Macedonian and imperial reinforcements that were the product of Philip's replacement system.

Wars occur within the political context that makes them possible. This context is often more important than the armies, troops and equipment required. Alexander's campaign against Persia would not have been possible had Philip not first established a civic peace among the warring Greek states. More than anything, it was Philip's peace and its accompanying guarantee that the Greek states would observe their obligations to the League of Corinth that made Alexander's attack on Persia possible. Without this guarantee, no Macedonian commander would have dared risk invading Persia while exposing himself to revolt and attack in his rear. Without the Athenian assurance to use its navy to oppose any Persian attempt to attack Greece by sea while Alexander was in the field, Alexander's expedition risked being cut off and destroyed piecemeal. The initial crossing into Asia also depended upon Philip's previous successes. Alexander's crossing into Asia at the Hellespont was possible because Philip had previously secured Thrace and the Chersonese in a year-long military campaign, creating the strategic platform from which Alexander could launch his invasion. Had Philip not accomplished this, no invasion of Persia was possible.

The strategic vision of taking a Greek army into Asia and conquering Persia was Philip's, not Alexander's. The idea had been around for at least a decade, espoused by men such as Isocrates as a way of stopping Greek civil strife by bringing the warring states together in the common effort against Persia, and then exploiting the country as a prize of war. Before Philip, the idea was less than fully formed, and the political conditions necessary to render an invasion possible were absent until Philip brought them into being. It was only after he had done so that a war against Persia with some expectation of success became possible. Philip gave the strategic idea operational possibility, and he planned the invasion in detail. Alexander carried out the invasion, but it was Philip who first transformed thought into action and gave practical expression to the strategic vision itself.

It was Philip's military genius, not Alexander's, in devising and introducing new infantry and cavalry formations, expanding their tactical roles and increasing exponentially their combat killing power, that created the military instrument that provided Alexander with the strong advantage in battle that made his victories possible. Robert Gaebel summed up this advantage in the following terms: 'Except for numbers, Alexander always had superior fighting ability at his disposal, so that a significant military asymmetry existed between his forces and those of his enemies. Most of this superiority resulted from the inherent qualities of the Macedonian army and was based on discipline, training, arms skill, professionalism, and cultural outlook, all of which had been enhanced by experience.'[9] Had Philip not invented a new Macedonian army, the odds are very good that there would have been no Alexander the Great.

It is no exaggeration to say that Philip was a military genius whose tactical and operational innovations revolutionized the Greek way of war, bringing into existence new and more powerful combat capabilities without which Philip's conquests in Greece and Alexander's in Asia would not have been possible. Philip's invention of a new form of infantry warfare constructed around a new combat formation, the pike-phalanx, armed with a new weapon, the *sarissa,* and capable of greater flexibility, stability and manoeuvre than the hoplite phalanx, bequeathed Alexander his main combat arm for controlling the battlefield. The new phalanx could be employed in a number of new ways: defensively to offset the numerical superiority of the Persian infantry, offensively to strike at the Persian line with sufficient force to penetrate it, and as a platform of manoeuvre to anchor the battle line and freeze enemy dispositions while the Macedonian cavalry sought a weak spot through which to penetrate and turn inside the Persian lines. Philip's introduction of the long pike also afforded his infantry a great advantage in close combat over the Persian infantry, which was armed mostly with short spear, shield, bow and little armour, making it far less formidable than Macedonian heavy infantry.

Philip also revolutionized the killing capability of Greek cavalry. Until Philip, cavalry in Greece had been only a minor combat arm with little killing power, incapable of offensive action, limited in the pursuit and unable to break infantry formations. Philip changed all this by replacing the short cavalry javelin with the long *xyston* lance and introducing the Thracian cavalry wedge to drive through infantry formations. He also taught the Macedonian cavalry to fight as units instead of individual combatants, and trained them in close combat and horsemanship to a level heretofore unseen in Greece. Unlike traditional Greek cavalry, Philip's cavalry was tactically designed to close with the enemy, shatter its formations and kill it where it stood. If the enemy took flight, Macedonian cavalry was expert in the lethal pursuit, something mostly absent in Greek warfare until then, hunting the enemy in small groups and striking it down with lance and sabre.

Philip's cavalry innovations transformed Macedonian cavalry from an impotent combat arm into the Macedonian army's combat arm of decision. It was the killing power of the Macedonian cavalry in close combat that made Alexander's cavalry so effective against both Persian infantry and cavalry. Persian cavalry was employed mostly in the traditional manner, for riding close to the enemy and throwing javelins, skirmishing and closing here and there with the sabre. As such, it lacked the ability for effective close combat against both disciplined infantry and aggressive cavalry. Again and again, Alexander used his cavalry to close the distance with the enemy and bring the killing power of his cavalry to bear upon his adversaries at close quarters. If Alexander had been equipped with traditional Greek cavalry, his combat arm of decision against the Persians would have been practically useless.

Another innovation that made Alexander's success possible was Philip's creation of an engineering and siege capability for the first time as an integral part of a Greek field army. Philip's siege engineers had almost two decades of field experience before Alexander took them to Asia, and were equipped with the new Macedonian torsion catapult that gave Alexander's army the capability to batter down city walls. Alexander's chief engineer, Diades, had been trained by Polyeidos, Philip's chief engineer. The siege corps itself had been trained to a fine edge by Philip, who employed them in at least eleven sieges in his previous campaigns.[10]

The importance of a siege capability to Alexander's success cannot be overestimated. Having landed in Asia unopposed and defeated a Persian army at the Granicus River, Alexander had to secure his hold on the Asian coast. He had to quickly reduce the major coastal cities to avoid being caught from behind by the Persian army, as almost happened at Issus, and to deprive the Persian navy of bases from which to launch a sea-borne attack against Greece. It was Philip's veteran engineers and sappers who reduced Miletus, Hallicarnasus, Tyre and Gaza in relatively short order.[11] Alexander also used his siege capability to great effect in Sogdiana and especially in India, where most city walls and fortifications were made of wood and wattle.[12] Without Philip's engineers, Alexander would have been forced to rely upon the usual Greek siege practice of isolation and starvation, and would not have got much beyond the Ionian coast, giving the Persian army plenty of time to reassemble.

Another major innovation upon which Alexander depended heavily was Philip's commissariat corps. Philip introduced the science of logistics to Greek armies, allowing his armies to march long distances and sustain themselves in the field for months on end. By Alexander's time, Philip's logisticians had been at their work for two decades. Alexander's march up country lasted a decade and covered 10,000 miles. It was Philip's logistics officers that made this projection of force possible by finding the means to supply the army. The Persians were excellent logisticians themselves, and as Alexander moved inland he captured the extensive system of Persian supply depots holding food and military equipment. The Persian system of interior roads also aided Alexander, as did the Persian practice of requiring each satrap to collect supplies for the army on a semi-annual basis.[13] Once Alexander moved east through Bactria, Sogdiana and into India itself, however, he depended heavily upon his own Macedonian logistics officers, who had been trained by Philip. Once in India, supplying the army became easier due to the astonishing fertility of the Indian river valleys and plains, that produced two harvests a year.[14] Here, the staple diet for the army was rice.

While Alexander is often given credit for being a good tactician, in fact his tactics were no different from those Philip had developed and used for the army.[15] There is no evidence of any sort of tactical innovation or employment in any of Alexander's campaigns, or even individual battles. Even the famous story of using mountaineers to scale the Sogdian Rock was but a repeat of Philip's having used the same tactic to outflank a blocking force in Thessaly.[16] Alexander's famous night crossing of the Hydaspes River against Porus was another repeat of Philip's earlier night crossing of the Danube. Alexander's reputation as a tactical genius is largely overrated and quite unsubstantiated.

In Alexander's early battles against the Persian army, the Persian advantage in numbers presented the risk of single or double envelopment of Alexander's formations by Persian cavalry. Alexander countered this threat with a swift penetration of the enemy line, turning inward toward the enemy commander's position and assaulting the interior ranks as he advanced. The key to a successful penetration of the Persian line was the ability of Alexander's cavalry to close with the enemy, engaging in violent close combat until it drove through the line and exploded behind it. It was Philip who first used his infantry as a platform of manoeuvre, while unleashing his cavalry to achieve penetration of the enemy line. Philip first used this tactic in his battle with Bardylis, and then again at Chaeronea. The whole point of training and equipping the Macedonian heavy cavalry was to give it the ability to penetrate an enemy infantry line, a tactical capability that Philip invented by adopting the Thracian wedge formation for his cavalry squadrons.

Alexander's infantry was always deployed in the centre-left of the line, across from the location of the enemy commander, and used primarily as a platform of manoeuvre to hold the enemy infantry in check while the Companion cavalry, always deployed on the right under Alexander's personal command, manoeuvred until it found a weak spot in the enemy infantry line through which to attack. To weaken the ability of the enemy cavalry across from him to resist his cavalry assault, Alexander employed mounted skirmishers in front of his cavalry to engage the enemy and force it to throw its javelins and expend its energy defensively. This done, Alexander attacked with his fresh Macedonian cavalry.

A successful attack by Alexander's cavalry depended greatly upon the ability of Parmenio's reduced cavalry force to hold the other wing against an attack by numerically superior Persian cavalry, something Parmenio accomplished at the Granicus, Issus and Gaugamela. Philotas, Parmenio's son and a fine cavalry commander in his own right, may have been correct when he told his mistress that it was he and his father more than Alexander who had won the battles! An analysis of Alexander's battle tactics reveals no innovations or even significant differences in his use of cavalry from that of Philip.

Alexander always possessed a significantly more powerful and tactically sophisticated force than any of his opponents. Alexander's campaign was really three different campaigns, each one fought against an opponent with different military capabilities, none of which were a match for Alexander's. Alexander's victories over the Persians are often cited to support his claim to military brilliance. In truth, the Persian army was hollow, its excellent Median troops comprising only a minority of the fighting force, their infantry lightly armoured and equipped with bow and short spear. Most of the Persian cavalry was light cavalry, and even the famed Median cavalry was less well-armed and armoured than the Macedonians. The rest of the Persian force was comprised of levied national and tribal forces that received only limited training, wore different uniforms, carried minor weapons, spoke a variety of languages, fought in different ways, were commanded by their own chiefs and were highly unreliable. These circumstances made it impossible for Persian commanders to develop coordinated battle tactics. To ensure that these native units did not break and run, Persian commanders were forced to occupy the centre of the line with their own reliable infantry, and place their cavalry on the flanks and rear to create a tactical container within which the various national units were deployed. The Persian army was not a tactically integrated fighting force and could not be deployed in many tactically different ways, nor relied upon to fight effectively as a whole.

Persian tactics were ill-designed to deal with an opponent possessing the combat power of the Macedonian army. The Persian way of war was centred around skirmishing, hit-and-run tactics and using missile weapons (bows, thrown javelins, slings) to hit the enemy from a distance, while relying on the weight of numbers and light cavalry to carry the day.[17] The Persians usually formed up with the light infantry and archers acting as skirmishers in the front, trying to inflict as much damage with their missiles and javelins as possible. As the two lines clashed, the Persians would attempt to strike the flanks and rear with their cavalry and chariots to scatter the enemy, using their usually large numerical advantage to attack from several directions at once. Once enemy infantry began to scatter, cavalry could ride it down and finish it off with lance and javelin.[18]

The success of this tactical design depended upon the inability of the enemy infantry to withstand the initial Persian assault. Persian armies usually fought against rebellious nationalities on the eastern rim of the empire, whose level of military skill, tactics, logistics, armament, training and strength was far below that of the Persians. Under these circumstances, the Persian army's lack of tactical integration and, most important, lack of heavy infantry did not matter very much, since its enemies also lacked these assets. Where this deficiency did matter, of course, was in Persia's battles with the Macedonian war machine developed by Philip and now commanded by Alexander.

The ability of disciplined Macedonian infantry to stand fast against Persian skirmishing attacks and close with the enemy on command, and whose weapons outranged and could easily pierce Persian infantry armour, essentially gave command of the battlefield and its tempo to the Macedonians. With Macedonian heavy cavalry on the left holding fast even against superior numbers of Persian, mostly light, cavalry, Alexander's Companion cavalry could easily penetrate the Persian infantry line almost at a point of his choosing. Macedonian cavalry also seems to have had little difficulty in attacking through Persian cavalry, which generally fought in an unorganized and individualized manner. These Persian weaknesses, disguised by centuries of military success against equally flawed enemies, brought the empire to its knees before the unequalled combat power of Macedonian heavy infantry and cavalry.

The tale of Alexander's pursuit of Darius was one of the most widely told battle stories to demonstrate Alexander's use of strategic pursuit in his campaigns. But here again we witness Alexander doing what Philip did first. Philip made strategic pursuit possible by creating a logistics system that made sustaining his forces in the field over long-distance forced marches a practical possibility. Philip not only used pursuit to destroy fleeing enemy armies, but for strategic, political ends as well. He often conducted lethal pursuits with the political objective of destroying as many of the enemy's leadership corps and aristocracy as possible, to make it easier for the survivors to come to terms with him. Alexander used it for the same purposes in hunting down Darius. Later, he used pursuit to destroy the leadership of the insurgency that followed Darius' murder. The invention and effective use of strategic pursuit within the context of Greek warfare must be credited to Philip, however, and by Alexander's day it was a stock element in the Macedonian commander's tactical repertoire.

Alexander faced a much different opponent in Bactria and Sogdiana when he attempted to put down the national insurgency that erupted after Darius' defeat. The insurgents ran Alexander ragged, inflicted heavy casualties and tied down his army in a guerrilla war that lasted for three years (330–327 BC). The area of operations ranged from Afghanistan to Bukhara, from Lake Seistan to the Hindu Kush, against the fiercest, most indomitable opposition Alexander had ever faced. In Afghanistan, Alexander was facing some of the most warlike tribes known to history, descendants of the Aryan invaders and warriors known for their horse-culture and cavalry fighting. These Aryan tribes – Ashvakas, Aspasians, Assakenoi and Asvayanas – were tough highlanders and excellent horsemen, like the Macedonians themselves.[19] Alexander lost more men in this campaign than in any other, against generals who proved his equal.[20]

Refusing to offer set-piece battles, the guerrillas fought a war of ambush, deception and surprise with highly mobile light cavalry units that were expert at these tactics.[21] While besieging Cyropolis, Alexander sent a force of 3,000 infantry and 800 Companion cavalry to block Spitamenes' route to Maracanda. Curtius tells us that Spitamenes trapped the Macedonians in a deadly ambush, killing 2,000 infantry and 300 cavalrymen.[22] Arrian says the casualties were even worse, and only 'forty of the cavalry and three hundred infantrymen escaped with their lives'.[23] He says the cavalrymen were all 'true-born Macedonians and Companions of the king', among them four general officers – Pharnuches, Andromachus, Menedemus and Caranus.[24] The losses amount to almost 10 per cent of Alexander's field force! Alexander swore the few survivors to secrecy under penalty of death. In another case, fifty Companions were deceived by the hospitality of a tribe and killed while they slept.[25] Unable to bring the enemy to battle, Alexander undertook a policy of systematic destruction of the civilian population.

Alexander is often given credit for his innovations in assembling units of mixed arms for specific missions. Arrian identifies twenty-seven examples of Alexander's combining forces of different arms for specific tactical missions.[26] Most of Arrian's examples apply to the counter-insurgency operations that Alexander mounted in Afghanistan and the Swat Valley, where his opponents were highly mobile units armed with bow and javelin. While specialty units (archers, slingers, *peltasts*, javeliners, etc.) had been used by Greek armies for decades, albeit in minor roles, it was Philip who first incorporated them into a regular standing military force. Philip's wars in the mountains of western Macedonia and the Balkans forced him to deal with highly mobile tribal forces operating in difficult terrain. During the Thracian campaign, Philip used mixed forces with some regularity when he found himself short of regular infantry and had to request replacements from Macedonia. Specialty units – archers, *peltasts*, light cavalry, etc. – are recorded by Diodorus as being among the troops in the invasion force.[27]

There was never a national army fighting against Alexander in Afghanistan. The insurgency consisted of an assembly of local warlords banded together against a common foe. Most battles were small in scale and mostly inconclusive, except in their ability to inflict casualties on the invader. There was no large army for Alexander to lure into a decisive battle. Alexander had only one significant victory in open field operations, that against the Scythians. All others were against fixed positions, such as the Sogdian Rock and the Rock of Chorines, or against towns that were taken with great slaughter. Most of the casualties were civilians, not enemy combatants.

It was politics and not battlefield victories that finally ended the war in Afghanistan. The key leaders of the insurgency were all assassinated by political rivals. Eventually, the barons and their tribes grew weary of the war and, one by one, came to an accommodation with Alexander in which they mostly retained their lands and local authority as they had under the Persian king, an approach now being tried to bring the present war in Afghanistan (2016) to an end.

The cost of the war to Alexander's army was high. Forced marches through the highlands of eastern Afghanistan caused large numbers of soldiers to suffer frostbite, snow blindness and chronic fatigue. The crossing of the Hindu Kush through the highest and most snow-driven passes caused many additional deaths and injuries. On his march to the Oxus, Alexander drove his men across a burning, waterless desert in which many died from heatstroke. The harsh conditions caused some Thessalian units and Philip's older veterans to mutiny, and demand to be demobilized. Alexander had little choice but to agree. Hundreds of additional troops died from dehydration following too much drinking of alcohol. All these losses left Alexander short of first-rate troops, forcing him for the first time to recruit local 'barbarian' troops into the field army.[28]

Alexander's known manpower losses exceeded 7,000 men in this campaign alone, perhaps as much as one quarter of his field force and more than he had lost in all the battles and sieges against Darius.[29] Within months of Alexander's departure for India, a regional governor and the *hyparch* assigned to the Assacenians were assassinated. Afghanistan remained in a state of sporadic civil war, as local barons and tribes manoeuvred for power. Alexander's campaign in Afghanistan was over, but it had been nasty business indeed, leaving Alexander with a reputation more for brutality than military brilliance.

Alexander's Indian campaign, after his set-piece battle with Porus, was more pointless slaughter than anything else, conducted more out of personal anger and a desire to punish his troops than to attain any military objective. Except for one or two battles when the tribes chose to fight, Alexander could easily have avoided most of his violent encounters with the Indians.

Alexander always had the advantage against his Indian opponents. Indian tribal infantry was light infantry, armed with bows and javelins, no match for Alexander's heavy infantry.[30] Indian infantry usually fought without body armour, or were equipped only with jackets of padded cotton.[31] Some infantry carried a two-handed broadsword and a small wicker or wooden shield, but without helmet or armour were easy prey for Macedonian infantry and cavalry.[32] Nearchus tells us that among the Indians, 'to ride on a single horse is low', meaning that horse cavalry ranked below elephant riders, the four-horse chariot and camel mounts in social status.[33] What horse cavalry they had was light cavalry, unarmoured, armed with two throwing javelins and sometimes the bow, and completely ineffective against Macedonian cavalry.[34] The same can be said for Indian elephant, chariot and camel cavalry, all evident in small numbers, lightly armed with javelin and bow and unable to match the Macedonian cavalry in speed and manoeuvrability. They were simply no match for Alexander's heavy Macedonian cavalry.

The construction of Indian towns and fortifications was extremely vulnerable to Alexander's siege and storm capabilities. Nearchus tells us that most Indian towns located on rivers or on the coast were constructed of wood, because 'if they were built of brick, they could not last long because of the moisture due to the rain, and to the fact that the rivers overflow their banks and fill the plains with water'.[35] Only when the towns or forts were 'situated in commanding and lofty places' were they built of brick and clay, as was Sangala.[36] Alexander's route took him down the river valleys, where few fortifications of this type were evident. We often hear of Indian forces retreating to their towns and forts to make a stand, only to have their fortifications easily overcome by Alexander's engineers or quickly stormed by the infantry. With the Indians trapped, terrible slaughter usually followed. There is little in the accounts of Alexander's victories in India that merits the claim of military brilliance.[37]

Great generals are not the only causes of their greatness. War is a cooperative enterprise by its nature, heavily dependent upon the talents and abilities of others, orchestrated by the commander into a coherent whole of activity. The quality of leadership and experience is vitally important at all levels of command to the overall success of any army. Perhaps it is in the qualities of leadership, training and experience of the Macedonian officer and non-commissioned officer corps that Alexander owes his greatest debt to Philip. Most of the important officers in Alexander's army had served with Philip at various levels of command over the years. They included Parmenio, the old war horse, who was Philip's best field commander; his sons, Philotas and Nicanor, commanding the horse and foot guards respectively; and Cleitus, the commander of the Royal Squadron. Even some of Alexander's peers had seen their first combat under Philip, including, perhaps, Hephaestion, Alexander's closest friend and later the commander of half the Companion cavalry; Craterus, commander of the left half of the phalanx; Seleucus, commander of the foot guards; Antigonus the One-Eyed; and Ptolemy, a fellow-student with Alexander under Aristotle's tutelage.[38]

Perhaps more important were the unnamed and unremembered battalion commanders, squadron commanders, file leaders and section leaders, the small unit officer and non-commissioned officer corps upon which the combat effectiveness of an army depends most, who had served under Philip. The army staff system was comprised of officers who had also served Philip in previous wars. For a young officer with such limited experience as Alexander possessed, these officers and small unit combat leaders were critical to the army's operational success. Perhaps no general in history had ever received a better-trained, experienced and well-led army than Alexander did as his legacy from Philip.

Both Philip and Alexander were heads of state as well as field generals, a fact that radically changes the meaning of military greatness. In modern times, and even at times in antiquity, generals were most often not simultaneously heads of government. Accordingly, they are properly judged only by their achievements on the field of battle, and not held responsible for larger political concerns. In these circumstances, military performance may be regarded as an end in itself. But Alexander must be judged by a different standard, that is by the degree to which his military achievements worked to support his strategic objectives not only as a military man, but as a head of government. In these circumstances, military competence becomes not an end, but a means to additional ends for which the general is also responsible. The concerns of the general as a general are the tactical and operational elements of war; those of the general as statesman are the strategic objectives of the national state or people he leads.

For the general as strategist, war is but one means to achieve national objectives in the political and cultural context within which wars are fought for specified goals. Philip always properly saw war as a means to his strategic goals, and much preferred to achieve his objectives by other 'less kinetic' means, such as diplomacy. Even to so Homeric a warrior as Philip, the search for glory and heroism had but little place in his strategic thinking. Alexander, by contrast, was the prototypical Homeric warrior fighting for personal glory and reputation, a military adventurer almost entirely lacking in strategic vision. One is hard-pressed to discern in accounts of Alexander's adventures any strategic vision that might have reasonably been achieved by his many campaigns. When the Indian philosopher Dandamis met Alexander, he seems to have grasped Alexander's strategic mettle correctly when he asked, 'For what reason did Alexander make such a long journey hither?'[39]

Only in the early Persian campaign can one discern a strategic objective: the conquest of Persia. Having achieved this, Alexander didn't seem to have any idea how to govern the country or for what purpose. The Bactrian and Sogdiana campaigns were designed to suppress the insurgency, but again, to what strategic end is unclear. Alexander's efforts gained a temporary peace there, but the country fell back into civil war within a few months of his leaving for India. The Indian campaign makes no strategic sense at all, and none of our sources makes an effort to explain just why Alexander undertook it, save for personal reputation and glory. Even this objective evaporated when the army mutinied, and Alexander was forced to turn back, subjecting his army to a number of pointless and lethal conflicts with Indian tribes. The crossing of the Gedrosian Desert was undertaken not for any strategic or tactical reasons, but to surpass the achievements of other generals. Nearchus tells us that, 'Alexander chose it, we are told, because with the exception of Semiramis, returning from her conquests of India, no one had ever brought an army successfully through it ... the Persian king, Cyrus the Great, supposedly had lost all but seven of his men when he crossed it. Alexander knew about these stories, and they had inspired him to emulate and hopefully surpass Cyrus and Semiramis.'[40] There was no strategic point to the adventure.

It is difficult to credit Alexander with being a brilliant strategist. One can point to any number of serious strategic mistakes committed by Alexander. Here are a few of them: (1) Despite the massacre and destruction of Thebes, far more Greeks fought against Alexander than ever fought with him. He never regained support in Greece after the Theban massacre, and Sparta rose in open revolt three years later. When Alexander died, all Greece rejoiced; (2) Because of the hatred of the Greeks, Alexander was never able to make good use of the Athenian navy because he couldn't trust them. When he disbanded his fleet at Tyre, he kept a few squadrons of Athenian ships and crews with him to use as hostages in case of Athenian treachery; (3) The sieges of Halicarnarsus and Miletus, as brutal as they were, did not frighten Tyre into surrendering. Alexander still had to take the port city by force; (4) The massacres at Tyre did not stop the Persians at Gaza from putting up a six-month fight that almost killed Alexander; (5) The burning of Persepolis did not stop the Persian nobility from leading a three-year insurgency against Alexander. The destruction of Persepolis, the religious capital of the country, only created popular support for the insurgency; (6) Afghanistan was a disaster that cost Alexander thousands of troops and gained him nothing. Despite slaughter after slaughter, the next town or tribe always resisted, often to the end. The Soviet policy of 'migratory genocide' in Afghanistan over ten years had the same effect; (7) The victory over Porus had no strategic effect except to unify the Indian tribes on the other side of the Hydaspes River to rally and prepare to fight Alexander together. Confronted with this opposition and the mutiny of his troops, Alexander was forced to abandon his Indian campaign; (8) The transit down the Indus River saw Alexander perpetrate one slaughter after another. None of them convinced the next tribe to forego resistance. As can be seen, there is precious little in the way of sound strategic thinking that can be credited to Alexander.

In Alexander's mind, war was the arena of fame and glory, an end in itself, his achievements the stuff of history and legend by which he would be remembered and, ultimately, fashioned into a god. Like his hero, Achilles, Alexander 'seems to have been possessed of some sort of restless, almost irrational desire for glory unchecked by a larger political sense',[41] that is, by any strategic vision or calculation. Without a sense of strategy or a national vision for his people, it is difficult to see how Alexander can be judged a great general or a great king. In the end, he was, at most, a savage *conquistador* who cared little for anything or anyone beyond himself.

Alexander was one of antiquity's most notorious mass murderers. He slaughtered thousands of innocent victims, mostly women and children, and, at times, his own countrymen. Almost every one of his military campaigns was marked by an atrocity. Alexander's murdering ferocity falls into five categories: the sheer carnage he inflicted upon enemies on the battlefield; the routine slaughter of defenders and civilians in sieges; the wholesale and genocidal extermination of tribes and villagers during his guerrilla wars in Iran, Afghanistan and Pakistan; the toll taken on his own soldiers and their thousands of camp followers during his crazed and unnecessary crossing of the Gedrosian desert; and the crass murders of his rivals, family and an entire generation of Macedonian generals and officers whom Alexander, in his paranoia, came to see as threats.[42]

Even in the early days of his adventure, Alexander showed himself to be irascibly cruel, as when he destroyed Thebes, Tyre and Gaza. But his cruelty, now mostly militarily pointless, became much worse after Alexander suffered a severe head wound at the siege of Cyropolis in 328 BC. Curtius tells us that, 'Alexander was struck so severely on the neck by a stone that everything went dark and he collapsed unconscious. The army wept for him as if he were dead.'[43] Arrian says the injury was to the back of the head and neck, while Plutarch says it was to the back of the neck and the side of the neck, that is the occipital and parietal area of the skull.[44] The Latin text can be interpreted to mean that Alexander lost his sight, and Plutarch says 'for many days he was in fear of becoming blind'.[45] We do not know for how many days Alexander was without his sight, only that he eventually recovered it. Two months later, Curtius tells us that Alexander had still not recovered from his wound, 'and in particular had difficulty speaking'. He was so weak that 'Alexander himself could not stand in the ranks, ride a horse, or give his men instructions or encouragement'. His voice was so weak that in staff meetings he had his friends sit close to him so that they could hear 'without him having to strain his voice'.[46] At a later meeting, Alexander proposed to take the field against Spitamenes, but 'Alexander's words were spoken in a quivering voice that became increasingly feeble, so that it was difficult even for those next to him to hear'.[47] It was another several weeks before Alexander's symptoms disappeared, and he was able to put on his cuirass and 'walk to the men, the first time he had done so since receiving the most recent wound'.[48] Altogether, Alexander was out of action for at least two months.[49]

The blow to Alexander's head caused a very severe concussion that resulted in transient cortical blindness.[50] Alexander's difficulties with balance, walking and speaking, however, suggest more extensive damage to the brain. The symptoms of concussion were known to Greek physicians, and appear in several case studies in the *Corpus Hippocraticum*. Most symptoms, as in Alexander's case, are eventually self-resolving. Less evident to the Greeks were the long-term emotional and behavioural consequences of the injury that Alexander suffered.[51]

The damage caused by the blow to the back and side of Alexander's head was not confined to that area. A blow to the back of the head drives the fluid surrounding the brain forward, propelling the frontal lobe of the brain into the bony structure of the skull, causing damage to the frontal lobe of the cerebral cortex. In this type of 'contra-coup' injury, the functions of the frontal lobe can be greatly affected, as they appear to have been in Alexander's case. Alexander continued to show physical symptoms of his concussion for at least two months after the injury, a clinically prolonged period that suggests considerable trauma to the brain and frontal cortex.

Long-term emotional effects of concussion include depression, explosive anger, irritability, shortened temper, paranoia, memory loss and inappropriate displays of emotion, all dysfunctions of the frontal lobe. Certain conditions – traumatic brain injury, psychiatric disorders, severe concussion and substance abuse – can create a state of reduced control over one's behaviours, impulses, attention and emotions. Physicians refer to this condition as disinhibition, the opposite of inhibition, a state of control over one's responses. Individuals under the influence of alcohol, for example, exhibit disinhibition as a consequence of the depressant effect of alcohol on the brain's higher functioning. Disinhibition can affect motor, instinctual, emotional, cognitive and perceptual aspects with symptoms similar to the diagnostic criteria for mania. Hyper-sexuality, hyperphagia (obsessive compulsive behaviour regarding food or drink) and aggressive outbursts are common effects of disinhibited instinctual drives.[52] Severe concussion can, over time, also result in chronic traumatic encephalopathy, producing severe emotional outbursts and paranoid states. It is telling in this regard that Alexander's symptoms of brain damage continued to get worse from 328 BC, when he was injured at Cyropolis, until his death in 323 BC.

Alexander was 27 when he was injured at Cyropolis, and had been at war for seven years. He had already begun to show symptoms of post-traumatic stress disorder: explosive anger, cruelty, paranoia, depression, heavy drinking and suicidal impulses. The expressions of these behaviours became even more dramatic after this injury. From Cyropolis to the end of his life, Alexander's symptoms of post-traumatic stress became more severe, as he increasingly lost his ability to control his impulses, emotions and behaviour.

A brief review of Alexander's behaviour *after* the injury reveals this to have been the case. At Maracanda, Alexander killed Cleitus with a spear in a fit of drunken anger; his paranoia became more acute, and he had Callisthenes and the Pages executed when he believed they were involved in a conspiracy to kill him; four senior generals were executed out of fear that they could no longer be trusted; upon his return from India, Alexander ordered scores of Macedonian and Persian officials killed in a mass purge; any common soldier guilty of an offence was routinely executed without trial; his depression became worse and more frequent, and on at least two occasions he was suicidal; Alexander's homosexuality became more blatant and public; and he ordered the execution of Persian officials on the whim of his lover, Bagoas. He even had a mentally ill man who had accidentally sat upon his throne executed, and Alexander became more convinced that he was divine, paying excessive attention to even the smallest events as signs of his divinity. It was only a few months after his injury at Cyropolis that he attempted to require the Macedonians to prostrate themselves in his presence.

Alexander's behaviour became more brutal than before his injury. At Cyropolis, he ordered the death of 7,000 enemy prisoners who had surrendered. In the attack on Maracanda in 328 BC, he ordered a sweep of the area, destroying every village and town, killing every man of military age. When he captured the city, Alexander ordered the population butchered to a man. In 327 BC, Alexander returned to Sogdiana and destroyed every village, town and tribe encountered en route of the line of march. Estimates of the losses begin at 120,000 people. Forty thousand were killed in a single engagement. After taking the town of Massaga in the Kabul Valley, he granted the Indian mercenary force safe passage, then surrounded them and their families and killed every man, woman and child, some 7,000 people in all.[53]

After defeating Porus at the Hydaspes River, Alexander's Indian campaign continued with the slaughter of the entire town of Sangala in 326 BC. Seventeen thousand people were killed and 70,000 taken prisoner. The refugees fled, leaving 500 sick and wounded behind. When Alexander came upon them, he ordered them killed. Alexander moved on to a neighbouring town, bringing it under siege. He set fire to it, burning most of the inhabitants alive. In 325 BC, Alexander attacked the Malians, destroying their towns and villages and slaughtering the inhabitants. Some 50,000 souls were slain in this single campaign. A few months later, he encountered the Brahmins at Sambus. In a fit of anger at their resistance, Alexander once more ordered a terrible massacre. If Curtius and Diodorus are to be believed, 80,000 people were systemtatically slaughtered. Later, he marched through the territory of the Oreitae, killing and setting fire to homes, towns and villages as he went, all without any provocation. Six thousand were killed in a single engagement. In 324 BC, Alexander and his army spent forty days in a campaign against the Cossaeans, again without provocation. The entire nation was put to the sword. This was done to soothe Alexander's grief at the death of his lover.[54]

Even allowing for exaggeration by our sources, it is clear that Alexander had changed markedly, and his brutality was much worse after his injury at Cyropolis than it had previously been. Much of the slaughter seems to have had no military purpose, and was committed out of Alexander's personal anger or, perhaps, the psychological need to bring on the berserk state as a way of calming his turbulent mind. Whatever had inhibited Alexander's rage and psychological drives before Cyropolis seems to have lessened or disappeared altogether after he was injured. J.M. O'Brien summed up the changes that occurred in Alexander at this time: 'This change, which deepened during the last seven years of his life, was marked by a progressive deterioration of character. He became increasingly suspicious of friends as well as enemies, unpredictable, and megalomaniacal. Towards the end, he was almost totally isolated, dreaded by all, a violent man capable of anything.'[55]

It might also be said that Alexander was not much of a king, and this may well have been his greatest strategic shortcoming. Having inherited the government of the first truly national state in Western history, Alexander attempted nothing with it. He promptly turned over effective national authority to Antipater when he left for Asia, and Antipater governed and protected Macedonia until the end of his life. Alexander never returned to Macedonia, nor, as far as we know, ordered any governmental action to be carried out by Antipater.

Nor did Alexander make much of an attempt to govern Persia, being content to leave most satraps in place, or to replace them with other loyal Persians more often than Macedonians. And he seems to have cared equally little for the survival of the Argead dynasty. He took no steps to secure the succession, barely fathering an heir before he died and designating no clear successor on his deathbed. It was his Macedonian officers who protected the dynastic line by insisting that Roxanne's child, though not fully Macedonian, retain the claim to the Argead throne. That Alexander cared nothing for governance of anything seems clear enough.

Notes

1. For an analysis of Philip's achievements, see Richard A. Gabriel, *Philip of Macedonia: Greater Than Alexander* (Dulles, VA, Potomac Books, 2010).
2. Diodorus Siculus of Sicily, trans. C. Bradford Welles, (Cambridge, MA, Harvard University Press, 1983), 17.3–5. Peter Green, *Alexander the Great and the Hellenistic Age* (London, Orion Books, 2008), p.158.
3. N.G.L. Hammond, 'Casualties and Reinforcements of Citizen Soldiers in Greece and Macedonia', *Journal of Hellenic Studies* 109 (1989), p.68.
4. Ibid.
5. Ibid.
6. P.A. Brunt, *Nearchus' Indica* (Cambridge, MA, Harvard University Press, 1983), pp.489–90.
7. Ibid.
8. Green, *Alexander the Great and the Hellenistic Age*, p.413.
9. Robert E. Gaebel, *Cavalry Operations in the Ancient World* (Norman, OK, University of Oklahoma Press, 2002), p.213.
10. For an account of Philip's innovations in Macedonian siege capability, see E.W. Marsden, 'Macedonian Military Machinery and Its Designers Under Philip and Alexander', *Ancient Macedonia* (1968), pp.211–23.
11. An analysis of Alexander's six sieges can be found in *Ancient Warfare*, iv, no. 2 (2012), pp.17–21.
12. Brunt, *Indica*, p.335.
13. Richard Gabriel, 'The Persian Army and Alexander the Great', in Gabriel, *Empires At War*, vol. 1 (Westport, CT, Greenwood Press, 2005), pp.313–14.
14. Brunt, *Indica*, p.453.
15. For Alexander's tactics, see A R. Burn, 'Alexander the Great', *Greece and Rome* 12, no. 2 (October 1965), pp.146–54. See also Gaebel, *Cavalry Operations*, pp.183–93.
16. With his advance blocked in Thessaly, Philip had his soldiers cut steps out of the rock of a mountain cliff, crossed the mountain and took the enemy by surprise. Gabriel, *Philip of Macedonia*, pp.117–21.
17. Christopher Matthew and W.W. How, 'Arms, Tactics, and Strategy in the Persian Wars', *Journal of Hellenic Studies* 43.2 (2013), pp.117–32.
18. Jim Lacey, 'The Persian Fallacy', *Military History* (July 2012), pp.50–51.
19. Buddha Prakash, *History of the Punjab* (Punjab University, Patiala Publications Bureau, 1997), p.225.
20. Green, *Alexander the Great and the Hellenistic Age*, p.338.
21. Valerii Nikonorov, *The Armies of Bactria, 700 BC–450 AD* (Stockport, PA, Montvery Publications, 1997), for the tactics of the Bactrian combatants that Alexander faced.

22. Quintus Curtis Rufus, *The History of Alexander*, trans. John Yardley (London, Penguin Books, 2001), 7.7.39.
23. Arrian, *The Campaigns of Alexander*, trans. Aubrey De Selincourt (London, Penguin Books, 1971), 4.6.
24. Frank L. Holt, *Into the Land of the Bones: Alexander the Great in Afghanistan* (Berkeley, CA, University of California Press, 2005), p.57.
25. Curtius, 6.17.
26. Arrian, 1.5.10; see also Gaebel, *Cavalry Operations*, p.194, for other citations in Arrian dealing with the same subject.
27. Diodorus, 17.17.3–5.
28. Green, *Alexander the Great and the Hellenistic Age*, p.353.
29. Holt, *Into the Land of The Bones*, p.107.
30. Nearchus, *Indica,* 16.1–9.
31. Duncan Head, *Armies of the Macedonian and Punic Wars, 359 BC to 146 B C* (Sutton, UK, Wargames Research Group, 1982), p.137.
32. Nearchus, *Indica,* 9.17.
33. Ibid.
34. Head, *Armies of the Macedonian and Punic Wars*, p.139.
35. Nearchus, *Indica*, 10.2–9.
36. Ibid.
37. A.K. Narin, 'Alexander in India', *Greece and Rome*, vol. 12, no. 2 (1965), pp.155–65.
38. A.R. Burn, 'The Generalship of Alexander', *Greece and Rome*, vol. 12, no. 2 (1965), pp.142–43, for Alexander's debt to his officers.
39. Guy MacLean Rogers, *Alexander: The Ambiguity of Greatness* (New York, Random House, 2004), p.222.
40. Ibid.
41. George Cawkwell, *Philip of Macedon* (London, Faber and Faber, 1978), p.164.
42. Victor David Hanson, 'Alexander', *Military History Quarterly* (summer 1998), p.12.
43. Curtius, 7.22.
44. John Lascartos, 'The Wounding of Alexander the Great in Cyropolis: The First Reported Case of the Syndrome of Transient Cortical Blindness', *History of Ophthalmology* 42 (November–December 1977), p.286.
45. Christine F. Salazar, *The Treatment of War Wounds in Greek and Roman Antiquity* (Boston, Brill, 2000), p.199, citing Plutarch.
46. Curtius, 7.5–6.
47. Ibid., 7.19.
48. Ibid., 8.3.

49. We may take Curtius' account as reliable. Hammond notes that this section of Curtius' work draws heavily upon Aristobulus, who was a staff officer with Alexander and is generally considered reliable. See N.G.L. Hammond, *Three Historians of Alexander the Great: The So-Called Vulgate Authors* (Cambridge, Cambridge University Press, 1983), whose work makes a bold attempt to assess the reliability of the ancient sources.

50. Lascaratos, 'The Wounding of Alexander the Great in Cyropolis', pp.284–85.

51. Until recently, the traditional medical view of the symptoms of concussion was that they were largely self-resolving, with little in the way of long-term effects. Only with the recent investigations in the United States of the death and suicides of National Football League players have physicians begun to appreciate the long-term physiological, emotional and behavioural consequences of severe and/or repeated concussions.

52. I am indebted to my friend, John Cowan, former Chair of the Physiology Department of the Faculty of Medicine at the University of Ottawa, for much of the medical information in this section.

53. Richard A. Gabriel, *The Madness of Alexander the Great and the Myth of Military Genius* (Barnsley, Pen and Sword, 2015), pp.48–51.

54. Ibid.

55. John M. O'Brien, 'The Enigma of Alexander: The Alcohol Factor', *Annals of Scholarship* (1980), p.32.

SELECTED BIBLIOGRAPHY

Thutmose III

'Ancient Egyptian Joint Operations in Lebanon Under Thutmose III', *Semaphore: Newsletter of the Sea Power Center of Australia*, 16 (August 2006), pp.1–2. http://www.navy.gov.au/spc/

Bagnall, R.S., *Egypt in Late Antiquity* (Princeton, NJ, Princeton University Press, 1993).

Bietak, Manfred, 'The Thutmoside Stronghold of Perunefer', *Egyptian Archaeology* 26 (spring 2005), pp.13–14.

Breasted, James Henry, *Ancient Records of Egypt, vol. 2:* The *Eighteenth Dynasty* (Urbana, Ill., University of Illinois Press, 2001).

Bryan, Betsy M., 'Administration in the Reign of Thutmose III', in *Thutmose III: A New Biography*, pp.69–122.

Cline, Eric, and O'Connor, David, *Thutmose III: A New Biography* (Ann Arbor, MI, University of Michigan Press, 2008).

——, *The Battles of Armageddon* (Ann Arbor, University of Michigan Press, 2000).

Cottrell, Leonard, *The Warrior Pharaohs* (New York, Dutton, 1969).

Dorman, Peter F., 'The Early Reign of Thutmose III: An Unorthodox Mantle of Coregency', in *Thutmose III: A New Biography,* pp.39–68.

Edgerton, William F., 'Ancient Egyptian Ships and Shipping', *American Journal of Semitic Languages and Literature* 39, no.2 (January 1923), pp.109–35.

——, 'Dimensions of Ancient Egyptian Ships', *American Journal of Semitic Languages and Literature* 46, no. 3 (April 1930), pp.145–49.

——, 'Egyptian Seagoing Ships of One Hundred Cubits', *American Journal of Semitic Languages and Literature* 47, no. 1 (October 1930), pp.50–51.

——, 'Ancient Egyptian Steering Gear', *American Journal of Semitic Languages and Literature* 43, no. 4 (July 1927), pp.255–65.

Erman, Adolf, *Life in Ancient Egypt*, trans. H.M Girard (New York, Dover Books Reprint, 1971).

Faulkner, R.O., 'The Euphrates Campaign of Thutmose III', *Journal of Egyptian Archaeology* 32 (1947), pp.39–42.

——, 'The Battle of Megiddo', *Journal of Egyptian Archaeology* 28 (1942), pp.2–15.

——, 'Egyptian Military Organization', *Journal of Egyptian Archaeology* 39 (1953), pp.32–47.

——, 'Egyptian Sea-going Ships', *Journal of Egyptian Archaeology* 16 (1940), pp.3–17.

Forbest, Dennis, 'Menkheperre Djehutymes: Thutmose III, A Pharaoh's Pharaoh', *KMT* 9, no. 4 (winter, 1998–1999), pp.44–65.

Fox, Troy, 'Siege Warfare in Ancient Egypt', www.touregyptnet/featurestories/siegewarfare.

——, 'Military Architecture of Ancient Egypt', www.toureegyptnet/features/fortresses/htm.

——, 'Defensive Equipment of the Egyptian Army', www.touregyptnet/featurestories/defense.htm.

——, 'The Egyptian Navy', www.touregyptnet/featurestories/navy.htm.

Gabriel, Richard A., *Thutmose III: The Military Biography of Egypt's Greatest Warrior Pharaoh* (Dulles, VA, Potomac Books, 2009).

—— and Metz, Karen. S., *From Sumer To Rome: The Military Capabilities of Ancient Armies* (Westport, CT, Greenwood Press, 1991)

Gardiner, Sir Alan, *Egypt of the Pharaohs* (Oxford, Oxford University Press, 1961).

——, 'The Defeat of the Hyksos by Kamose: The Carnarvon Tablet, No. 1', *Journal of Egyptian Archaeology* 3 (1916), pp.95–110.

Gichon, Mordecai, 'Military Camps in Egyptian and Syrian Reliefs', *Assaph: Studies in Honor of Asher Ovadiah* (Tel Aviv, Department of Art History, 2005), pp.569–93.

Goedicke, Hans, *The Battle of Megiddo* (Baltimore, MD, Halgo Inc., 2000).

——, 'Egyptian Military Actions in Asia in the Middle Kingdom', *Revue d'egyptologie* 42 (1991), pp.89–94.

Grimal, Nicholas, *A History of Ancient Egypt*, trans. Ian Shaw (Oxford, Blackwell, 1988).

Hansen, Kathy, 'The Chariot in Egypt's Age of Chivalry', *KMT* 5, no. 1 (1994), pp.50–61, 82–83.

Kozloff, Arielle P., 'The Artistic Production of the Reign of Thutmose III' in Cline and O'Connor, *Thutmose III: A New Biography*, pp.314–23.

Laskowski, Pitor, 'Monumental Architecture and the Royal Building Program of Thumose III', in *Thutmose III: A New Biography*, pp.183–237.

Nelson, Harold Hayden, *The Battle of Megiddo* (Chicago, IL, University of Chicago Library, 1913).

O'Connor, David, 'The Hyksos Period in Egypt', in *The Hyksos: New Historical and Archaeological Perspectives*, pp.43–56.

——, 'Thutmose III: An Enigmatic Pharaoh', in *Thutmose III: A New Biography*, pp.1–38.

O'Connor, David, and Cline, Eric, *Thutmose III: A New Biography* (Ann Arbor, MI, University of Michigan Press, 2008).

Partridge, R.B., *Faces of Pharaohs: Royal Mummies and Coffins From Ancient Thebes* (London, Rubicon Press, 1994).

Petty, William, 'Hatshepsut and Thutmose III Reconsidered', *KMT* 8, no. 1 (spring 1997), pp.45–53.

Pritchard, James B, *Ancient Near Eastern Texts* (Princeton, NJ, Princeton University Press, 1955).

Redford, Donald B., *History and Chronology of the Eighteenth Dynasty of Egypt* (Toronto, University of Toronto Press, 1967).

——, *Egypt, Canaan, and Israel in Ancient Times* (Princeton, NJ, Princeton University Press, 1992).

——, 'The Northern Wars of Thutmose III', in *Thutmose III: A New Biography*, pp.325–43.

——, *The Wars in Syria and Palestine of Thutmose III* (Boston, Brill, 2003).

——, 'The Coregency of Thutmose III and Amenophis II', *Journal of Egyptian Archaeology* 51 (1965), pp.107–22.

——, 'On the Chronology of the Egyptian Eighteenth Dynasty', *Journal of Near Eastern Studies* 25, no. 2 (April 1966), pp.113–24.

Sandor, B. I., 'Tutankamun's Chariots: Secret Treasures of Engineering Mechanics', in *Fatigue and Fracturing of Engineering Materials and Structure* (London, Blackwell, 2004), pp.637–46.

——, 'The Rise and Decline of the Tutankhamun-Class Chariot', *Oxford Journal of Archaeology* 23, no. 2 (2004), pp.153–75.

Save-Soderbergh, Torgny, *The Navy of the Eighteenth Egyptian Dynasty* (Uppsala, Sweden, Uppsala University Press, 1946).

Schulman, Alan R., *Military Rank, Title, and Organization in the Egyptian New Kingdom* (Berlin, Bruno Hassling Verlag, 1964).

Shaw, Ian, 'Egyptians, Hyksos, and Military Technology: Causes, Effects, or Catalysts?', in *The Social Context of Technological Change*, pp.59–71.

Spalinger, Anthony J., *War in Ancient Egypt* (Malden, MA, Blackwell, 2005).

——, 'Covetous Eyes South: The Background of Egypt's Domination Over Nubia by the Reign of Thutmose III', in *Thutmose III: A New Biography*, pp.344–69.

——, 'New Reference to an Egyptian Campaign of Thutmose III in Asia', *Journal of Near Eastern Studies* 37, no. 1 (January 1978), pp.35–41.

Stillman, Nigel, and Tallis, Nigel, *Armies of the Ancient Near East* (Sussex, Flexiprint Ltd., 1984).

'Thutmose III: The Napata Stela', http://www.terraflex.co.il/ad/egypt/napata_stela.htm

Townsend, Glen R., *The First Battle in History* (Ft. Leavenworth, KS, Command and General Staff School, 1935).

Weigall, Arthur, *A History of the Pharaohs* (New York, E.P. Dutton, 1927).

Weingartner, Steven, "Chariots Changed Forever the Way Warfare Was Fought', *Military Heritage* (August 1999), pp.18–26.

——, 'Near Eastern Bronze Age Chariot Tactics', *Military Heritage* (August 2002), pp.18–26, 79.

Winkelman, Betty, 'Buren: Blueprints of an Egyptian Fortress', *KMT* 6, no. 2 (summer 1995), pp.72–83.

Winter, Irene J., 'Carchemish', *Anatolian Studies* 33 (1983), pp.177–97.

Yadin, Yigael, *The Art of Warfare in Biblical Lands in Light of Archaeology* (New York, McGraw-Hill, 1963).

Moses

Alfred, Cyril, *Akhenaten: King of Egypt* (London, Thames and Hudson, 1988).

Assmann, Jan, *Moses the Egyptian* (Cambridge, MA, Harvard University Press, 1998).

Auerbach, Elias, *Moses*, trans./ed. Robert A. Barclay and Israel O. Lehman (Detroit, MI, Wayne State University Press, 1975).

Barnett, William S, 'Only the Bad Died Young in the Ancient Middle East', *International Journal of Aging and Human Development* 21, no. 2 (1985), pp.155–60.

Boling, Robert G., and Wright, G. Ernest, *Joshua: The Anchor Bible* (New York, Doubleday, 1982).

Breasted, James H., *The Dawn of Conscience* (New York, Charles Scribner, 1947).

Buber, Martin, *Moses: The Revelation and the Covenant* (Amherst, NY, Humanity Books, 1998).

Cleveland, Kerry O., 'Tularemia', *Medscape Reference*, http://emedicine.medscape.com/article/230923-overview

Curtius, Quintus, *History of Alexander*, Book V, ii, 7, trans. John C. Rolfe (Cambridge, MA, Harvard University Press, 1946).

Douglas, Mary, *In The Wilderness: The Doctrine of Defilement in the Book of Numbers* (Sheffield, Sheffield Academic Press, 1993).

Freud, Sigmund, *Moses and Monotheism* (New York, Vintage Books, 1939).

Gabriel, Richard A., *The Culture of War* (Westport, CT, Greenwood Press, 1990).

—— and Metz, Karen S., *From Sumer To Rome: The Military Capabilities of Ancient Armies* (Westport, CT, Greenwood Press, 1991).

——, *Soldiers' Lives Through History: The Ancient World* (Westport, CT, Greenwood Press, 2000).

——, *The Military History of Ancient Israel* (Westport, CT, Greenwood Press, 2003).

Gall, Reuven, *A Portrait of the Israeli Solider* (Westport, CT, Greenwood Press, 1986).

Gichon, Mordecai, 'The Siege of Masada', *Collection du Centre des Etudes Romaines et Gallo-Romaines*, no. 20 (Lyon, 2000), pp.541–43.

Gottwald, Norman K.,*Tribes of Yahweh* (Maryknoll, NY, Orbis Books, 1979).

Grant, Michael, *The History of Ancient Israel* (New York, Scribner, 1984).

Grimal, Nicholas, *History of Ancient Egypt* (London, Blackwell Publishers, 1992).

Herzog, Chaim, and Gichon, Mordechai, *Battles of the Bible* (Jerusalem, Steimatzky Agency, 1978).

Hobs, T.R., *A Time For War* (Wilmington, DE, Michael Glazer, 1989).

Homan, Michael M., 'The Divine Warrior in His Tent: A Military Model for Yahweh's Tabernacle', *Bible Review* 16, no. 6 (December 2000), pp.22–33.

Isaac, Eric, 'Circumcision as a Covenant Rite', *Antropos* 59 (1965), pp.442–43.

Isserlin, B.S.J., *The Israelites* (London, Thames and Hudson, 1998).

Josephus, *Contra Apion*, Book 1, 82–92.

Kirsch, Jonathan, *Moses: A Life* (New York, Ballantine Books, 1998).

Klein, Joel T., *Through the Name of God* (Westport, CT, Greenwood Press, 2001).

Lucas, A., 'The Number of Israelites at the Exodus', *Palestine Exploration Quarterly* (1944), pp.164–68.

Mendenhall, George E., 'The Census List of Numbers 1 and 26', *Journal of Biblical Literature* 77 (1958), pp.52–66.

Neville, Edouard, 'The Geography of the Exodus', *Journal of Egyptian Archaeology* 10 (1924), pp.19–25.

Pritchard, James B., *Ancient Near East Texts Relating to the Old Testament* (Princeton, NJ, Princeton University Press, 1955).

Propp, William H.C., *Exodus 1–8: The Anchor Bible* (New York, Doubleday, 1998).

Redford, Donald B., *Akhenaten: The Heretic King* (Princeton, NJ, Princeton University Press, 1984).

Rowley, H.H., *From Joseph to Joshua* (London, Oxford University Press, 1948).

Schulman, A.R., 'Some Remarks on the Military Background of the Amarna Period', *Journal of the American Research Center in Egypt* 3 (1964), pp.51–70.

Smith, Morton, *Jesus The Egyptian* (New York, Barnes and Noble, 1997).

Stillman, Nigel, and Tallis, Nigel, *Armies of the Ancient Near East* (Sussex, Flexiprint Ltd., 1984).

Trevisanato, Siro Igino, 'The Hittite Plague: An Epidemic of Tularemia and the First Record of Biological Warfare', *Medical Hypotheses* 69, 6 (2007), pp.1,371–74.

Weiner, H.M., 'The Historical Character of the Exodus', *Ancient Egypt* IV (1926), pp.104–15.

Wright, George Ernest, and Filson, Floyd Vivian, *Westminster Historical Atlas of the Bible* (Philadelphia, PA, Westminster Press, 1945).

Yadin, Yigael, *The Art of Warfare in Biblical Lands in Light of Archaeological Discovery* (New York, McGraw-Hill, 1963).

Yasuda, A.S., 'The Osiris Cult and the Designation of Osiris Idols in the Bible', *Journal of Near Eastern Studies* 3 (1944), pp.194–97.

Sargon the Great

Brinkman, J.A., 'Merodach-Baladan II', in *Studies Presented to A. Leo Oppenheim* (Chicago, Oriental Institute, 1968), pp.3–33.

Contineau, Georges, *Everyday Life in Babylon and Assyria* (London, Edward Arnold, 1954).

Gabriel, Richard A., 'The Iron Army of Assyria', in *Empires At War: From Sumer to the Persian Empire*, vol. 1 (Westport, CT, Greenwood Press, 2005), p.177.

——, *Great Captains of Antiquity* (Westport, CT, Greenwood Press, 2001), p.54.

—— and Metz, Karen S., *From Sumer To Rome: The Military Capabilities of Ancient Armies* (Westport, CT, Greenwood Press, 1991).

Gordon, D.H., 'Fire and Sword: Techniques of Destruction', *Antiquity* 27 (1953), 159–62.

Hawkins, J.D., 'Assyrians and Hittite', *Iraq* 36 (1974), pp.67–83.

Kramer, Samuel N., *The Cradle of Civilization* (New York, Time Inc., 1969).

Littauer, M.A., and Crouwel, J., *Wheeled Vehicles and Ridden Animals in the Ancient Near East* (Leiden, E.J. Brill, 1979).

Lloyd, Seton, *The Archaeology of Mesopotamia* (London, Thames and Hudson, 1978).

Luckenbill, Daniel David, *Ancient Records of Assyria and Babylonia*, vol. 2 (Chicago, University of Chicago Press, 1926).

Manitius, W., 'The Army and Military Organization of the Assyrian Kings', *Zeitschrift fur Assyriologie* 24 (1910), pp.90–107.

Nada'v, Na'aman, and Zadok, Ron, 'Sargon's Deportations to Israel and Philistia (716–108 BC)', *Journal of Cuneiform Studies*, vol. 40, no. 1 (spring 1988), pp.36–46.

Oates, D., 'Fort Shalamaneser: An Interim Report', *Iraq* 21 (1959), pp.98–129.

Olmstead, A.T., *The History of Assyria* (Chicago, University of Chicago Press, 1951).

Oppenheim, A. Leo, *Ancient Mesopotamia* (Chicago, University of Chicago Press, 1971).

Piotrovsky, R., *The Ancient Civilization of the Urartu* (London, Cresses Press, 1969).

Postdate, J.N., *Taxation and Conscription in the Assyrian Empire* (Rome, Biblical Institute Press, 1974).

Pritchard, James B, *Ancient Near Eastern Texts* (Princeton, NJ, Princeton University Press, 1955).

Radnor, Karen, 'Sargon II, King of Assyria (721–705 BC)', in *Assyrian Empire Builders* (London, University College London, 2012), p.27.

Reades, J., 'The Neo-Assyrian Court and the Army', *Iraq* 34 (1972), pp.141–49.

Roux, Georges, *Ancient Iraq* (New York, Penguin, 1964), p.314.

Saggs, H.W.F., *The Might That Was Assyria* (London, Sedgwick and Jackson, 1984).

Saggs, H.W.F., 'Assyrian Warfare in the Sargonid Period', *Iraq*, vol. 25, no. 2 (1963), pp.148–54.

Tadmor, Hayim, 'The Campaigns of Sargon II of Assur: A Chronological-Historical Study', *Journal of Cuneiform Studies*, vol. 12, no. 1 (1958), pp.22–40; part 2 of the study appears in the same journal, vol. 12, no. 3 (1958), pp.77–100.

——, 'The Struggle of King Sargon of Assyria against the Chaldaean Merodach-Baladan (710–707)', Leiden, *Annual of the Oriental Society of the Orient and Light*, no. 25 (1978), pp.1–13.

Wiseman, D.J., 'The Assyrians', in Sir John Hackett, *Warfare in the Ancient World* (London, Sedgwick and Jackson, 1989).

Philip of Macedon

Adcock, F.E., *The Greek and Macedonian Art of War* (Berkeley, CA, University of California Press, 1957).

Aeschines, *The Speeches of Aeschines*, trans. Charles Darwin Adams (Whitefish, WI, Kissinger Publishers, 2007).

Anderson, J.K., *Ancient Greek Horsemanship* (Berkeley, CA, University of California Press, 1961).

Andronikos, Manolis, 'The Royal Tombs at Aigai (Vergina)', in Miltiades Hatzopoulos and Louisa Loukopoulos (eds.), *Philip of Macedon* (Athens, Ekdotike Athenon, 1980), pp.188–231.

——, 'Sarissa', *Bulletin de Correspondence Hellenique* 94 (1970), pp.98–99.

Arnett, William S, 'Only The Bad Died Young in the Ancient Middle East', *International Journal of Aging and Human Development* 21, no. 2 (1985), pp.155–60.

Arrian, *The Anabasis of Alexander*, trans. P.A. Brunt and E. Cliff Robson (Cambridge, MA, Loeb Classics Library, 1983).

Badian, E., 'Philip and the Last of the Thessalians', *Ancient Macedonia* 6 (1999), pp.117–20.

——, 'Greeks and Macedonians', in *Macedonia and Greece in Late Classical and Early Hellenistic Times* (Washington, DC, 1982), pp.33–51.

——, 'The Death of Philip', *Phoenix* 17, no. 4 (winter 1963), pp.244–50.

Bartsiokas, A., 'The Eye Injury of King Philip II and the Skeletal Evidence from the Royal Tomb at Vergina', *Science* 288, no. 5465 (April 2000), pp.511–14.

Borza, Eugene N., 'Philip II and the Greeks', *Classical Philology* 73, no. 3 (July 1978), pp.236–43.

Buckler, J., *Philip and the Sacred War* (Leiden, Brill, 1989).

Bugh, G.R., *The Horsemen of Athens* (Princeton, Princeton University Press, 1988).

Burke, Edmund S., 'Philip and Alexander the Great', *Military Affairs* 47, no. 2 (April 1983), pp.66–70.

Carney, Elizabeth, *Women and Monarchy in Macedonia* (Norman, OK, Oklahoma University Press, 2000).

——, 'Macedonians and Mutiny: Discipline and Indiscipline in the Army of Philip and Alexander', *Classical Philology* 91, no. 1 (January 1996), pp.19–44.

——, 'The Politics of Polygamy: Olympias, Alexander, and the Murder of Philip', *Historia* 41, no. 2 (1992), pp.169–89.

Cawkwell, George, 'Philip and Athens', in Hatzopoulos and Loukopoulos (eds), *Philip of Macedon* (Athens, Ekdotike Athenon, 1980), pp.100–11.

——, 'Philip and the Amphictyonic League', in Hatzopoulos and Loukopoulos (eds), *Philip of Macedon* (Athens, Ekdotike Athenon, 1980), pp.78–89.

——, *Philip of Macedon* (London, Faber and Faber, 1978).

Curtius, Quintius Rufus, *History of Alexander*, trans. John Yardles (London, Penguin, 1984).

Dell, Harry J., 'The Western Frontier of the Macedonian Monarchy', *Ancient Macedonia* 1 (1970), pp.115–26.

——, 'Philip and Macedonia's Northern Neighbors', in Hatzopoulos and Loukopoulos (eds), *Philip of Macedon* (Athens, Ekdotike Athenon, 1980), pp.90–99.

Demosthenes, *Demosthenes Orations*, 7 vols, trans. H.Vince (Cambridge, MA, Loeb Classical Library, 1930).

Develin, R., 'The Murder of Philip II', *Antichthon* 15 (1981), pp.86–99.

Devine, A.M., 'Macedonia From Philip II to the Roman Conquests', *Classical Review* 45, no. 2 (1995), pp.325–26.

Diodorus Siculus, *The Reign of Philip II, The Greek and Macedonian Narrative From Book XVI*, trans. E.I. McQueen (London, Bristol Classical Press, 1995).

Ellis, John R., 'Macedonia Under Philip', in Hatzopoulos and Loukopoulos (eds), *Philip of Macedon* (Athens, Ekdotike Athenon, 1980), pp.146–65.

——, 'The Assassination of Philip II', in *Ancient Macedonian Studies in Honor of Charles E. Edson* (Thessalonika, Institute for Balkan Studies, 1981), pp.99–137.

——, 'The Stepbrothers of Philip II', *Historia* 22 (1973), pp.350–54.

——, 'The Unification of Macedonia', in Hatzopoulos and Loukopoulos (eds), *Philip of Macedon* (Athens, Ekdotike Athenon, 1980), pp.36–47.

Fears, J.R., 'Pausanias: The Assassin of Philip', *Atheneum* 53 (1975), pp.111–35.

Fredricksmeyer, E.A., 'Alexander and Philip: Emulation and Resentment', *Classical Journal* 85, no. 4 (April–May 1990), pp.300–15.

——, 'Persian Influence at Philip's Court', *Amerian Journal of Archaeology* 85, no. 3 (July 1981), pp.328–37.

Frontinus, Sextus Julius, *Strategemata*, Lucus-Curtis website trans., 2007.

Gabriel, Richard A., 'Philip of Macedon', in *Great Captains of Antiquity* (Westport, CT, Greenwood Press, 2004).

——, *Philip of Macedonia: Greater Than Alexander* (Dulles, VA, Potomac Press, 2010).

——, 'The Genius of Philip II', *Military History* (February–March 2009), pp.40–44.

——, *The Great Captains of Antiquity* (Westport, CT, Greenwood Press, 2004).

——, and Boose, Donald Jr, 'The Greek Way of War: Marathon, Leuctra, and Chaeronea', in Gabriel and Boose, *Great Battles of Antiquity* (Westport, CT, Greenwood Press, 1994).

Gaebel, Robert E., *Cavalry Operations in the Ancient Greek World* (Norman, OK, University of Oklahoma Press, 2002).

Ginouves, R., *Macedonia from Philip II to the Roman Conquest* (Princeton, NJ, Princeton University Press, 1994).

Green, Peter, *Alexander of Macedon: A Historical Biography* (Berkeley, CA, University of California Press, 1991).

Griffith, G.T., 'Philip as a General and the Macedonian Army', in Hatzopoulos and Loukopoulos (eds), *Philip of Macedon* (Athens, Ekotike Athenon, 1980), pp.58–77.

——, 'Philip of Macedon's Early Interventions in Thessaly (358–352 BC)', *The Classical Quarterly* 20, no.1 (May 1970), pp.67–80.

Hammond, N.G.L., 'Alexander's Campaign in Illyria', *Journal of Hellenic Studies* 94 (1974), pp.66–87.

——, *Alexander the Great: King, Commander, and Statesman* (Princeton, NJ, Princeton University Press, 1980).

——, 'Casualties and Reinforcements of Citizen Soldiers in Greece and Macedonia', *Journal of Hellenic Studies* 109 (1989), pp.56–68.

——, 'Cavalry Recruited in Macedonia Down to 322 BC', *Historia* 47, no.4 (1998), pp.404–25.

——, *Philip of Macedon* (Baltimore, MD, Johns Hopkins University Press, 1994).

——, 'Royal Pages, Personal Pages, and Boys Trained in the Macedonian Manner During the Period of the Temenid Monarchy', *Historia* 39 (1990), pp.261–90.

——, 'The Battle Between Philip and Bardylis', *Antichthon* 23 (1989), pp.1–9.

——, 'The End of Philip', in Hatzopoulos and Loukopoulos (eds), *Philip of Macedon* (Athens, Ekdotike Athenon, 1980), pp.166–75.

——, 'The King and the Land in the Macedonian Kingdom', *Classical Quarterly* 38 (1988), pp.382–91.

——, *The Macedonian State: Origins, Institutions, and History* (Oxford, Clarendon Press, 1989).

——, 'The Two Battles of Chaeronea', *Klio* 31 (1938), pp.186–218.

——, 'Training in the Use of the Sarissa and Its Effects in Battle, 359–333 BC', *Antichthon* 14 (1980), pp.53–63.

——, and Griffith, G.T., *A History of Macedonia*, 2 vols (Oxford, Oxford University Press, 1979).

Hatzopoulos, Miltiades B., and Loukopoulos, Louisa D. (eds), *Philip of Macedon* (Athens, Ekdotike Athenon,1980).

Jacoby, F., *Die Fragmente der Griechischen Historiker* (Berlin/Leiden, 1926).

Justin (Marcus Junianus Justinus), *Epitome of the Philippic History of Pompeius Trogus*, trans. John Shelby Watson (London, Henry G. Bohn Press, 1853).

Keyser, P.T., 'The Use of Artillery by Philip II and Alexander the Great', *Ancient World* 15 (1994), pp.27–49.

Kromayer, Johannes, and Keith, George, *Schlachten Atlas zur Antike Kriegsgeschichte* (Leipzig, Wagner and Debs, 1922–1928).

Leveque, Pierre, 'Philip's Personality', in Hatzopoulos and Loukopoulos (eds) *Philip of Macedon* (Athens, Ekdotike Athenon, 1980), pp.176–87.

Lloyd, A., 'Philip II and Alexander the Great: The Moulding of Macedon's Army', in Lloyd, *Battles in Antiquity* (London, 1996), pp.169–98.

Manti, P.A., 'The Macedonian Sarissa, Again', *Ancient World* 24, no.1 (1994), pp.77–91.

Markle, Minor M., 'Use of the Sarissa by Philip and Alexander of Macedon', *American Journal of Archaeology* 82, no.4 (autumn 1978), pp.483–97.

——, 'The Macedonian Sarissa, Spear, and Related Armor', *American Journal of Archaeology* 81, no.3 (summer 1977), pp.323–39.

Marsden, E.W., 'Macedonian Military Machinery and Its Designers Under Philip and Alexander', *Thessalonike* 2 (1977), pp.211–23.

McQueen, E.I., *Diodorus Sicuulus: The Reign of Philip II* (London, Bristol Classical Press, 1995).

Musgrave, Jonathan H., Prag, A.J., and Neave, R., 'The Skull from Tomb II at Vergina: King Philip II of Macedon', *Journal of Hellenic Studies* 104 (1984), pp.60–78.

Pausanias, *The Complete Collectin of Pausanias in Four Volumes*, trans. W.H.S. Jones (Cambridge, MA, Harvard University Press, 1966).

Polyaenus, *Strategies of War* (Chicago, Ares Publishers, 1994).

Prag. J.N., 'Reconstructing King Philip: The Nice Version', *American Journal of Archaeology* 94, no.2 (April 1990), pp.237–47.

Rahe, P.A., 'The Annihilation of the Sacred Band at Chaeronea', *American Journal of Archaeology* 85 (1981), pp.84–87.

Riginos, Alice Swift, 'The Wounding of Philip II of Macedon: Fact and Fabrication', *Journal of Hellenic Studies* 114 (1994), pp.103–19.

Roebuck, Carl, 'The Settlements of Philip II with the Greek States in 338 BC', *Classical Philology* 43, no.2 (April 1948), pp.73–92.

Ryder, T.T.B., 'The Diplomatic Skills of Philip II', in Ian Worthington (ed.) *Ventures into Greek History* (Oxford, Oxford University Press, 1994), pp.228–57.

Spence, I.G., *The Cavalry of Classical Greece* (Oxford, Oxford University Press, 1993).

Theopompus and Pilochorus, F. Jacoby. *Die Fragmente der Griechischen Historiker.* (Berlin, 1926).

Tomlinson, R.A., 'Ancient Macedonian Symposia', *Ancient Macedonia* 1 (1970), pp.308–15.

Worley, L.J., *Hippeis: The Cavalry of Ancient Greece* (Boulder, CO, Westview Press, 1994).

Worthington, Ian, *Philip of Macedon* (New Haven, CT, Yale University Press, 2008).

Xenophon, *On The Art of Horsemanship*, trans. G.W. Bowersock (Cambridge, MA, Harvard University Press, 1968).

——, *The Cavalry Commander*, trans. G.W. Bowersock (Cambridge, MA, Harvard University Press, 1968).

Scipio Africanus

Adock, F.E. *The Roman Art of War Under the Republic* (Cambridge, MA, Harvard University Press, 1940).

Antonelli, Giuseppe, *Scipione l'africano: L'uomo che conquista Cartagine* (Rome, Newton and Compton, 1999).

Austin, N.J.E., and Rankov, Boris, *Exploratio: Military and Political Intelligence in the Roman World From the Second Punic War to the Battle of Adrianople* (London, Routledge, 1995).

Bagnall, N., *The Punic Wars* (London, Hutchison, 1990).

Balsdon, J.P., 'The Ides of March', *Historia* 7 (1958), pp.80–94.

Bell, M.J.V., 'Tactical Reform in the Roman Republican Army', *Historia* 14 (1965), pp.404–22.

Bennett, Charles E., *Frontinus: The Strategemata* (New York, Loeb, 1925).

Bettenson, Henry S., *Rome and the Mediterranean* (London, Penguin, 1976).

Boardman, John, Griffen, Jasper, and Murray, Olwyn, *The Oxford History of Greece and the Hellenistic World* (Oxford, Oxford University Press, 1991).

Brizzi, Giovanni, 'Hannibal: Punier und Hellenist', *Das Altertum* (1991), pp.201–10.

Brunt, P.A., *Italian Manpower, 225 BC to AD 14* (London, Clarendon Press, 1971).

Caven, Bruce, *The Punic Wars* (London, Weidenfeld and Nicholson, 1980).

Cornell, Tim, Rankov, Boris, and Sabin, Philip (eds), *The Second Punic War: A Reappraisal* (London, Institute of Classical Studies, 1996).

Cottrell, Leonard, *Hannibal: Enemy of Rome* (New York, Holt, Rinehart and Winston, 1960).

Delbruck, Hans, *The History of the Art of War, vol. 1, Warfare in Antiquity*, trans. Walter J. Renfroe Jr. (Westport, CT, Greenwood Press, 1990).

Develin, Robert, 'Scipio Africanus Imperator', *Latomus* 36 (1977), pp.110–13.

Dio Cassius, *Bibliotheca Historica* (Cambridge, MA, Harvard University Press, 1947).

Diodorus Siculus, *Diodorus of Sicily*, trans. Francis R. Walton, 12 vols (Cambridge, MA, Harvard University Press, 1937).

Doornik, Francis, *Origins of Intelligence Services* (New Brunswick, NJ, Rutgers University Press, 1974).

Dorey, Thomas A., 'Scipio Africanus as a Party Leader', *Klio* 39 (1961), pp.191–98.

Dorey, Thomas, and Reynolds, Dudley, *Rome Against Carthage* (Garden City, NJ, Doubleday, 1972).

Fournie, Daniel A., 'Clash of the Titans at Zama', *Military Review* 16, no.6 (2000), pp.27–33.

——, 'Harsh Lessons: Roman Intelligence in the Hannibalic War', *International Journal of Intelligence and Counterintelligence* 17, no.3 (2004), pp.502–38.

Gabriel, Richard A., *Scipio Africanus: Rome's Greatest General* (Dulles, VA, Potomac Press, 2008).

——, *The Great Captains of Antiquity* (Westport, CT, Greenwood Press, 2001).

——, 'Zama: Turning Point in the Desert', *Military History* (January/February 2008), pp.50–57.

Gartner, Thomas, 'Die praemilitaerische Ausbildun des Scipio Africanus', *MAIA*, vol.55, no.2 (May–August 2003), pp.315–22.

Grant, Michael, *The Army of the Caesars* (New York, Charles Scribner's Sons, 1974).

Gruen, Erich S., *Culture and National Identity in Republican Rome* (Ithaca, NY, Cornell University Press, 1992).

Hafner, G., 'Das Bildnis des P. Cornelius Scipio Africanus', *Archaeologischer Anzeiger* (1972), pp.474–92.

Haywood, Richard M., *Studies on Scipio Africanus* (Baltimore, MD, Johns Hopkins University Press, 1932).

Hoyos, B.D., 'Hannibal: What Kind of Genius?', *Greece and Rome*, 2nd Ser., vol.30, no.2 (October 1983), pp.171–80.

Italicus, Sirius, *Punica*, trans. J.D. Duff (Cambridge, MA, Harvard University Press, 1934).

Knapp, Robert, *Aspects of the Roman Experience in Iberia, 206–100 BC* (Spain, Valladolid, 1977).

Lazenby, John, *Hannibal's War* (Warminster, Aris and Phillips, 1978).

Lendon, J.E., *Soldiers and Ghosts: A History of Battle in Classical Antiquity* (New Haven, Yale University Press, 2005).

Liddell-Hart, B.H., *Scipio Africanus: Greater Than Napoleon* (New York, Da Capo Press, 1994).

Livy, *The History of Rome from its Foundation: The War With Hannibal*, trans. Aubrey De Selincourt (London, Penguin, 1965).

Lovejoy, Jack, 'The Tides of New Carthage', *Classical Philology* 67, no.2 (1972), pp.110–11.

Marks, Raymond, *From Republic To Empire: Scipio Africanus in the Punica of Sirius Italicus*, (New York, Peter Lang, 2005).

McDonald, A.H., 'Scipio Africanus and the Roman Politics of the Second Century BC', *Journal of Roman Studies* 28, pt.2 (1938), pp.153–64.

Meiklejohn, K.W., 'Roman Strategy and Tactics from 509 to 202 BC', *Greece and Rome*, vol.7, no.2 (May 1938), pp.169–77.

Messer, William Stuart, 'Mutiny in the Roman Army: The Republic', *Classical Philology* 15, no.2 (1920), pp.158–75.

Nicorescu, Paul, 'La Tomba delgli Scipioni', *Ephermeris Daca-romana*, I, pp.1–56.

Parker, James, *Comparing Strategies of the Second Punic War* (Carlisle, PA, U.S. Army War College, 2001).

Picard, G. C., *Hannibal* (Paris, C. Klincksiek, 1967).

Polybius, *The Histories of Polybius*, trans. Evelyn S. Shuckburgh (Bloomingon, University of Indiana Press, 1962).

Riddley, R.T., 'Was Scipio Africanus at Cannae?', *Latomus* 36 (1977), pp.110–13.

Sabin, Philip, 'The Mechanics of Battle in the Second Punic War', in T. Cornell, B. Rankov and P. Sabin (eds), *The Second Punic War: A Reappraisal* (London, Institute of Classical Studies, University of London, 1996).

Scullard, Howard H., 'A Note on the Battle of Ilipa', *Journal of Roman Studies* 26, pt. 1 (1936), pp.19–23.

——, *Scipio Africanus in the Second Punic War* (Cambridge, Cambridge University Press, 1933).

——, *Scipio Africanus: Soldier and Politician* (Ithaca, NY, Cornell University Press, 1970).

Sheldon, Rose Mary, *Tinker, Tailor, Caesar, Spy: Espionage in Ancient Rome* (Ann Arbor, MI, University Microfilms International no. 8720338, 1987).

——, *Intelligence Activities in Ancient Rome: Trust in the Gods, But Verify* (New York, Frank Cass, 2005).

Valori, Francesco, *Scipione l'Africano* (Torino, Societa Editrice Internationale, 1955).

Walbank, F.W., 'The Scipionic Legend', *Proceedings of the Cambridge Philological Society* 13 (1967), pp.54–69.

——, *Polybius II: A Historical Commentary on Polybius* (Oxford, Oxford University Press, 1970).

Warry, John, *Warfare in the Classical World* (London, Salamander Books, 1980).

Williams, Mary Francis, 'Shouldn't You Have Come and Talked to Me About It? Democracy and Mutiny in Scipio's Army', *Ancient History Bulletin* 15, no.4 (2001), pp.143–53.

Wise, Terence, *Armies of the Carthaginian Wars: 265–1436 BC* (London, Osprey, 1982).

Hannibal Barca

Appian, *Roman History*, trans. H.E. White (Cambridge, MA, Harvard University Press, 1992).

Aranegui, C., and De Hoz, J., 'Una falcata decorada con inscription iberica. Juegos gladiatorios y venationes', in Tribute to Enrique Pla Ballester, Trabajos Various del SIP, pp.319–44.

Astin, A.E., 'Saguntum and the Origins of the Second Punic War', *Latomus* (1967), pp.577–96.

Bagnall, Nigel, *The Punic Wars: 264–146 BC* (London, Osprey, 2002).

Barcelo, A., *Karthago und die iberische Halbinsel vor den Barkiden* (Bonn, 1988).

Beer, Sir Gavin de, *Hannibal's March* (New York, Dutton, 1955).

——, *Hannibal* (New York, Viking, 1969).

Briscoe, John, 'The Second Punic War', *Cambridge Ancient History* 2nd ed., vol.8 (Cambridge, Cambridge University Press, 1989), pp.44–80.

Brizzi, Giovanni, 'Hannibal: Punier and Hellenist', *Das Altertum* (1991), pp.201–10.

Canter, H.V., 'The Character of Hannibal', *Classical Journal* 24, no.8 (May 1929), pp.564–77.

Caven, Brian, *The Punic Wars* (London, Weidenfeld and Nicolson, 1980).

Clack, Jerry, 'Hannibal's Gait', *The Classical World* 70, no.3 (November 1976), p.181.

Consiglio, Alberto, *Scipione e la conquista del Mediterraneo* (Milan, Fratelli Treves, 1937).

Cornell, Tim, Rankov, Boris, and Sabin, Philip, *The Second Punic War: A Reappraisal* (London, Institute for Classical Studies, University Of London, 1996).

Davis, E.W., 'Hannibal's Roman Campaign of 211 BC', *Phoenix* 13, no.3 (autumn 1959), pp.113–20.

Dawson, A., 'Hannibal and Chemical Warfare', *The Classical Journal* 63, no.3 (December 1967), pp.117–25.

De Sanctis, G.B., *L'eta delle guerre puniche: Storia dei Romani* III (Torino, Fratelli Bucca, 1916–1917).

Diana, Bettina, 'Annibale e il passaggio deli Appennini', *Aevum* 61 (1987), pp.108–12.

Diodorus Siculus, *Diodorus of Sicily in 12 Volumes*, trans. Francis R. Walton (Cambridge, MA, Harvard University Press, 1937).

Dorey, Thomas A., and Reynolds, Dudley, *Rome Against Carthage* (Garden City, NJ, Doubleday, 1972).

Eckstein, A.M., 'Hannibal at New Carthage', *Classical Philology* 84, no.1 (January 1989), pp.1–15.

Erdkamp, Paul, *Hunger and the Sword: Warfare and Food Supply in Roman Republican Wars, 264–30 BC* (Amsterdam, J.C. Gieben Publishers, 1998).

——, 'Polybius, Livy, and the Fabian Strategy', *Ancient Society* 23 (1992), pp.127–47.

Erskine, Andrew, 'Hannibal and the Freedom of the Italians', *Hermes* 121, no.1 (1993), pp.58–62.

Feliciani, N., 'la Seconda Guerra Punica Nella Spagna', *Studi e Documenti di Storia Diritto* (1904), pp.249–65.

Fitton-Brown, A.D., 'After Cannae', *Historia* 8, no.3 (July 1959), pp.365–71.

Fournie, Daniel A., 'Clash of Titans at Zama', *Military Review* 16, 6 (February 2000), pp.27–33.

Gabriel, Richard A., and Metz, Karen S., *From Sumer To Rome: The Military Capabilities of Ancient Armies* (Westport, CT, Greenwood Press, 1991).

Gabriel, Richard A., *Scipio Africanus, Rome's Greatest General* (Washington, DC, Potomac Books, 2008).

——, 'Siege craft and Artillery', *Soldiers' Lives Through History: The Ancient World* (Westport, CT, Greenwood Press), pp.132–43.

——, *The Battle Atlas of Ancient Military History* (Kingston, Ontario, Canadian Defence Academy Press, 2008).

——, *The Campaigns of Hannibal* (Carlisle Barracks, PA, US Army War College Monograph, 1992).

——, 'The Carthaginian Empire and Republican Rome', in Gabriel, *Empires At War* III (Westport, CT, Greenwood Press, 2005), pp.369–434.

——, 'The Roman Navy: Masters of the Mediterranean', *Military History* 29, no.9 (December 2007), pp.36–43.

——, 'Why Hannibal Lost', *Military History* (March 2016), pp.40–44.

Gilliver, C. M., *The Roman Art of War* (London, Shroud, 1999).

Goldsworthy, Adrian, *Cannae: Hannibal's Greatest Victory* (London, Orion Books, 2007).

——, *Roman Warfare* (London, Clarendon Press, 2000).

Hallward, B.L., 'The Roman Defensive', *Cambridge Ancient History* 8 (Cambridge, Cambridge University Press, 1930).

Hanson, Victor David, 'Cannae', in R. Crowley (ed.), *Experience in War* (New York, Putnam, 1992).

Head, D., *Armies of the Macedonian and Punic Wars* (Cambridge, Wargames Research Group, 1982).

Hoyos, B.D., 'Barcid Proconsuls and Punic Politics, 237–218 BC', *Rheinisches Museum fur Philologie* 137 (1994), pp.246–74.

——, *Hannibal's Dynasty: Power and Politics in the Western Mediterranean, 247–183 BC* (London, Routledge, 2003).

——, 'Hannibal: What Kind of Genius?', *Greece and Rome* 2nd Series, 30, 2 (1983), pp.171–80.

Johnston, Mary, 'Hannibal and the Duke of Wellington', *The Classical Weekly* 29, no.3 (28 October 1935), pp.21-22.

Kromayer, Johannes, and Veith, Georges, *Antike Schlachtfelder*, 4 vols (Berlin, Wiedmannsche Buchhandlung, 1912).

Kromayer, Johannes, and Veith, Georges, *Schlachten Atlas zur Antiken Kriegsgeschichte* (Leipzig, Wagner and Debbs, 1922).

Lancel, Serge, *Carthage: A History*, trans. Antonia Nevill (Malden, MA, Blackwell Publishers, 1995).

——, *Hannibal* (Malden, MA,: Blackwell Publishers, 1999).

Lazenby, John, *Hannibal's War* (Warminster, Aris and Philips, 1978).

——, 'Was Maharbal Right?', in T. Cornell, B. Rankov and P. Sabin (eds), *The Second Punic War: A Reappraisal* (London, Institute of Classical Studies, University of London, 1996), pp.39–48.

Lehmann, Konrad, 'Der letzte Feldzug des hannibalischen krieges', in vol. 21 of *Jahrbucher fur klassische Philologie* (Leipzig, B.G. Teubner), pp.556–69.

Livy, *The War With Hannibal*, trans. Aubrey De Selincourt (London, Penguin, 1965).

Marks, Raymond, *Scipio Africanus in the Punica of Silius Italicus* (New York, Peter Lang, 2005).

Nepos, Cornelius, *Hannibal*, trans. John C. Rolfe (Cambridge, MA, Harvard University Press, 1984).

Nofi, Albert A., 'Roman Mobilization During the Second Punic War', *Military Chronicles* (May–June 2005), p.10.

O'Bryhim, S., 'Hannibal's Elephants and the Crossing of the Rhone', *The Classical Quarterly* 41, no.1 (1991), pp.121–25.

Parker, James, *Comparing Strategies of the Second Punic War* (Carlisle Barracks, PA, US Army War College Monograph, 2001).

Polybius, *The Histories of Polybius*, trans. Evelyn S. Shuckburgh (Bloomington, IN, University of Indiana Press, 1962).

Pomeroy, Arthur J., 'Hannibal at Nuceria', *Historia* 38, no.2 (1989), pp.162–76.

Proctor, Dennis, *Hannibal's March in History* (Oxford, Clarendon Press, 1971).

Rankov, Boris, 'The Second Punic War at Sea', in T. Cornell, B. Rankov and P. Sabin (eds), *The Second Punic War: A Reappraisal* (London, Insitute of Classical Studies, University of London, 1996), pp.49–58.

Rankov, B, and Sabin, P. (eds), *The Second Punic War: A Reappraisal* (London, Institute of Classical Studies, University of London, 1996), pp.81–90.

Reid, J.S., 'Problems of the Second Punic War: Rome and Her Italian Allies', *Journal of Roman Studies* 5 (1915), pp.87–124.

Rich, John, 'The Origins of the Second Punic War', in T. Cornell, B. Rankov and P. Sabin (eds), *The Second Punic War: A Reappraisal* (London, Institute of Classical Studies, University of London, 1996), pp.1–37.

Russell, W.H., *Polybius on Hannibal and Scipio Africanus* (Annapolis, MD, Academic Fellowship, 1963).

Salmon, E.T., 'Hannibal's March on Rome', *Phoenix* 11, no.4 (winter 1957), pp.153–63.

——, 'The Strategy of the Second Punic War', *Greece and Rome* 7, no.2 (October 1960), pp.131–42.

Samuels, M., 'The Reality of Cannae', *Militargeschichtliche Mittelungen* 47 (1990), pp.7–29.

Scullard, Howard H., 'The Carthaginians in Spain', *Cambridge Ancient History*, 2nd ed., vol. 8 (Cambridge, 1989), pp.17–43.

Seibert, Jakob, *Hannibal* (Darmstadt, Eissenschaftliche Buchgesellschaft, 1993).

Shean, John F., 'Hannibal's Mules: The Logistical Limitations of Hannibal's Army and the Battle of Cannae, 216 BC', *Historia* 45, no.2 (1996), pp.159–87.

Shuckburg, Evelyn S., 'Punic War in Spain Between 211 and 206 BC', *Classical Review* 6, 9 (November 1892), pp.381–85.

Smith, Philip, *Scipio Africanus and Rome's Invasion of Africa: A Historical Commentary on Titus Livius, Book XXIX* (Amsterdam, J.C. Gieben Publisher, 1993).

Spaeth, John W., 'Hannibal and Napoleon', *The Classical Journal* 24, no.4 (January 1929), pp.291–93.

Stevenson, G.H., 'Hannibal as Statesman', *The Classical Review* 43, no.5 (November 1929), p.190.

Storey, Glen R., 'The Population of Ancient Rome', *Antiquity* (December 1997), pp.1–14.

Sumner, G.V., 'Rome, Spain and the Outbreak of the Second Punic War', *Latomus* 31, no.2 (1972), pp.469–80.

Terrell, Granville, 'Hannibal's Pass Over the Alps', *The Classical Journal* 17, no.9 (June 1922), pp.503–13.

Toynbee, A.J., *Hannibal's Legacy* (London, Oxford University Press, 1965).

Walbank, F.W., *A Historical Commentary on Polybius*, vol. 1 (Oxford, Oxford University Press, 1957).

Wise, Terrence, and Hook, Richard, *Armies of the Carthaginian Wars: 265–146 BCE* (London, Osprey, 1982).

Wolters, Edward J., 'Carthage and Its People', *The Classical Journal* 47, no.5 (February 1952), pp.191–204.

Julius Caesar

Africa, T.W., 'The Mask of an Assassin: A Psychological Study of M. Junius Brutus', *Journal of Interdisciplinary History* 8 (1978), pp.599–626.

Appian, *The Civil Wars* (London, Waxkeep Press, 2013).

Balsdon, J.V..P., *Julius Caesar and Rome* (Harmondsworth, Penguin, 1971).

——, 'The Ides of March', *Historia* 7 (1958): pp.80–94.

Caesar, Julius, *Caesar: The Alexandrian War, African War, and Spanish War*, trans. A.G. Way (Cambridge, MA, Loeb Classic Series, 1955).

——, *Commentaries on the Gallic War* (New York, Penguin, 1982).

——, *The Civil War* (New York, Penguin, 1988).

——, *The Civil War*, trans. Jane P. Gardner (New York, Penguin Classics, 1976).

——, *The Gallic Wars*, trans. H.J. Edwards (Cambridge, MA, Harvard University Press, 1917).

Collins, John H., 'Caesar and the Corruption of Power', *Historia* 4 (1955), p.445–65.

Connolly, Peter, *Greece and Rome At War* (Englewood Cliffs, NJ, Prentice-Hall, 1981).

Delbruck, Hans, *History of the Art of War – Antiquity* (vol. 1) (Westport, CT, Greenwood Press, 1990).

Deutsche, Monroe E., 'Veni, Vidi, Vici', *Philological Quarterly* 4 (1925), pp.151–56.

——, 'Caesar's Triumphs', *Classical Weekly* 19, 13 (25 January 1926), pp.101–06.

Epstein, David, 'Caesar's Personal Enemies on the Ides of March', *Latomous* 46 (1987), pp.569–70.

Fritz, Kurt von, 'Pompey's Policy Before and After the Outbreak of the Civil War', *Transactions and Proceedings of the American Philological Association* 73 (1942), pp.145–80.

Fuller, J.F.C., *A Military History of the Western World – From Earliest Times to the Battle of Lepanto* (New York, Da Capo, 1954).

——, *Julius Caesar: Man, Soldier, Tyrant* (New York, Da Capo, 1965).

Gabriel, Richard A., and Metz, Karen S., *From Sumer To Rome: The Military Capabilities of Ancient Armies* (Westport, CT, Greenwood Press, 1991).

Gelzer, Matthias, *Caesar: Politician and Statesman* (Cambridge, MA, Harvard University Press, 1968).

Goldsworthy, Adrian, *Caesar: Life of a Colossus* (New Haven, CT,Yale University Press, 2008).

——, *The Roman Army at War, 100 BC – AD 200* (Oxford, Clarendon Press, 1996).

Grant, Michael, *Caesar* (Chicago, Follett Publishing Company, 1974).

——, *The Army of the Caesars* (New York, Charles Scriber's Sons, 1974).

Greece and Rome, vol. iv, no.1 (Oxford University Press , March 1957). A commemmorative volume of essays on the bi-millennium of Caesar's death.

Hackett, General Sir John, *Warfare in the Ancient World* (London, Sidgwick & Jackson, 1989).

Kahn, A.D., *The Education of Julius Caesar* (New York, Schocken Books, 1986).

Morgan, J.D., 'Palapharsalus: The Battle and the Town', *American Journal of Archaeology* 87 (1983), pp.23–54.

O'Connell, Robert L., 'The Roman Killing Machine', *Quarterly Journal of Military History* (autumn 1988), pp.36–39.

Payne-Gallwey, Ralph, 'The Artillery of the Carthaginians, Greeks, and Romans', *Journal of the Royal Artillery,* vol. LVIII, no.1 (April 1931), pp.34–40.

Peaks, Mary Bradford, 'Caesar's Movements January 21 to February 14, 49 BC', *Classical Review* 18 (1904), pp.347–49.

Pelling, C.B.R., 'Pharsalus', *Historia* 22 (1973), pp.249–59.

Plutarch's *Lives*, trans. B. Perrin (London, William Heinemann, 1920).

Sabben-Clare, James, *Caesar and Roman Politics, 60–50 BC* (London, Oxford University Press, 1971).

Storch, Rudolph H., 'Relative Deprivation and the Ides of March: Motive for Murder', *Ancient History Bulletin* 9, 1 (1995), pp.45–52.

Suetonius, *The Twelve Caesars* (Harmondsworth, Penguin Books, 1979).

Sumner, G.V., 'A Note on Julius Caesar's Great Grandfather', *Classical Philology* 71 (1976), pp.341–44.

Taylor, Lily Ross, 'Caesar's Early Career', *Classical Philology* 36 (1941), pp.113–32.

——, 'On the Chronology of Caesar's First Consulship', *American Journal of Philology* 72 (July 1951), pp.254–68.

——, 'The Rise of Julius Caesar', *Greece and Rome* 4 (1957), pp.10–18.

——, *Party Politics in the Age of Caesar* (Berkeley, CA, University of California Press, 1961).

Tucker, Robert A., 'What Really Happened at the Rubicon', *Historia* 37 (1988), pp.245–48.

Watson, G.R., *The Roman Soldier* (Ithaca, Cornell University Press, 1969).

Wiseman, Ann, *Julius Caesar: The Battle For Gaul* (London, Chatto and Windus, 1980).

Marcus Agrippa

The ancient sources upon which this study draws are: Cassius Dio, *Roman History*, available in translation in the Loeb Classics series and Penguin Classics series; Appian, *The Civil Wars*, trans. John Carter (New York, Penguin Classics, 1996); Pliny, *Natural History*, available in many volumes from Loeb Classics series; and Nicholas of Damascus, *Life of Augustus*, trans. Clayton M. Hall (1923), available online. The only modern treatments of Agrippa's life can be found in Meyer Reinhold, *Marcus Agrippa: A Biography* (New York, Humphrey Press, 1933); J.M. Rodaz, *Marcus Agrippa* (Rome, Ecole Franchise de Rome, Palas Farnese, 1884); and Lindsay Powell, *Marcus Agrippa: Right-Hand Man of Caesar Augustus* (Barnsley, Pen and Sword, 2015).

Gabriel, Richard A., 'Agrippa Takes Charge: Rome's Shadow Emperor', *Military History Quarterly* (winter 2016), p.56.

——, *Great Captains of Antiquity* (Westport, CT, Greenwood Press, 2001), pp.183, 196–98.

——, 'Mark Antony', *Military History* (spring 2016), p.43.

——, 'The Roman Imperial Navy: Masters of the Mediterranean', *Military History* (December 2007), pp.36–43.

Huzar, Eleanor Holtz, *Mark Antony: A Biography* (Minneapolis, MN, University of Minnesota Press, 1978), pp.209–33.

Koppie, L., *The Making of the Roman Army from Republic to Empire* (London, Batsford, 1984), p.98.

Paoli, U. E., *Rome, Its People, Life, and Customs* (London, Longman 1963), pp.169–70.

Reinhold, Meyer, *Marcus Agrippa* (Geneva, NY, Humphrey Press, 1933), p.49, citing Pliny 36.121.

Rogers, K., 'Sextus Pompeius: Rebellious Pirate of Imitative Son', *Chrestomathy* 7 (2008) p.199–226.

Muhammad

The literature on Muhammad is vast. However, most of it either does not address Muhammad's military exploits at all or does so only in passing, and is of little use to the military historian. This is a selected bibliography, and lists only those works I found most important to understanding and researching Muhammad's military life. It is not intended to address other areas of scholarly interest concerning Muhammad's life. The purpose of any bibliography is to help other scholars check one's work, criticize it or build upon it. Thus, the focus is on only the sources most useful to the subject at hand. I have included in a separate section the original Arabic sources so that Arabic scholars and historians can use them in a similar manner. I have made occasional notes regarding those entries which I thought may be particularly valuable to the military researcher.

* * *

Arberry, A.J., *The Seven Odes* (London, Unwin and Allen, 1957). Valuable for the military facts that may be extracted from a very close reading of the material.

Becker, Carl. H., 'The Expansion of the Saracens', *The Cambridge Medieval History*, vol. II (New York, 1913), pp.332–38. The classic Western view of the forces which shaped both the *riddah* and the Arab conquest.

Beeston, A.F.L., *Warfare in Ancient South Arabia* (London, Luzac, 1976).

Bostom, Andrew, *The Legacy of Jihad: Islamic Holy War and the Fate of Non-Muslims* (Amherst, NY, Prometheus Books, 2005).

Bousquet, G.H., 'Observations sur lat nature et les causes de lat conquete arabe', *Studia Islamica* 6 (1956), pp.37–52.

Breasted, James H., *The Development of Religion and Thought in Ancient Egypt* (New York, Harper and Brothers, 1959).

Brockelmann, Carl, *History of the Islamic Peoples*, trans. J. Carmichael and M. Perlmann (New York, Capricorn Books, 1960).

Buhl, Franz, *Das Leben Muhammeds*, trans. H.H. Schaeder (Leipzig, 1930). A compact biography full of scholarly notes of great value.

Caetani, Leone, *Annali dell Islam*, 10 vols (Milan, 1905–1926). Probably the most comprehensive treatment of the history of the Arabs in which all the extant Arabic sources can be found, year by year, quoted, analyzed and compared. It has not been translated into English so far as I am aware.

Cook, David, *Understanding Jihad* (Berkeley, CA, University of California Press, 2005).

Crone, Patricia, 'The Early Islamic World', in Kurt Raaflaub and Nathan Rosenstein, *War and Society in the Ancient and Medieval World* (Washington, DC, Center for Hellenic Studies, 1999).

Doughty, C.M., *Travels in Arabia Deserta* (London, Jonathan Cape, 1936).

Dupuy, R. Ernest, and Trevor, N., *The Encyclopedia of Military History* (New York, Harper and Rowe, 1986).

Firestone, Reuven, *Jihad: The Origins of Holy War in Islam* (London, Oxford University Press, 1999).

Gabriel, Richard A., *Empires At War*, 3 vols (Westport, CT, Greenwood Press, 2005). Useful as a basic reference for the wars, armies, equipment, weapons, tactics and commanders for wars fought in antiquity from 4000 BCE to the fall of Constantinople in 1453 CE.

Gods of Our Fathers: The Memory of Egypt in Judaism and Christianity (Westport, CT, Greenwood Press, 2002).

——, *Jesus The Egyptian: The Origins of Christianity and the Psychology of Christ* (New York, iUniverse, 2006).

——, *Muhammad: Islam's First Great General* (Norman, OK, University of Oklahoma Press, 2007).

——, *Soldiers' Lives: Military Life and War in Antiquity* (Westport, CT, Praeger, 2006).

——, 'The Crusaders', in *Empires At War*, vol. 3 (Westport, CT, Greenwood Press, 2005), pp.791–836.

——, *The Military History of Ancient Israel* (Westport, CT, Greenwood Press, 2003).

——, 'The Wars of Arab Conquest, 600–850 CE', in Richard A. Gabriel, *Empires At War*, vol. 2 (Westport, CT, Greenwood Press, 2005), pp.639–58.

——, 'War to the Knife', *Military History* (September 2014), pp.34–39.

——, and Boose, Donald W. Jr, *The Great Battles of Antiquity: A Strategic and Tactical Guide to the Great Battles That Shaped The Development of War* (Westport, CT, Greenwood Press, 1994).

Glubb, Sir John, *A Short History of the Arab Peoples* (New York, Stein and Day, 1969).

——, *The Life and Times of Muhammad* (New York, Cooper Square Press, 2001). Glubb was a professional soldier who lived and served with Arab units for many years. His experiences provide valuable insights in this small volume.

Goldschmidt, Arthur Jr, *A Concise History of the Middle East* (Boulder, CO, Westview Press, 1988).

Guillaume, A., *The Life of Muhammad: A Translation of Ibn Ishaq's Life of Muhammad.* (Oxford, Oxford University Press, 1967). Perhaps the most important source and most easily accessible for understanding the detail and context of Muhammad's military life.

Hamidullah, Muhammad, *The Battlefields of the Prophet* (Paris, Revue des Etudes Islamiques, 1939). Mostly useful for the maps and terrain descriptions of the battlefields.

Hitti, Philip K., *History of the Arabs* (Hampshire, Palgrave, 2002). First published in 1937 and still one of the best historical sources available.

Hoyland, Robert G., *Arabia and the Arabs: From the Bronze Age to the Coming of Islam.* (London, Routledge, 2001).

Huntington, Samuel P., *The Clash of Civilizations and the Remaking of the World Order* (New York, Torchstone, 1996).

Ibn Ishaq, *The Life of Muhammad*, trans. A. Guillaume (Oxford, Oxford University Press, 2007).

Kirsch, Jonathan, *Moses: A Life* (New York, Ballantine Books, 1998).

Laoust, Henri, *Les Schismes dans l'Islam* (Paris, 1965).

Lewis, Bernard (ed.), *Historians of the Middle East* (London, Holt, 1962).

——, *The Arabs in History* (London, Arrow Books, 1958).

Lings, Martin, *Muhammad: His Life Based on the Earliest Sources* (Rochester, VT, Inner Traditions International, 1983). An excellent narrative history based strongly in original sources.

Lowin, Shari, 'Muslims and Circumcision', *JTS Magazine* 10, 1 (Fall 2000), pp.18–21.

Macdonald, M.C.A., 'Hunting, Fighting, and Raiding: The Horse in Pre-Islamic Arabia', in David Alexander (ed.), *Furusiyya: The Horse in the Art of the Near East* (Riyadh, King Abdulaziz Public Library, 1996), pp.73–83.

Murphy, Thomas Patrick (ed.), *The Holy War* (Columbus, OH, Ohio State University Press, 1976).

Nicolle, David, and McBride, Angus, *The Armies of Islam, 7th–11th Centuries* (London, Osprey Publishers, 1982). A good source for descriptions of Arab military equipment.

Parry, V.J., and Yapp, M.E., *War, Technology and Society in the Middle East* (London, Oxford University Press, 1975). A useful collection of articles dealing with Arab warfare at different periods, with emphasis on technical detail.

Payne, James L., *Why Nations Arm* (Oxford, Blackwell Books, 1889). One of the first books published in the modern West that deals with Muhammad as a soldier.

Peters, Rudolph, *Jihad In Classical and Modern Islam* (Princeton, Marcus Wiener Publishers, 1996).

Rodinson, Maxime, *Muhammad* (New York, The New Press, 1980). Contains an excellent section on Muhammad's military exploits.

Roth, Jonathan P., *The Logistics of the Roman Army at War* (Boston, Brill, 1999). Chapter One, 'Supply Needs and Rations', is particularly valuable for information dealing with the soldier's nutritional needs and the military capabilities of animals of war.

Shoufani, Elias S., *Al-Riddah and the Muslim Conquest of Arabia* (Toronto, University of Toronto Press, The Arab Institute for Research and Publishing, 1973). The definitive work on the *Riddah* in English.

Watt, W. Montgomery, 'Islamic Conceptions of Holy War', in Thomas Patrick Murphy (ed.), *The Holy War* (Columbus, OH, Ohio State University Press, 1976), pp.141–56.

——, *Muhammad At Mecca* (Oxford, Clarendon Press, 1953).

——, *Muhammad At Medina* (Oxford, Oxford University Press, 1956).

Wellhausen, Julius, *Skizzen und Vorarbeiten*, 6 vols (Berlin, 1884–1889). Like Caetani's work, a classic in the field that deals with all the sources and the conflicts between them.

Yadin, Yigael, *The Art of Warfare in Biblical Lands in Light of Archaeological Discovery*, 2 vols (New York, McGraw-Hill, 1964).

Original Arabic Sources

Abu Yusuf, al-Kufi, Ya'qub ibn Ibrahim (731–798), *Kitab al-Kharaj* (Cairo, 1933).

al-Baghdadi, 'Abd al-Qahir ibn Tahir (d. 1037), *al-Farq bayn al-firaq*, Muhammad 'Abd al-Hamid (ed) (Cairo, 1959).

al-Baladhuri, Ahmad ibn Yahya ibn Jabir (d. 892), *Ansar al-ashraf*, vol. I, Muhammad Hamidullah (ed.) (Cairo, 1959).

ibn Hisham, 'Abd al-Malik (d. 834), *Sirat al-nabi*, Muhammad 'Abd al-Hamid (ed.), 4 vols (Cairo, 1963).

Ibn Sa'd, Muhammad (d. 845), *Biographen Muhammeds* (known as *al-Tabaqat al-kubra*), Edward Sachau (ed.) (Leiden, 1904–1940).

al-Maqrizi, Ahmad ibn 'Ali (1364–1442), *Kitab al-niza wa-al-takhasum fi ma bayn bani, UUmayyah wa-bani Hashim* (Cairo, 1937).

al-Tabari, Muhammad ibn Jarir (838–923), *Annales*, 15 vols, M.J. de Goeje (ed.) (Leiden, 1879–1901).

al-Tufayl, Amir, *The Poems of Diwan*, Sir Charles Lyall (ed.), E.J.W. Gibb Memorial, XXI (1913).

al-Waqidi, Muhammad ibn 'Umar (747–823), *Kitab al-Maghazi*, 3 vols, Marsden Jones (ed.) (Oxford, 1966).

al-Ya'qubi, Ahmad ibn Abi Yaqub (d. 897), *Tarikh al-Ya'qubi*, 2 vols (Beirut, 1960).

Alexander the Great

Aldrete, Gregory S., Bartell, Scott, and Alorete, Alicia, *Reconstructing Ancient Linen Body Armor: Unraveling the Linothorax Mystery* (Baltimore, MD, Johns Hopkins University Press, 2013).

Andronikos, Anolis, 'The Royal Tombs at Agae (Vergina)', in Hatzopoulous and Loukopoulos (ed.), *Philip of Macedon* (Athens, Ekdotike Athenon, 1980), pp.188–231.

Arrianus, Lucius Flavius, *The Campaigns of Alexander*, trans. Aubrey De Selincourt (London, Penguin Books, 1971).

Athenaeus, trans. C.B. Gluick (London, Loeb Classical Library, William Heinemann Ltd, 1930).

Badian, Ernst, 'Alexander the Great and the Loneliness of Power', in E. Badian (ed.), *Studies in Greek and Roman History* (New York, Barnes and Noble, 1964), pp.192–205.

——, 'Conspiracies', in Ian Worthington (ed.), *Alexander the Great: A Reader* (London, Routledge, 2003), pp.277–95.

——, 'The Death of Parmenio', *Transactions and Proceedings of the Americal Philological Association* 91 (1960), pp.324–38.

——, 'The Deification of Alexander the Great', in J. Roisman, *Alexander the Great: Answers and Modern Perspectives* (Lexington, MA, D.C. Heath, 1995), pp.188–201.

Balsdon, J.P.V.D., 'The Divinity of Alexander', *Historia* 1, no.3 (1950), pp.363–88.

Bertolotti, M., *La Critica Medica Nell Storia Alessandro Magno.* (1933).

Borza, Eugene, 'Malaria in Alexander's Army', *Ancient History Bulletin* 1, 2 (1987), pp.36–38.

——, 'Origins of the Royal Macedonian House', *Hesperia* 19 (1982), pp.7–13.

——, 'The Symposium at Alexander's Court', *Ancient Macedonia* 3 (1983), pp.45–55.

Bosworth, A.B., *Conquest and Empire: The Reign of Alexander the Great* (Cambridge, Cambridge University Press, 1988).

——, 'The Death of Alexander the Great: Rumor and Propaganda', *Classical Quarterly* 1 (May 1971), pp.112–36.

Brunt, Peter, *Nearchus' Indica* (Cambridge, MA, Harvard University Press, 1983).

——, 'The Aims of Alexander', *Greece and Rome* 12, no 2 (October 1965), pp.205–15.

Burn, A.R., 'Alexander the Great', *Greece and Rome* 12, no.2 (October 1965), pp.146–54.

——, 'The Generalship of Alexander', *Greece and Rome* 12, no.2 (1965), pp.140–47.

Carney, Elizabeth, 'The Politics of Polygamy: Olympias, Alexander, and the Murder of Philip', *Historia* 41, no.2 (1992), pp.169–89.

Cartledge, Paul, *Alexander the Great* (New York, Vintage Books, 2005).

Cawkwell, George, *Philip of Macedon* (London, Faber and Faber, 1978).

Curtius, Quintius Rufus, *History of Alexander*, trans. John Yardley (London, Penguin Classics, 1984).

Davidson, James, 'Bonkers About Boys', *London Review of Books* (1 November 2013), pp.7–10.

——, *The Greeks and Greek Love* (London, Weidenfeld, 2007).

Diagnostic and Statistical Manual of Mental Disorders, American Psychiatric Association, Fourth Edition Revision (2000).

Diodorus of Sicily, *Histories*, trans. C. Bradford Welles (Harvard, MA, Harvard University Press, 1963).

Dover, Kenneth, *Greek Homosexuality* (Cambridge, MA, Harvard University Press, 1978).

Edmunds, Lowell, 'The Religiosity of Alexander', in Joseph Roisman (ed.), *Alexander the Great: Answers and Modern Perspectives* (Lexington, MA, D.C. Heath, 1995), pp.172–88.

Ellis, J.R., 'The Stepbrothers of Philip II', *Historia* 22 (1973), pp.348–56.

Engels, Donald, 'A Note on Alexander's Death', *Classical Philology* 73 (July 1978), pp.224–28.

Foss, Clive, 'The Battle of the Granicus: A New Look', *Ancient Macedonia* (August 1977), pp.495–502.

Fredricksmeyer, E.A., 'Alexander and Philip: Emulation and Resentment', *Classical Journal* 85, no.4 (April–May 1990), pp.300–15.

Fuller, J.F.C., *The Generalship of Alexander the Great* (New York, Da Capo Press, 1960).

Gabriel, Richard A., 'Alexander the Monster', *Military History Quarterly* (summer 2013), pp.11–14.

——, *Between Flesh and Steel: A History of Military Medicine from the Middle Ages to the War in Afghanistan* (Dulles, VA, Potomac Books, 2013).

——, *Man and Wound in the Ancient World: A History of Military Medicine from Sumer to the Fall of Constantinople* (Dulles, VA, Potomac Books, 2012).

——, *No More Heroes: Madness and Psychiatry in War* (New York, Hill and Wang, 1987).

——, *Philip of Macedonia: Greater Than Alexander* (Dulles, VA, Potomac Books, 2010).

——, *The Madness of Alexander the Great and the Myth of Military Genius* (Barnsley, Pen and Sword 2015).

——, 'The Persian Army and Alexander the Great', in *Empires At War* (Westport, CT, Greenwood Press, 2005), pp.306–68.

——, 'The Roman Military Medical Corps', *Military History* (January 2011), pp.39–44.

——, 'War, Madness, and Military Psychiatry', *Military History* (forthcoming, 2016), pp.45–49.

Gaebel, Robert E., *Cavalry Operations in the Ancient World* (Norman, OK, University of Oklahoma Press, 2002).

Garrison, Elise P., 'Attitudes Toward Suicide in Ancient Greece', *Transactions of the American Philological Association* 121 (1991), pp.1–34.

Gerig, Bruce, 'Greek Homosexuality', internet epistle 1–10, epistle.us/hbarticles/greeks.html (2013).

Ginsberg, Eli., *The Lost Divisions* (New York, Columbia University Press, 1950).

Graham, James, *The Secret History of Alcoholism* (Virginia, Aculeus Press,1994).

Green, Peter, *Alexander of Macedon: A Historical Biography* (Berkeley, University of California Press, 1991).

——, *Alexander the Great and the Hellenistic Age* (London, Orion Books, 2008).

Grossman, David, *On Killing: The Psychological Cost of Learning to Kill in War and Society* (Boston, Little Brown, 2009).

Hamilton, J.R., 'Alexander and His So-Called Father', *Classical Quarterly* 3 (1953), pp.151–57.

——, 'Alexander's Early Life', *Greece and Rome*, vol. 12, no.2 (October 1965), pp.117–24.

Hammond, N.G.L., 'Alexander's Campaign in Illyria', *Journal of Hellenic Studies* 94 (1974), pp.66–87.

——, 'Alexander's Personality', in Ian Worthington (ed.), *Alexander the Great: A Reader* (London, Routledge, 2003), pp.299–302.

——, *Alexander the Great: King, Commander, and Statesman* (Princeton, NJ, Princeton University Press, 1980).

——, 'Casualties and Reinforcements of Citizen Soldiers in Greece and Macedonia', *Journal of Hellenic Studies* 109 (1989), pp.56–68.

——, 'Royal Pages, Personal Pages, and Boys Trained in the Macedonian Manner During the Period of the Temenid Monarchy', *Historia* 39 (1990), pp.261–90.

——, *The Macedonian State: Origins, Institutions, and History* (Oxford, Clarendon Press, 1989).

——, *Three Historians of Alexander the Great: The So-Called Vulgate Authors* (Cambridge, Cambridge University Press, 1983).

——, and Griffith, G.T., *A History of Macedonia*, 2 vols (Oxford, Oxford University Press, 1979).

Hanson, Victor Davis, 'Alexander the Killer', *Great Commanders* (Fall 2002), pp.55–60.

Hatzopouloss, Miltiades B., and Loukopoulos, Louisa D. (eds), *Philip of Macedon* (Athens, Ekdotike Athenon, 1980).

Head, Duncan, *Armies of the Macedonian and Persian Wars* (Sutton, War Games Research Group, 1982).

Heckel, Waldemar, 'The Conspiracy Against Philotas', *Phoenix* 31, no.1 (spring 1977), pp.14–22.

——, *The Wars of Alexander the Great* (London, Routledge, 2002).

Herman, J., *Trauma and Recovery* (New York, Global Books, 1997).

Herodotus, *The Histories*, trans. G.C. Macaulay (New York, Barnes and Nobles, 2004).

Holt, Frank L., *Into the Land of Bones: Alexander the Great in Afghanistan* (Berkeley, University of California Press, 2005).

Jacoby, F., *Die Fragmente der griechischen Historiker* (FgrH) (Berlin and Leiden, 1923).

Justin, Marcus Junianus, *Epitome of the Philippic History of Pompeius Trogus*, trans. John Shelby Watson (London, Henry G. Bohn Press, 1853).

Kouretas, D., 'The Oracle of Trophonius: A Kind of Shock Treatment Associated with Sensory Deprivation in Greece', *British Journal of Psychiatry* 113, no.505 (1979), pp.1,441–46.

Lacy, James, 'The Persian Fallacy', *Military History* (July 2012), pp.50–54.

Lascaratos, John, 'The Wounding of Alexander the Great in Cyropolis: The First Reported Case of the Syndrome of Cortical Blindness', *History of Ophthalmology* 42 (November–December 1997), pp.285–86.

Li Donnici, Lynn R., *The Epidaurian Miracle Inscriptions: Texts, Translations, and Commentary* (Atlanta, GA, Scholars Press, 1995).

Lorenzi, Rossella, 'Laminated Linen Protected Alexander the Great', paper at *Annual Conference of the Archaeological Institute of America* (Anaheim, CA, 10 January 2010).

Marsden, E.W., 'Macedonian Military Machinery and Its Designers Under Philip and Alexander', *Ancient Macedonia* (1968), pp.211–23.

Matthew, Christopher, 'Testing Herodotus', *Ancient Warfare* (May 2011), pp.41–46.

Matthew, Christopher, and How, W.W., 'Arms, Tactics, and Strategy in the Persian Wars', *Journal of Hellenic Studies* 43, no.2 (2013), pp.117–32.

McKeon, Richard, *The Basic Works of Aristotle* (New York, Random House, 1941).

McKinley, A., 'Ancient Experience With Intoxicating Drinks: Non-Attic States', *Quarterly Journal of Studies On Alcohol* 10 (1949), pp.309–16.

Miller, Emanuel, *Neuroses in War* (New York, Macmillan, 1942).

Musgrave, Jonathan H., Prag, A.J., and Neave, R., 'The Skull from Tomb II at Vergina: King Philip II of Macedon', *Journal of Hellenic Studies* 104 (1984), pp.63–78.

Narin, A.K., 'Alexander in India', *Greece and Rome*, vol. 12, no.2 (1965), pp.155–65.

Nikonorov, Valerii, *The Armies of Bactria: 700 BC–450 AD* (Stockport, PA, Montvery Publications, 1997).

O'Brien, John M., 'Alexander and Dionysus: The Invisible Enemy', *Annals of Scholarship* 1 (1980), pp.31–46.

——, *Alexander the Great: The Invisible Enemy* (London, Routledge, 1992).

——, 'The Enigma of Alexander: The Alcohol Factor', *Annals of Scholarship* 1 (1980), pp.31–46.

Ogden, Daniel, 'Alexander's Sex Life', in Waldemar Heckel and Lawrence A. Trittle, *Crossroads of History: Alexander the Great* (Routledge, 2012) 202-17.

Oldach, David W., Richmond, Robert E., Borza, Eugene N., and Benitez, R. Michael, 'A Mysterious Death', *New England Journal of Medicine* 338 (Boston, 11 June 1998), pp.1,764–70.

Papageorgiu, M.G., 'Incubation as a Form of Psychotherapy in the Care of Patients in Ancient Greece', *Psychotherapy* 26 (1975), pp.35–38.

Parke, H.W., 'The Massacre of the Branchidae', *Journal of Hellenic Studies* 105 (1985), pp.59–68.

Plutarch, *Moralia*, trans. P. Clement, VIII (London, 1969).

——, *The Parallel Lives*, trans. Bernadette Perin (Loeb Classical Library, 1919).

Prakash, Buddha, *History of the Punjab* (Punjabi University Patiala Publications Bureau, 1997).

Rogers, Guy MacLean, *Alexander: The Ambiguity of Greatness* (New York, Random House, 2004).

Rolleston, J.D., 'Alcoholism in Classical Antiquity', *British Journal of Inebriety* 24 (1927), pp.101–20.

Romano, Jon, 'Temples, Asylums, or Hospitals?', *Journal of the National Association of Private Psychiatric Hospitals* 9, no.4 (summer 1978), pp.5–12.

Sabin, Philip, 'The Face of Roman Battle', *Journal of Roman Studies* 90 (2000), pp.15–29.

——, 'The Mechanics of Battle in the Second Punic War', in Tim Cornell, Boris Rankov and Philip Sabin (eds), *The Second Punic War: A Reappraisal* (London, Institute for Classical Studies, University of London, 1966), pp.34–72.

Salazar, Christine F., *The Treatment of War Wounds in Graeco-Roman Antiquity* (Boston, Brill, 2000).

Sarton, George, *Galen of Pergamon* (Lawrence, KS, University of Kansas Press,1954).

Shay, Jonathan, *Achilles in Vietnam* (New York, Scriber, 1994).

Swank, Roy L., and Marchand, Walter E., 'Combat Neuroses: The Development of Combat Exhaustion', *Archives of Neurology and Psychiatry* 55 (1946), pp.232–54.

The Complete Plays of Sophocles: Ajax, trans. Richard Claverhouse Jebb (London, Bantam, 1982).

Thomas, Carol, 'What You Seek Is Here: Alexander the Great', *Journal of the Historical Society* 7 (March 2007), pp.61–83.

Trittle, Lawrence A., 'Alexander and the Killing of Cleitus the Black', in Heckel (ed.), *Crossroads of History: Alexander the Great* (2002), pp.127–46.

——, *From Melos to My Lai* (New York, Routledge, 2000).

Wagner, Robert B., and Slivko, Benjamin 'History of Nonpenetrating Chest Trauma and Its Treatment', *Maryland Medical Journal* 37 (April 1988), pp.297–304.

Weiner, I.B., and Craig, W.E., *The Corsini Encyclopedia of Psychology* (Hoboken, NJ, John Wiley & Sons, 2010).

Worthington, Ian, 'How Great Was Alexander the Great?', *Ancient History Bulletin* 13 (1999), pp.44–49.

Xenophon, *Anabasis*, trans. W.H.D. Rouse (Ann Arbor, University of Michigan Press, 1958).

INDEX

OTHER BOOKS

By Richard A. Gabriel

God's Generals: The Military Lives of Moses, the Buddha and Muhammad (2016)

The Madness of Alexander the Great and the Myth of Military Genius (2015)

Between Flesh and Steel: Military Medicine from the
Middle Ages to the War in Afghanistan (2013)

Man and Wound in the Ancient World (2012)

Hannibal: The Military Biography of Rome's Greatest Enemy (2011)

Philip II of Macedonia: Greater than Alexander (2010)

Thutmose III: Egypt's Greatest Warrior King (2009)

The Battle Atlas of Ancient Military History (2008)

Scipio Africanus: Rome's Greatest General (2008)

Muhammad: Islam's First Great General (2007)

The Warrior's Way: A Treatise on Military Ethics (2006)

Soldiers' Lives: Military Life and War in Antiquity: 4,000 BCE to 1453 CE (2006)

Jesus The Egyptian: The Origins of Christianity
and the Psychology of Christ (2005)

Ancient Empires at War, 3 vols. (2005)

Subotai The Valiant: Genghis Khan's Greatest General (2004)

Lion of the Sun (2003)

The Military History of Ancient Israel (2003)

Great Armies of Antiquity (2002)

Sebastian's Cross (2002)

Gods of Our Fathers: The Memory of Egypt in Judaism and Christianity (2001)

Warrior Pharaoh (2001)

Great Captains of Antiquity (2000)

Great Battles of Antiquity (1994)

A Short History of War: Evolution of Warfare and Weapons (1994)

History of Military Medicine: Ancient Times to the Middle Ages (1992)

History of Military Medicine: Renaissance to the Present (1992)

From Sumer to Rome: The Military Capabilities of Ancient Armies (1991)

The Culture of War: Invention and Early Development (1990)

The Painful Field: Psychiatric Dimensions of Modern War (1988)

No More Heroes: Madness and Psychiatry in War (1987)

The Last Centurion (French, 1987)

Military Psychiatry: A Comparative Perspective (1986)

Soviet Military Psychiatry (1986)

Military Incompetence: Why the US Military Doesn't Win (1985)

Operation Peace for Galilee: The Israeli-PLO War in Lebanon (1985)

The Antagonists: An Assessment of the Soviet and American Soldier (1984)
The Mind of the Soviet Fighting Man (1984)
Fighting Armies: NATO and the Warsaw Pact (1983)
Fighting Armies: Antagonists of the Middle East (1983)
Fighting Armies: Armies of the Third World (1983)
To Serve With Honor: A Treatise on Military Ethics (1982)
The New Red Legions: An Attitudinal Portrait of the Soviet Soldier (1980)
The New Red Legions: A Survey Data Sourcebook (1980)
Managers and Gladiators: Directions of Change in the Army (1978)
Crisis in Command: Mismanagement in the Army (1978)
Ethnic Groups in America (1978)
Program Evaluation: A Social Science Approach (1978)
The Ethnic Factor in the Urban Polity (1973)
The Environment: Critical Factors in Strategy Development (1973)